The Multilingual Muse
Transcultural Poetics in the Burgundian Netherlands

LEGENDA

LEGENDA is the Modern Humanities Research Association's book imprint for new research in the Humanities. Founded in 1995 by Malcolm Bowie and others within the University of Oxford, Legenda has always been a collaborative publishing enterprise, directly governed by scholars. The Modern Humanities Research Association (MHRA) joined this collaboration in 1998, became half-owner in 2004, in partnership with Maney Publishing and then Routledge, and has since 2016 been sole owner. Titles range from medieval texts to contemporary cinema and form a widely comparative view of the modern humanities, including works on Arabic, Catalan, English, French, German, Greek, Italian, Portuguese, Russian, Spanish, and Yiddish literature. Editorial boards and committees of more than 60 leading academic specialists work in collaboration with bodies such as the Society for French Studies, the British Comparative Literature Association and the Association of Hispanists of Great Britain & Ireland.

The MHRA encourages and promotes advanced study and research in the field of the modern humanities, especially modern European languages and literature, including English, and also cinema. It aims to break down the barriers between scholars working in different disciplines and to maintain the unity of humanistic scholarship. The Association fulfils this purpose through the publication of journals, bibliographies, monographs, critical editions, and the MHRA Style Guide, and by making grants in support of research. Membership is open to all who work in the Humanities, whether independent or in a University post, and the participation of younger colleagues entering the field is especially welcomed.

ALSO PUBLISHED BY THE ASSOCIATION

Critical Texts
Tudor and Stuart Translations • *New Translations* • *European Translations*
MHRA Library of Medieval Welsh Literature

MHRA Bibliographies
Publications of the Modern Humanities Research Association

The Annual Bibliography of English Language & Literature
Austrian Studies
Modern Language Review
Portuguese Studies
The Slavonic and East European Review
Working Papers in the Humanities
The Yearbook of English Studies

www.mhra.org.uk
www.legendabooks.com

EDITORIAL BOARD

Chair: Professor Jonathan Long (University of Durham)
For *Germanic Literatures*: Ritchie Robertson (University of Oxford)
For *Italian Perspectives*: Simon Gilson (University of Warwick)
For *Moving Image*: Emma Wilson (University of Cambridge)
For *Research Monographs in French Studies*:
Diana Knight (University of Nottingham)
For *Selected Essays*: Susan Harrow (University of Bristol)
For *Studies in Comparative Literature*: Duncan Large
(British Centre for Literary Translation, University of East Anglia)
For *Studies in Hispanic and Lusophone Cultures*:
Trevor Dadson (Queen Mary, University of London)
For *Studies in Yiddish*: Gennady Estraikh (New York University)
For *Transcript*: Matthew Reynolds (University of Oxford)

Managing Editor
Dr Graham Nelson
41 Wellington Square, Oxford OX1 2JF, UK

www.legendabooks.com

The Multilingual Muse

Transcultural Poetics in the Burgundian Netherlands

Edited by
Adrian Armstrong and Elsa Strietman

Modern Humanities Research Association
2017

Published by Legenda
an imprint of the Modern Humanities Research Association
Salisbury House, Station Road, Cambridge CB1 2LA

ISBN 978-1-781885-49-9 (HB)
ISBN 978-1-78188-550-5 (PB)

First published 2017

All rights reserved. No part of this publication may be reproduced or disseminated or transmitted in any form or by any means, electronic, mechanical, photocopying, recording or otherwise, or stored in any retrieval system, or otherwise used in any manner whatsoever without written permission of the copyright owner, except in accordance with the provisions of the Copyright, Designs and Patents Act 1988, or under the terms of a licence permitting restricted copying issued in the UK by the Copyright Licensing Agency Ltd, Saffron House, 6–10 Kirby Street, London EC1N 8TS, England, or in the USA by the Copyright Clearance Center, 222 Rosewood Drive, Danvers MA 01923. Application for the written permission of the copyright owner to reproduce any part of this publication must be made by email to legenda@mhra.org.uk.

Disclaimer: Statements of fact and opinion contained in this book are those of the author and not of the editors or the Modern Humanities Research Association. The publisher makes no representation, express or implied, in respect of the accuracy of the material in this book and cannot accept any legal responsibility or liability for any errors or omissions that may be made.

Trademark notice: Product or corporate names may be trademarks or registered trademarks, and are used only for identification and explanation without intent to infringe.

© Modern Humanities Research Association 2017

Copy-Editor: Charlotte Brown

This work was supported by the Arts and Humanities Research Council (AHRC) [grant number AH/J001481/1].

Arts & Humanities Research Council

CONTENTS

Acknowledgements ix

Notes on the Contributors x

Introduction 1
ADRIAN ARMSTRONG

1 'Frenchified': A Contact-based Approach to Transculturation and Linguistic Change in Holland-Zeeland (1428/33–c. 1500) 12
DIRK SCHOENAERS

2 'Gescryfte met letteren na elcxs geval gegraueert en oic dyveerssche ymagyen': Uses of Code-Switching in Dutch and French 42
CATHERINE EMERSON

3 Printing in French in the Low Countries in the Early Sixteenth Century: Patterns and Networks 54
MALCOLM WALSBY

4 Rhetorical Encounters: *Puys*, Chambers of Rhetoric, and the Urban Literary Culture of the Burgundian Low Countries and Northern France 71
ANNE-LAURE VAN BRUAENE

5 Target Languages: Multilingual Communication in Poetic Descriptions of Crossbow Competitions 84
LAURA CROMBIE

6 Wrapped in Rhetoric: The *Cent Nouvelles nouvelles* and Dutch *Rederijker* Literature 106
DIRK COIGNEAU

7 Cross-Cultural Intersections in the Middle Dutch Translations of *Le Chevalier délibéré* by Olivier de La Marche 132
SUSIE SPEAKMAN SUTCH

8 The Blind Leading the Blind? Choreographing the Transcultural in Pierre Michault's *La Dance aux aveugles* and Gheraert Leeu's *Van den drie blinde danssen* 149
REBECCA DIXON

Bibliography 162

Index 185

ACKNOWLEDGEMENTS

This volume originated in a colloquium of the same name, held at Murray Edwards College, Cambridge in September 2013. The colloquium contributed to a wider collective research project, 'Transcultural Critical Editing: Vernacular Poetry in the Burgundian Netherlands, 1450–1530', supported by the Arts and Humanities Research Council (AHRC) between 2012 and 2016 [grant number AH/J001481/1]. We are immensely grateful both to the AHRC for its financial support, and to the staff of Murray Edwards College for providing a superbly organized and comfortable setting for our discussions. A number of colloquium participants are not represented in this book, but made important contributions to our individual and collective understanding of this richly cross-disciplinary subject by delivering papers, chairing sessions, and engaging in discussions. Our heartfelt thanks, then, go to Estelle Doudet, Margriet Hoogvliet, Bas Jongenelen, Jelle Koopmans, Claude Thiry, and Arjan van Dixhoorn; and to Katell Lavéant, Samuel Mareel, and Johan Oosterman, the other members of the 'Transcultural Critical Editing' team, who facilitated workshops at the colloquium and from whom we have learned so much about language and culture in the Burgundian Netherlands throughout the project's lifespan. Joel Grossman and Sophia Wilson provided able editorial assistance with the index and bibliography respectively.

A.A., E.S., July 2017

NOTES ON THE CONTRIBUTORS

Adrian Armstrong is Centenary Professor of French at Queen Mary University of London. He is the author of *Technique and Technology: Script, Print, and Poetics in France, 1470–1550* (2000) and *The Virtuoso Circle: Competition, Collaboration, and Complexity in Late Medieval French Poetry* (2012), and co-author with Sarah Kay of *Knowing Poetry: Verse in Medieval France from the Rose to the Rhétoriqueurs* (2011). Between 2012 and 2016 he was Principal Investigator on the project 'Transcultural Critical Editing: Vernacular Poetry in the Burgundian Netherlands, 1450–1530', supported by the Arts and Humanities Research Council (AHRC) (grant number AH/J001481/1).

Dirk Coigneau is a former Professor of Dutch Literature at Ghent University. He is the author of *Refreinen in het zotte bij de rederijkers* (1980–83) and editor of *Mariken van Nieumeghen* (1982, 1996), and has published extensively on the work of Dutch-speaking rhetoricians. He is chair of the Ghent chamber of rhetoric De Fonteine, which was formally recognized in 1448 and which since 1943 has published a *Jaarboek* devoted to the historical study of *rederijker* culture and literature.

Laura Crombie is currently a teaching fellow in medieval history at the University of Leicester, having previously taught at the University of York. Her publications, including her first monograph *Archery and Crossbow Guilds in Medieval Flanders* (2016), focus on urban culture and civic groups, particularly shooting guilds and connections between court and civic societies. She is currently researching towns and war, and cultural and diplomatic connections between Scotland and the Burgundian Low Countries *c.* 1384–1477.

Rebecca Dixon is Lecturer in French at the University of Liverpool. Her work has focused on late medieval Burgundian culture, vernacular prose and verse literature, text/image relations in manuscript and early print, and costume and material culture. Her forthcoming monograph, *A Romance Spectacular: Mises en Prose, Cultural Consumption, and Lifestyle Aspiration in Burgundy (1445–67)*, and the critical edition of the *Roman de Buscalus* which she is preparing, bring together these varied interests.

Catherine Emerson lectures in French at the National University of Ireland, Galway. Her research mainly focuses on the historical writing of the Burgundian court, on early printed editions of medieval texts, and on Belgium. She is the author of *Olivier de La Marche and the Rhetoric of Fifteenth-Century Historiography* (2004) and *Regarding Manneken Pis: Culture, Celebration and Conflict in Brussels* (2014), and is a contributor to the international project 'Charlemagne: A European Icon', funded by the Leverhulme Trust (2015–18).

Dirk Schoenaers (PhD University of Liverpool) has held postdoctoral positions at University College London ('Medieval Francophone Literary Culture Outside France', 2011–15) and the University of St. Andrews ('The *Jacquerie* and Late Medieval Revolts', 2015). He is mainly interested in manuscript studies, transcultural contact in the Burgundian Low Countries, and the ways in which historiographical narratives are reframed to suit new political contexts. His current activities include a collaborative book project on the history of translation in the Low Countries (with Theo Hermans, Cees Koster, Inger Leemans, and Ton Naaijkens) and research into Jean d'Enghien's *Livre des croniques* (Brabant, *c.* 1470).

Elsa Strietman is a former Senior Lecturer in Dutch and Fellow of Murray Edwards College, Cambridge. Her research focuses on the dramatic and theatrical culture of the Low Countries in the fifteenth and sixteenth centuries, particularly chambers of rhetoric and their significance in urban society. She has translated a number of medieval and sixteenth-century plays from the Low Countries into English, and is also active as a translator of medieval and sixteenth-century poetry, seventeenth- and eighteenth-century satirical poetry and prose, and neo-classical drama.

Susie Speakman Sutch is a postdoctoral researcher in the History Department at Ghent University. Her research encompasses the contribution of chambers of rhetoric, devotional brotherhoods, book production, and translation as cultural interface to urban culture in the Dutch-speaking Low Countries during the late fifteenth and early sixteenth centuries. She has recently published on the Brussels Seven Sorrows Confraternity, and on politics and printing in the region.

Anne-Laure Van Bruaene teaches early modern cultural history and urban history at Ghent University. Most of her work concerns the Low Countries in the period from *c.* 1450 to *c.* 1650. She is the author of *De Gentse memorieboeken als spiegel van stedelijk historisch bewustzijn (14de tot 16de eeuw)* (1998) and *Om beters wille: Rederijkerskamers en de stedelijke cultuur in de Zuidelijke Nederlanden (1400–1650)* (2008). In 2016 she co-edited *Gouden eeuwen: stad en samenleving in de Lage Landen, 1100–1600* (with Bruno Blondé and Marc Boone), and a themed issue of *BMGN-Low Countries Historical Review* on iconoclasm (with Koenraad Jonckheere and Ruben Suykerbuyk).

Malcolm Walsby is a lecturer at the University of Rennes II and co-director of the Universal Short Title Catalogue. He is the author of *The Counts of Laval: Culture, Patronage and Religion in Fifteenth- and Sixteenth-Century France* (2007) and *The Printed Book in Brittany (1480–1600)* (2011). He has also edited two volumes on European book history, as well as three bibliographies of French and Netherlandish books. Most recently he has published *Entre l'atelier et le lecteur: le commerce du livre imprimé dans la France de la Renaissance* and *The French Provincial Book Trade Index 1470–1600* (both 2017).

INTRODUCTION

Adrian Armstrong

Exchange and negotiation were fundamental to life in the late medieval Burgundian Netherlands.[1] In economic terms, the exceptional importance of trade and commerce in the region caused its major cities to become European hubs as well as manufacturing centres. In political terms, relations of power and consent were played out between so many parties — including the Dukes of Burgundy and their régime, urban élites in the various and often competing cities, local nobility, and the multiple institutions within the Church, not to mention neighbours such as the kingdom of France — that delicate balances constantly had to be struck anew.[2] In cultural terms, activities ranging from the plastic arts to popular culture were sustained and encouraged by a mixture of patronage, commissions, and institutions (such as chambers of rhetoric and crossbow guilds) that promoted both collaboration and competition.[3] Scholars in diverse disciplines have widely acknowledged all these types of interaction. Very few, however, have reflected on a hugely important form of exchange: between the vernacular languages spoken in the region, and the cultural products realized in those languages.

Communication between native speakers of French and Dutch was of course essential not only to take best advantage of trading opportunities, but also for political purposes in the broadest sense.[4] A few instances of this communication are well known to specialists, albeit often at second hand: George Chastelain, the ducal *indiciaire* [poet and historian] who was born into a family of Ghent shippers but discharged his literary duties exclusively in French; the professional advantages of multilingualism for ducal administrators; the practice in some families of sending children to live for a time with a family who spoke the other vernacular; the existence of phrase books and vocabularies, in both manuscript and print.[5] Yet literary historians of the Burgundian Netherlands have overwhelmingly focused exclusively on either French or Dutch, notwithstanding some excellent studies of works translated from one to the other.[6] There are doubtless multiple reasons for this tendency: the limitations of researchers' training, the shortage of models (whether published studies or individual scholars) to emulate, the disciplinary strictures of scholarly institutions and associations, or indeed assumptions of an ideological kind.[7] The result is a denial, or at least a serious distortion, of the intertextual and interdiscursive contexts within which vernacular writing in the region acquired its meanings.[8] Certainly the formally elaborate devotional poetry of Jean Molinet, Chastelain's successor as *indiciaire*, cannot be considered in isolation from its most obvious analogues, the religious verse composed within the kingdom of France around the same time.⁹ Yet Dutch-speaking poets in the Burgundian Netherlands produced similarly sophisticated work — most notably the Marian poetry of Molinet's Bruges contemporary, Anthonis de Roovere. As contributions to the region's lively culture of vernacular verse piety, the compositions of Molinet and De Roovere demand to be read against each other, regardless of whether any relationships of influence can be posited.¹⁰

To read specific forms of French- and Dutch-language Burgundian writing side by side is just one way of revealing the multiple affiliations between these cohabiting literatures. Other approaches include the analysis of translated texts; of lexical borrowing and code-switching; of the cross-cultural dimensions of book production in the region; of the ways in which writers in one language represent users of the other; and of institutions and cultural practices that encouraged interactions between speakers of different languages. In conjunction, these perspectives indicate that writing in the Burgundian Netherlands is a *transcultural* activity: it is informed by interactions between different cultures, languages, and communities, which it in turn helps to shape. This is particularly true of poetry, as opposed to the other major literary forms of the region, prose romance and historiography.¹¹ In late medieval western Europe, verse was a more public medium than prose: it was much more frequently produced by or for collective bodies, whether these were courts, chambers of rhetoric, or theatre audiences.¹² Consequently, verse has much greater potential for dissemination outside its immediate public, and hence for resonating across cultures.

These insights were the basis for a collective research project, co-directed by the editors of this book, entitled 'Transcultural Critical Editing: Vernacular Poetry in the Burgundian Netherlands, 1450–1530' and supported by the Arts and Humanities Research Council (AHRC) between 2012 and 2016. The main priority of the project was to produce new scholarly editions of poetry from the region, with an apparatus that paid especial attention to its transcultural dimensions. Complementing this editorial activity, a colloquium on transcultural aspects of poetry in the Burgundian Netherlands was held in September 2013 in Murray Edwards College, Cambridge. In satisfyingly mimetic fashion, the colloquium created a space of exchange between researchers with disparate disciplinary and linguistic specialisms: the project team presented and discussed the editions in progress, while other speakers shared their work on interactions between languages, texts, and cultures in the region. The result was an unprecedented collective engagement with the issues, bearing witness to the recent emergence of scholars with the skills, intellectual commitment, and readiness to collaborate that now make it possible to envisage sustained and extensive research in the field. Hence the 'Transcultural Critical Editing' project built on the limited number of existing studies, and engaged in fruitful dialogue with simultaneous ventures that were similarly capitalizing on a new critical mass of expertise.¹³

The studies collected in this volume, revised (often significantly) from papers delivered at the colloquium, encompass the diverse forms of contact between French- and Dutch-language poetry noted above. Lexical borrowing and code-switching, and the shifting relationship between them, are addressed by the first two pieces. Dirk Schoenaers re-evaluates the use of French loan-words in Middle Dutch literature in Holland and Zeeland, as both a symptom of linguistic and social modernity and a means of negotiating power and identity. The process is closely intertwined with linguistic changes that produce a 'mixed idiom' in the language of administration, an effect of the integration of these northern counties into the composite Burgundian state. Far from reflecting the dubious linguistic or stylistic competence of Dutch-speaking authors, loans demonstrate the authors' facility in French, and therefore enable them to share in the prestige associated with the ducal authorities. Catherine Emerson considers code-switching in the work of the three major authors we have already encountered: Chastelain, Molinet, and De Roovere. Striking patterns emerge from the distribution of Dutch/French switches according to context, function, and genre. While Dutch terms in French-language texts tend to have an 'ethnographic' value, conveying a flavour of Dutch-speaking communities, French terms in Dutch-language texts are often difficult to distinguish from Latin vocabulary.[14] Indeed, switches from either language involve Latin much more often than the other vernacular. At the same time, the medium of verse proves perhaps surprisingly amenable to loans and switches. Both Schoenaers and Emerson identify various occurrences at the rhyme — the point at which a poem is most obviously a poem, and whose structural prominence cannot but emphasize the process of borrowing.

Malcolm Walsby's account of printing in the Low Countries reveals a broad shift in the patterns of French-language printing. Literary publication dwindled in importance after the fifteenth century, while Antwerp's dominance in francophone printing was even more pronounced than its preponderance in the industry as a whole. The vernaculars co-existed in various publication contexts: not only in dictionaries and vocabularies, but also in books published simultaneously in both languages, usually by bilingual printers. Walsby notes the significance of distribution networks, reminding us that the book culture of the Low Countries cannot be considered in isolation. Texts composed in one area were often published in another; the books that people bought and read had not always been produced in the region; the region's printers did not necessarily cater for an exclusively local market. We might identify further complications of the linguistic and cultural landscape: the relationship between Latin and vernaculars; diversity within vernaculars; the important presence of English translators, publishers, and readers in the region.[15] Hence binary distinctions between French and Dutch can only ever be a heuristic convenience. In this light, a transcultural perspective might best be considered as an antidote to the limitations of inherited literary-historical concepts and terminology.

Anne-Laure Van Bruaene and Laura Crombie address different kinds of performative activity that brought together French-speaking and Dutch-speaking individuals and communities. Van Bruaene discusses the early development of both Dutch- and French-speaking chambers of rhetoric in the Burgundian Netherlands, focusing particularly on the relationship between the French-speaking *puys mariaux*, poetry competitions in honour of the Virgin Mary, and the early Dutch-speaking chambers devoted to the Holy Ghost or Trinity. Both types of institution, and the cultures within which they developed, were marked — albeit to varying degrees — by different forms of competition, collective and individual. Mutual influences were significant: chambers and *puys* adapted and influenced elements from each other; French terminology percolated into Dutch-speaking bodies, and some contests were bilingual. Crombie examines archery and crossbow competitions, in which urban communities from across the Low Countries performed a set of shared values that transcended linguistic difference and commercial self-interest. The events could involve spectacular entry ceremonies, and were sometimes commemorated in verse. Reading two poems against each other, a Dutch account of the entries into Ghent for its competition of 1498, and a French poem celebrating the shoot at Tournai a century earlier, Crombie shows not only how they document the participating communities' self-understanding, but also how the medium of verse is particularly appropriate for commemorative purposes.

While performative institutions foster broadly parallel trends in the French- and Dutch-language poetry produced within and around them, traffic between the languages is manifested in cases of 'rewriting', André Lefevere's powerfully synthetic notion that embraces multiple forms of adaptation as well as translation in the more conventional sense.[16] Yet while Lefevere — aptly enough a native of Belgium — insists on the ways in which rewriting is governed by the target culture's ideology and aesthetics, the translations and adaptations produced in the Burgundian Netherlands often manifest a more two-way interplay between source and target cultures. Aspects of the language, form, and values of French-language texts can exert a certain impact on their Dutch rewritings. Even highly interventionist rewritings exemplify the competitive ethos that permeates the poetic cultures of both languages, in the *puys* and chambers of rhetoric and elsewhere — the difference is simply that the competition takes place between author and translator/adaptor, rather than between authors who speak the same vernacular.[17] Hence, as Dirk Coigneau reveals, prose stories from the famous fifteenth-century Burgundian court collection *Les Cent Nouvelles nouvelles* are transformed into something altogether more complex when Dutch-speaking rhetoricians use their plots as the basis for verse drama. Colijn van Rijssele's *Spieghel der minnen* and Cornelis Everaert's *Esbatement van den visscher* not only emphasize different themes, but also adopt the more formally challenging medium of verse and confront the structural and logistical complexities of theatre. In this sense, Van Rijssele and Everaert outdo their sources in compositional sophistication; a subtle 'interplay of dependence and empowerment' is at work, which can also be seen in a later verse adaptation by Jan Fruytiers and in some of the amplifications in prose translations (*Dat bedroch der vrouwen, Die ontrouwe der mannen*). Susie Speakman Sutch and Rebecca Dixon analyze more conventional cases of interlingual translation, where the impact of French-language sources reveals itself in diverse and sometimes surprising ways. Focusing on two Dutch translations of Olivier de La Marche's *Chevalier délibéré*, Sutch demonstrates that French lexis is strikingly present in Johannes Pertcheval's *Camp vander doot*, whereas Pieter

Willemsz's *Vanden ridder welghemoet* relies considerably less on loan-words yet often conveys nuances of the source text more effectively. Both translators demonstrate their understanding of francophone cultural productions, Pertcheval by drawing on the cross-cultural literary idiom of Brussels and Willemsz by engaging carefully with his source. Dixon considers the impact of form rather than vocabulary, by examining the role of verse in *Van den drie blinde danssen*, a translation of Pierre Michault's *prosimetrum* allegory *La Dance aux aveugles*. Michault's verse sections evince meaningful contrasts in line length, which cannot be reproduced directly in a language where versification is stress-based rather than syllabic; accordingly, the translator conveys these contrasts through variations in stanzaic form. On one level this constitutes what scholars of translation studies call 'compensation': 'a technique for making up the loss of a source text effect by recreating a similar effect in the target text through means that are specific to the target language and/or the target text'.[18] On another level, however, various features of the Dutch verse indicate competition rather than compensation: the stanzaic structures of *Van den drie blinde danssen* are technically more challenging than in *La Dance aux aveugles*.

From these complementary approaches a number of common threads emerge, relevant not only to the poetic culture of the Burgundian Low Countries but also to the nature of transcultural exchange in pre-modern societies more generally. In the first place, it is clear that the region's transcultural productions often go beyond the indigenous vernacular speech communities of French and Dutch. This partly reflects the importance of Latin as a shared language for educated speakers. Besides its fundamental role as the medium of expression in the Church, in educational institutions, and in diplomacy, Latin served more generally to facilitate trans-regional communication in the Low Countries as it did elsewhere in Europe. Indeed, it could aid comprehension of a reader's own vernacular: varieties of Dutch were sometimes translated into Latin for speakers of other varieties, as Emerson notes, while Latin glosses are used to distinguish between French homophones in Jean Molinet's *Art de rhétorique*.[19] In principle at least, then, Latin provided more opportunities for speakers of different vernaculars to interact in the cultural sphere. These vernaculars were not solely French and Dutch: various audiences and patrons were speakers of English, Spanish, Italian, or varieties of German not native to the region. The presence of these languages in the Low Countries is further attested by trilingual or translated vocabularies.[20] Certain audiences, moreover, were competent in two or more of these vernaculars: such facility was not at all unique to translators. Sutch observes, for instance, that the Brussels readers of Pertcheval's *Camp vander doot* must have been familiar with literary French. Equally, the Aragonese and Catalan merchant community in Bruges comprised the audience of a Dutch-language verse play, *Tspel dat ghespeilt was voor de Aragoenoysen*, which Cornelis Everaert composed for a theatre competition to celebrate Charles V's victory over Francis I at Pavia in 1525.[21] Francophone Burgundian reactions to Pavia are less directly connected with such audiences: poets such as Julien Fossetier and Nicaise Ladam direct their work towards the emperor who now resides in Spain, rather than towards Spanish aristocrats or merchants who had journeyed in the opposite direction.[22] Nevertheless, the relationships that gave rise to Everaert's play, between Iberian power structures — both courtly and mercantile — and cultural activity in the Low Countries, generated various other transcultural products during and after the period under consideration. The Spanish affiliations of Philip the Handsome loom large in the career and output of the francophone poet and chronicler Nicaise Ladam (1465–1547), while the so-called 'Flemish Chapel' (*capilla flamenca*) of Charles V was made up of court musicians drawn from the Low Countries but based primarily in Spain.[23]

At the same time, book producers often solicited readers of different languages. Pertcheval's translation is again a case in point: its printer, Otgier Nachtegael of Schiedam, also produced an edition of La Marche's original poem in French.[24] A wider point is at issue here, one that is vital to an understanding of the transcultural qualities of so much writing in the region. Those involved in the cultural productions of the Burgundian Netherlands are not just authors, but also — as so many contributors to this volume demonstrate — translators, patrons, scribes, printers, and illustrators. In this respect the Low Countries are no different from elsewhere in late medieval Europe, and the diversity of cultural agents is surely crucial to transcultural processes in all pre-modern societies. However, in this region such diversity acts as a particularly strong multiplier on the possibilities for interaction between speakers of different vernaculars. Hence transcultural activity covers not only interlingual translation, but also public performance, book production, and much else besides.[25] This activity sometimes took place in musical contexts, appropriately enough in a period when poetry was regarded as having a fundamental connection with music.[26] The second songbook of Margaret of Austria (Brussels, Bibliothèque royale de Belgique, ms. 228) contains a Dutch song by Pierre de la Rue as well as French and Latin works; the *chansonnier* of Hieronymus Lauweryn van Watervliet (London, British Library, Add MS 35087) contains polyphonic songs based on texts in Dutch, French, and Latin.[27] More generally, the public performance of music — an important element of political and ceremonial culture in the Burgundian Netherlands — potentially created complex soundscapes involving both melodies and texts in different languages, a 'supermusicality' that no listener could apprehend in its entirety.[28]

In the same way as transcultural activity involves many more processes and participants than interlingual translation alone, so the formal and thematic echoes between texts in different languages cannot be ascribed solely to the rewriting of identifiable sources. Motifs and techniques from a common cultural store may be actualized in different linguistic and socio-literary settings, and in different media (for instance in narrative, drama, and song). Coigneau's contribution comes closest to addressing these phenomena, which are interdiscursive and transmedial rather than intertextual.[29] In early modern theatrical contexts, the term 'theatregram' has gained currency as a means of designating elements that are re-used across traditions in this way: it has the merit of covering characters and stylistic devices, as well as what scholarship has traditionally designated as topoi.[30] The same process is also apparent in other cultural forms, however. To the examples noted above —

the devotional poetry of Molinet and De Roovere, the literary responses to Pavia — we might add the rewriting of work by Jean Molinet for posthumous print publication, which is stimulated and facilitated by underlying narrative patterns or 'masterplots'.[31]

There is undoubtedly scope for further investigation into some of the individual areas touched on here: the transcultural qualities of the musical repertory, the place of poetry in English and Spanish, prevailing patterns in the use of theatregrams (or maybe 'scriptograms', since they are not at all limited to theatre). What is most important, however, is that these and other areas are interdependent; and that, in conjunction, they tell us something significant about poetry in the Burgundian Netherlands. We are apt to think of poetry as 'what gets lost in translation', as Robert Frost has been widely misquoted as claiming; a medium uniquely resistant to transmission across linguistic and cultural boundaries.[32] Yet the contributions to this volume demonstrate that poetry — an inherently public medium, disseminated by diverse cultural agents and in varying physical contexts (manuscript, print, performance) — in fact has a profoundly transcultural character in the region. Interactions between Dutch- and French-speakers in the sphere of poetry, whether direct or indirect, were more numerous and varied than historians of literature or culture have assumed. The editors seek not only to chart the range and significance of these interactions, but also to stimulate corresponding exchanges between the scholars of the future.

Notes to the Introduction

1. The historical literature on the region is vast. On what follows, see especially David Nicholas, *Medieval Flanders* (London: Longman, 1992); Walter Prevenier and Wim Blockmans, *The Burgundian Netherlands*, trans. by Peter King and Yvette Mead (Cambridge: Cambridge University Press, 1986); Bertrand Schnerb, *L'État bourguignon 1361–1477* (Paris: Perrin, 1999); *Networks, Regions and Nations: Shaping Identities in the Low Countries, 1300–1650*, ed. by Robert Stein and Judith Pollmann (Leiden: Brill, 2010); Richard Vaughan, *Philip the Good: The Apogee of Burgundy*, rev. edn, foreword by Graeme Small (Woodbridge: Boydell Press, 2002).
2. It is perhaps time to abandon the venerable commonplace observation that the region was frequently riven by conflict, and to ask instead why such conflicts did not take place more often.
3. See, for example, Till-Holger Borchert, 'The Mobility of Artists: Aspects of Cultural Transfer in Renaissance Europe', in *The Age of Van Eyck: The Mediterranean World and Early Netherlandish Painting 1430–1530*, ed. by Till-Holger Borchert, trans. by Ted Alkins and others (Bruges: Ludion, 2002), pp. 32–51; Laura Crombie, 'French and Flemish Urban Festive Networks: Archery and Crossbow Competitions Attended and Hosted by Tournai in the Fourteenth and Fifteenth Centuries', *French History*, 27 (2013), 157–75; Katell Lavéant, *Un théâtre des frontières: la culture dramatique dans les provinces du Nord aux XVe et XVIe siècles* (Orleans: Paradigme, 2011); Reinhard Strohm, *Music in Late Medieval Bruges*, rev. edn (Oxford: Clarendon Press, 1990); Arjan van Dixhoorn, *Lustige geesten: Rederijkers in de noordelijke Nederlanden (1480–1650)* (Amsterdam: Amsterdam University Press, 2009). Among the extremely rich scholarly literature on the culture of the late medieval Low Countries should also be noted the Brepols publication series Burgundica, and the publications of the Centre européen d'études bourguignonnes.
4. In accordance with standard usage in literary and historical research, 'Dutch' is used throughout this volume to refer to the totality of varieties of the West Germanic language spoken in the Low Countries. Terms such as 'Flemish' are used only to distinguish specific dialects. On the

context and varieties of Middle Dutch, see Roland Willemyns, *Dutch: Biography of a Language* (Oxford: Oxford University Press, 2013), pp. 48–77.

5. See Estelle Doudet, *Poétique de George Chastelain (1415–1475): 'Un cristal mucié en un coffre'* (Paris: Champion, 2005), pp. 120–33; C. A. J. Armstrong, 'The Language Question in the Low Countries: The Use of French and Dutch by the Dukes of Burgundy and their Administration' [1965], in *England, France and Burgundy in the Fifteenth Century* (London: Hambledon, 1983), pp. 189–212; Gilbert Degroote, 'Taaltoestanden in de Bourgondische Nederlanden', *De Nieuwe Taalgids*, 49 (1956), 303–09; *Le Livre des mestiers de Bruges et ses dérivés: quatre anciens manuels de conversation*, ed. by Jean Gessler (Bruges: Le Consortium des Maîtres Imprimeurs Brugeois, 1931); Alison Hanham, 'Who Made William Caxton's Phrase-Book?', *The Review of English Studies*, new ser., 56 (2005), 712–29. More generally, Serge Lusignan, *Essai d'histoire sociolinguistique: le français picard au Moyen Âge* (Paris: Garnier, 2012), pp. 187–233, discusses contact between Picard French and Middle Dutch.

6. Cynthia Brown, Susie Speakman Sutch, and Samuel Mareel, 'Polemics in Print in the Low Countries: *Venegien*: Transcription with Introduction and English Translation', *Queeste*, 19 (2012), 140–72; Colijn Caillieu, *Dal sonder wederkeeren of pas der doot*, ed. by Paul de Keyser (Antwerp: De Sikkel, 1936), pp. 45–54; Bas Jongenelen, 'Jan Pertcheval's Translation of *Le Chevalier délibéré*: Den camp vander doot — Source, Translation and Public', *Publications du Centre européen d'études bourguignonnes (XIVe–XVIe s.)*, 43 (2003), 199–212; Bas Jongenelen, 'Pieter Willemsz' vertaling van *Le Chevalier délibéré*: *Vanden ridder welghemoet* — Dichter tussen bron en lezers', in *Met eigen ogen: De rederijker als dichtend individu (1450–1600)*, ed. by Dirk Coigneau and Samuel Mareel, special issue of *Jaarboek De Fonteine*, 58 (2008), 233–51; Jan Pertcheval, *Den Camp vander doot*, ed. by Gilbert Degroote (Antwerp: De Sikkel, 1948), pp. xxvii–xxxiii.

7. Such assumptions, it must be stressed, do not necessarily reflect linguistic nationalism as expressed in modern political contexts (notably in Belgian party politics). Rather, they may involve unconscious attitudes to social class or other aspects of demography. For instance, the claim that French was the language of the Burgundian court while Dutch was the language of the cities — a claim occasionally encountered in historical writing on the region — rests upon the twin misconceptions that the feudal aristocracy and its entourage were exclusively francophone, and that no urban francophone communities existed in the region. On monolingual patterns in university teaching and research, see notably Samuel Mareel and Dirk Schoenaers, 'Introduction', *Literature and Multilingualism in the Low Countries (1100–1600)*, ed. by Samuel Mareel and Dirk Schoenaers, special issue of *Queeste*, 22.1 (2015), 1–7 (p. 3); Joep Leerssen, 'Philology and the European Construction of National Literatures', in *Editing the Nation's Memory: Textual Scholarship and Nation-Building in 19th-Century Europe*, ed. by Dirk van Hulle and Joep Leerssen (Amsterdam: Rodopi, 2008), pp. 13–27.

8. On interdiscursivity, see Cesare Segre, *Teatro e romanzo: due tipi di comunicazione letteraria* (Turin: Einaudi, 1984), p. 111.

9. On francophone devotional poetry of the period, see especially Gérard Gros, *Le Poète, la vierge et le prince du Puy: étude sur les Puys marials de la France du Nord du XIVe siècle à la Renaissance* (Paris: Klincksieck, 1992); Gérard Gros, *Le Poème du Puy marial: étude sur le serventois et le chant royal du XIVe siècle à la Renaissance* (Paris: Klincksieck, 1996); Denis Hüe, *La Poésie palinodique à Rouen (1486–1550)* (Paris: Champion, 2002).

10. In fact a persuasive case can be made that De Roovere adopted various techniques practised by Molinet and similar francophone poets, not all of them based in the Low Countries: see Johan Oosterman, 'Tussen twee wateren zwem ik: Anthonis de Roovere tussen rederijkers en rhétoriqueurs', *Jaarboek De Fonteine*, 49–50 (1999–2000), 11–29.

11. On prose romance, see Georges Doutrepont, *La Littérature française à la cour des ducs de Bourgogne* (Paris: Champion, 1909); Georges Doutrepont, *Les Mises en prose des épopées et des romans chevaleresques du XIVe au XVIe siècle* (Brussels: Palais des Académies, 1939); Bart Besamusca, 'The Medieval Dutch Arthurian Material', in *The Arthur of the Germans: The Arthurian Legend in Medieval German and Dutch Literature*, ed. by W. H. Jackson and S. A. Ranawake (Cardiff: University of Wales Press, 2000), pp. 187–228. On historiography, see *Littérature et culture historiques à la cour de Bourgogne*, ed. by Jean Devaux, special issue of *Le Moyen Âge*, 112.3–4 (2006);

Genoechlike ende lustige historiën: Laatmiddeleeuwse geschiedschrijving in Nederland, ed. by B. Ebels-Hoveling, C. Santing and C. P. H. M. Tilmans (Hilversum: Verloren, 1987); Graeme Small, *George Chastelain and the Shaping of Valois Burgundy: Political and Historical Culture at Court in the Fifteenth Century* (Woodbridge: Boydell Press, 1997); Michael Zingel, *Frankreich, das Reich und Burgund im Urteil der burgundischen Historiographie des 15. Jahrhunderts* (Sigmaringen: Thorbecke, 1995).

12. On these issues, see Adrian Armstrong and Sarah Kay, *Knowing Poetry: Verse in Medieval France from the 'Rose' to the 'Rhétoriqueurs'* (Ithaca, NY: Cornell University Press, 2011), pp. 199–200.
13. Previous studies include, in particular, *Rhetoric — Rhétoriqueurs — Rederijkers*, ed. by Jelle Koopmans and others (Amsterdam: North-Holland, 1995); Lavéant, *Un théâtre des frontières*; Oosterman, 'Tussen twee wateren'; Graeme Small, 'When Indiciaires Meet Rederijkers: A Contribution to the History of the Burgundian "Theatre State"', in *Stad van koopmanschap en vrede: Literatuur in Brugge tussen middeleeuwen en rederijkerstijd*, ed. by Johan Oosterman (Leuven: Peeters, 2005), pp. 133–61; and *The Reach of the Republic of Letters: Literary and Learned Societies in Late Medieval and Early Modern Europe*, ed. by Arjan van Dixhoorn and Susie Speakman Sutch, 2 vols (Leiden: Brill, 2008). Simultaneous work includes the AHRC-funded project 'Medieval Francophone Literary Culture Outside France', <http://www.ustc.ac.uk> [accessed 23 June 2014], and *Literature and Multilingualism in the Low Countries (1100–1600)*, ed. by Mareel and Schoenaers.
14. The incidences of switching in these French-language texts are strikingly reminiscent of those in French documents written by Dutch-speakers in Flanders and Brabant. Lusignan, pp. 199–202, notes that the Picard French in these documents is very close to that recorded in francophone regions; however, authors often fall back on Dutch to express locally specific technical, legal, and administrative concepts for which they know no appropriate term in French.
15. Jelle Koopmans addressed these issues, among others, in a paper delivered at the Cambridge colloquium, 'Langues et cultures, politiques et pratiques — une vue sur la longue durée'.
16. See especially André Lefevere, *Translation, Rewriting, and the Manipulation of Literary Fame* (London: Routledge, 1992).
17. On this principle, see Adrian Armstrong, 'Translating Poetic Capital in Fifteenth-Century Brussels: From Amé de Montgesoie's *Pas de la Mort* to Colijn Caillieu's *Dal sonder Wederkeeren*', *Literature and Multilingualism in the Low Countries (1100–1600)*, ed. by Mareel and Schoenaers, pp. 47–61.
18. Keith Harvey, 'A Descriptive Framework for Compensation', *The Translator: Studies in Intercultural Communication*, 1 (1995), 65–86 (p. 66).
19. Jean Molinet, *L'Art de rhétorique*, in *Recueil d'arts de seconde rhétorique*, ed. by Ernest Langlois (Paris: Imprimerie Nationale, 1902), pp. 214–52 (p. 252). On the relationship between Latin and Dutch in a book collection of the late fourteenth century, see Renée Gabriël, 'Boekenlijsten en *Material Philology*: Methodologische overwegingen bij de boekenlijst van Michael van der Stoct (ca. 1394)', *Queeste*, 16 (2009), 83–111.
20. Previous research on English book culture has occasionally noted the relevance of translations or publications from the Low Countries, albeit in the context of a broader perspective (such as the continental book trade, or literature in French) within which the region's cultural products do not receive a sustained treatment. Two excellent studies of this kind are Martha W. Driver, *The Image in Print: Book Illustration in Late Medieval England and its Sources* (London: The British Library, 2004), esp. pp. 36–39, 41–42, 67, 131; and Anne E. B. Coldiron, *English Printing, Verse Translation, and the Battle of the Sexes, 1476–1557* (Farnham: Ashgate, 2009), esp. p. 3. I am grateful to Johan Oosterman for pointing out that a number of manuscripts from Flanders, most of them probably produced in Bruges, contain texts in German: they include Copenhagen, Kongelige Bibliotek, MS GKS 79 (*Spegel der minschliken zalicheid*); New York, Pierpont Morgan Library, MS M 76 (Book of Hours); Glasgow, University Library, MS Gen. 2 (prayers); Wolfenbüttel, Herzog August Bibliothek, Cod. Guelf 84.2.1 Aug 12° (prayer book of Albrecht of Brandenburg); and Kassel, Universitätsbibliothek, 4° Ms. poet. et roman. 5 (*Dance of Death*). On translated vocabularies, see Hanham, 'Who Made William Caxton's Phrase-Book?'. An example of a trilingual vocabulary, with appropriate text on its title-page, is *Vocabulario para aprender Franches,*

Espannol y Flamincq | Vocabulaire pour apprendre Franchoys, Espagnol et Flaming | Vocabulaire om te leerene Wallich, Spaensch, ende Vlaemich (Antwerp: Willem Vorsterman, 1520) (USTC 78033) (see *Universal Short Title Catalogue*, <http://www.ustc.ac.uk> [accessed 9 July 2014]). Throughout this volume, quotations from manuscripts and early printed books have been normalized in accordance with standard editorial practice: hence abbreviations have been expanded, *i/j* and *u/v* distinguished, capitalization regularized, and so forth. Translations are the contributors' own unless otherwise stated.

21. See Cornelis Everaert, *De spelen*, ed. by W. N. M. Hüsken, 2 vols (Hilversum: Verloren, 2005), I, 274–99.
22. See Estelle Doudet, 'Un chant déraciné? La poésie bourguignonne d'expression française face à Charles Quint', *e-Spania*, 13 (2012), <DOI: 10.4000/e-spania.21220>. On francophone literary reactions to Pavia more generally, see Claude Thiry, 'L'Honneur et l'Empire: à propos des poèmes de langue française sur la bataille de Pavie', in *Mélanges à la mémoire de Franco Simone* (Geneva: Slatkine, 1980), pp. 297–324.
23. The presence of Philip in Ladam's work was illuminatingly traced by Claude Thiry in a paper delivered at the Cambridge colloquium, 'Nicaise Ladam et Philippe le Beau'. On the 'Flemish Chapel', see Bruno Bouckaert, 'The *Capilla Flamenca*: The Composition and Duties of the Music Ensemble at the Court of Charles V, 1515–1558', in *The Empire Resounds: Music in the Days of Charles V*, ed. by Francis Maes (Leuven: Leuven University Press, 1999), pp. 36–45.
24. The phenomenon is not limited to French- and Dutch-speaking audiences, nor to printing. See Lotte Hellinga, 'William Caxton, Colard Mansion, and the Printer in Type 1', *Bulletin du bibliophile* (2011), 86–114.
25. This observation is developed further in Adrian Armstrong, '"Imprimé en la ville marchande et renommée d'Anvers": Antwerp Editions of Jean Molinet's Poetry', in *Between Stability and Transformation: Textual Traditions in the Medieval Netherlands*, ed. by Johan Oosterman, special issue of *Queeste*, 23.2 (2016), 123–37. See also Margriet Hoogvliet, 'Middle Dutch Religious Reading Cultures in Late Medieval France', in *Literature and Multilingualism in the Low Countries (1100–1600)*, ed. by Mareel and Schoenaers, pp. 29–46.
26. See especially Philipp Jeserich, *Musica naturalis: Speculative Music Theory and Poetics, from Saint Augustine to the Late Middle Ages in France*, trans. by Michael J. Curley and Steven Rendall (Baltimore, MD: Johns Hopkins University Press, 2013); Nelleke Moser, *De strijd voor rhetorica: Poëtica en positie van rederijkers in Vlaanderen, Brabant, Zeeland en Holland tussen 1450 en 1620* (Amsterdam: Amsterdam University Press, 2001), pp. 98–130.
27. Ignace Bossuyt, 'Charles as a Young Man at the Court of Marguerite of Austria', in *The Empire Resounds*, ed. by Maes, pp. 85–93 (pp. 88, 90–91).
28. On music at the Burgundian court, see Honey Meconi, 'Foundation for an Empire: The Musical Inheritance of Charles V', in *The Empire Resounds*, ed. by Maes, pp. 19–34; Emily Snow, 'The Lady of Sorrows: Music, Devotion, and Politics in the Burgundian-Habsburg Netherlands' (unpublished doctoral dissertation, Princeton University, 2010). The notion of the 'supermusical' is coined in Emma Dillon, *The Sense of Sound: Musical Meaning in France, 1260–1330* (Oxford: Oxford University Press, 2012), p. 8; see also pp. 59–61 on soundscapes in the context of medieval cities. Strohm, *Music in Late Medieval Bruges*, pp. 102–50, notes Dutch, French, and Latin material in the musical repertory of one of the region's major cities.
29. On interdiscursivity, see n. 8 above. On transmediality, see Irina O. Rajewsky, 'Intermediality, Intertextuality, and Remediation: A Literary Perspective on Intermediality', *Intermédialités*, 6 (Autumn 2005), 43–64 (p. 46). I am indebted to Estelle Doudet for the perspectives outlined in this paragraph, which she is developing in ongoing work on late medieval theatre.
30. See Louise George Clubb, *Italian Drama in Shakespeare's Time* (New Haven, CT: Yale University Press, 1989), p. 6.
31. Armstrong, '"Imprimé en la ville marchande et renommée d'Anvers"', p. 133, discusses the role of masterplots in Antwerp editions of work by Molinet. Strohm, *Music in Late Medieval Bruges*, p. 108, notes aspects of form and content that recur across French- and Dutch-language songs in late medieval Bruges.
32. The misquotation derives from Frost's suggestion that 'I could define poetry this way: It is that

which is lost out of both prose and verse in translation' (Robert Frost, *Conversations on the Craft of Poetry*, ed. by Cleanth Brooks and Robert Penn Warren, 3rd edn (New York: Holt, Rinehart and Winston, 1961), p. 7).

CHAPTER 1

'Frenchified': A Contact-based Approach to Transculturation and Linguistic Change in Holland-Zeeland (1428/33–c. 1500)[1]

Dirk Schoenaers

The *Lexicon Balatronicum or A Dictionary of Buckish Slang, University Wit, and Pickpocket Eloquence* defines 'frenchified' as 'infected with the venereal disease'. A few lines up the page, the example for 'French Disease' ('He suffered by a blow over the snout with a French faggot stick; i.e. he lost his nose by the pox') identifies this imported affliction as syphilis.[2] Today, 'to frenchify' could be paraphrased more generally as 'to make something more French(-sounding)'. Nonetheless, the slang meaning gives a clear insight into the popular appreciation of French origins in England at the beginning of the nineteenth century. At the same time, this vulgar sense of 'to frenchify' also applies to the largely negative scholarly evaluation of French lexical influences on official and literary texts written in the Dutch-speaking part of the Low Countries during the later Middle Ages.[3] In previous centuries, literary scholars and linguists have claimed that the tumultuous liaison between francophone and Dutch culture in that period — absolutely smitten with each other in the thirteenth century, seemingly less passionate in the fourteenth century, and the passion eventually rekindled in the fifteenth century — left the written vernacular with a burning itch.[4] However, more recently it has become increasingly clear that this obsession with unsullied language is entrenched in nationalistic ideology and sustains the purist discourse of homogenizing and prescriptive early-modern grammars, rather than properly reflecting the complexity of late medieval linguistic reality.[5] Moreover, the tendency to distinguish firmly between the impact of French in administrative sources and in literary texts may very well be based on questionable grounds. Accordingly, in what follows I propose a more open-minded, contact-based, and multicausal view of French lexical influence in the fifteenth century.

French Lexical Influence in Administrative and Literary Language: A Brief State of the Art

In the past, scholars have repeatedly emphasized that documents issued by regional and municipal administrations in the Dutch-speaking part of the Low Countries during the fourteenth and fifteenth centuries are riddled with French-sounding words. The presence of these borrowings is usually ascribed to the incorporation of the various principalities in this area into the Burgundian conglomerate.[6] Over a period of nearly a century, the individual regions of Flanders (1384), Brabant (1396/1406–30), Holland and Zeeland (1427/28–1433), and finally also Guelders (1473), all for the most part Dutch-speaking, were brought together under the rule of the dukes of Burgundy. These Valois princes were all bilingual to some degree, meaning that they spoke and understood Dutch. Nonetheless, to all intents and purposes, they were francophone. In this respect it comes as no surprise that, although these foreign rulers did not enforce a strict language policy, in most of the regional chanceries the dynastic change also caused a notable shift in the balance of power between the Dutch and French vernaculars.[7] In practice, local dialects continued to serve as the administrative language for day-to-day government. However, correspondence with the supra-regional level was to be drafted in French, in the Dutch-speaking parts of the conglomerate as elsewhere.[8] Obviously this twin-track linguistic policy required a considerable degree of bilingualism on the part of regional officials, who needed not only to understand but also to be able to translate official documents between Dutch and French (or Latin). In a brief discussion first published in 1931, C. G. N. de Vooys characterized the ensuing French influence on official documents pejoratively as 'overwoekering' [overgrowth] and detrimental to the expressivity of the Dutch language.[9] About sixty years later, and despite recognizing that French language skills could facilitate social advancement, Roland Willemyns tentatively attributed the gallicisms of administrative 'vertalingsnederlands' [translationese] to 'de onvoldoende taalcompetentie van sommige "verfranste" ambtenaren' [the linguistic incompetence of certain 'frenchified' bureaucrats].[10]

The connection between these linguistic developments in regional administrations and a similar trend in literary language has not always been fully appreciated.[11] In 1906, J. J. Salverda de Grave called the 'werkelik [sic] misbruik' [genuinely excessive use] of French words by the 'beperkte kring der Rederijkerkamers' [restricted circle of chambers of rhetoric] a temporary fad. He further added that borrowings in the poetic lexicon should be considered separately from administrative jargon, since '[d]e talrijke veranderingen die het centrale gezag [...] heeft ondergaan, hebben de letterkundige schrijftaal veel minder aangetast dan de officiële taal' [the numerous changes of authority [...] have affected literary writing far less than the official language].[12] Explanations for fashionable French loans in literary texts, as opposed to official documents, have tended to include stylistic preference and the influence of French examples. For instance, in his discussion of *De spiegel der minnen* [The Mirror of Love], written by the Brussels rhetorician Colijn van Rijssele (c. 1430/40–c. 1500), Gerard Knuvelder acknowledged that the negative scholarly evaluation of late medieval literary style was probably due to the prejudiced application of a modern aesthetic:

> Desondanks is dit stuk voor de moderne lezer vrijwel ongenietbaar. Ons hoofdbezwaar geldt de taal, waarin het geschreven werd; ook de grootste bewonderaars kunnen niet ontkennen, dat 'de verfranschte vormelijke liefdeszangen, dikwijls in onverstaanbare rederijkerstaal' geschreven zijn.[13]
>
> [Nonetheless, this play is practically indigestible to a modern readership. Our main objection is to the language in which it was written; even its greatest admirers cannot deny that the 'frenchified formal love lyrics [are] often [composed] in the gibberish of rhetoricians'.]

With reference to the story's long-winded elaboration, Knuvelder anachronistically wondered: 'Zullen Colijns tijdgenoten ook ons bezwaar gedeeld hebben [...]?' [Would Colijn's contemporaries have shared our objections?]. However, Colijn van Rijssele's use of French-sounding words was at least partly justified by his desire 'een echt réderijkers-toneelstuk te schrijven, waarin rijkheid aan klank door middel van welklinkende woorden, rondelen, overdadige rijmen en knutselarijen moest domineren' [to write a real rhetorician's play, dominated by the opulence of sound created by the use of sonorous words, roundels, extravagant rhyme, and ornamentation].[14] More recently, Herman Pleij described the linguistic characteristics and style of the *Spiegel* as 'die van een volbloed rederijker' [those of a thoroughbred rhetorician]. Abstaining from further modern value judgments, Pleij argued that the formal features of late medieval Dutch rhetoricians' literature should be evaluated against the backdrop of an intellectual, emancipatory programme partly inspired by French literary models.[15]

These partial explanations and evaluations of French lexical influence are mostly negative. Nonetheless, it seems justified to suggest an alternative line of reasoning, which sets the linguistic innovations caused by language contact in the Burgundian administrative apparatus in a more positive light. Indeed, the appropriate use of terminology, as well as a considerable degree of bilingualism, must have been invaluable in the daily routine of those involved in cross-cultural interaction: chancery clerks, secretaries, legal and financial experts, diplomats, and others. In this respect it seems plausible that the mixed idiom was not the result of linguistic incompetence, but rather that lexical borrowing (or code-switching between vernaculars) was a sign that these officials deeply appreciated the importance of linguistic usage in the negotiation of power relations and professional identities.[16] Furthermore, recent prosopographical studies have demonstrated that contemporary cultural and administrative networks overlapped.[17] It therefore seems fair to advance the hypothesis that certain stylistic features of official writing and literature in the Burgundian Netherlands can be seen more productively as two interlocking circuits rather than, as previously suggested, the products of two largely distinct worlds.

Contact Explanations for Linguistic Change in Holland: Multiple Causation

In her definition of contact-induced linguistic change, Sarah Thomason notes that 'contact is a source of linguistic change if it is less likely that a particular change would have happened outside a specific contact situation'. Interestingly, she pauses to point out that changes often occur for multiple reasons, and adds that 'a growing body of evidence suggests that multiple causation [...] is responsible for a sizable number of changes'. In other words, it has become increasingly clear that there is no one-to-one mapping of contact-related cause onto linguistic effect. In an additional caveat Thomason advises that 'efforts to argue for contact-induced change without identifying a contact situation in which it could have occurred are doomed to failure'.[18] Bearing this in mind, I will first further specify the contact situations (political/administrative, cultural, and commercial) that are most likely to have prompted changes in the administrative and poetic idiom. For each of these situations, a number of potentially related examples from literary texts will be discussed. For reasons explained below, the focus will be on the counties of Holland and Zeeland in the most northern part of the Low Countries.

It hardly needs repeating that even before the integration of the Low Countries into the Burgundian conglomerate, language contact was ubiquitous in the principalities that would later become the *pays de par-deçà*. In the first place, daily routine was deeply permeated by the cohabitation of Latin and the local vernaculars, most importantly in the fields of religion, education, administration, and science.[19] No less frequent, however, was contact between the local Germanic and Romance dialects. Flanders and Brabant were both bilingual regions, traversed by a fluid language frontier that virtually divided the mainly Dutch-speaking areas in the north from the Romance territories to the south.[20] Nonetheless, the flourishing production of French-language manuscripts in urban centres in Flanders during the second half of the thirteenth century and the first decades of the fourteenth, together with contemporary Dutch translations and adaptations of francophone epic and romance, provide ample evidence of the exceptional degree of cultural osmosis between these two seemingly distinct linguistic areas. Indeed, in previous centuries, French — which in these areas meant Picard — had become a cultural lingua franca of elite networks, in the Low Countries as elsewhere. Possibly even more important was that, along with other European vernaculars such as Italian, Spanish, German, and English, French was widely used as a common tongue in commercial exchange.[21]

This heteroglossic climate was by no means confined to the border regions in the South. Similar tendencies were also noted in the northern territories of the Dutch language area. In the *Rijmkroniek van Holland* [Verse Chronicle of Holland], written *c.* 1280 and continued *c.* 1301/14, it is mentioned that once her nephew Florent V (1254–96) was of an appropriate age, Adelaide of Holland (*c.* 1230–84), the widow of John of Avesnes, Count of Hainaut, ensured that her ward would 'Walsch ende Dietsch leren wel' [become proficient in French and Dutch].[22] Even if this statement does not accurately reflect biographical reality, it indicates the appreciation of bilingualism and language teaching in contemporary aristocratic circles in Holland.

After the untimely death of Florent's son, John I of Holland (1284–99), the county was subsumed in a personal union with Hainaut and was ruled by the francophone Avesnes dynasty for over half a century (1299–1358).

Even after the Bavarian Duke Albert of Wittelsbach had assumed regency in Holland in 1358, French remained an important language at the court. Although the native vernacular of the Bavarian counts was a German dialect, they entertained excellent relations with French courtly circles in Paris. Albert's son, William VI of Holland, frequently resided there to manage the affairs of his princely son-in-law, John of Touraine.[23] In 1406, William's only daughter and heir, Jacqueline, was betrothed to the French dauphin; the princely couple were raised and educated at the castle of Le Quesnoy.[24] The Wittelsbachs had also inherited the Avesnes' territories in Hainaut. In Holland, a *walschclerc* or French secretary processed documents relating to these French-speaking areas.[25] The entertainment at the itinerant court had international appeal and was undoubtedly multilingual.[26] In his much-praised monograph *Court and Culture*, Frits van Oostrom has highlighted the importance of the Dutch authors Willem van Hildegaersberch, Claes Heynenzoon (Bavaria Herald), and Dirc van Delft.[27] However, there was undeniably also room for French literature at the Wittelsbach court. In 1372, an entertainer from France named Cudelier performed before the counts of Holland-Hainaut, no doubt also reciting short fiction in French.[28] In his *Joli Buisson de jonece*, the Hainaut poet and chronicler Jean Froissart listed Albert and William among his patrons.[29] Although Froissart's claim still awaits documentary confirmation, it suggests that authors with a francophone background saw the Bavarian counts of Holland as potential and attractive sources of patronage.

In 1385, Albert's son William married Margaret of Burgundy, daughter of Philip the Bold; on the same occasion William's sister, Margaret of Holland was given in matrimony to Philip's eldest son and heir, John of Nevers. After the Valois-Wittelsbach intermarriage, Burgundian francophone culture no doubt became even more prominent at the comital residence in The Hague. It has been suggested, for instance, that the Bavarian in-laws commissioned the French poem that commemorates the wedding festivities at Cambrai.[30] Van Oostrom cites another, telling example of patronage that strikingly illustrates the literary influence of the Burgundians at The Hague. In 1408, a 'man from France' delivered a book of new (unmistakably French) poetry to Margaret of Burgundy, at the time countess of Holland.[31] This demonstrates that, although Holland and The Hague were relatively remote from the more important centres of francophone culture, the aristocratic in-groups still managed to keep up with the newest literary vogue from France.

Despite their remoteness, we might expect that the linguistic effects of Burgundian integration will be more easily gauged in the case of Holland than in the other Dutch-speaking principalities of the Low Countries, especially Flanders, where a French presence had been much more prominent for a great deal longer.[32] As early as the twelfth century, the sovereigns of the county were primarily oriented towards francophone culture, and French also played an important role in government at a local level. Even in Dutch-speaking areas, the *baljuws* [sheriffs], local representatives of comital authority, drew up their administration in French.[33] In municipal chanceries, Picard was used not only in correspondence with the comital court or other francophone addressees but also, albeit far less frequently, in exchanges with other Dutch-speaking cities.[34] Francophone literary culture dominated the Flemish court and the local aristocratic, and possibly also urban, elites.[35] Significantly, the particularly dashing literary style of Flemish epics written during the thirteenth and fourteenth centuries is marked by the use of French-sounding words, even when indigenous Dutch alternatives were available.[36] Moreover, in contrast with Holland to the north and Brabant to the east, the greater part of Flanders was feudally associated with the French crown and not with the Germanic-speaking empire. The effects of this association were also felt on a linguistic level. From the second half of the fourteenth century, administrations in imperial Brabant used the local Dutch vernacular much more frequently in official communication and record-keeping than did their counterparts in 'Crown' Flanders.[37] A final justification for focusing on Holland is that, in comparison with other regions, the relation between French and Dutch in the northern part of the Burgundian territories has not yet attracted scholarly attention.[38]

Political Networks: Professionalization and Regularization

The incorporation of Holland into the Burgundian conglomerate entailed significant structural changes in the administrative apparatus and legislation. In the regional and municipal chanceries of Holland, lexical change may have been facilitated by at least two associated factors. First, the presence of foreign, mostly bilingual government officials, along with the use of French for specific governmental purposes, undoubtedly created a fertile context for code-switching. This allowed the local Dutch vernacular to assimilate gradually the foreign language of supra-regional administration. Secondly, from the 1440s, a programme of increased professionalization in the administrative apparatus introduced a series of fiscal and legal innovations primarily based on French models and Roman canonical law. At the level of legislation and jurisdiction, these changes were intimately linked to the recruitment of both foreign and indigenous academics, who shared a Romance-based legal idiom, which also affected the linguistic usage in local chanceries.

The historian Mario Damen has calculated that between 1425 and 1483 around twenty-five per cent of all salaried regional officials in Holland were foreign immigrants. That a staggering eighty per cent of these originated from (Walloon) Flanders clearly demonstrates the need for bilingual workforces. These foreign dignitaries chiefly occupied the prominent positions of governor and general prosecutor. Because these executive offices managed the first line of communication between the supra-regional, francophone branches of Burgundian administration and local municipal governments, they required a (near-)native command of French, but also of Dutch.[39] In 1427, even before the Treaty of Delft (3 July 1428) had finally ended the long-drawn-out war of succession between Jacqueline of Bavaria and various other claimants, Philip the Good had assured those 'baenraedsen, ridderen, knapen, steden ende goede luden' [barons, knights, squires, cities, and notables] who had recognized him as their sovereign that after he left, his subjects would be able to understand and talk to those he would leave in charge.[40] This statement obviously entailed that these governors needed to have fairly advanced Dutch language skills. Other workers with knowledge of foreign languages were employed in the Council, chancery, and finance. At least part of the paperwork relating to these functions needed to be translated from Dutch or edited in French. The ordinance for the Court of Holland approved by Charles of Charolais in September 1462 stipulated, for instance, that all legal documentation pertaining to judicial cases tried before the Court of Holland 'overghestelt ende getranslateert wesen sullen in Latijn of in Walschen by eenen van den rade van den Hove voorsz., by den griffier of by een van den twee secretarissen' [shall be translated into Latin or French by one of the councillors, by the registrar, or by one of the two secretaries]. The translators should be paid two Flemish *groten* for each double-sided leaf, of at least twenty-eight lines per page and ten words per line.[41] In the financial department, bilingual accountants (e.g. Bartholomeus à la Truye from Tournai) monitored the Dutch-language records and added marginal notes in French, mostly requests for additional documentation or comments on the style of bookkeeping.[42] The Council forwarded ducal decrees to 'baeljuwen, drossaten, scouten, tolnaeren, boden, burgmeysteren, scepenen, raide, goeden luyden ende ondersaten' [bailiffs, governors, sheriffs, tax collectors, messengers, mayors, aldermen, councillors, notables, and subjects] as appropriate. These messages succinctly paraphrased the most important decisions, but also attached were the Dutch translations of the original French documents.[43] Finally, administrators were sent to the Burgundian court on behalf of the Council and emissaries embarked on diplomatic missions to French-speaking territories, at times accompanied by urban delegates. Damen has asserted that it was not at all typical for indigenous government officials from Holland to have been appropriately trained in French.[44] In January 1440, councillor Willem van Egmond and general receiver Willem van Naaldwijk joined Philip the Good and his wife at Arras. The emissaries were sent on to Saint-Omer to negotiate with 'den Oisterlingen ende den Spangiarden' [the Hanseatic merchants and the Spanish] on behalf of the cities of Holland. Significantly, Egmond and Naaldwijk took with them public prosecutor Jacob Bossaert, a native Fleming, who was already in Arras. Bossaert's task was to 'translateren uten Duytsschen in Walssche ende uten Walsschen in Duytssche, alle die saken die doe dair getracteert werden' [translate from Dutch to French and from French to Dutch everything that was negotiated there]. This can be construed more broadly as a reference to Bossaert's function as an interpreter between the Germanic- and Romance-speaking partners. However, it may also indicate that the diplomats from Holland were reluctant to enter into these negotiations without the proper linguistic assistance.[45]

Robert Stein has recently characterized the Burgundian system of regional administration as a combination of continuity and radical innovation.[46] Regional councils and *chambres de comptes* took over the governmental and judicial roles of the indigenous princely courts and treasuries. Although the process leading up to institutional change was complex and followed different paths in the various principalities, the innovations in fiscal and legal policy were at least partially indebted to existing French and Roman-canonical models, which were gradually adopted and disseminated throughout the Burgundian lands.[47] Interestingly, this trajectory, which led from Paris to the north, also left its mark on the linguistic usage of regional administrations. For instance, when Flanders was absorbed into the composite Burgundian state in 1384, Parisian French gradually usurped Picard as the dominant variant of French in Flemish regional government.[48] Likewise, the Romance terminology used in foreign administrative centres found its way to the administration of Holland. This is demonstrated most clearly by the case of the (Flemish?) accountancy clerk Gijsbrecht Pijn. In 1448, after his appointment to the *Chambre de comptes* at The Hague, Pijn requested to stay on longer at Lille 'pour tousiours mieulx apprendre la langaige François et le stile de compte' [to become ever more proficient in French and accounting techniques].[49] In jurisdiction and legislation, university-educated legal experts — especially among the councillors, general prosecutors, and registrars — contributed to the introduction of standardized legal procedures. This may provide an additional explanation for the Romance (i.e. French and/or Latin) terminology used in legal documents.[50]

Indeed, the regularization of Burgundian administration in Holland *c.* 1445 and the ensuing increase in professionalization coincide with a remarkable shift in the administrative lexis. After the installation of the regional *Chambre de comptes* in 1447, financial documents were no longer glossed in French. Instead, accountants started to use Dutch versions of the same formulae, which did not conceal their foreign origins. For instance, the example 'het is also gewoent' [it is customary that], quoted by Jansma in his study of Burgundian institutions in Holland, is clearly a calque of the French formula 'il est ainsi accoustumé'.[51] In approximately the same period, Romance jargon began to appear more frequently in official documents issued by the regional council and in the receiver's accounts. Some items were copied without further modification, and could be interpreted as clear instances of intra-sentential code-switching. A good example is the word *bellechiere*, from the French *bellechère* [sustenance]; used in travel expenses, mostly in combination with *wagenhuyr* [carriage rental; transport], it is first recorded *c.* 1452. Other technical terms were morphologically and phonologically 'dutchified' by adding appropriate affixes: *affirmieren* for *affirmer* [to confirm]; *examinieren* for *examiner* [to examine]. Although these words were also used earlier, mainly in Flanders and less frequently also in Holland, their breakthrough in the north came only after *c.* 1445.[52] Finally, the word order in the regularly used *raide geordiniert* for *conseil ordonnés* [commissioners], and the more sporadic *informatie precedente* [prior evidence], betrays an orientation towards French exemplars.

Such usages also confirm De Vooys's assertion that in official discourse Dutch terms were frequently substituted for equivalents borrowed from Latin or French.[53] Examples listed are *dadinghe/composeren* [legal act]; *bestel/arrestement* [arrest]; *bevelinghe/commissie* [commission]. A search for 'comis*'/'commis*' in the online edition of the *Bronnen voor de geschiedenis der dagvaarten van de Staten en steden van Holland vóór 1544*

[Sources relating to the general meetings between the estates and cities of Holland] suggests that the related Dutch *commissaris* [commissioner] (from the Latin, but potentially via French) makes its first appearance in the official records of Holland in 1440.[54] Surely coincidentally, the search yields the French counterpart *commissaire* in the same year.[55] *Commissie* [commission], is first listed in 1445, in a document issued by the nobility of Holland.[56] Very many instances of both words occur after these dates. The Dutch *bevelinge* [order] (search for 'beveli★'), first occurs a century earlier in 1353; a final instance is found in 1477.[57] In general, however, *bevelinge* is not used very frequently, even before 1433: the documents relating to the general meetings list three occurrences before that date, and eleven afterwards. A further three instances combine the older and newer terminology into a bilingual doublet, *commissie ende bevelinghe*. These occur in a document issued by Philip the Good, signed by the bilingual accountant Andries van der Cruce (also de la Croix) in 1452.[58] A similar pattern can be noted for the other word pairs. *Dading* [negotiation] (search for 'daeding★'/'dading★'), appears first in the municipal chancery of Dordrecht in 1311, last in Leiden in 1493.[59] The last recorded instance in the comital chancery is 1492.[60] A first instance of *composicie/composeren* [negotiation/to negotiate] (search for 'compos★'), is dated 1422 (municipal chancery of Haarlem).[61] Nonetheless, the vast majority of occurrences are again dated after 1433. *Composicie/composeren* also appears in tautological doublets with the older *dadinge/dadingen*. Both occasionally figure with the synonymous *tractaet/tractieren* [negotiation/to negotiate], first recorded in 1362 in the archives of Blois.[62] After about ten examples dated before 1433, the search ('tract★') returns hundreds of instances in Latin, French, but primarily Dutch from documents composed after the Burgundian takeover. Many similar binary pairs can be added to De Vooys's list: *vonnis* ('vonni★', 1324) and *sentencie* ('senten★', 1405, but again mostly after 1433, also in doublets) [verdict]; *houden* and *reserveren* ('reserv★', 1445, also in doublets) [to reserve]; *overhoorigheit* ('overho★', 1325, but mostly after 1433) and *rebellicheit* ('rebel★', one instance in 1426; many more after 1433, also in doublets) [rebellion]; *vestigen* ('vest★', 1423, more instances after 1433) and *confirmeren/confirmacie* ('confirm★', seven instances before 1433, some thirty-five after, doublets with *bestagen, stijven, vestigen, houden, besegelen*) [to confirm].[63]

It is important to note that the dates and figures listed here are by no means absolute, and can only be regarded as indicative. This is primarily due to the nature and limited coverage of this corpus of excerpts from regional and municipal sources, which were selected on the basis of their content. Nonetheless, the results of this preliminary investigation probably approximate the contemporary linguistic situation in the administrations of Holland. These examples clearly illustrate that after their incorporation into the Burgundian conglomerate, regional and municipal chanceries were inclined to adopt Romance-influenced administrative terminology, but that this new lexis did not completely replace indigenous practice. Although jargon with a Romance background became dominant, older Dutch synonyms did not fall out of use. That indigenous terms continued to appear, both independently and in bilingual doublets alongside the new 'Burgundian' alternatives, demonstrates that the 'frenchified' official vocabulary did not fill a lexical gap.

In this respect, the situation differs significantly from the examples of intra-sentential code-switching reported by Lusignan in the municipal administration of Calais.[64] In these cases, the use of Dutch technical terms in a French matrix text probably demonstrates that the accountant or scribe did not know (or at least could not come up with) the appropriate French jargon. When it comes to the simultaneous use of foreign and indigenous terminology in the administration of Holland, neither the 'translationese' nor the 'linguistic incompetence' hypotheses are completely satisfactory. The specific distribution is better explained as a side-effect of standardization and professionalization in the administrative apparatus. As the dukes of Burgundy aspired to a certain degree of regularization in their composite lands, standard Burgundian terminology piggybacked a ride on foreign experts and university-educated lawyers who took up governmental functions in the newly acquired territories. Undoubtedly, the same terminology was used in interregional communication. The connection to supra-regional conventions and professionalization also makes it plausible that Burgundian linguistic usage became a locus of authority and expertise, and thus an attractive means for staging professional identity. It is therefore very likely that Gijsbrecht Pijn's ambition fully to grasp the *stile de compte* (see above) was not limited to methodological concerns, but also involved specialist linguistic proficiency.[65]

This brief exploration also shows that the influences of Romance-based jargon extended well beyond the administrative milieu of the regional Council and were adopted in the municipal chanceries. This no doubt reflects frequent contact with (foreign) regional administrators, in person as well as in writing, but again can be associated with professionalization and a growing number of academics who performed duties in urban administrations.[66] Additionally, some city governments hired specialized personnel to accommodate foreign (French-speaking) merchants, which to some extent may also have affected the jargon used in the municipal chanceries. This will be discussed further below.

Elsewhere I have proposed that the language of the Middle Dutch translation of Jean Froissart's *Chroniques* by Gerrit Potter (c. 1395–1454) is closely linked to the administrative and linguistic context outlined above.[67] After the death of the former countess Jacqueline of Bavaria in 1436, Potter held a number of offices from Philip the Good and quickly rose in the ranks of Burgundian administration. In 1445 he became a salaried member of the Council of Holland, a seat he would hold until his death. A comparison of the Dutch and French texts, and the extant manuscript evidence, strongly suggests that Potter's Froissart translation was aimed at an audience of (indigenous) peers in regional government.[68] Because of its use of Romance-inspired neologisms, Potter's translation would undoubtedly have sounded modern to a contemporary public. About six per cent of the lexical items are clearly borrowed from French or, in some unclear cases, Latin; around thirty-five per cent of these are conventionally dated to the fifteenth century or later, half of them after 1450. However, the translator's style may also have verged on management-speak. Even when Froissart's French text contains other, synonymous terms, Potter frequently turns to Romance-based jargon. The abundant use of bilingual doublets, and of anaphora such as *voirscreven* [aforementioned], are other elements that characterize the language of accounts and judicial registers. Nonetheless, interference or the formal influence of source text lexical and syntactic patterns on Potter's style cannot be ruled out. The possibility remains, for instance, that the translator emulated Froissart's tautological phrasing, intentionally or otherwise. Furthermore, the use of doublets was also a common stylistic device in Dutch literary texts.[69] Nonetheless, because of the very specific contact situation in which the translation was produced, it is too reductive to explain Potter's style as reflecting linguistic or stylistic interference. Rather, it seems probable that deliberate use of the appropriate linguistic and stylistic register also conferred an aura of Burgundian, administrative expertise upon the translation. Moreover, the colophons of the extant manuscripts firmly associate this text with Gerard Potter's name, again suggesting that the intended readership was well acquainted with its author. In this light, it seems highly unlikely that a careerist like Potter would have risked tarnishing his professional credibility by producing a text whose authority might be compromised by stylistic inaccuracies.

It is difficult to substantiate similar processes in other literary texts written in Holland during the same period. Yet the same stylistic features are also found elsewhere, for instance in the *Doctrinael des tijts*. A translation of Pierre Michault's didactic *Doctrinal du temps present* (1466), which transforms many of the verse passages in Michault's *prosimetrum* into prose, the *Doctrinael* was 'volendt tot Haerlem in Holland' (completed [meaning printed?] in Haarlem in Holland) on 24 July 1486.[70] Various lexical and orthographical particularities situate the translator in North Holland, possibly Haarlem (pp. 80–82); numerous minor alterations 'domesticate' Michault's allegory for a northern audience. These include references to Frisian rather than French nicknames (p. 98); the insertion of 'Coninc van Vrieslant' [King of Frisia] into a list of titles (p. 137); and the replacement of 'escus' and 'flourins' by local units of currency, 'cronen' and 'Rijnsguldens' (p. 140).

Wilhelmus Schuijt characterized the anonymous translator as 'een echt rederijker' [a true rhetorician] (p. 81), but ascribed the frequent Romance loans and doublets — bilingual as well as indigenous — to the influence of the 'Bourgondische kanselarijstijl' [Burgundian chancery style] (p. 80). Although some instances can be explained by lexical interference, such as 'rechts cours' for 'droit cours' [directly] (p. 101) and 'balie balie' for 'baille baille' [giving and taking] (p. 103), others occur independently of the French source: 'alligieren' [refer to] for 'il fait' (p. 96); 'u [...] inployeert' [apply yourselves] for 'vous habiletés' (p. 105); 'simelerende' [feigning] for 'faignez' (p. 108); 'dangierlic' [dangerous] for 'perilleux' (p. 158).[71] Examples of 'modern' French loans, typically dated after *c.* 1400, are found throughout. These words are related to the fields of administration (*officie* [function]; *propoest* [proposition]; *expert* [expert]), law (*accusacie* [accusation]; *procederen* [to litigate]; *rebelder* [rebellious]), and finance (*financye* [finance]), but also pertain to other contexts: *flatteren* [to flatter]; *creacy* [creation]; *excusatie* [excuse]; *faetsoen* [manner]; *proberen* [to prove]; *affectie* [affection]; *alligieren* [to gather]; *conceptie* [conception], and so forth. Like Potter's text, the *Doctrinael des tijts* is marked by the abundant use of (bilingual) doublets. The most eye-catching examples from the first quarter of the text are:

formeerde ende maecte [formed and made] (p. 92);
ghereparect ende gebetert [repaired and made better]; bi wille ende consente [with volition and consent]; intencie ende meninghe [intention and opinion] (p. 94);
magnificeren ende groot maken [to magnify and enlarge]; certificeren ende zweren [to certify and swear] (p. 98);
costelic ende sumptuoselic [preciously and sumptuously] (p. 100);
divers ende van velen stijlen [diverse and in many styles]; subsidy ende secours [help and assistance] (p. 101);
wetten ende statuten [laws and statutes] (p. 104);
propoeste ofte meninghe [propositions or opinions] (p. 105);
mode ende maniere [manners and ways]; sonder dangier ende sonder sorge [without danger and without sorrow] (p. 106);
bereyt ende dyligent [willing and diligent] (p. 107);
pylage of hoefsche dieverye [pillaging or courteous theft]; verwoetheit ende vyolencie [savagery and violence] (p. 108);
groot gheruft of exclamacie [noise or exclamation] (p. 109);
rebelicheyt ende woelinghe [rebellion and turbulence] (p. 111);
purgatorien of vegevieren [purgatory or limbo]; dwalinghe ende erreur [errant ways and faults] (p. 119);
middelen ende manieren [means and ways]; peynsen ende ymaginacye [thoughts and imagination] (p. 138);
Concupisency, dats Begheerlicheit [concupiscence; that is, desire]; dangereux ende vreeselic [dangerous and frightful] (p. 139);
convoteux ende begeerlic [covetous and desirous] (p. 141).

These stylistic features may suggest that the *Doctrinael*'s anticipated audience also belonged to the 'early adopters' in administrative circles. They confirm Schuijt's characterization of the translator as well acquainted with legal terminology, and a skilled — hence educated — Latinist (p. 82).[72] This profile corresponds remarkably well to that of the administrative and legal professionals discussed above. It is, therefore, not at all implausible that the *Doctrinael*'s translator served in regional or municipal administration or pursued a legal career elsewhere. From this perspective, the stylistic features noted here could be at least partly understood as reflecting the translator's professional activities. Obviously, this does not rule out that the translator may also have belonged to a local chamber of rhetoric, as Schuijt tentatively suggested. Prosopographical studies by Van Dixhoorn and Damen have indeed demonstrated that in Holland administrative and cultural networks clearly overlapped.[73]

Cultural Networks: Book Collectors, Printers, and Chambers of Rhetoric

The integration of Holland into the composite Burgundian state coincides with an increasing interest in French(-inspired) literary culture. Various channels assisted in this process, many of which had direct connections to regional and local administrations. The following will highlight the importance of the web of Burgundian bibliophiles, printing networks, and the chambers of rhetoric. In these cases also, previously incorporated territories, most importantly Flanders, served as hubs promoting linguistic change.

During the 1460s and 1470s, luxuriously executed French-language manuscripts from Flemish ateliers became highly popular with Burgundian aristocrats.[74] Although we are not very well informed about late medieval book ownership among indigenous aristocratic families, this trend was also felt in Holland. The early generation of prestigious immigrant administrators were men of letters, among them for instance the governors Hugues de Lannoy (*stadtholder*, 1433–40) and his relative Jean (*stadtholder*, 1448–60), who authored didactic treatises in French and owned manuscripts of French literary texts.[75] Guillaume de Lalaing (*stadtholder*, 1440–45) was councillor-chamberlain to Philip the Good. As *chevalier d'honneur* of the duke's wife, Isabella of Portugal, he was right at the centre of the cultural splendour displayed by the Burgundian court.[76] However, the most prolific book collector was undoubtedly the *stadtholder* Louis of Bruges, Lord of Gruuthuse (*stadtholder*, 1462–77). Over 140 volumes from his collection are still extant today: Gruuthuse's bibliophilia was second only to that of his sovereign.[77]

The enduring cross-cultural contacts between indigenous and foreign officials, along with Holland-Burgundian intermarriages, enhanced the susceptibility of indigenous magnates to the francophone preferences of these Burgundian book owners. This tendency is exemplified by the Zeeland nobleman Wolfert VI van Borsselen (*stadtholder*, 1477–79). In 1468, he married Charlotte de Bourbon-Montpensier, a cousin of Isabella, the late wife of Charles of Charolais. Between 1460 and 1480, Borsselen compiled a handsome collection of manuscripts, mostly copies of French historical and didactic texts illustrated in Flanders, completely in line with the latest trends in Burgundian book collecting.[78] Borsselen is also mentioned as the patron of the anonymous French translation of Johannes de Beka's *Chronographia* (*c.* 1455), a regional chronicle of Holland, which was dedicated to Philip the Good.[79] Some decades earlier, in 1445, another important Holland aristocrat, Reinoud II van Brederode, married Yolande de Lalaing, the eldest daughter of Guillaume.[80] Yolande was educated at the court of Isabella of Portugal and it seems plausible that she and her husband owned an appreciable collection of French romances. At any rate, two sixteenth-century inventories of the family possessions kept at the castle of Batestein include numerous French books and, very interestingly, also a now-lost luxury copy of Gerard Potter's Froissart translation.[81] Yolande was the driving force behind the composition of the Brederode family chronicle, and possibly also its French translation. The purpose of these texts was most probably to clear the Brederode name after a bitter conflict between her husband's clan and David of Burgundy, Bishop of Utrecht and an illegitimate son of Philip the Good.[82]

In spite of the modernity of these book collections, Hanno Wijsman has also noted a converse trend among northern aristocrats. It seems, for instance, that the important Zeeland nobleman Frank van Borsselen, a relative of Wolfert VI and fourth husband to Jacqueline of Bavaria, preferred to commission manuscripts of Dutch texts. There is evidence to suggest that the manuscript of the Froissart translation now kept at The Hague (Koninklijke Bibliotheek, MS 130 B 21) may have been copied at his request, though this evidence is less than complete.[83] Given that Borsselen frequently entertained prominent members of the ducal family, he must also have been well-versed in French. The same is probably true for Reinoud II van Brederode. As noted above, his wife was Hainaut-born and a native speaker of French. Nonetheless, at the Chapter of the Golden Fleece in 1456, where he was accused of disloyalty and prioritizing family bonds over his duties to the Order and its prince, Brederode decided to make his case in Dutch, and not in French or Latin as was customary. In order to prepare, he requested linguistic assistance from three bilingual fellow members and a Dutch translation of the Order's statutes. Brederode's strategy has been explained in numerous ways: linguistic incompetence (rather unlikely), filibustering, or open defiance. Whatever the case, these examples bear out the same complexity that was signalled in the relationship between French and Dutch in regional administration.[84]

From the 1480s, the introduction of the printing press in Holland modestly promoted francophone literature among lower-ranked administrators.[85] Susie Speakman Sutch has convincingly argued that the commissioning patron of the Gouda edition of *Le Chevalier délibéré* (Collaciebroeders?, 1489) was Jan van Cats, a local government official, who had served in the Council of Holland. She further notes that the luxuriously executed edition was probably intended for an audience of peers in regional administration.[86] Although the vast majority of titles in the back catalogues of local printers in the northern Low Countries were in Latin or Dutch, some entrepreneurs, such as Gheraert Leeu and Jacob Bellaert, also turned out editions of French texts. In Gouda, Leeu first produced *Le Dialogue des creatures moraligié* (1482), a collection of Latin fables translated into French. After his presses had relocated to Antwerp in Brabant, other French titles followed. The Gouda printer was well acquainted with the editions of William Caxton (and vice versa), which demonstrates that Leeu's network reached beyond the boundaries of Holland and out into Flanders.[87] At any rate, from 1484 he was registered as a member of the guild of St John in Bruges. Various linguistic features of *Van den drie blinde danssen* (Gouda, 1482) point towards Flanders, possibly Bruges, as the place of composition.[88] It may thus also have been in Bruges that Leeu procured the exemplar for this Dutch version of Pierre Michault's *Dance aux aveugles*, translated by a 'clercxken' [young clerk] called Martijn.[89]

Although other explanations remain possible, it is plausible that the exemplars for at least some of the editions printed by Leeu's Haarlem associate Jacob Bellaert followed a similar trajectory from Flanders to Holland. Like Leeu, Bellaert produced a small number of luxuriously executed Dutch and French editions of literary texts that were firmly connected to the Burgundian court. These include Raoul Lefèvre's stories of Jason and Troy, which elaborated on key motifs in Burgundian mythology and had been dedicated to Philip the Good, as had Pierre Michault's *Doctrinal du temps present*. Both Lefèvre and Michault held offices in the vicinity of the Burgundian court.[90] Manuscripts of their texts were in the Burgundian library and illustrious members of the dukes' entourage, such as Margaret of Austria, Louis of Bruges, and Philip of Cleves, had their own private copies.[91] It is also significant that William Caxton dedicated his *Recuyell of the Historyes of Troye* (completed 1471;

printed c. 1473–74), an English translation of Lefèvre's Trojan history, to Margaret of York, the third wife of Charles the Bold.

As Table 1.1 indicates, the texts by Michault and Lefèvre also survive in slightly older editions printed in Flanders.

Title	Place/Printer/Date	Edition Holland	Dutch translation
Raoul Lefèvre, *Recueil des histoires de Troie*	Ghent or Bruges?: David Aubert for William Caxton?, 1474–75 (USTC 37521)	Haarlem: Bellaert, c. 1486–88 (USTC 71249)	Haarlem: Bellaert, 1485 (USTC 435730)
Raoul Lefèvre, *Fais et prouesses du chevalier Jason*	Ghent or Bruges?: David Aubert for William Caxton?, c. 1477 (USTC 71243)	Haarlem: Bellaert, c. 1486–88 (USTC 71245)	Haarlem: Bellaert, c. 1483–85 (USTC 435612)
Jean Boutillier, *La Somme rurale*	Bruges: Colard Mansion, 1479 (USTC 70933)	—	Delft: van der Meer, 1483 (USTC 435578)
Pierre Michault, *Doctrinal du temps present*	Bruges: Colard Mansion, c. 1479–81 (USTC 71375)	—	Haarlem: Bellaert, 1486 (USTC 435827)
Pierre Michault, *Danse aux aveugles*	Bruges: Colard Mansion, c. 1479–81 (USTC 71369)	—	Gouda: Leeu, 1482 (USTC 435522)

TABLE 1.1. Editions of French texts printed in Flanders with later French/Dutch versions in Holland

Lotte Hellinga has convincingly demonstrated that the contents of the Dutch *Historie vanden vromen ridder Jason* 'closely follow the French version as printed c. 1477 in Flanders' and 'a copy of the book printed in Flanders may first have served the translator before being used in the printing house as printer's copy'.[92] She also suggests that the Jason Master, who painted the illustrations of Bellaert's exemplar (London, British Library, MS Additional 10290), may also have worked for Gheraert Leeu in Haarlem (pp. 328–34). Her observation that some of the drawings were executed before the text was copied puts some dialectical features of the text, as copied in the only extant manuscript, into a new perspective. While it was previously thought that the text was copied in Flanders and afterwards illustrated in Holland by an artist from Haarlem, it now seems more likely that the manuscript as a whole was produced in Holland, using an exemplar written by a scribe 'used to spelling with the idiomatic characteristics of West-Flanders and Zeeland', the most eye-catching of which is probably the 'unetymological h' (p. 321). Given the exceptional degree of professional mobility in the Burgundian conglomerate, and the fact that Bellaert also used a copy of the French edition while preparing his Dutch edition, an alternative explanation for the manuscript's distinct linguistic features — namely that a Flemish immigrant translated and copied the French text in Haarlem — does not seem entirely implausible.[93] Interestingly, the second compositor working in Bellaert's printing house deemed these southern dialectical traits in the exemplar too exotic for the Holland market. In the printed text, certain variants (e.g. 'up' for 'op', forms with h-deletion, but also instances of hypercorrect use of 'h' in initial position) were replaced by indigenous northern forms. Additionally, various French-sounding borrowings were apparently considered too regional. Conversely, doublets — mostly indigenous pairs — were added throughout the text, possibly indicating their stylistic value.[94]

The anticipated audience of the 'Francophile' books printed in Haarlem probably differed little from that of the Gouda edition of *Le Chevalier délibéré*. Heraldic evidence in the illustrations of at least six Bellaert editions suggests that the patronage of these volumes was somehow connected to the eminent Van Ruyven family.[95] Several members of this clan held important offices in the municipal administration of Haarlem. The most probable candidate for sponsorship is the high-profile government official Klaas van Ruyven (1446/47–1492). Although Van Ruyven operated on a more local basis, most importantly as sheriff of Haarlem, he can be characterized as an ambitious Burgundian careerist, like Gerrit Potter a generation before.[96] Van Ruyven's wife, Maria, was a second cousin of Jan van Cats, who had commissioned the Gouda edition of La Marche's *Chevalier*. Jan's brother Jacob had married Van Ruyven's sister, Elisabeth.[97] In this light it is not surprising that the driving force behind *Vanden ridder welghemoet*, the first of two Dutch translations of the *Chevalier*, was Klaas van Ruyven.[98]

The business arrangement between Jacob Bellaert and the Van Ruyven family (if not Klaas alone) was surely advantageous to both parties. On the one hand, the Van Ruyvens provided access to their social and professional contacts, which increased the market potential of Bellaert's output.[99] On the other hand, it is also plausible that, for someone like Klaas van Ruyven, Bellaert's luxury editions of Burgundian best-sellers (in French as well as Dutch) were valuable tools for networking and professional advancement. Van Ruyven's patronage of these editions not only provided a cultural mooring-point for Burgundian ideology in the north; it also claimed an identifiable space for the local elite within the larger discourse community of the composite state. In this respect, the sheriff's cultural activities may also have enhanced his professional and social status among his peers and possibly also his superiors.[100]

It is surely no coincidence that these books were all printed during a time of relative political stability in Holland, while resistance against Maximilian persisted in the surrounding principalities. After the death of Charles the Bold in 1477, the long-drawn-out rivalry between *Hoeken* [Hooks] and *Kabeljauwen* [Cods] had resurfaced (1477–80/83). Maximilian had reacted firmly, replacing the regional Council and installing supportive urban governments. As the most active insurgents had been banished from the county, the years leading up to the *Jonker Fransenoorlog* [Revolt of Squire Frans van Brederode] of 1488–91 and the 1492 *Opstand van het*

Kaas- en Broodvolk [Bread and Cheese Revolt] were mostly tranquil.[101] Elsewhere, especially in Flanders, Maximilian's regency remained heavily contested. In these circumstances, it is not unlikely that Van Ruyven's cultural activities also had a more symbolic dimension as a token of his loyalty to Maximilian. In the end this cost him dearly: during the Bread and Cheese Revolt he was brutally murdered, precisely because of his support for Maximilian's policies. The Burgundian *indiciaire* Jean Molinet records that during the capture of Haarlem by rebels from Kennemerland, Van Ruyven's throat was cut by one of the insurgents after he had been knocked to the ground by a battle-axe.[102] In his translation of the *Chevalier délibéré*, Pieter Willemsz commemorates the sheriff's *onnoselen doot* [innocent death].[103] There is no contemporary evidence to confirm the gossip that Van Ruyven's body was dismembered and the remains delivered in a basket at his wife's doorstep with a note saying 'Widow van Ruyven, now nibble on these quarters'.[104] However, if there is any truth to the story, the dismemberment, and possibly even the rumouring of it, may have been a political act reflecting the way in which Van Ruyven had supposedly 'mutilated' the body politic by supporting Maximilian's excessive taxes. At any rate, it is probable that in the minds of the administrative elite the 'frenchified' stylistic register, by virtue of its connection to Burgundian authority, also conveyed a political message and displayed membership of the administrative in-group. Its presence in the textual production traditionally linked with Van Ruyven may suggest that the language of those texts, as well as their subject-matter, expressed loyalty to Burgundy and possibly also to Maximilian's rule.

In this respect, it is interesting that two of three poems written shortly after the *Jonker Fransenoorlog*, copied in Rotterdam, Gemeentearchief, MS 1534, are also clearly marked by Romance jargon. These texts present a negative perspective on the uprising led by Frans van Brederode, a younger son of Reinoud II and Yolande de Lalaing; they are clearly written from a pro-Maximilian standpoint, and are possibly linked with an early chamber of rhetoric. In view of their subject, it comes as no surprise that the lexical borrowings relate mostly to the fields of diplomacy (*tracteerden* [negotiated]), justice (*correxie* [punishment]; *punieren* [to punish]; *corrigieren* [to bring to justice]), and warfare (*dominerende* [dominating]; *pilgieren* [to pillage]; *vaelyant* [courageous]; *fytaelge, provande* [provisions]; *paysieren* [to pacify]; *ghetriumfeert* [triumphed]; *violencie* [violence]); but there are also terms referring to the world of poetry and entertainment (*rhetorike, musijke, alrehande melodije* [rhetoric, music, and all kinds of melodies]). Notable also are the following items, which may have some connection to administrative jargon: *faelgieren* [to diminish]; *adverteren* [to notify]; *confuyse* [confusion]; *gheabondoneert* [abandoned]; *obediencie* [obedience]; *gecorrumpeert* [corrupted]; *gheaviseert* [advised]; *gedeputeert* [delegated]; *costuymen* [the usual].[105]

The bibliophilia of Burgundian aristocrats, and early printing activities in Gouda and Haarlem, have already demonstrated the extremely mobile nature of contemporary literary culture in the Low Countries. This is further evidenced by the dissemination of rhetoricians' poetry. Herman Brinkman has shown that, even before chambers of rhetoric in Holland and Zeeland are recorded in surviving documents, local administrative and cultural elites entertained relations with rhetoricians in Flanders and Brabant.[106] The literary compilation Berlin, Staatsbibliothek Preussischer Kulturbesitz, MS Germ. Qu. 557, is an important witness of this contact across regional borders.[107] The manuscript was copied intermittently between *c.* 1473 and 1481 by the Leiden city clerk Jan Phillipsz, who also was its first owner. Brinkman analyzed the dialects of the texts in the collection and found that most were written in Holland or Utrecht. However, a group of six refrains (nos. 102–07 in Brinkman's edition) on the same topic — what is the most efficient cure for diabolical temptation? — were probably composed in Brabant and the border area with Holland and Flanders, possibly for a Brabantine competition organised in 1478.[108] Each of the six provides evidence of Romance influence in its use of older terms such as *temptacie* [temptation], *collacie* [comparison], *regieren* [to rule], and *conforteren* [to comfort]. The first and last refrains in particular, both from (Western) Brabant, also show examples of modern influence, traditionally dated to the (later) fifteenth century, such as *arguacie* [argument, belief], *jubilacie* [praise, joy], *versolacien* [to comfort], and *deputeren* [to delegate]. Interestingly, these foreign loans often occur in rhyming position. This placement, which is also the case in the poems on the *Jonker Fransenoorlog*, possibly draws further attention to the words' exotic nature. Another example from the same manuscript, the emulation of Anthonis de Roovere's *Sacramentslof* by Willem van Wassenaar, shows the direct influence of a Flemish rhetorician's text on a composition from Holland.[109]

Arjan van Dixhoorn has drawn further attention to the importance of the Burgundian integration process for the genesis of an international network of rhetoricians, and to the frequent organization of interregional meetings during the period in which chambers were introduced into Holland (1475–94). In 1493 Leiden organized an international festival; this was followed by similar gatherings in Mechelen (1493) and Antwerp (1496). In addition to textual dissemination in manuscript and print, personal contacts and the organization of these cross-regional competitions undeniably contributed to the standardization of literary language.[110] Adrian Armstrong has recently argued that Dutch- and French-speaking rhetoricians from the southern Low Countries participated in a collective culture of literary competition and shared a common capital of poetic devices.[111] In her essay in this volume (Chapter 4), Anne-Laure van Bruaene shows that the organizational model of the chambers in the south was at least partly fashioned on the lines of examples from the French-speaking Low Countries. This contact across linguistic borders also influenced the poetic language of the Dutch-speaking rhetoricians, which is most obvious from their use of technical terms, such as *rhetorike* [rhetoric], and *prince* [prince, president]; and from their designations of literary forms: *refrain* [refrain]; *rondel* (rondeau); *ballade* (ballade); *virelai* (virelai).[112] It is within reason that, in the terms suggested by Armstrong, the shared poetic capital of francophone and Dutch-speaking rhetoricians was not confined to formal or stylistic devices, but also extended to this Romance-based linguistic register. In the context of interregional contact and competition, it is quite plausible that northern authors wanted to conform to the established poetic idiom, which ultimately derived from networking rhetoricians from the south.[113] Additionally, Serge ter Braake and Van Dixhoorn have previously demonstrated that the literary circuit of the Holland chambers was closely connected to the pro-Burgundian administrative networks mentioned above.[114] Besides their acceptance of the 'universal rhetoricians' discourse', this may further explain the relative ease with which late medieval authors in Holland adopted a mixed idiom.[115]

Commercial and Urban Networks

Much of the evidence adduced above has already demonstrated the susceptibility of urban centres in the north to foreign literary and linguistic influences. Yet a number of further contact situations deserve attention. By the fifteenth century, local mercantile elites in the cities of Holland had built international commercial networks with Flanders and Brabant, the British Isles, and francophone regions in the southern Low Countries and northern France.[116] The data on transcultural contact through commerce is copious, and exemplarily evidenced in the source publications by Smit and Unger. While this is not the place to outline the trade relations of Holland and Zeeland in any detail, it should be underlined that these commercial contacts entailed that, ideally speaking, merchants from Holland should also be proficient in French. As of the fifteenth century, private teachers, often immigrants from the southern Low Countries, established mercantile schools (*bijscholen* or *Franse scholen* [French schools]) in the north. Here students from the merchant classes were educated in arithmetic and accounting, but also followed courses in business correspondence and foreign languages for specific purposes, most importantly French. Didactic materials included bilingual conversation manuals, of which the best-known example is the Bruges *Livre des mestiers* (1349).[117]

Other tradesmen housed their apprentices with francophone merchants in order for them to be immersed in a foreign-language milieu. An agreement dated 13 May 1484 between Cornelis Oirtsz from Reimerswaal in Zeeland and Nicolas Vassal, a merchant from Rouen, is particularly informative on this practice. Vassal agreed to provide Oirtsz's nephew, Oele Clausz, with appropriate lodging, food, and drink for the period of one year 'om te leeren de tale van den lande' [in order to learn the region's language, i.e. French]. In exchange, Vassal would receive two Flemish pounds. Oirtsz declared that he would continue to vouch for the reliability of his young relative and promised to reimburse 'enige scade oft scande' [any damage or dishonour] caused by his nephew 'alsoewel voir dit voirscr. jair als van alle den tyde, dien de voirscr. Oele namails met hem soude moegen woenen' [during this period of one year as well as the entire duration of the aforementioned Oele's stay thereafter]. Apparently the agreement could be prolonged if it proved satisfactory to both parties.[118] This kind of arrangement was by no means limited to the northern Low Countries. In December 1520 it was recorded that a certain 'Jorijs [George?] Bertram' from Newcastle had stayed with 'Peter [Pierre?] Bousin' at Tournai, 'om Wals te leeren' [to learn French].[119]

Nonetheless, it appears that French did not always come easy to merchants from the northern regions of the Low Countries. In 1472, Jan de Ruysscher jr., a shipper from Mechelen, declared before the judicial court of Bergen-op-Zoom that he had sold English cloth at Bourgneuf for the benefit of Jan Lastman, Jan Poort, and Laureys Aelleman, three merchants from Amsterdam, 'overmits dat hy bat Walsch conde dan zy' [because he spoke French better than they did]. The Dutchmen rewarded de Ruysscher with 'een couslaken' [fabric for trousers].[120] At the turn of the fifteenth century, the city administration of Middelburg in Zeeland repeatedly reimbursed Jan Adam for reading and responding to French-language correspondence addressed to the city, and for helping locally based merchants with business conducted in French. It appears that Adam's clientele for assistance with foreign-language business correspondence comprised foreign as well as indigenous merchants. In 1399 and 1407–08 he received forty shillings for a year's service.[121]

Evidence from Haarlem and Leiden suggests that other cities outsourced translation activities on a more ad hoc basis. Translators included local clerks and secretaries.[122] However, since municipal representatives frequently attended to official business in Flanders or Brabant, they also called on the services of translators while they were on the road.[123] For instance, on 9 September 1458, a mayor and treasurer of Haarlem, Aert Pietersz and Allijn Claesz, travelled with a servant to Lille, where they were to appear before Philip the Good and his Great Council. They spent twenty-two shillings eight pence to have the proper legal documents translated from Dutch into French. Afterwards, a bailiff called *magister* Adriaen van Dordrecht was given four Holland pounds to prepare additional documents, presumably also in French.[124] On 23 January 1459, another of Haarlem's four mayors, Simon Noirtich, travelled to Brussels and had 'XIII articlen' [thirteen legal clauses?/documents?] translated there.[125] In other instances, cities shared the translation costs incurred in collective actions and reimbursed Burgundian officials, such as registrar Willem Dommesent, for their services.[126] At any rate, for translations of official and legal documents, city administrations in Holland apparently turned to the same categories of professionals who also translated literary works: clerks (cf. the local 'clercxken' Martijn, the author of *Van den drie blinde danssen*), secretaries, and legal administrators (cf. the anonymous *Doctrinael* translator). That the examples recorded here mostly involve translations from Dutch to French may at first sight seem peculiar. However, an obvious explanation is that the official documents from the Burgundian administration that were forwarded by the Council at The Hague to local city administrations had been translated beforehand by regional councillors or secretaries.

That the use of French occasionally became problematic, in spite of these practices, raises interesting questions. With regard to Flanders, Marc Boone has demonstrated that — however infrequent the evidence — at times of discord between the Burgundian prince and his Flemish subjects, linguistic usage could become an integral part in the development of the conflict.[127] In May 1526 the municipal government of Middelburg received an imperial edict ordering the release of a number of Scottish trade vessels that had been captured on 28 April. When Jehan du Bois, the *huissier d'armes* [bailiff] sent by Charles V to investigate the matter, confronted members of the Middelburg city council with their disobedience, they pleaded linguistic ignorance and claimed that they did not understand the French document. Although utterly unconvincing, this must have seemed a convenient excuse. That the councillors later informed Du Bois of their intention to challenge the edict in a higher court of appeal edges towards insubordination.[128] The refusal of the Estates of Holland and Zeeland to come before Maximilian in Ypres on 29 September 1477 appears more openly defiant. The main point of this meeting, to which representatives of other regions had also been invited, was the protracted conflict with France. The Estates had replied that:

> Alsoe den voirs. mijns genadichs heeren brief in walsche gescreven was, ende dat zij oic buyten den voirs. landen bescreven waeren te trecken, dat beyde tegens die nyeuwe privilege was, dat zij dairom in deser sake niet en wisten te doen dan te blijven bij den inhouden van huere voirscreven previlege.[129]

> [Since the aforementioned letter of our grace was written in French, and additionally because they were ordered to travel outside the aforementioned region — two things that were in breach of the new privilege — they could not react otherwise in this matter than to abide by the contents of their aforementioned privilege.]

On 14 March 1477 Mary of Burgundy had issued a new privilege for Holland, Zeeland, and West Frisia. It stipulated not only that the Council of Holland would henceforth be populated with indigenous administrators (§ 4), but also that in future all communication with these regions should be in Dutch (§ 20). Article 35, concerning supplementary financial support from the region (the so-called *beden*), stated that any request for additional funding was to be made in person 'ten behoorliken ende gewoonliken plecken' [at the customary locations] in Holland, Zeeland, and Frisia. The representatives of the Estates should not be made to cross county borders. Moreover, all commands in breach of the privilege would be void (§ 21).[130] The Council of Holland had forwarded this reply to Maximilian of Austria and Mary of Burgundy, leaving it up to them how to respond. Eventually the meeting was suspended.

A Transregional Discourse Community

That the Estates turned down Maximilian's offer to meet at Ypres of course demonstrates the determination with which different social groups in Holland held on to the privileges they had received six months before. However, it also indicates how precious the balance between French, the Burgundian language of power, and Dutch, the native vernacular of Holland, really was. I have demonstrated above that the integration of Holland into the Burgundian conglomerate had a significant impact on linguistic usage in regional and urban councils. Immigrant professionals imported the French jargon of administration, financial management, and jurisdiction; for these administrators, the resulting mixed idiom may have become a locus of authority and an important factor in the construction of social identities. In the essentially diglossic context of the composite Burgundian state, French clearly occupied the role of 'high variant' while Dutch was the 'low form'. In some circles, the hybrid language of administration may have become some kind of 'mesolect' or 'intermediate form'. In this respect, it is unsurprising that the mixed idiom also established itself as an appropriate code in other areas of communication, such as cultural expression.

Given the overlap between administrative and cultural networks, the linguistic changes in the field of administration may also have affected the literary language. Important government officials subscribed to the Burgundian vogue for collecting French literary and historiographical texts, preferably in the form of luxury manuscripts that were copied and illustrated in Flanders. Local officials translated French texts that were popular in Burgundian surroundings (Gerrit Potter, the *Doctrinael* translator) or supported their dissemination in print (Klaas van Ruyven). The entrepreneurship and mobility of local printers such as Gheraert Leeu and Jacob Bellaert, who enjoyed the patronage of these cultural brokers, influenced the selection of material for printing, but also promoted the importation of French and Flemish exemplars from the south.

Even before the first chambers of rhetoric were established in Holland and Zeeland, local agents (again linked to administrative circles, as in the case of Jan Phillipsz) maintained relations with literary networks from the south. There was a notable Burgundian impulse in establishing the first chambers in the north. The membership of these new institutions was clearly marked by its connections to local administrations. Cross-border contacts, the circulation of texts in manuscript and print, and interregional competitions all stimulated the dissemination of a shared poetic idiom. Finally, urban chanceries increasingly needed professional jurists and skilled translators, especially in their dealings with foreign merchants (e.g. Middelburg) and supraregional government.

In view of all this, it seems fair to say that Burgundian integration stimulated the emergence of a trans-regional discourse community, at least in some circles (needless to say, the majority of the population was probably unaffected). The process was furthered by professional and cultural mobility across regional borders. In the fields of administration as well as literature, the southern, bilingual regions acted as hubs promoting linguistic change. In some ways this process was not an obvious one. Not all regional administrators in Holland were sufficiently trained to use French in their daily routine. The example of Bellaert's *Jason* suggests that in the 1480s some still hesitated to accept French neologisms in Dutch literary texts. It is possible that the hybrid linguistic usage limited the literary market to administrative in-groups: as a by-product of the overlap between international administrative and literary networks, the mixed idiom became characteristic of a newly established discourse community that probably excluded large parts of the populace. But there are strong grounds for suspecting that, in the end, members of the in-group — the likes of Jan van Cats and Klaas van Ruyven — did not mind. To them 'frenchified' was most certainly not a dirty word.

Notes to Chapter 1

1. The research for this article was carried out in the context of the AHRC-funded project 'Medieval Francophone Literary Culture Outside France', <http://www.medievalfrancophone.ac.uk>, which ran between 2011 and 2015 at King's College London, the University of Cambridge, and University College London.
2. Francis Grose, *Lexicon Balatronicum or, A Dictionary of Buckish Slang, University Wit, and Pickpocket Eloquence* (London: C. Chappel, 1811).
3. 'French' and 'francophone' are used here as hypernyms and refer to a group of Romance dialects including Parisian French and Picard. Likewise, the term '(Middle) Dutch' collectively refers to the regional variants spoken in Flanders, Holland, and Brabant.
4. For the changing attitude towards French literature in the fourteenth century, particularly in Brabant and Flanders, see Remco Sleiderink, 'From Francophile to Francophobe: The Changing Attitude of Medieval Dutch Authors towards French Literature', in *Medieval Multilingualism: The Francophone World and Its Neighbours*, ed. by Christopher Kleinhenz and Keith Busby (Turnhout: Brepols, 2010), pp. 127–43.
5. For instance, Gijsbert Rutten, '"Ghelyck wy zien dat de Fransóyzen doen": Dialoog en dialogisme in de *Twe-spraack vande Nederduitsche letterkunst*', *Yang*, 40 (2004), 477–85, illuminatingly discusses H. J. Spiegel's *Twe-spraack vande Nederduitsche letterkunst* (1584). See also Pierre Michault, *Doctrinael des tijts*, ed. by W. J. Schuijt (Wageningen: Veenman, 1946), p. 80; Willem Frijhoff, 'Verfransing? Franse taal en Nederlandse cultuur tot in de revolutietijd', *Bijdragen en mededelingen betreffende de geschiedenis in Nederland*, 104 (1989), 592–609.
6. Roland Willemyns, 'Taalpolitiek in de Bourgondische tijd', *Verslagen en mededelingen van de Koninklijke Vlaamse Academie voor Taal- en Letterkunde*, 104 (1994), 162–77; Roland Willemyns, 'Laatmiddelnederlands (circa 1350–1550)', in *Geschiedenis van de Nederlandse taal*, ed. by M. C. van den Toorn and others (Amsterdam: Amsterdam University Press, 1997), pp. 147–219; Willemyns, *Dutch: Biography of a Language*, pp. 57–65; Nicoline van der Sijs and Roland Willemyns, *Het verhaal van het Nederlands: Een geschiedenis van twaalf eeuwen* (Amsterdam: Bakker, 2009), pp. 204–05.
7. See, for instance, Lusignan, *Essai d'histoire sociolinguistique*, pp. 223–24. I use the term 'vernacular' here as an equivalent for locally used variants of Dutch and French as opposed to Latin, and not as the lower-status language in a diglossic situation. In this latter interpretation, French, when it became the preferred language for supra-regional communication, would no longer be perceived as a 'vernacular'.
8. Willemyns, 'Taalpolitiek in de Bourgondische tijd'; Willemyns, 'Laatmiddelnederlands (circa 1350–1550)'; Armstrong, 'The Language Question in the Low Countries'; Marc Boone, 'Langue, pouvoirs et dialogue: aspects linguistiques de la communication entre les ducs de Bourgogne et leurs sujets flamands (1385–1505)', *Revue du Nord*, 91 (2009), 9–33; Mario Damen, *De staat van dienst: De gewestelijke ambtenaren van Holland en Zeeland in de Bourgondische periode (1425–1482)* (Hilversum: Verloren, 2000).
9. C. G. N. de Vooys, *Geschiedenis van de Nederlandse taal* (Groningen: Wolters-Noordhoff, 1970), p. 45. De Vooys is quoting Z. W. Sneller, *Walcheren in de vijftiende eeuw* (Utrecht: Oosthoek, 1917), p. 57.
10. Willemyns, 'Taalpolitiek in de Bourgondische tijd', p. 168.
11. Exceptions to this general rule include J. W. Muller, 'Gerijt Potter van der Loo en zijne vertaling van Froissart', *Tijdschrift voor Nederlandsche Taal- en Letterkunde*, 8 (1888), 264–95; Michault, *Doctrinael*, ed. by Schuijt, p. 80.
12. J. J. Salverda de Grave, *De Franse woorden in het Nederlands* (Amsterdam: Johannes Muller, 1906), pp. 115, 116–17. The strict division between explanations for lexical influence on official and literary discourse is repeated in Willemyns, 'Taalpolitiek in de Bourgondische tijd', p. 163.
13. G. P. M. Knuvelder, *Handboek tot de geschiedenis der Nederlandse letterkunde*, 4 vols (Den Bosch: Malmberg, 1971–78), I, 496–97. Knuvelder is quoting the introduction to Colijn van Rijssele, *De spiegel der minnen*, ed. by Margaretha W. Immink (Utrecht: Oosthoek, 1913), p. xxv.
14. Knuvelder, *Handboek tot de geschiedenis der Nederlandse letterkunde*, I, 497–98.

15. Herman Pleij, *Het gevleugelde woord: Geschiedenis van de Nederlandse literatuur 1400–1560* (Amsterdam: Bert Bakker, 2007), pp. 408, 321.
16. See also Dirk Schoenaers, '"Getranslateerd uuten Franssoyse": Gerard Potter's Dutch Translation of Froissart's *Chroniques*' (unpublished doctoral thesis, University of Liverpool, 2010), pp. 48–54; Dirk Schoenaers, 'The Middle Dutch Translation of Froissart's Chronicle (*c.* 1450): Historiography in the Vernacular and the Ruling Elite of Holland', *Dutch Crossing*, 36 (2012), 98–113 (pp. 103–05).
17. Van Dixhoorn, *Lustige geesten*; Damen, *De staat van dienst*, pp. 441–502.
18. Sarah Thomason, 'Contact Explanations in Linguistics', in *The Handbook of Language Contact*, ed. by Raymond Hickey (Oxford: Blackwell, 2010), pp. 31–47 (p. 32).
19. Godfried Croenen, 'Latijn en de volkstalen in de dertiende-eeuwse Brabantse oorkonden', *Taal & Tongval*, 12 (1999), 9–34; Thérèse de Hemptinne and Walter Prevenier, 'La Flandre au Moyen Âge: un pays de trilinguisme administratif', in *La Langue des actes: Actes du XIe Congrès international de diplomatique (Troyes, jeudi 11–samedi 13 septembre 2003)*, ed. by Olivier Guyotjeannin (Paris: Éditions en ligne de l'École des chartes, 2005), pp. 1–16, <http://elec.enc.sorbonne.fr/CID2003/de-hemptinne_prevenier> [accessed 15 March 2015].
20. Lusignan provides a more detailed overview of the contact between French (Picard) and Dutch, see *Essai d'histoire sociolinguistique*, pp. 187–233, 235–73.
21. De Hemptinne and Prevenier, 'La Flandre au Moyen Âge'.
22. *Rijmkroniek van Holland (366–1305) door een anonieme auteur en Melis Stoke*, ed. by J. W. J. Burgers (The Hague: Instituut voor Nederlandse Geschiedenis, 2004), v. 4507.
23. Antheun Janse, *Een pion voor een dame: Jacoba van Beieren (1401–1436)* (Amsterdam: Balans, 2009), p. 58.
24. Ibid., pp. 61–65.
25. Th. van Riemsdijk, *De tresorie en kanselarij van de graven van Holland en Zeeland uit het Henegouwsche en Beyersche huis* (The Hague: Martinus Nijhoff, 1908), pp. 226–27.
26. Jeanne Verbij-Schillings, 'Hofcultuur en hofvermaak: Het Haagse hof in de middeleeuwen (1248–1462)', in *In den Haag geschied*, ed. by Han Foppe (The Hague: Sdu Uitgevers, 1998), pp. 33–53.
27. Frits van Oostrom, *Court and Culture: Dutch Literature, 1350–1450*, trans. by Arnold J. Pomerans (Berkeley: University of California Press, 1992), pp. 37–76, 126–218. Another unmistakably multilingual court in Holland, also discussed by Van Oostrom (p. 12), was that of the counts of Blois.
28. W. J. A. Jonckbloet, *Geschiedenis der Middelnederlandsche dichtkunst*, 3 vols (Amsterdam: Van Kampen, 1851–55), III, 601. He is referred to as 'Cudelier, des conincs spreker van Vrancrike' [Cudelier, 'speaker' of the king of France]. *Sproken*, the genre usually associated with these entertainers, were short rhymed texts, often with a moralizing or didactic tenor and meant to be performed in a variety of circumstances and before different audiences (at aristocratic courts, but also before city magistrates or in convents). Given that Cudelier was employed by the French king, he probably recited poetry in French. This may have included *fabliaux* or religious compositions.
29. Jean Froissart, *Le Joli Buisson de jonece*, ed. by Anthime Fourrier (Geneva: Droz, 1975), p. 57.
30. *Epithalame pour les mariages de Jean, comte de Nevers, avec Marguerite de Bavière et de Guillaume d'Ostrevant avec Marguerite de Bourgogne*. See Alexandre Pinchart, 'Jean de Malines, poète français du quatorzième siècle', *Bulletin du bibliophile belge*, 12 (1856), 28–37.
31. Van Oostrom, *Court and Culture*, p. 25.
32. Frits van Oostrom, *Stemmen op schrift: Geschiedenis van de Nederlandse literatuur vanaf het begin tot 1300* (Amsterdam: Bert Bakker, 2006), pp. 218–26 (pp. 224–25); Lusignan, *Essai d'histoire sociolinguistique*, pp. 229–31.
33. Lusignan, *Essai d'histoire sociolinguistique*, pp.189–91.
34. Ibid., p. 197.
35. Mary D. Stanger, 'Literary Patronage at the Medieval Court of Flanders', *French Studies*, 9 (1957), 214–29; Willy Van Hoecke, 'La Littérature française d'inspiration arthurienne dans les anciens Pays-Bas', in *Arturus Rex: Volumen 1, Catalogus, Koning Artur en de Nederlanden, la matière*

de Brétagne et les anciens Pays-Bas, ed. by W. Verbeke, J. Janssens, and M. Smeyers (Leuven: Universitaire Pers Leuven, 1987), pp. 189–260; Van Oostrom, Stemmen op schrift, pp. 216–33; Catherine Gaullier-Bougassas, L'Histoire ancienne jusqu'à César ou histoires pour Roger, châtelain de Lille, de Wauchier de Denain: l'histoire de la Macédoine et d'Alexandre le Grand (Turnhout: Brepols, 2012).

36. Joost Van Driel, Meesters van het woord: Middelnederlandse schrijvers en hun kunst (Hilversum: Verloren, 2012), pp. 23–31.
37. Lusignan, Essai d'histoire sociolinguistique, pp. 229–31; Croenen, 'Latijn en de volkstalen in de dertiende-eeuwse Brabantse oorkonden'.
38. Boone, 'Langue, pouvoirs et dialogue', investigates Burgundian language policy mostly in relation to Flanders. Lusignan's study of Picard devotes attention to linguistic contact in Flanders and to a lesser extent Brabant, but hardly makes reference to the relation between French and Dutch in Holland. Most of the evidence referenced in Willemyns, 'Taalpolitiek in de Bourgondische tijd', 'Laatmiddelnederlands (circa 1350–1550)', and Dutch, and in Armstrong, 'The Language Question in the Low Countries', relates to the southern Low Countries.
39. Damen, De staat van dienst, pp. 185–86.
40. Holland bestuurd: Teksten over het bestuur van het graafschap Holland in het tijdvak 1299–1567, ed. by J. A. M. Y. Bos-Rops, J. G. Smit, and E. T. van der Vlist (The Hague: Instituut voor Nederlandse Geschiedenis, 2007), pp. 230–31 (p. 230).
41. Ibid., p. 318.
42. T. S. Jansma, Raad en rekenkamer in Holland en Zeeland tijdens hertog Philips van Bourgondië (Utrecht: Instituut voor Middeleeuwse geschiedenis; Leipzig: Verlang von Duncker und Humblot, 1932), pp. 156–69; Damen, De staat van dienst, p. 190; Robert Stein, De hertog en zijn staten: De eenwording van de Bourgondische Nederlanden ca. 1380–ca. 1480 (Hilversum: Verloren, 2014), pp. 224–29.
43. See for instance, Bronnen tot de geschiedenis van den handel met Engeland, Schotland en Ierland 1150–1585, ed. by H. J. Smit (The Hague: Instituut voor Nederlandse geschiedenis, 1928–1950), I.2, pp. 931 no. 1457 (quoted); 1097 no. 1737 n. 3.
44. Damen, De staat van dienst, p. 189.
45. Bronnen voor de geschiedenis der dagvaarten van de staten en steden van Holland voor 1544: Deel 2 (1433–1467) Tweede stuk: Teksten, ed. by J. G. Smit (The Hague: Instituut voor Nederlandse geschiedenis, 2005), 2.2, p. 134, no. 179b (hereafter referred to as Dagvaarten).
46. Stein, De hertog en zijn staten, pp. 126, 171–73.
47. Damen, De staat van dienst, p. 190; Stein, De hertog en zijn staten, p. 217.
48. Lusignan, Essai d'histoire sociolinguistique, pp. 223–24.
49. Damen, De staat van dienst, p. 190.
50. Stein, De hertog en zijn staten, pp. 159, 171, 180–81. Damen, De staat van dienst, pp. 291–92, shows that in Holland at least twenty-five per cent of the salaried government officials held a university degree. However, only around a third of these had studied wholly or partly in France, in Paris or Orléans. At least about half graduated from a faculty of law.
51. Jansma, Raad en rekenkamer in Holland en Zeeland tijdens hertog Philips van Bourgondië, p. 173.
52. Holland bestuurd, ed. by Bos-Rops, Smit, and van der Blist, p. 321; Instituut voor Nederlandse Lexicologie, De geïntegreerde taal-bank, <http://gtb.inl.nl/> [accessed 15 February 2015]; Etymologiebank, ed. by Nicoline van der Sijs (2010), <http://etymologiebank.nl/> [accessed 15 February 2015].
53. De Vooys, Geschiedenis van de Nederlandse taal, p. 45; Willemyns, 'Taalpolitiek in de Bourgondische tijd', p. 163.
54. Dagvaarten, 2.2, p. 138, no. 182e. Other resources related to Holland, available via Historici. nl: Werken aan de geschiedenis van Nederland, <https://www.historici.nl/resources> [accessed 15 February 2015] (Bronnen tot de geschiedenis van de handel met Frankrijk tot 1585; Bronnen tot de geschiedenis van de Leidsche textielnijverheid 1333–1795; Bronnen tot de geschiedenis van den handel met Engeland, Schotland en Ierland 1150–1585; Bronnen tot de geschiedenis van den Oostzeehandel; Bronnen tot de geschiedenis van Middelburg in den landsheerlijken tijd; Bronnen voor de geschiedenis der dagvaarten van de staten van Zeeland 1318–1572; De tol van Iersekeroord. Documenten en rekeningen 1321–1572; Holland bestuurd. Teksten over het bestuur van het graafschap Holland in het tijdvak 1299–1567), do not

give earlier results. *Rekeningen graafschap Holland 1358–1361* has one match for 1361. In any case, it is noteworthy that these words become increasingly common in documents issued after the Burgundian takeover.
55. *Dagvaarten*, 2.2, p. 147, no. 192.
56. Ibid., 2.2, p. 301, no. 334e.
57. Ibid., 1.2, p. 116, no. 189 (A.G.H. no. 221); 4.2, p. 64, no. 37b.
58. Ibid., 2.1, pp. 33–34.
59. Ibid., 1.2, p. 15, no. 32; 4.2, p. 1130, no. 903.
60. Ibid., 4.2, p. 1091, no. 874.
61. Ibid., 1.2, p. 607, no. 1005.
62. Ibid., 1.2, p. 202, no. 289.
63. The information in brackets lists the search term, the year of the first result yielded by the *Dagvaarten*, and use in foreign/indigenous doublets.
64. Lusignan, *Essai d'histoire sociolinguistique*, pp. 202–03.
65. Damen, *De staat van dienst*, p. 190.
66. Ibid., p. 209.
67. Schoenaers, '"Getranslateerd uuten Franssoyse"', pp. 157–206; Schoenaers, 'The Middle Dutch Translation of Froissart's Chronicle (*c.* 1450)'.
68. Schoenaers, '"Getranslateerd uuten Franssoyse"', pp. 206–24.
69. *Lanceloet: De Middelnederlandse vertaling van de 'Lancelot en prose' overgeleverd in de 'Lancelotcompilatie': Pars 2 (vs. 5531–10750) met inleidende studie over de vertaaltechniek*, ed. by Bart Besamusca (Hilversum: Verloren, 1991), pp. 46–48.
70. Michault, *Doctrinael des tijts*, ed. by Schuijt. Further references are supplied in the text. The only extant copy of the 1486 edition (The Hague, Koninklijke Bibliotheek, 168 G 34) is incomplete; a digitization can be freely accessed at <https://archive.org/details/ned-kbn-all-00001830-001> [accessed 14 October 2015]. On the *Doctrinael*'s use of verse, see Adrian Armstrong, '"Half dicht, half prose gheordineert": vers et prose de moyen français en moyen néerlandais', *Le Moyen Français*, 76–77 (2015), 7–38.
71. I have compared the *Doctrinael* in Schuijt's edition with the French *Doctrinal* printed by Colard Mansion ([1479]; USTC 71375), available in a digitization of Paris, Bibliothèque nationale de France, Rés. Ye-89: <http://gallica.bnf.fr> [accessed 14 October 2015].
72. For instance, the author inserts phrases in Latin that are absent from his source, or further elaborates on them. He adds 'flectamus genua' (p. 106); develops 'Car chascun scet que argent se nomme art gent' into 'Quia argentum est compositum ab ar, quot est ardere. Et gentum quot est gens quasi ardes gentem' (p. 119); renders Michault's French into Latin as 'Qui est occasion cause, est occasion de re causata' (p. 138), followed by a Dutch translation; and supplies 'de virtute activa' for 'de force active' (p. 140) and 'Virtuten [*sic*] passivam' for 'vertu passive' (p. 141).
73. Van Dixhoorn, *Lustige geesten*; Damen, *De staat van dienst*, pp. 441–502.
74. Hanno Wijsman, *Luxury Bound: Illustrated Manuscript Production and Noble and Princely Book Ownership in the Burgundian Netherlands (1440–1550)* (Turnhout: Brepols, 2010), pp. 525, 545.
75. Schoenaers, '"Getranslateerd uuten Franssoyse"', p. 56; Wijsman, *Luxury Bound*, pp. 410–17.
76. Damen, *De staat van dienst*, p. 471.
77. Wijsman, *Luxury Bound*, pp. 356–69.
78. Ibid., pp. 261–69.
79. Johannes de Beka, *La Traduction française de la Chronographia*, ed. by W. Noomen (The Hague: Excelsior, 1954).
80. Antheun Janse, 'Yolande van Lalaing (1422–1497)', in *Yolande van Lalaing (1422–1497), kasteelvrouwe van Brederode*, ed. by Elizabeth den Hartog and Hanno Wijsman, special issue of *Jaarboek van de Kastelenstichting Holland en Zeeland* (2009), pp. 7–36 (p. 14).
81. Dirk Schoenaers and Hanno Wijsman, 'De *librie* van Batestein: De boeken van Brederode in de vijftiende en zestiende eeuw', in *Yolande van Lalaing (1422–1497)*, ed. by Hartog and Wijsman, pp. 69–98.
82. H. Bruch and R. E. V. Stuip, 'Een Franse kroniek van de heren van Brederode', *Holland,*

regionaal-historisch tijdschrift, 16 (1984), 35–42; René Stuip, 'Histoire des Seigneurs de Gavre dans la bibliothèque d'Antoine de Lalaing en 1548', in *Rencontres de Middelbourg/Bergen-op-Zoom (27 au 30 septembre 1990): les sources littéraires et leurs publics dans l'espace bourguignon (XIVe–XVIe s.)*, ed. by Jean-Marie Cauchies (Neuchâtel: Centre européen d'études bourguignonnes, 1991), pp. 189–98.

83. Schoenaers, '"Getranslateerd uuten Franssoyse"', pp. 41–42, 236–40; Hanno Wijsman, 'Frank van Borssele en boeken', in *Het kasteel te Sint-Maartensdijk en zijn bewoners*, ed. by Elizabeth den Hartog and others (Haarlem: Kastelenstichting Holland en Zeeland, 2010), pp. 105–68 (pp. 111–15).

84. On this conflict, see Janse, 'Yolande van Lalaing (1422–1497)', p. 21; Sonja Dünnebeil, *Die Protokollbücher des Ordens vom Goldenen Vlies I, Herzog Phillip der Gute, 1430–1467* (Stuttgart: Thorbecke, 2002), pp. 117–22.

85. By the end of the fifteenth century many of the most important printing offices in Holland had disappeared, because of discontinuation, bankruptcy, or relocation to the southern Low Countries. This has led scholars to conclude that the market in Holland was too limited for printed literary texts in the vernacular, especially for luxury editions such as those of Jacob Bellaert at Haarlem. See, for instance, Herman Pleij, *Nederlandse literatuur van de late middeleeuwen* (Utrecht: H & S, 1990), pp. 148–49; Wilma Keesman, 'Jacob Bellaert en Haarlem', in *Haarlems Helicon: Literatuur en toneel te Haarlem vóór 1800*, ed. by E. K. Grootes (Hilversum: Verloren, 1993), pp. 27–48; Herman Brinkman, *Dichten uit liefde: Literatuur in Leiden aan het einde van de middeleeuwen* (Hilversum: Verloren, 1997), p. 113.

86. Susie Speakman Sutch, 'De Gouda-editie van *Le Chevalier délibéré*: Een boek uitgegeven in eigen beheer', in *Geschreven en gedrukt: Boekproductie van handschrift naar druk in de overgang van middeleeuwen naar moderne tijd*, ed. by Herman Pleij and Joris Reynaert (Ghent: Academia Press, 2004), pp. 137–55.

87. In Antwerp, Leeu delivered an edition of *La Complainte de dame Marguerite* (1491 or 1492; USTC 71327), Gaspar Laet the Elder's *Pregnostications pour l'an 1493* (1492; USTC 71221), and Charles Soillot's *Le Debat de felicité* (between 1489 and 1492; USTC 71473). A first redaction of the latter text had been composed in 1462 and was offered to Charles the Bold; this is the text printed by Leeu. A later version (1477) was dedicated to Louis of Bruges and Philippe de Croÿ. Leeu also published no fewer than four different editions of the prose romance *Paris et Vienne*: in French (1487; USTC 70568), Dutch (1487 and 1492; USTC 435854, 436061), Low German (1488; USTC 438824), and in Caxton's English translation, *Thy Storye of the Right Noble and Worthy Knyght Parys and of the Fayre Vyenne the Dolphyns Doughter of Vyennoys* (1492; USTC 438825). Caxton based his *Historye of Reynart the Foxe* (after 6 June 1481; USTC 500045) on Leeu's Dutch edition, *Historie van Reynaert die vos* (17 August 1479; USTC 435458); in turn, Leeu produced editions of other translations by Caxton.

88. Pierre Michault, *Van den drie blinde danssen*, ed. by W. J. Schuijt (Amsterdam: Wereldbibliotheek, 1955), p. xlvii. It is of course also possible that an emigrant clerk from Flanders translated the text elsewhere.

89. In the epilogue (Michault, p. 104), the translator calls himself 'Dijn scamel scoelkint ende clerxcken martijn' [Your humble student and clerk Martijn]. The 'schoolboy' reference should probably not be taken literally, but rather be read as a *captatio benevolentiae*. For this text, see also the essay by Rebecca Dixon in this volume (Chapter 8).

90. Lefèvre was in the service of Jean de Créquy, and may have been chaplain to Philip the Good. In 1466 Michault was given the honorific title of *secrétaire signant* to Charles of Charolais; in 1473 he was appointed *maître de requêtes* at the Parliament of Mechelen (Michault, *Doctrinael des tijts*, ed. by Schuijt, p. 57).

91. See: *Luxury Bound: A Corpus of Manuscripts Illustrated in the Netherlands (1400–1550)*, <http://www.cn-telma.fr/luxury-bound/index/> [accessed 16 October 2015]; *JONAS: Répertoire des textes et des manuscrits médiévaux d'oc et d'oïl*, <http://jonas.irht.cnrs.fr/> [accessed 16 October 2015].

92. Lotte Hellinga, *Texts in Transit: Manuscript to Proof and Print in the Fifteenth Century* (Leiden: Brill, 2014), pp. 63, 82–83, 304–65, 415 (quotations from pp. 312–13). Further references are supplied in the text.

93. For yet another line of reasoning suggesting that a Flemish illustrator later moved to Haarlem, see Johan Oosterman, 'De fascinerende symbiose van handschrift en druk. Naar aanleiding van: J. M. M. Hermans & K. van der Hoek (red.), *Boeken in de late middeleeuwen: Verslag van de Groningse Codicologendagen 1992'*, special issue of *Queeste*, 3 (1996), 76–80 (p. 79).
94. R. Nieuwstraten, 'Overlevering en verandering: De pentekeningen van de Jasonmeester en de houtsneden van de Meester van Bellaert in de *Historie van Jason*', in *Boeken in de late middeleeuwen: Verslag van de Groningse Codicologendagen, 1992*, ed. by J. M. M. Hermans and K. van der Hoek (Groningen: Forsten, 1994), pp. 111–24.
95. See Keesman, 'Jacob Bellaert en Haarlem'; Sutch, 'De Gouda-editie van *Le Chevalier délibéré*'; Saskia Bogaart, *Geleerde kennis in de volkstaal: 'Van den proprieteyten der dinghen' (Haarlem 1458) in cultuurhistorisch perspectief* (Hilversum: Verloren, 2004), pp. 52–53. The Van Ruyven family arms feature in the opening woodcut of Bellaert's Dutch and French editions of Lefèvre's works, and in the *Doctrinael des tijts*. The Van Ruyven and Van Cats family arms figure together in Bellaert's *Der sonderen troest* [A Consolation for Sinners] (1484; USTC 435684), a Dutch version of Jacobus de Teramo's *Consolatio peccatorum* (*c*. 1382). They appear as elements of the decor in stained glass windows in several illustrations, most of which are repeated throughout the edition (e.g. fol. j8^r). Two other insignia, one of which is also found in the Van Cats-Van Ruyven woodcut, are as yet unidentified (e.g. fols i1^v, i2^r). Wilma Keesman has suggested that the first could be Bellaert's trademark (p. 29); however, this identification remains hypothetical. Since these other emblems do not correspond to the family arms of Van Mathenesse or Oem van Wijngaerden (the maternal lineages of Jacob and Maria van Cats), nor those of Van Rietwijk (the maternal lineage of Klaas and Elisabeth van Ruyven), it would be rash to conclude that the print run of *Der sonderen troest* was financed by a couple from the Van Cats and Van Ruyven families (see for instance Keesman, pp. 30, 41–42). A digitization of The Hague, Koninklijke Bibliotheek, 168 E 5 is available at <https://archive.org/details/ned-kbn-all-00001799-001> [accessed 3 April 2017].
96. In 1471 Klaas was *rentmeester* [steward] of West-Frisia and *baljuw* [sheriff] of Kennemerland (1471–76). In 1475–77 he was *baljuw* of Beverwijk. He is mentioned as *schout* [sheriff] of Haarlem in 1475, and still held that office when he died (*Dagvaarten*, 3, p. 368 no. 335b; 4.1, p. 72). In 1476 he is recorded as *kastelein* [castellan] of Teilingen. In 1478–79, a Klaas van Ruyven is listed as *schepen* [alderman] of Haarlem; in subsequent years he is repeatedly recorded as performing duties for the city government.
97. Arie van Steensel, *Edelen in Zeeland: Macht, rijkdom en status in een laatmiddeleeuwse samenleving* (Hilversum: Verloren, 2010), pp. 240–41, 407.
98. On the two *Chevalier* translations, see the essay by Susie Speakman Sutch in this volume (Chapter 7).
99. This may be suggested by the early ownership of extant copies of Bellaert's *Van den proprieteyten der dinghen* (1485; USTC 435725) linked with the Burgundian administration in Flanders and Brabant. Admittedly, in this case there is no verifyable connection with Van Ruyven. Bogaart argues, however, that the text's subject and the material realization of the printed book fit in very well with Van Ruyven's Burgundian predelictions and was probably aimed at a similarly affluent audience belonging to the urban elites (*Geleerde kennis in de volkstaal*, pp. 52–53). All of this does not confine, of course, the audience of Bellaert's books to a network of Burgundian administrators.
100. Bogaart, *Geleerde kennis in de volkstaal*, pp. 52–53, 160–62; Sutch, 'De Gouda-editie van *Le Chevalier délibéré*', p. 140.
101. M. J. Van Gent, *'Pertijelike saken': Hoeken en kabeljauwen in het Bourgondisch-Oostenrijkse tijdperk* (The Hague: Stichting Hollandse Historische Reeks, 1994), pp. 370–75.
102. Jean Molinet, *Chroniques*, ed. by Georges Doutrepont and Omer Jodogne, 3 vols (Brussels: Palais des Académies, 1935–37), II, 292.
103. Pieter Willemsz, *Vanden ridder welghemoet* (Leiden: Jan Seversz, 1507), fol. [f4^v].
104. H. A. van Vessem, 'De dood van Claes van Ruven', *Haerlem: Jaarboek 1977*, 9–16.
105. An Faems, 'Een rederijkersgedicht over de Jonker Fransenoorlog: Achtergronden en editie', *Spiegel der letteren*, 40 (1998), 55–88. I quote from this edition here. The significantly lower frequency of Romance loans in the second poem may suggest that the three texts were not

written by the same author, or at least that the authorship of the second piece was different. In this respect, it may seem strange that the second and third poem are both preceded by 'Jesus. Maria. Ursula. Cecilia', and concluded by the same motto: 'A. Al bin ic onconstich | Ic blive gejonstich J.' [A. Even if I am unskilled | I still remain good-humoured J.]. The first text ends with 'fac semper bene semper fac' [do always well always do]. Although these opening and closing formulae have been associated with the anonymous authors of these texts, it is of course also possible that they are interventions by the scribe, and have nothing to do with authorship.

106. Van Dixhoorn, *Lustige geesten*, p. 100; Herman Brinkman, 'De weerklank van de Bourgondische hofliteratuur in het Middelnederlands', *Millennium: Tijdschrift voor middeleeuwse geschiedenis*, 8 (1994), 125–33; *Het handschrift-Jan Phillipsz.: Hs. Berlijn, Staatsbibliothek Preussischer Kulturbesitz, Germ. Qu. 557*, ed. by Herman Brinkman (Hilversum: Verloren, 1995); Brinkman, *Dichten uit liefde*, p. 262.

107. Van Dixhoorn, *Lustige geesten*, p. 39; *Het handschrift-Jan Phillipsz.*, ed. by Brinkman.

108. *Het handschrift-Jan Phillipsz.*, ed. by Brinkman, pp. 108–18 (nos. 102–07); Brinkman, *Dichten uit liefde*, pp. 359–62; Van Dixhoorn, *Lustige geesten*, p. 38.

109. *Het handschrift-Jan Phillipsz.*, ed. by Brinkman, pp. 122–33 (nos. 111–12); Brinkman, *Dichten uit liefde*, pp. 173–78.

110. Van Dixhoorn, *Lustige geesten*, pp. 39, 206–07. Van Dixhoorn also notes, however, that after 1506 chambers tended to meet within the same region; it was rare for meetings or competitions to be organized on an interregional basis (p. 234).

111. Adrian Armstrong, 'Translating Poetic Capital in Fifteenth-Century Brussels'.

112. See also Pleij, *Het gevleugelde woord*, pp. 297, 321; Arjan van Dixhoorn, 'The Multilingualism of Dutch Rhetoricians: Jan van den Dale's 'Uure van den doot' (Brussels, *c.* 1516) and the Use of Language', in *Bilingual Europe: Latin and Vernacular Cultures. Examples of Bilingualism and Multilingualism c. 1300–1800*, ed. by Jan Bloemendal (Leiden/Boston: Brill, 2015), pp. 50–72 (53–58). Van Dixhoorn notes: 'Why exactly the Dutch rhetorical language became such a hybrid is not clear. It is evident however that the transformation, if not initiated, at least was furthered by the establishment of the chambers of rhetoric and their adaptation of the rhetorical knowledge and practices of the *seconde rhétorique*. The communities of rhetoricians of the Dutch-speaking areas borrowed the core of their technical terms from the world of the *seconde rhétorique* of France and the French-speaking Low Countries' (p. 54).

113. For notions of an innovative linguistic and artistic project looking to French models, see Pleij, *Het gevleugelde woord*, pp. 321, 329–33, 338–40; Van Dixhoorn, *Lustige geesten*, p. 189.

114. Serge ter Braake and Arjan van Dixhoorn, 'Engagement en ambitie: De Haagse rederijkerskamer "Met Ghenuchten" en de ontwikkeling van een burgerlijke samenleving in Holland rond 1500', *Jaarboek voor de middeleeuwse geschiedenis*, 9 (2006), 150–90 (pp. 166–83); Van Dixhoorn, *Lustige geesten*, pp. 99–101; Brinkman, *Dichten uit liefde*, p. 263.

115. The chambers in the southern regions also chiefly recruited among men of letters. Some of these were local administrators, and thus equipped to compose texts in the vernacular. It would be interesting to examine to what extent the lexis of the innovative literature composed and disseminated by rhetoricians in Flanders and Brabant is rooted in the frenchified jargon of Burgundian administration. For the composition of local chambers of rhetoric in Flanders and Brabant, see Pleij, *Het gevleugelde woord*, p. 312, which lists amongst others administrators, judicial officers, teachers, secretaries, notaries, and scribes. In Holland, the emergence of chambers of rhetoric during the last decades of the fifteenth century has been associated not only with the political and cultural considerations noted above, but also with growing economic prosperity and expansion: Pleij, *Het gevleugelde woord*, p. 300.

116. Van Dixhoorn, *Lustige geesten*, p. 36; *Handel met Engeland, Schotland en Ierland; Bronnen tot de geschiedenis van den handel met Frankrijk. Eerste deel*, ed. by Z. W. Sneller and W. S. Unger (The Hague: Martinus Nijhoff, 1930).

117. Ben van der Have, 'Taalonderwijs: Vier triviumteksten', in *Een wereld van kennis: Bloemlezing uit de Middelnederlandse artesliteratuur*, ed. by E. Huizinga, O. S. H. Lie, and L. M. Veltman (Hilversum: Verloren, 2002), pp. 37–62 (pp. 47–60); Bogaart, *Geleerde kennis in de volkstaal*, p. 19. Another Dutch-French phrasebook, copied in the northern Netherlands and dated to the first

decades of the sixteenth century, is transmitted in The Hague, Haags Gemeentearchief, MS 36, fols 123^v–138^r.
118. *Handel met Frankrijk*, ed. by Sneller and Unger, pp. 194–95.
119. *Bronnen tot de geschiedenis van den handel met Engeland, Schotland en Ierland*, ed. by Smit, 2.1, p. 345, no. 451 n. 3.
120. *Handel met Frankrijk*, ed. by Sneller and Unger, 1, p. 145, no. 264.
121. *Bronnen tot de geschiedenis van Middelburg in den landsheerlijken tijd*, ed. by Willem Sybrand Unger (The Hague: Martinus Nijhoff, 1926), 2, pp. 240, no. 197 (anno 1399), 265, no. 203 (anno 1411); *Handel met Frankrijk*, ed. by Sneller and Unger, p. 36, no. 85 (anno 1407–1408).
122. *Dagvaarten*, 2.2., p. 589, no. 668e, 'Wouter Janssoen, clerck'; p. 773, no. 881b, 'meester Lodewijc secretaries der stede van Harlem'.
123. Ibid., 2.2, pp. 589, no. 668e, 594, no. 676c; 3, p. 43 no. 49e.
124. Ibid., 2.2, p. 648, no. 724c.
125. Ibid., 2.2, p. 656, no. 739e.
126. Ibid., 2.2, pp. 1004, no. 1108e, 1021, no. 1127c.
127. Boone, 'Langue, pouvoirs et dialogue', pp. 29–30.
128. *Bronnen tot de geschiedenis van den handel met Engeland, Schotland en Ierland*, ed. by Smit, 2.1, p. 352, no. 459 n. 1.
129. *Dagvaarten*, 4.2, p. 64, no. 37b.
130. *Holland bestuurd*, ed. by Bos-Rops, Smit, and van der Vlist, pp. 338–51, no. 80 (quotation from p. 346); A. G. Jongkees, 'Het groot privilege van Holland en Zeeland (14 maart 1477)', in *Burgundica et varia*, ed. by E. O. van der Werff, C. A. A. Linssen, and B. Ebels-Hoveling (Hilversum: Verloren, 1990), pp. 48–51.

CHAPTER 2

'Gescryfte met letteren na elcxs geval gegraueert en oic dyveerssche ymagyen': Uses of Code-Switching in Dutch and French

Catherine Emerson

The quotation which forms the title of this contribution, from Anthonis de Roovere's *Droom van Rovere op die doot van hertoge Kaerle van Borgognnyen saleger gedachten*, illustrates something which we think we know about transcultural poetics in a multilingual society.[1] Poets are not constrained by linguistic boundaries in their search for novel poetic forms or material, and, in a literary culture that prizes verbal dexterity, we can expect that they will not be constrained by linguistic boundaries in their choice of vocabulary either.[2] At first sight, De Roovere's line appears to contain evidence of language contact: words such as *gegraueert*, *dyveersch*, and *ymagyen* come to Dutch from French — or possibly Latin — and seem to suggest that the author is enlarging his vocabulary by engaging in what linguists might term 'code-switching': the 'use of material from two (or more) languages by a single speaker in the same conversation'.[3] Initially presumed to be a consequence of speakers' shortcomings in one language, code-switching is now recognized as implying a large degree of verbal competence, such as one might expect in administrative circles in a society like the Burgundian Netherlands.[4] The three poets examined in this chapter, De Roovere himself, George Chastelain, and Jean Molinet, come from three distinct linguistic backgrounds, but can all be presumed (with a greater or lesser degree of certainty, as will be demonstrated) to have been familiar with the three languages of Burgundian society: Dutch, French, and Latin. The varying way in which they deploy vocabulary from one language in matrix texts in another language suggests conscious and deliberate choice indicating a different set of cultural values attached to each of the three languages.

Before embarking on this analysis, however, it is important to note that the use of the term code-switching requires some circumspection. On the one hand, it might be argued that code-switching is a verbal phenomenon only, and cannot really be studied in a written environment, where different constraints operate. Clearly, the use of a word or phrase in another language has a different implication when an author has sat down and considered its use, particularly in something as constructed as a poem, from its meaning when a speaker makes a decision on the spot to switch into another language, possibly in the light of cues from an interlocutor. However, linguistically, the phenomena turn out to be quite similar. Herbert Schendl has examined a range of texts produced in Norman England and found that the types of switches found are the same in the medieval written and the contemporary oral corpus.[5] The same, that is, apart from one of the most common sorts of switch, the emblematic switch, tags such as 'yeah', 'right', 'you know', and negative and affirmative particles — the sort of language habit that it is hard to suppress, even when one is speaking another language. Emblematic switches make up anything from ten to thirty per cent of code-switches in modern oral studies and they are almost entirely absent from Schendl's corpus.[6] Schendl attributes this to the difference between spoken and written language, which seems plausible. Otherwise, he affirms that medieval written language in a multilingual society employs the same sorts of switches as modern spoken language.

Another difficulty, which appears to face all linguists who address the question of code-switching and which seems particularly complicated in the case of a historical corpus, is that of distinguishing switches from borrowings. At the extremes the two seem very different: a conversation that begins in one language and ends in another has clearly undergone a switch, but the shorter the portion of discourse that is from a second language, the harder it is to say whether the speaker — or indeed the writer — perceives it to be a switch into another language or an adoption of a foreign element to enrich the matrix language. Questioning speakers as to how they perceive their own language use has not provided very reliable information on this point, and this is even harder in a historical investigation, where the speakers and writers are long dead.[7] Besides, linguists are divided on the extent to which single-word borrowings and switches can be distinguished, and on the importance of drawing the distinction. As will be demonstrated here, there is a great deal of overlap between the two phenomena, as is the case in modern contexts: Donald Winford points to studies that suggest that speakers in modern Brussels (to take just one example) who use the largest number of borrowed words are also likely to employ more switches.[8] We can, of course, distinguish words that originally come from one language but have been in current use in another for some time from those which appear to be used for the first time by a given writer. However, even here, it is difficult to know in the case of established borrowings whether that writer perceives such words as borrowed or whether they are seen as fully integrated into the lexis of the matrix language. To take the example of the title again, *ymagyen* is a word in church Latin that is also found in French literature and in Dutch.[9] When De Roovere uses it, is he consciously selecting a word from another language (and, if so, which?) or is he simply using the Dutch word without awareness of its origins? Such questions are difficult to answer, but we need to bear them in mind when considering the semantic impact of a switched or borrowed word. The question is, of course, further complicated if we consider the impact that a borrowed word might have on a reader or listener, particularly if we assume a reader whose degree of competence in the relevant language differs significantly from that of the poet. A reader with no familiarity with the language from which borrowed elements derive will have a very different experience of a poem from someone who is completely bilingual, and both may be unable to access an experience of understanding with effort that the poet may have envisaged.

The three writers considered in this chapter each had a different relationship to the two vernaculars of the Burgundian Netherlands. George Chastelain was a native speaker of Dutch, working in French; Jean Molinet, his successor as official ducal poet and historiographer, also worked in French but it was his first language; Anthonis de Roovere worked in Dutch and, according to his first editor, spoke nothing else.[10] It is much rarer to find the fourth permutation: a poet whose native language was French but who worked in Dutch, for reasons which will become apparent in the course of this article, which will concentrate on examples taken from Chastelain, Molinet, and De Roovere. Each of the three men had a different working relationship to the vernaculars of the Burgundian Netherlands and a different familiarity with them: Chastelain had grown up in a Dutch-speaking environment, Molinet in a French-speaking one where there was frequent contact with Dutch. As for De Roovere, Eduard de Dene's affirmations regarding De Roovere's linguistic competence were made in a particular context, which means that we should perhaps not take them at face value. Firstly, De Dene did not necessarily intend to represent the truth of De Roovere's expertise in other languages, since his description aims to report the possible reasons why De Roovere had not found a publisher, in contrast to those poets who had written in French.[11] The use of pejorative terms stressing De Roovere's simplicity and lack of learning indicates that this is not De Dene's own view. Moreover, De Dene has a particular polemical purpose in seeking to portray the vitality of the Dutch language tradition, stressing De Roovere's natural genius and that of his fellow countrymen. We do not necessarily need to accept that De Roovere had no French, nor even that De Dene seriously meant to suggest that this was the case. De Roovere certainly had a great deal of cultural contact with the francophone ducal court. Johan Oosterman has detailed De Roovere's pension, which he carefully describes as having been granted on behalf of Duke Charles, and its effect on De Roovere's political positions.[12] At the same time, there are clear influences of francophone literary forms in his writing, both in his poetry and in his chronicle.[13] Whether this exposure to the francophone world translated into fluency in French cannot be determined, but evidence from his poems suggests that he knew enough French at least to adopt individual words.

By examining a sample of the work of these three poets, it is possible to draw some general conclusions about the status of the two vernaculars in Burgundian poetry. It is easy to assume that French was favoured, because it was the language of the court, but this can be nuanced. There is clear evidence that an individual's facility in both vernaculars was prized, both practically and culturally. Charles Armstrong cites a number of instances where knowing both French and Dutch was an advantage to an individual's career, and numerous scholars have pointed out the extent to which this was increasingly considered the ideal in the administration of the Valois dukes of Burgundy.[14] Moreover, when Jean Molinet and Olivier de La Marche enthusiastically point out that George Chastelain is a native speaker of Dutch but writes fluently in French, they do so in terms that celebrate his competence in both languages.[15] According to Molinet, Chastelain was 'prompt en trois langaiges' [eloquent in three languages].[16] Estelle Doudet points out that this phrase is consciously ambiguous: while actually referring to the three Burgundian administrative languages of Latin, French, and Dutch, it implies that Chastelain was fluent in the three sacred languages of Hebrew, Greek, and Latin.[17] Molinet is not simply expressing his admiration of an author who is able to write well in a language other than his own here; he is celebrating multilingualism as cultural capital. Chastelain is impressive not simply because he is skilled, but because he is a skilled multilinguist.

In doing so, Molinet draws attention to the importance of the third language of the Burgundian Netherlands, Latin. Latin was the language of the Church, of diplomacy, and of university education.[18] It was the way in which the Burgundian state communicated with the outside world, but it was also a way in which it communicated internally. Charles Armstrong cites several cases where speakers of different dialects of Dutch had their correspondence translated into Latin in order to avoid ambiguity.[19] In a world where much of the education was delivered by the Church and many of the opportunities for reading were either devotional or liturgical, being literate often meant knowing Latin. So, as in Norman England, there was a triad of languages, and speakers who mastered more than one could enlarge their vocabulary by employing borrowings from or switches into either of the others.[20]

The analogy between Chastelain's three languages and the three languages of scripture, however, hints that the poet was not unrestricted in the sorts of switches that could be made. In scriptural exegesis it was held that each of the divine languages had a different role to play in the revelation of God's plan, and this attitude seems to be echoed in other medieval multilingual settings as well as in contemporary multilingual societies.[21] Thus Schendl reports that most switches in Anglo-Norman texts take place between Latin, occupying the high status language position, and one of the two vernaculars, English or French, although there are also some instances of switching taking place between the vernaculars.[22] The same is true of the poets studied here, where switches between the vernacular and Latin are more frequent than switches between the two vernaculars. However, this general picture can be refined to give a more detailed picture of the relative positions of the three languages in the Burgundian Netherlands.

Firstly, many scholars who have worked on the vocabulary of Chastelain and Molinet, the first two Burgundian *indiciaires*, official historians to the dukes, have commented on the amount of Dutch in their lexis.[23] Both writers are known for their verbosity and their use of recondite vocabulary. However, in both cases the use of rare words in Latin far exceeds their employment of the same strategy in Dutch. Because Dutch vocabulary is less common in French writers of the period, it is seen as remarkable, but this should not allow us to overlook the fact that poets turn to Dutch much less frequently than to Latin. Moreover, Dutch borrowings and switches are used in a very specific set of circumstances. Firstly, they are found much more frequently in the prose than in the verse of the *indiciaires* and much more often in their chronicles than in their other works. In general these Dutch elements fulfil one of two functions, which can both loosely be described as 'lending local colour'. Either they designate a local word for an item that is perceived as being characteristic of the place — a dyke or a dune in Chastelain's chronicles; a boat, a bulwark, or again a dyke in those of Molinet[24] — or they quote words actually spoken on a particular occasion, as when Chastelain describes the crowd welcoming Charles the Bold into Ghent: 'Et alors tout d'une voix crièrent contre-mont: Hée! Wille-comme! Wille-comme!, bienviegné, bienviegné monseigneur' [And then with a single voice, they cried out, *Hey, Welcome! Welcome.* Welcome, Welcome My Lord].[25] In the first case, it appears that the Dutch word is used partly because the author has no other word with which to evoke a particular landscape. Dykes and dunes belong to the Dutch-speaking north, and so to describe this landscape a writer must use this language. The point is reinforced when we realize that these Dutch loan-words have entered the modern French vocabulary, indicating that they designate something for which there is no native word in French, or something that occurs much more frequently in Dutch, so that the Dutch word has been preferred.[26] Additionally, there are many more Dutch words in Chastelain's and Molinet's chronicles than would normally be the case in French because the chroniclers are writing about a society where objects are frequently named in Dutch. Doudet has pointed out that Chastelain often uses a phrase containing synonyms in Dutch and French, such as 'doyens et hoefmans' [deans and chief officers].[27] This allows the author to convey the cultural specificity of the society described, without sacrificing clarity to a francophone readership. It also, as Doudet suggests, places the chronicler on an almost ethnographic footing in his reporting, positioning him as a mediator between the netherlandophone subjects of his narrative and his francophone readers.[28] In addition, it allows Chastelain to display his verbal dexterity and the extent of his vocabulary.

When Chastelain quotes words spoken in Dutch, he creates an impression of verisimilitude. These were the words really spoken, he implies, and so this is a faithful account of what took place. Of course he could, and does, translate remarks, or paraphrase them in French, but conveying them in the original language lends colour to the account. It also has a rhetorical force, persuading the reader of the objectively factual nature of what is narrated. Perhaps poetry is not supposed to be factual in the same way, and this is one reason why Dutch words are much less in evidence in the poetry of both Chastelain and Molinet. Noël Dupire cites some instances in Molinet's poetry, for example when he renounces beer drinking in favour of wine:

> Fy de brassin, de queute, de briemart,
> De foudrine, de cervoise et de let;
> Fy de galant, de miel, de hacquebart,
> D'amboursebier, de biere et citoullet
> De ripauppé et de coqueplumet,

> Fy de perré, d'ambours, de houppedalle,
> De cherise, de cidre, de goudalle
> Et de fonteine a tous abandonnee,
> Car desormés, pour mieux emplir me dalle,
> Je me tenray a la bonne vinee.²⁹
>
> [Pooh to brew, to light ale, to Bremen's best;
> To sloe gin, to unhopped beer, and to milk;³⁰
> Pooh to muscat, to mead, to weak beer,
> To amber ale, to beer, and Bremen-style brews,
> To plonk and paintstripper;
> Pooh to perry, Hamburg's produce, and hoppy ale,
> Cherry beer, cider, heavy,
> And to the fountain that everyone can drink from;
> From now on, to better fill my throat,
> I'll stick to good vintages.]

Briemart, hacquebart, amboursebier, ambours, goudale, and we could probably add *houppedalle*: Molinet knows his beers, and names them using their Dutch names. This is the equivalent of the prose usage of Dutch, where a regionally specific word is used to give precision in the meaning (not just quality beer, but the sort of quality beer appreciated by Dutch-speakers). However, it is one of the rare instances where we find an evocation of regional specificity in francophone poetry, and therefore one of the rare cases where words are unambiguously and consciously borrowed from Dutch.

Elsewhere, we find both poets writing in French using words with generally Germanic or specifically Dutch roots, without much indication of whether they are considered as foreign loans. *Estrif* [strife], for example, was presumably sufficiently established in French by this stage for speakers to regard it as a native lexical element, though someone whose first language was Dutch, like Chastelain, might still recognize it as a cognate of *strijd*.³¹ His use of the rarer *estrivée* in a line in *Le Miroer des nobles hommes de France* might come from a desire to use a word form which was less recognizably related to Dutch.³² At the same time it might equally stem from exigencies of metre and rhyme: particularly since *estrivée* appears in the final rhyme position: 'Voit-on bien sourdre une dure estrivée' [we see a bitter struggle arise]. Similar considerations may be behind Chastelain's use of one of his few Dutch words in poetry, *remme* [cord], in the *Dit de verité*, where it appears in a rhyme position, rhyming with *baptême* and with the line that follows:

> La où foy une, un fons et un baptême
> Un bers, un sang, un lien doit estraindre
> Et traire tout ensemble à une remme
> Là vient malheur qui les regnans achemme
> Et fait leurs cœurs enfroidir et refraindre.³³
>
> [There where one faith, one font, and one baptism,
> One cradle, one blood, and one bond should draw together,
> Pulling all together with one cord,
> There comes misfortune, which shames rulers
> And cools and calms the ardour of their hearts.]

The rhyme-word *achemme*, which appears in the source as *schemme*, has caused some problems for Kervyn de Lettenhove, Chastelain's editor, partly because the meaning is not clear, but also because the line is hypometric, which suggests a faulty reading. The editor attempts to resolve the dilemma by emending it to *achesmer*, 'to decorate', whilst acknowledging that this does not seem to fit the context of the stanza. It seems much more plausible that it is also a Dutch loan-word, formed from *schemen*, a cognate of the English 'shame'. The significance of two Dutch words in prominent final rhyme positions could be interpreted as conveying some sort of message, perhaps located socio-linguistically, about the shaming of rulers; but we must be cautious, since phonological similarities mean that once one loan-word is employed in a final position, loans from the same language may present themselves to complete the rhyme.

Whilst interesting, these momentary switches into Dutch pale into insignificance when compared with the extensive recourse that both Chastelain and Molinet have to the vocabulary of Latin. Latin loan-words make up by far the greatest element in the lexical innovation of both poets, and Molinet in particular employs extensive shifts between Latin and French in macaronic poems. A favourite technique of Molinet's is to build up a Latin prayer, acrostic-style, using the first word of a verse or stanza in Latin, while the rest of the poem is in French.[34] The poem can thus be read in two ways: vertically it makes up one sentence in Latin, but horizontally, the Latin and the French interact to convey a message that in most cases makes sense. I say in most cases, because it is sometimes possible to read a line without reference to the meaning of the Latin, either because the French text does not integrate the Latin or because it repeats it. Examples of both can be found in the poet's *Pater Noster*, which opens with the couplet:

> *Pater noster*, vray amateur,
> Nostre Dieu, nostre plasmateur[35]
>
> [*Our Father*, true lover,
> Our God, our creator]

and later contains the lines:

> *Adveniat regnum tuum*
> Et si fort nous esvertuon
> Que gaignons le regne des cieulx. (vv. 57–59)
>
> [*Thy Kingdom come*
> And may we deploy all our strength
> So that we attain the kingdom of heaven.]

In the second example, the French even seems to contradict the Latin, in that Molinet envisages the believer as ascending to heaven, while the prayer speaks of heaven coming to the believer. In any case, lexically and syntactically, the sentence does not integrate the Latin and the French, even though the switch into French takes place at a conjunction, which implies continuity. If the definition of code-switching requires that the switch take place within the same conversation, does an incoherent or unlinked set of statements, in which different languages mark different perspectives, really qualify as an example of code-switching? The first example is even more complex, in that the terms that follow the Latin, *amateur*, *Dieu*, and *plasmateur* (the last a learned borrowing from Greek, meaning 'creator'), translate and gloss the Latin phrase *Pater noster*. A father is someone who creates and loves, and this is why God is called a father. There is no doubt here that the subject-matter is the same, since it is repeated. Molinet uses three nouns to translate the Latin and to explain what it means, but is this code-switching? One could argue that it is not, because it is not necessary to understand the Latin to understand the poet's message and so the poem is not fully bilingual. However, this sort of practice, where a switch contains the same information as has previously been enunciated in the other language, is typical of modern oral code-switching and in fact constitutes one of the most common types of switches in the language of bilingual speakers.[36] We have seen that Chastelain performs the same sort of switch in Dutch when writing prose, giving the local Dutch term and its French equivalent. Given the status of Latin as the specialist language of religion, we can argue that in this case too Molinet's switch performs the same function: allowing the poet to use the specialist term (regional when he uses Dutch, ecclesiastical when he uses Latin) and explain its meaning, or how he understands its meaning, in French.

Elsewhere in *Pater Noster* we find Molinet switching from Latin to French without providing a translation. So, for example:

> *Debitoribus nostris* sont
> Les cinq sens naturels qui font
> A l'ame trop grant vitupere. (vv. 183–85)
>
> [*Those who lead us into temptation* are
> The five natural senses which do
> Very great damage to the soul.]

Lexically this makes sense: the Latin words have the same meaning in the sentence as they would if they were French words. However, Molinet does not respect the grammatical quality of the Latin element, which is dative — an indirect object, governed by the preceding verb *dimittimus*. By making it the subject of the verb *être*, he demonstrates that it is the meaning of the words used in the switch which is significant, not their form.

A comparison with a poem by Anthonis de Roovere, also called *Pater Noster* and also operating under the same macaronic constraint, reveals a similar picture. In De Roovere's poem, the Latin elements are more closely grouped, since he places a Latin word at the beginning of every verse, rather than a word or two at the start of each stanza, as Molinet does. Nevertheless, we see the same sorts of switches that we found in Molinet — and others that we did not see. The first stanza serves as an illustration:

> Pater eewich sonder beghinsel
> Noster zijdy sonder insel
> Qui ons gheeft dat eewich leuen
> Es dat wy die sonden vergheuen
> In aerdtrijk worden Marien sone

> Celis/Schepper vanden throone
> Sanctificetur eewelijcke
> Nomen Jesu op aerdtrijcke
> Tuum is al luyde oft stille
> Adveniat Heere my uwen wille
> Regnum naer dit corte leuen
> Tuum moet dy mijnder sielen gheuen
> Fiat lieue Heere Godt
> Voluntas te behoudene v ghebodt.[37]
>
> [*Father* eternal without beginning
> *Ours* be you without end
> *Who* grants us, that we might live forever
> *Art* so we forgive sins
> *On* earth become Mary's son
> *In Heaven* creator of the throne
> *Hallowed be* eternally
> *The Name* of Jesus on Earth
> *Thine* is everything, whether loud or quiet
> *May it come*, Lord, your will to me
> *The Kingdom* after this short life
> *Of yours* may you give my soul
> *Be done*, dear Lord God
> *Your Will*, to keep your command.]

Here, there has been a greater effort to respect the grammatical quality of the words used, and not just their lexical meaning. *Celis*, for example, seems to retain the sense of the preposition *in*, providing a contrast between the earthly and the heavenly domain in De Roovere's text. There are other complexities too, not seen in Molinet's poem. The way that De Roovere has chosen to impose the acrostic constraint, as a single-word element at the start of each verse, means that he is obliged to use words from all grammatical categories, such as relatives like *qui* and prepositions like *in*, which Molinet subsumes into phrases that he deploys as a single element. By contrast, De Roovere takes these individual words and employs them just as he would their Dutch equivalents. Indeed, the meaning of *in* is identical in Dutch and in Latin, and so the switch site here is blurred: it is not clear where Latin ends and Dutch begins. The use of *in* in the initial position of the verse signals that it must be understood as a Latin word, since all words in this position are Latin, but nothing else about the word indicates that a switch has taken place. In the previous verse, *Es* is simultaneously the second person singular present indicative of the Latin verb *esse* and a Dutch relative, part of 'es dat'. Depending on whether the reader is reading vertically, the Latin prayer, or horizontally, the Dutch poem, the element has a different meaning. Later in the poem, the Latin conjunction *et* stands for the Dutch pronoun *het* ('et is tijd') with similar effect.

Like Molinet, then, De Roovere makes intelligent and innovative use of switches between Latin and the vernacular to achieve poetic effect. The fact that both poets do this, is further testament — if any were needed — to the formal influence of poems in one vernacular on those in the other. However, as in Norman England, regardless of the influence of French poetic *form* on Dutch and vice versa, most of the *linguistic* switches take place between the vernacular and Latin. We can conclude that this is because, in the Burgundian Netherlands as in Norman England, Latin was the high-status literary language. However, we should also note that this is especially true in devotional poems, where the influence of church Latin might be expected to be strongest. When Molinet writes about drinking, for example, he uses a little Dutch.

By contrast, De Roovere employs French borrowings more frequently. Or rather, he uses words with a Romance origin that have most likely come via French. It is sometimes difficult to tell whether such elements are to be considered French or Latin words. The 'imagyen' of the *Droom van Rovere* is a case in point. The palatalization of the *g* suggests that it has entered Dutch via French, rather than coming straight from Latin *imago*. The nativization displayed in the addition of the Dutch plural suffix, suggests that it is being treated as a borrowing rather than a switch: De Roovere does not switch into French when discussing the statues he sees in his dream, but he uses French vocabulary to describe them. Like Chastelain, we find him using groups of such borrowed words in rhyme positions, particularly in this poem, in clusters of French-inspired rhyme-words, 'ymageneringe'/'arguwerynge', 'Vysieren'/'Obedieren'.[38] This last seems directly borrowed from Latin, since it contains the etymological *d*, but it may be a learned back-formation comparable to the large number of etymological letters being reinserted into French words in the period. There are other words in De Roovere's vocabulary, for example *tyrannen* (v. 38), which are spelled in a way that reflects their etymology (the *y* appearing as in Greek) but where the meaning demonstrates awareness of the French usage, where it is exclusively applied to violent leaders. We cannot measure the contribution of the scribe to such decisions but it is surely significant: the *y* may have been used to create a visual impression on the page, or to remove ambiguity, or the scribe may have had a greater — or lesser — awareness of etymology than the poet, and may have therefore opted for a particular orthography which may not have been that of the poet. Such examples illustrate how hard it is to disentangle French from classical borrowings in De Roovere's poetry. This reflects the linguistic similarity of French and Latin, of course, but also the similarity in status, since De Roovere turns to both when looking for a specialist word, particularly in the lexical field of religion.

Context is clearly very important here: De Roovere's borrowings are much more unequivocally Latin in his macaronic devotional poems, much more influenced by French when he is writing about the death of the duke and the reaction surrounding the court. Molinet and Chastelain use numerous Latin borrowings, but Latin switches also occur mainly in devotional poetry. Dutch borrowings and switches occur in prose or very occasionally in poems describing everyday life. The two vernaculars of the Burgundian Netherlands, therefore, do not occupy the same place in the literary culture, even though all our poets have the linguistic resources to draw on both. Dutch appears in a French context only where it describes the environment and practices of the Dutch-speaking populace. This is not often considered a proper subject for poetry, and so recourse to Dutch in French poetry is rare. French is the principal language of the court, to some extent the language of literature, and is a vehicle for Latin vocabulary in Dutch. It appears in some Dutch-language poetry but is often substantially nativized. For poets writing in both French and Dutch, Latin is the high-status language; and it is to Latin, rather than to either of the vernaculars, that they turn for preference.

Notes to Chapter 2

1. 'Decorated with letters engraved in every way, and also diverse images', Anthonis de Roovere, *De gedichten*, ed. by J. J. Mak (Zwolle: Tjeenk Willink, 1955), pp. 351–59 (p. 352). All translations are my own.
2. For an exploration of interlinguistic formal influences, see Oosterman, 'Tussen twee wateren zwem ik'.
3. Sarah G. Thomason, *Language Contact: An Introduction* (Washington, DC: Georgetown University Press, 2001), p. 132.
4. Shana Poplack, 'Sometimes I'll Start a Sentence in Spanish *y termino en español*: Toward a Typology of Code-switching' [1980], in *The Bilingualism Reader*, ed. by Li Wei (London: Routledge, 2000), pp. 221–56.
5. Herbert Schendl, 'Syntactic Constraints on Code-Switching in Medieval Texts', in *Placing Middle English in Context*, ed. by Irma Taavitsainen and others (Berlin: Mouton de Gruyter, 2000), pp. 67–86.
6. Ibid., p. 78.
7. Suzanne Romaine, *Bilingualism*, 2nd edn (Malden: Blackwell, 1989).
8. Donald Winford, *An Introduction to Contact Linguistics* (Malden: Blackwell, 2003), pp. 37–39. The research referred to is reported in Jeanine Treffers-Daller, 'Borrowing and Shift-induced Interference: Contrasting Patterns in French-Germanic Contact in Brussels and Strasbourg', *Bilingualism: Language and Cognition*, 2.1 (1999), 1–22.
9. For etymological information relating to Dutch, see the *Geïntegreerde taal-bank*, combining the *Oudnederlands woordenboek* (2009), the *Vroegmiddelnederlands woordenboek*, the *Middelnederlandsch woordenboek*, the *Woordenboek der Nederlandsche taal*, and the *Woordenboek der Friese taal*: Instituut voor Nederlandse Lexicologie, *De geïntegreerde taal-bank*, <http://gtb.inl.nl> [accessed 9 July 2014]. The *Vroegmiddelnederlands woordenboek* gives the etymology of *image* as Vulgar Latin through French, with the earliest use attested in 1285. The *Dictionnaire étymologique de l'ancien français* lists *image* as a word appearing in the early eleventh century, also from Latin: <http://www.deaf-page.de> [accessed 9 July 2014].
10. Anthonis de Roovere, *Rethoricale wercken van Anthonis de Roovere, Brugghelinck, Vlaemsch doctoor ende gheestich Poete*, ed. by Eduard de Dene (Antwerp: Jan van Ghelen, 1562), fols a2^v–a3^r: 'maer een idiotz ende simpel leeck ongheleert ambachsman was, niet hebbende dan zijn vlaemsche ingheboren lanttale oft spraecke' [[he] was merely an uneducated man, a simple unschooled lay craftsman, possessing only the Flemish language or speech of his native land].
11. A complete transcription of De Dene's 'Foreword' can be found in 'De *Chronike van den lande van Vlaendre*: Studie van het handschrift en uitgave van f° 148v. tot f° 415v', ed. by Simon Vandekerckhove, 2 vols (unpublished thesis, University of Ghent, 2007), I, 66–67.
12. Johan Oosterman, 'Oh Flanders, Weep! Anthonis de Roovere and Charles the Bold', in *The Growth of Authority in the Medieval West*, ed. by Martin Gosman, Arjo Vanderjagt and Jan Veenstra (Groningen: Forsten, 1999), pp. 257–67.
13. Oosterman, 'Tussen twee wateren wateren zwem ik'.
14. Armstrong, 'The Language Question in the Low Countries'; Degroote, 'Taaltoestanden in de Bourgondische Nederlanden'; Luc Hommel, *Marie de Bourgogne ou le grand héritage* (Brussels: Goemaere; Paris: Presses universitaires de France, 1951), pp. 154–56. See also Dirk Schoenaers's contribution to this volume (Chapter 1).

15. La Marche describes Chastelain as 'natif flameng, toutesfois mettant par escript en langaige franchois' [a Flemish native nevertheless writing in the French language] (Olivier de La Marche, *Mémoires*, ed. by Henri Beaune and Jean d'Arbaumont, 4 vols (Paris: Société de l'Histoire de France, 1883–88), I, 14).
16. Molinet, *Chroniques*, ed. by Doutrepont and Jodogne, II, 593.
17. Doudet, *Poétique de George Chastelain (1415–1475)*, p. 121.
18. For an exploration of the significance of the universities in the Burgundian administration, see Francis Rapp, 'Universités et principautés: les états bourguignons', in *À la cour de Bourgogne: le duc, son entourage, son train*, ed. by Jean-Marie Cauchies (Turnhout: Brepols, 1998), pp. 51–65.
19. Armstrong, 'The Language Question in the Low Countries', p. 190.
20. Schendl, 'Syntactic Constraints on Code-Switching in Medieval Texts', especially pp. 78–80.
21. Irven M. Resnick, 'Lingua dei, lingua hominis: Sacred Language and Medieval Texts', *Viator*, 21 (1990), 51–74.
22. Schendl, 'Syntactic Constraints on Code-Switching in Medieval Texts', p. 79.
23. For instance, Kenneth Urwin, *Georges Chastellain: la vie, les œuvres* (Paris: André, 1937), p. 87: 'Le flamand exerçait une influence considérable sur le français, surtout dans la région que connaissait notre auteur. Des mots d'origine néerlandaise furent très employés'.
24. Georges Chastellain, *Œuvres*, ed. by Joseph Marie Bruno Constantin Kervyn de Lettenhove, 8 vols (Brussels: Heussner, 1863–66), IV, 27; VI, 87; I, 71. Noël Dupire, *Jean Molinet: la vie — les œuvres* (Paris: Droz, 1932), pp. 241, 254; see Molinet, *Chroniques*, ed. by Doutrepont and Jodogne, II, 316; I, 31; I, 41.
25. Chastellain, *Œuvres*, ed. by Kervyn de Lettenhove, V, 269.
26. The *Trésor de la langue française* gives no synonym for *dune*, but gives *levée* as a synonym for *digue*, adding that it is much rarer than the word derived from Dutch: <http://atilf.atilf.fr/> [accessed 9 July 2014].
27. Chastellain, *Œuvres*, ed. by Kervyn de Lettenhove, II, 223.
28. Doudet, *Poétique de George Chastelain (1415–1475)*, pp. 127–28.
29. Jean Molinet, 'Response a Anthoine Busnois', in *Faictz et dictz*, ed. by Noël Dupire, 3 vols (Paris: Société des Anciens Textes Français, 1936–39), II, 798–801 (vv. 81–90). This poem is discussed in Adrian Armstrong, 'Boire chez (et avec) Molinet', in *Jean Molinet et son temps: Actes des rencontres internationales de Dunkerque, Lille et Gand (8–10 novembre 2007)*, ed. by Jean Devaux, Estelle Doudet, and Élodie Lecuppre-Desjardin (Turnhout: Brepols, 2013), pp. 237–48 (p. 241).
30. The *Dictionnaire du moyen français* lists *let* only as a variant spelling of *lait*, so I have translated accordingly. See ATILF CNRS/Université de Lorraine, *Dictionnaire du moyen français*, 2012 version, <http://www.atilf.fr/dmf> [accessed 9 July 2014].
31. Frédéric Godefroy, *Dictionnaire de l'ancienne langue française et de tous ses dialectes du IXe au XVe siècle*, 10 vols (Paris: Vieweg, 1880–1902), III, 652–53, lists many examples of the word from before 1300.
32. Chastellain, *Œuvres*, ed. by Kervyn de Lettenhove, VI, 204–15 (p. 208). *Estrivée* also appears in the *Dictionnaire de l'ancienne langue française*, and in the *Dictionnaire du moyen français*, though in both cases with fewer cited examples. The words were clearly both in use, with *estrif* being more frequently employed than *estrivée*.
33. Chastellain, *Œuvres*, ed. by Kervyn de Lettenhove, VI, 219–42 (p. 223).
34. This is not unusual in devotional poetry of the period. It is discussed, along with a variety of more complex forms, in Gérard Gros, *Le Poète marial et l'art graphique: étude sur les jeux de lettres dans les poèmes pieux du Moyen Âge* (Caen: Paradigme, 1993).
35. Molinet, *Faictz et dictz*, II, 491–98 (vv. 1–2). Further references are supplied in the text.
36. Winford, *An Introduction to Contact Linguistics*, p. 117. The study cited is Peter Auer, 'The Pragmatics of Code-Switching: A Sequential Approach', in *One Speaker, Two Languages*, ed. by Lesley Milroy and Pieter Muysken (Cambridge: Cambridge University Press, 1995), pp. 115–35 (p. 120).
37. Anthonis de Roovere, 'Pater Noster', in *De gedichten*, ed. by Mak, pp. 216–18 (vv. 1–14).
38. De Roovere, *De gedichten*, ed. by Mak, pp. 351–59 (vv. 4–5, 29–30).

CHAPTER 3

Printing in French in the Low Countries in the Early Sixteenth Century: Patterns and Networks

Malcolm Walsby

When printing in the Low Countries during the sixteenth century is evoked, one inevitably thinks of the rise of the Reformation, the Dutch revolt, and the publications of Plantin. However, in the first decades of the century, the political and religious events that were to dominate the Netherlandish print world of the later Renaissance were by and large absent. Certainly, they had virtually no impact on printing in French. Martin Luther's message initially found only a limited echo in the Low Countries with no more than 170 pamphlets printed during the 1520s and 1530s, in stark contrast with the phenomenal tidal wave of *Flugschriften* that swept over the Holy Roman Empire during these same years.[1] Furthermore, very few of these short texts were published in French: Dutch dominated the vernacular language imprints that promoted or condemned the Protestant faith in the Netherlands.

Plantin's production, on the other hand, was heavily francophone. Born near Tours, Christophe Plantin established himself as the foremost printer in Antwerp in the second half of the century. Between 1555 and 1589, he created one of the most successful publishing houses in Europe, printing hundreds of editions in French and exporting many thousands of books to his homeland.[2] His success created a template of involvement with the French market which was to continue in the Netherlands over the following centuries by publishers such as Elzevier and others in Leiden, Amsterdam, and The Hague. But his business was predicated on a model that he had devised and had carefully nurtured. It tells us little about the multilingual exchanges that existed between France and the Netherlands during the first half of the sixteenth century.

Early French printing is, therefore, often absent from the traditional dominant narratives of sixteenth-century publishing in the Low Countries. Yet the importance and influence of this phenomenon should not be underestimated — and not just in the francophone parts of the southern Netherlands. After looking at the development of printing before 1540, this essay will highlight the place occupied by French in the industry and evoke the interaction between French texts and the Dutch public.

Map 3.1. Printing Locations in the Low Countries up to 1600

Printing in the Low Countries Before 1540

For many years some scholars suggested that the printed book was first devised in the Low Countries by a Breton prototypographer. Belgian historians of the eighteenth, nineteenth, and early twentieth centuries claimed that Gutenberg was not the inventor of the printing press.[3] They asserted that this honour should be bestowed on the Bruges scribe and later printer Jan Brito. This claim was based on the translation of two lines in Latin published in the colophon of an undated incunabulum volume: 'Inveniens artem nullo monstrante mirandam | Instrumenta quoque non minus laude stupenda' [Discovering the admirable art [of printing] without having been shown, with his own instruments, which are no less worthy of praise]; this allowed for sufficient ambiguity for nineteenth-century nationalistic historians, perhaps, but not for the contention to be taken seriously today. It was simply the assertion of a proud man who had learnt his art alone, rather than a claim to be the inventor of the printed book. Brito's career as a printer was, in reality, modest. It began in the early 1460s, some twenty years after Gutenberg had started to develop the printing press, and led to the production of a handful of imprints of unequal quality.[4]

Truth be told, the Low Countries were not at the centre of the early incunabulum world. Before 1480, cities in the Holy Roman Empire and in the Italian states dominated output. But Netherlandish printers and booksellers were ideally placed to play an important role in the developing book trade. They benefited from their strategic location at one extremity of what has been described as the 'paper valley'.[5] In the incunabula era four centres of print dominated output: Deventer, Louvain, Zwolle, and Antwerp. Each centre had its specialisms. Deventer concentrated on the production of lucrative school books that could be printed and distributed in great numbers. Louvain made the most of the presence of its celebrated university by engaging in the production of theological works and other scholarly publications. Zwolle was also a centre for religious and educational book production. In contrast Antwerp adopted a more mercantile approach. It was here that books destined for foreign markets such as England or Denmark were printed.[6]

Over the following years, printing spread rapidly through the Low Countries and, by the end of the sixteenth century, over fifty different towns and cities had welcomed the printing press within their walls (see Map 3.1). The geographic dispersion of these towns throughout both the northern and southern Netherlands must not, however, disguise the statistical importance of one centre during the Renaissance: Antwerp. As Andrew Pettegree has argued, it is possible to differentiate three different types of print culture: the dispersed model (exemplified by Germany) where many centres produce a large number of editions; the centralized model (exemplified by England) where publishing is concentrated in one city; and the dominated model (exemplified by France) where printing is mainly focused in one or two leading centres but with other secondary places of production.[7] Within this paradigm, the Low Countries can be seen as belonging to this last dominated model. During the first half of the sixteenth century, Antwerp represented over sixty per cent of the printed production.[8]

Bookselling in the Netherlands grew rapidly in the late fifteenth century as the local market for texts was particularly strong. High levels of urbanization, the rising wealth of the population, and one of the highest rates of literacy in Europe were all important facets of Netherlandish society that were favourable to the printed book trade.[9] This undoubtedly helped the emergence of regional print centres, but it also encouraged the development of a strong network of booksellers. In this regard too, the Low Countries were perfectly situated. The Rhine and other rivers that flowed towards the North Sea were traditional trade routes that ferried huge quantities of goods. Barrels and bales of printed sheets could easily be added as extra consignments to boats using pre-existing merchant networks. This helped the creation of strong import and export markets, a phenomenon further aided by the dynamism of trading centres such as Antwerp. All of this was particularly important with regard to exchanges between the francophone and Dutch-speaking regions of Europe. Indeed, the early sixteenth century saw the development of a durable bond between the French and Netherlandish print worlds.

Printing in French and the Low Countries

The connections between members of the book trade in the Netherlands and France were very strong in the first decades of the sixteenth century. These links were not simply predicated on common economic goals or shared interest in certain texts, but were the result of emigration and immigration. The printer and bookseller Martin Lempereur was a case in point. Born in France, he began his career in Paris, where he learned his trade before relocating to Antwerp in 1525. In the following twelve years he published a large portfolio of texts (over 200 editions) that demonstrated his versatility and multilingual capacities. Most of his production was in Latin, but he also published over fifty editions in French and over thirty in Dutch. His multilingual aspirations were emphasized by the fact that he readily used different versions of his surname, translating it to 'De Keyser' on the title-page of Dutch imprints and 'Caesar' on Latin ones. The mainstay of his production consisted of numerous Latin and French school books and humanist works that found a wide readership both in the Low Countries and beyond. He also printed covert translations of Luther and Erasmus that reveal his continued links not just with French printers and booksellers in cities such as Paris and Lyon but also in smaller centres such as Alençon, where the Protestant printer Simon Dubois was based.[10] His influence was such that some of his editions were rapidly republished in Paris by other printers. This was true both of French texts, such as Jean Thibault's *Le Thresor du remede*, and of Latin ones such as the *Fons vitæ*.[11]

Other printers and booksellers chose to go the other way. This type of emigration is perhaps best illustrated by the career of the humanist printer Josse Bade. Bade was born in Ghent but chose to move to Lyon in 1492, before later settling in Paris.[12] There he became an integral part of the Paris book world and published hundreds of erudite, mainly Latin, editions. His successful career allowed him to become, for a while, the main printer of the most famous of his compatriots, Erasmus. This represented an important change, as Erasmus had previously published his works in the Low Countries with Thierry Martens. The transfer of Erasmus's custom was a major blow for the Deventer printer, and emphasizes just how integrated the European book market had become. Having the privilege of printing Erasmus's texts first ensured quick sales and international fame. Martens would have to wait for over a decade before once more being the first to print one of Erasmus's texts.[13]

As the importance of Paris and Lyon as centres of print grew, so their imprints became more widely distributed in neighbouring countries. In Paris, in particular, the large quantities of Latin works produced for the powerful booksellers of the rue Saint-Jacques were perfectly suited to the needs of the international book trade.[14] Texts neither written in France nor in French but published in Paris became increasingly available and influential in the Low Countries. In the case of Josse Bade, his Latin publications rapidly infiltrated the Netherlandish market. In many cases his commercial success encouraged others to undertake new editions that faithfully copied his Parisian imprints. This was true of a number of publications that came off presses located in the Low Countries. The editions of Quintus Horatius Flaccus produced in Deventer by Jacobus de Breda in 1515, and in 's-Hertogenbosch by Laurens Hayen in 1521, for instance, were both based on the work Bade had done in Paris.[15] This trend was not limited to classical works: the influential writings of the near-contemporary author Battista Spagnoli of Mantua saw numerous editions produced in Antwerp, Deventer, and Zwolle that all used texts prepared and previously published by Bade in Paris. This was all the easier to do as the editions produced in France would not have benefitted from any commercial protection against competing Netherlandish imprints. The French booksellers would, at best, have been protected by the developing privilege system that depended on official letters issued either by local sovereign courts, such as the Paris Parlement, or by the King of France, neither of which had any legal authority in the Low Countries.[16]

This type of transcultural interaction was a fundamental aspect of the nascent international book trade. It demonstrates the level of exchange between the francophone and the Dutch-speaking worlds. But if this was true for Latin texts that would easily have found a market of educated readers in both linguistic zones, how common was the transmission and publication of French texts in the early sixteenth-century Low Countries? Only one tenth of the titles printed in the Netherlands during the Renaissance were published in French; far fewer than in Dutch. However, this statistic hides an interesting trend: over the first four decades of the sixteenth century more and more books were being printed in French. Between 1501 and 1540 the percentage of books printed in Latin fell from seventy-five per cent to less than half of overall production, whilst the quantity of French titles rose significantly and represented almost ten per cent of total output by the end of this period (see Table 3.1). Though this percentage remained modest when compared with that of Dutch-language texts, the rise was much more rapid than that of books published in other vernacular languages in the Low Countries over the same decades.

This signal success was solely associated with one place: Antwerp.[17] During this period five sixths of French titles printed in the Low Countries were published in that city. The rest were virtually all products of presses active in the French-

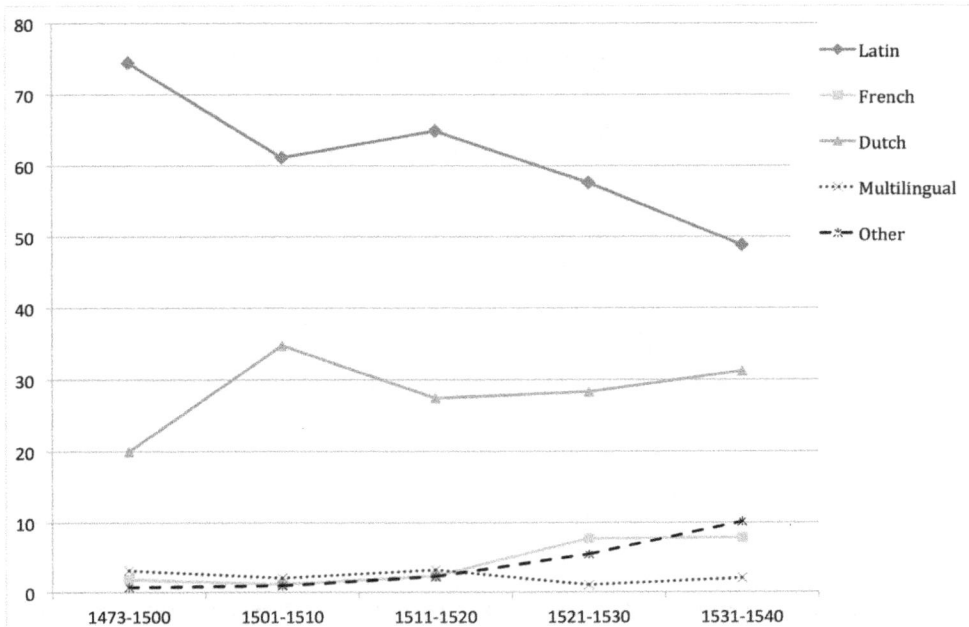

TABLE 3.1. Printing in the Low Countries by Language, 1473–1540 (number of editions)

speaking areas of the Southern Netherlands. The rise of Antwerp as a centre of French-language printing was a new phenomenon. During the incunabulum period, this had been heavily dominated by Bruges — a very different type of city.[18] This change is vital to our understanding of the nature of the evolving trade in French-language editions in the Low Countries. It was intricately linked to a radical alteration in the type of text printed in French. Bruges was a town closely connected to the Burgundian court. It mainly produced books for the consumption of the aristocratic elite and their entourage: romances, poetry, and other literary texts that sought to entertain and to deliver moral or religious messages. This was a highly literate world with a long tradition of cultural patronage which had yielded some of the most magnificent manuscript books of the later medieval period. Successive dukes had been important collectors and amassed considerable libraries.[19] The printed output of the Bruges presses was heavily influenced by this legacy. Alongside these upmarket imprints, the southern presses also produced a large number of religious editions. These were meant for a wider, but still very local, readership as printers sought to meet the needs of the large francophone population of the Southern Netherlands for basic texts of popular piety.

The rise of Antwerp at the very end of the incunabulum period changed the geography of the Netherlandish print world: it led to a sustained domination of the local book market that was to last for most of the sixteenth century. Compared to Bruges, the city catered for a far larger and socially diverse population. Antwerp had profited from the burgeoning Portuguese spice trade, which had contributed to drain Bruges of much of the city's economic activity.[20] The aristocratic nucleus

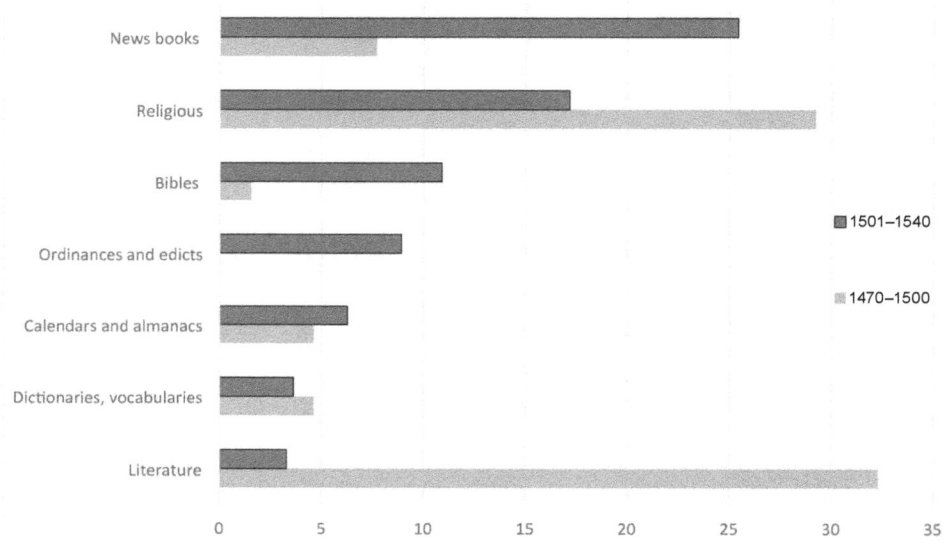

TABLE 3.2. Printing in the Low Countries by Subject, pre- and post-1500

around the Burgundian court in Bruges gave way to a much larger readership formed of merchants, lawyers, and literate artisans in Antwerp. This meant that publishers selected a very different type of texts for the local book market. The first result of this change was the rise of cheap print (see Table 3.2). In the first half of the sixteenth century, production in Antwerp was dominated by short works in smaller formats that required the use of fewer sheets of paper. As this was the main cost in the printing of a book, it meant that publishers could make these titles available at very low prices.[21] This enabled new readers to acquire books for the first time. The French books produced in this way were not the literary texts that had dominated Bruges publishing in the fifteenth century. The new works were characterized by their usefulness. The cheap imprints were mainly local edicts and ordinances that informed people of changes in the law, and calendars and almanacs that helped burghers and farmers organize their year. The latter works were also of interest for their entertainment value and in this they were joined by the most common type of imprint: news books.

News books in many ways typified the French-language books produced in Antwerp during the first half of the sixteenth century. They seldom consisted of more than three sheets of paper, which made them cheap commodities. They could be of great use to merchants, investors, and others who depended on the international trade — arguably one of the defining traits of Renaissance Antwerp. They were also entertaining: they were not short paragraphs of texts that sought solely to inform, as was more the case with the handwritten *avvisi* that were already an established feature of the European news world.[22] The description of the siege of Vienna in 1529 published in Antwerp by Michel de Hoochstraten is a perfect example of this type of text.[23] The title-page draws the potential buyer in by using a large, if crude, woodcut that focuses on the moment the cavalry of both armies clashed, with bodies and armour strewn across the ground in front of a large walled town. If this representation might seem generic, the title highlights a figure that greatly fascinated contemporary readers: the Turk, here described as the 'grand ennemy de Chrestienté' [great enemy of Christendom].[24] The date is also included in the title to underline the freshness of the news: it had made its way from Vienna onto the printed page in less than two months, something that was clearly seen by the publisher as a selling point. The desirability of this imprint was not simply limited to speed of production. The issue of trustworthiness was broached; the authors, though anonymous, were described as noblemen present at the siege. Finally, the title emphasized that the imprint was protected by a privilege. Printed using a single sheet, this was the archetypal news book, cheap but attractive, with many details of the siege, both informative and entertaining.

That such texts were printed in French poses an interesting question. What was the intended market for these books? In a predominantly Dutch-speaking area, who was supposed to read such texts? The production of an ever-increasing number of editions in Dutch meant that there was ample printed matter in the local vernacular. Furthermore, much of what was published in Dutch was similar to the French material: cheap, short, useful, informative, and entertaining. Certainly, news books were not the preserve of French-language imprints. Perhaps one of the keys to understanding the publication of these works is to look at the relationship between these editions and literate Dutch-speakers.

French Texts and the Dutch

One of the notable traits of publishing in the Low Countries was the large number of early multilingual dictionaries printed by Netherlandish presses. More than any other languages, these works sought to provide equivalences for those wishing to translate words and expressions between French and Dutch. In the first half of the sixteenth century over twenty editions of dictionaries or vocabularies offered readers a way to navigate between these two languages.[25] The market for these books was, perhaps unsurprisingly, cornered by printers based in the Southern Netherlands, where a large proportion of the population was francophone. But it was in Antwerp, a predominantly Dutch-speaking city, where most of these works were produced. The city was an international centre for trade where merchants from all over Europe met and exchanged. As the Florentine Lodovico Guicciardini commented, Antwerp was a 'cité vrayement des principales en quelque chose que ce soit, mais en trafficque marchant très-principale, entre toutes les autres du monde' [truly one of the leading cities in all respects, but absolutely foremost in commercial traffic, ahead of all others in the world].[26] In such circumstances, these dictionaries would have been a crucial tool for local businessmen seeking to interact with foreign merchants and in particular with their French counterparts.

Noël de Berlaimont's *Vocabulare van nieus gheordineert* was a good example of the need for such multilingual handbooks.[27] The emphasis placed on applied everyday use of the book was clear from the title-page, which announced that the goal was 'om lichtelijc Francoys te leeren lesen, scrijven ende spreken' [to teach people how to read, write, and speak French easily].[28] Published in an easy-to-use quarto format, this was a practical manual. The contents confirmed the target audience: after common conversations were handled in a first part, the second part was devoted to buying and selling, the third to the issue of counting and how to recover a debt, whilst the fourth taught the reader how to write commercial letters and financial documents. This was a book destined for merchants with international business concerns and not for readers with either literary or theological concerns. The only non-economic matter in this publication was aimed at everyday religious practice: the Credo, the Ten Commandments, or the paternoster were inserted at the very end of the volume, almost as an afterthought.

This contrasts with the far more serious approach adopted by some of the more substantial dictionaries printed during this period. During the first decades of the sixteenth century, Ambrogio Calepino's multilingual dictionaries became more widespread, with a number of editions of his five-language dictionary appearing in the Low Countries in the 1540s.[29] Such works were very different from those typified by Berlaimont's vocabulary. Not only did the words and phrases included in the book cover a much wider variety of subjects, but they were large and far more expensive ventures. For instance, Gilles Coppenius's 1546 edition of Calepino's *Pentaglottos* required the use of no fewer than 183 sheets per copy, as opposed to just ten for Berlaimont's *Vocabulare*.[30] The price of the Calepinos would have been far higher and the sheer size of the volumes indicates a very different usage: this was not the sort of book one could carry around for use on the quayside or during negotiations in a tavern. It was meant to sit on a shelf in a study and was undoubtedly primarily destined for a different readership.

If such works allowed speakers of either language to communicate and exchange on everyday matters as well as understand more serious books, readers would have mainly relied on the publication of translations to gain access to foreign-language texts. This was particularly true for literary works. Alongside the publication of local romances such as *Karel ende Elegast* or *Jonathas ende Rosafiere*, Netherlandish printers also produced a significant corpus of traditional French tales.[31] We know, for instance, of nine Dutch editions of *Sidrach*, six of *Paris et Vienne*, and four of *Melusine* printed in the first decades of the sixteenth century. Alongside these bestsellers, there were one-off publications of works such as *Floire et Blancheflor* or *Pierre de Provence*.[32] Both of these editions are known to us thanks to a single exemplar and this poor survival rate suggests that such imprints undoubtedly circulated far more than these statistics indicate. These were popular works that were probably victims of their own success and were read to destruction. The success of this genre of translation emphasizes the extent to which linguistic difference did not constitute an insurmountable barrier for traditional literary texts in the early Renaissance Low Countries.

The ease with which literary works moved from one language area to the other is underlined by the translation of the writings of contemporary francophone authors. The celebrated French poet Jean Bouchet saw his work *Les Regnars traversant les perilleuses voyes des folles fiances de ce monde*, originally published in Paris by Anthoine Vérard, translated and printed in Brussels during his lifetime.[33] This was not a one-way process: there were also instances of Dutch works translated for a francophone readership, as is the case with the edition of Jacob van Maerlant's *Wapene Martijn* printed by Jan Brito in Bruges.[34] Overall, the publication of contemporary works appears to have been much rarer than earlier, more traditional texts, though this phenomenon was not limited to the world of literary production. One of the most successful books of the first half of the sixteenth century was the work of the fourteenth-century jurist Jean Boutillier. *La Somme rurale*, originally published in Bruges in 1479, was translated into Dutch and published in that language in Delft just four years later.[35] The text quickly became a bestseller, with some twenty editions published all over France in towns as diverse as Lyon, Paris, Rouen, and even Abbeville before 1540. This commercial success was not limited to France with, in the Low Countries, four further Dutch editions published in Antwerp between 1503 and 1540.[36] This type of interaction between the Netherlandish and French book worlds highlights just how easily texts could go from one language to the next and retain their popularity.

The fluidity of exchanges between Dutch and French was further emphasized by the fact that foreign texts made their way into Dutch via French. For instance, the first translation into Dutch of the complete text of the Lives of Plutarch was not done directly from the Greek, but via the French translation of Jacques Amyot first published in Paris in 1559.[37] But it would be a mistake to confine the analysis of the interaction between the two languages to such literary works. As we have seen, the growth area for imprints produced in the Low Countries in French was precisely not this type of publication, but more accessible, cheap editions of useful and informative texts. And it is in the analysis of these works that we shall find the most interesting examples of interaction between French- and Dutch-language texts within the Netherlands.

Bilingual and Simultaneous Printing in French and Dutch

As the literary production that dominated the early years of Bruges French-language printing in the Low Countries gave way to the more ephemeral publications of Antwerp workshops, so the interaction between Dutch- and French-language imprints changed. With literary works, French editions were produced, distributed, and read before their commercial success enticed Dutch-speaking publishers to underwrite the costs of an edition in their own language. Each language generally had its own, distinct publisher, often located in a different town. In other words, such texts followed what might be seen as a traditional route from one language to another to appeal to different audiences and, for the most part, to be printed in workshops located in different cities. With the rising importance of cheap print, this pattern was jettisoned for a more integrated and commercially enterprising approach.

This new integrated approach centred on producing concurrently a text in both French and Dutch. The most obvious way of doing this was to present the content simultaneously in two languages on the same sheets. This method, however, remained rare. The printing of a text in one language on one page and in another language on the opposite page was a presentational device often reserved for educational books. When this involved two vernacular languages, the texts chosen were mainly either of a literary nature — as demonstrated by the versions of Juan de Flores's *L'Histoire d'Aurelio et Isabelle*, which was printed as a bilingual but also as a quadrilingual book — or religious, as with *Die historie van den ouden Tobias*, produced in Dutch and French.[38] The goal was very much to help readers learn a foreign language and entertain or instruct them as they went.

There are, however, a few examples of texts simultaneously in Dutch and French for more practical publications. In such cases, the use of both languages was seen as the most efficacious manner of informing a wide audience without having to print more than one edition of the original text. In the first half of the sixteenth century, surviving examples of this practice mainly seem to deal with the question of control over which coins in circulation were to be accepted as bona fide means of payment, and which were to be refused.[39] These short books were devised as practical works that were easy to use and were filled with woodcut images of the coins. The bilingual text meant that the book could be instantly referred to by merchants and artisans of both linguistic areas. It also meant that there was clear control over both the use of the woodcut images and their exactitude. The best example of this type of bilingual work is a book produced in Ghent by Josse Lambert. Printed in an oblong format for ease of reference, this scruffy imprint was to be sold throughout the Netherlands. The colophon indicated that the book was to be found in bookshops not just in Ghent, but also in Bruges, Ypres, Antwerp (two booksellers), Brussels, and Amsterdam (all these were only indicated in Dutch), and in Lille and Tournai (these two towns were only indicated in French).[40]

Whilst these types of works are intriguing, they remained rare. Antwerp publishers favoured a different approach when dealing with ephemeral works: they sought a more flexible alternative that would enable them to modulate their production in function of perceived demand for each language. Instead of producing a single print run, they began publishing simultaneously two parallel editions, one in French and one in Dutch. This could have been done through an agreement between two different publishers within the same town. The creation of such partnerships would have spread the risk involved in the initial investment and allowed the booksellers to make the most of their different sales networks — an approach that was commonly employed in France in the first decades of the sixteenth century.[41] However, in Antwerp local publishers preferred to undertake these parallel publications alone. As the works involved were short, they probably considered that the financial risk was small and that they would benefit from keeping the entire production process under their control.

Printing two parallel editions of the same text in different languages was a tactic that had both commercial advantages and disadvantages. On the one hand, by printing and selling the French and Dutch separately, printers were able to use fewer sheets of paper for each version. This meant that they would have been able to keep prices low — undoubtedly a priority when dealing with the lower end of the market.

On the other hand, producing two different editions meant that the labour involved was greater as the books had to be set and organized separately. Furthermore, the combined number of reams of paper necessary for the production of the text in both languages would have been greater than in a single bilingual edition: the duplication of the title page and unutilized blank end space would have necessitated the use of extra paper. This would have necessarily had an impact on the price of the imprints; buying both the French and the Dutch versions separately would have cost more than if they had been printed as a single edition. The publisher also had to determine the relative size of each print run rather than gauge demand for the subject matter as a whole. Having to evaluate whether subject matter would be of greater interest to the francophone or the Dutch-speaking community increased the chances of misinterpreting demand and being saddled with unsold items.

The two-edition strategy would, however, have offered another advantage: the French versions would have appealed to the francophone population of the Southern Netherlands, but they might also have proved more popular with foreign merchants and opened up the possibility of extra sales. In this regard, the question of the outward appearance of the imprints is interesting. Printed in French bastard gothic type, sheets of the French-language imprints would have been recognizable at a distance in the bookshops of the Low Countries. Set beside the Latin books printed using the Garalde material of each publisher, or the Dutch texts that used a more Germanic Fraktur gothic lettering, the French works would have been just as distinctive in their appearance as in the language used. This made them potentially more attractive to passing trade.

One of the features of these parallel publications is that they mainly involved ephemeral print. In particular, they seem to have been common for the news books that were being produced in increasing numbers in early sixteenth-century Antwerp. In this merchant city, such news imprints were clearly highly valued and were, as we have already argued, a growth market for the local publishing industry. Easy to transport and of low cost, they were also items that would have appealed to foreign visitors. In this context, they were perfect for the printing of parallel editions. The ten examples of this phenomenon included in Table 3.3 emphasize the importance of foreign events in the subject matter of these imprints. They cover events that ranged from the Mediterranean world (describing the latest events at the siege of Rhodes in 1522, for instance), to the Americas and Hernán Cortés's exploits in Mexico. The sample also shows that this type of printing was not the preserve of just one enterprising publisher: in the 1520s alone four different Antwerp workshops were printing simultaneously Dutch- and French-language news books with exactly the same content.

The extent to which the Dutch and French editions of these texts used the same template is emphasized by the comparison of two of the Willem Vorsterman imprints published in the wake of Charles V's imperial election in 1522.[42] In both cases the layout of the title-page is exactly the same: a first line in large type was followed by three lines of smaller type above a woodcut depicting Pope Clement VII and the emperor. In both cases the same woodcut was used and underneath it

USTC number	Author / heading	Short Title	Imprint
437088	Charles V	Die triumphe van dat cronemente vanden Keyser. Ende dye triumphelijcke incoemste van Aken	Antwerp, Willem Vorsterman, 1520.
437087	Charles V	Die triumphe van dat cronemente vanden keyser ende dye triumphelijcke incoemste van Aken	Antwerp, Willem Vorsterman, 1520.
72803	Charles V	Le triumphe du couronnement de l'empereur et l'entree triumphante en la ville d'Ayx	Antwerp, Willem Vorsterman, 1520.
77905	Charles V	La couronnation de l'empereur Charles cinquiesme de ce nom faicte a Boloingne la grasse	Antwerp, Willem Vorsterman, 1530.
77906	Charles V	La couronnation de l'empereur Charles cinquiesme de ce nom faicte a Boloingne la grasse	Antwerp, Willem Vorsterman, 1530.
400487	Charles V	Die crooninghe van den Keyser, gheschiet te Boloigne la grasse	Antwerp, Willem Vorsterman, 1530.
411035	Charles V	Die crooninghe van den Keyser, gheschiet te Boloigne la grasse	Antwerp, Willem Vorsterman, 1530.
437210	Cortés, Hernán	Les coutrees des iles et des paysages et conquis par le capitaine de tres illustre, tres puissant et invincible Charles elu empereur romain	Antwerp, Michel de Hoochstraten, [1523]
65921	Cortés, Hernán	De contreyen vanden eylanden ende lantdouwen ghevonden ende gheconquesteert byden capiteyn van Kaerle Roomsch Keysere	Antwerp, Michel de Hoochstraten, 1523
34094	France	S'ensuyt la maniere de la deffiance faicte par les heraulx des roys de France et d'Engleterre a l'empereur	Antwerp, Willem Vorsterman, 1528.
410523	France	In deser manieren zoe hebben die herraulten vanden coninck van Vranckerrijcke ende van den coninck van Inghelant den Keyser ghedeffiert	Antwerp, Willem Vorsterman, 1528.
57772	Ladam, Nicaise	Le double des lettres que le grant Truc escript a monsieur le grant maistre de Rodes	[Antwerp, Adriaen Van Berghen]: Antoine Membru, 1522.
437186	Ladam, Nicaise	Copie der brieven vanden grooten Turck ghescreven aen mijn Heere de grooten meestere van Rodes	Antwerp, [Adriaen van Berghen], 1522.
26124	Lemaire de Belges, Jean	La pompe funeralle des obseques du feu roy dom Phelippes	[Antwerp, Willem Vorsterman, 1507].
436747	Lemaire de Belges, Jean	Die funerallen ende deerlike triumphen oft pompen vander uutvaerden van wijle dom Philippus	[Antwerp, Willem Vorsterman], 1507.
55779	Montricharte	Memoires des nouvelles que l'osne Montricharte a apporte de Romme	Antwerp, Jacob van Liesvelt, [1527].
415552	Montricharte	Gherechtighe copie van der nieuwer tijdinghe welcke die jonghe Montrichart ghebracht heeft van Roomen	Antwerp, Jacob van Liesvelt, [1527].

402898	Pavia	Den strijdt gheschiet over tgheberchte voer de stadt van Pavye	Antwerp, Willem Vorsterman, 1525.
53928	Pavia	La bataille faicte par delà les mons devant la ville de Pavie	Antwerp, Willem Vorsterman, [1525].
42103	Rome	Nouvelles de Rome touchant l'empereur	Antwerp, Michel de Hoochstraten, 1536.
410810	Rome	Tijdinghe van Roome aengaende den keyser	Antwerp, Michel de Hoochstraten, [1536].
4206	Rome	Nouvelles de Rome touchant de l'empereur	Antwerp, Michel de Hoochstraten, 1536.
437429	Vienna	Dat beleg der stadt van Weenen in Oostenrijck vanden vervaerlicken Tyran ende verderver der Christenheyt den Turcschen Keyser	Antwerp, Michel de Hoochstraten, 1529.
13012	Vienna	Le siege de la ville de Vienne en Ostrice tenu par l'empereur de Turquie	Antwerp, Michel de Hoochstraten, 1529.

TABLE 3.3. Parallel French- and Dutch-language Editions, 1500–40

the statement 'Cum gratia et privilegio' [with grace and privilege]. Both editions were laid out in the simplest way possible, without paragraphs or breaks in the text; beneath the colophon, the same woodcut representation of the arms of the city of Antwerp appeared, with the large double-headed imperial eagle in the background. There was no attempt by the printer to differentiate between the two versions other than through the use of the different type in the main part of the text.

Conclusions

This type of interaction in news books between French and Dutch was to continue during later decades, as is shown, for instance, by the dual publication by Jan II van Ghelen following the election of Ferdinand, King of Bohemia and Hungary, as Emperor of the Holy Roman Empire in the aftermath of Charles V's abdication in 1558.[43] The model was clearly economically viable and adopted by several printers in Antwerp. Its success underlines the coexistence of a bilingual approach to publishing in the main centre of print in the Netherlands before the arrival of Plantin.

In the first decades of the sixteenth century, the French and Dutch book worlds were closely connected, encouraging not just cultural exchanges through the medium of Latin, the common European international language, but directly from one language to the next. French continued to be an important language in the Low Countries after the disappearance of the mainly francophone Burgundian court. With the rise of Antwerp and the development of its printing industry, French print changed in character, adapting to the requirements of a new market — a change that was particularly obvious in the production of parallel French and Dutch news books.

Notes to Chapter 3

1. This figure is given by Andrew G. Johnston in his 'L'Imprimerie et la Réforme aux Pays-Bas, 1520–c. 1555', in *La Réforme et le livre: l'Europe de l'imprimé (1517–v. 1570)*, ed. by Jean-François Gilmont (Paris: Cerf, 1990), pp. 155–86 (p. 155).
2. Malcolm Walsby, 'Plantin and the French Book World', in *International Exchange in the European Book World*, ed. by Sara Barker and Matt McLean (Leiden: Brill, forthcoming).
3. See Renaud Adam, 'Imprimeurs et société dans les Pays-Bas méridionaux et en principauté de Liège (1473–ca 1520)' (unpublished doctoral thesis, University of Liège, 2011) pp. 79–80.
4. *De vijfhonderdste verjaring van de boekdrukkunst in de Nederlanden: Catalogus* (Brussels: Koninklijke Bibliotheek Albert I, 1973), pp. 248–50.
5. This region stretched from London to Lombardy and comprised both the Rhine and Rhône valleys: Frédéric Barbier, *L'Europe de Gutenberg: le livre et l'invention de la modernité occidentale* (Paris: Belin, 2006) p. 220.
6. Andrew Pettegree, 'Printing in the Low Countries in the Early Sixteenth Century', in *The Book Triumphant: Print in Transition in the Sixteenth and Seventeenth Centuries*, ed. by Malcolm Walsby and Graeme Kemp (Leiden: Brill, 2011), pp. 3–25 (p. 23).
7. These models are outlined at greater length in Andrew Pettegree and Matt Hall, 'The Reformation and the Book: A Reconsideration', *Historical Journal*, 47 (2004), 785–808.
8. The statistics in this article are taken from USTC.
9. On the particular nature of the situation in the Low Countries, see Jan de Vries and Ad van der Woude, *The First Modern Economy: Success, Failure, and Perseverance of the Dutch Economy, 1500–1815* (Cambridge: Cambridge University Press, 1997).
10. Andrew G. Johnston and Jean-François Gilmont, 'L'Imprimerie et la Réforme à Anvers', in *La Réforme et le livre*, ed. by Gilmont, pp. 191–216 (p. 203).
11. Jean Thibault's *Le Thresor du remede preservatif et guerison bien experimentée de la peste et fievre pestilentialle* (Antwerp: Merten de Keyser, 1531) (USTC 57910), was copied the following year in Paris by Jean Bignon (USTC 53820). *Fons vitæ, ex quo scaturiunt suavissimæ consolationes, adflictis mentibus in primis necessariis, ne in adversitate et dolore protinus animum despondeant* (Antwerp: Merten de Keyser, 1533) (USTC 437659), was copied in 1537 for Richard du Hamel in Paris (USTC 185860).
12. On the question of his origins, see the debate analyzed by Philippe Renouard in his *Bibliographie des impressions et des œuvres de Josse Badius Ascensius, imprimeur et humaniste, 1462–1535*, 3 vols (Paris: E. Paul et fils et Guillemin, 1908), I, 4–6.
13. Renaud Adam and Alexandre Vanautgaerden, *Thierry Martens et la figure de l'imprimeur humaniste* (Turnhout: Brepols, 2009), p. 45.
14. On the statistical and economic importance of these Latin imprints to the Paris publishing world see most recently Sophie Mullins, 'Latin Books Published in Paris, 1501–1540' (unpublished doctoral thesis, University of St Andrews, 2013).
15. USTC 420783 and 410696.
16. On the limits and nature of French privileges, see Elizabeth Armstrong, *Before Copyright: The French Book-Privilege System 1498–1526* (Cambridge: Cambridge University Press, 1990).
17. On the dominance of Antwerp over other print centres in the Low Countries, see Hubert Meeus, 'Printing in the Shadow of a Metropolis', in *Print Culture and Peripheries in Early Modern Europe: A Contribution to the History of Printing and the Book Trade in Small European and Spanish Cities*, ed. by Benito Rial Costas (Leiden: Brill, 2013), pp. 147–70.
18. Over the incunabulum period, we know of thirty-eight editions published in French in Bruges, eleven in Antwerp, six in Valenciennes, three in Gouda, two in Haarlem and Oudenaarde, and just one item in Ghent, Louvain, and Schiedam.
19. On this see Wijsman, *Luxury Bound*; Hanno Wijsman, 'Les Manuscrits de Pierre de Luxembourg (ca 1440–1482) et les bibliothèques nobiliaires dans les Pays-Bas bourguignons de la deuxième moitié du XVe siècle', *Le Moyen Age*, 113 (2007), 613–37.
20. See the remarks made by the contemporary Florentine merchant Lodovico Guicciardini in his *Description de tout le Païs Bas autrement dict la Germanie inferieure, ou Basse-Allemagne* (Antwerp: Willem Silvius, 1567) (USTC 27799), pp. 113–14.

21. Léon Voet, in his research on the economics of Christophe Plantin's press in Antwerp in the second half of the sixteenth century, calculated that paper represented approximately two thirds of the cost of producing a book, though this could rise to three quarters of the cost for some large expensive projects. See his *The Golden Compasses: A History and Evaluation of the Printing and Publishing Activities of the Officina Plantiniana at Antwerp*, 2 vols (Amsterdam: Vangendt; London: Routledge and Kegan Paul; New York: Schram, 1969–72), II, 379.
22. On the *avvisi* and the emergence of printed news books, see most recently Andrew Pettegree, *The Invention of News: How the World Came to Know About Itself* (New Haven, CT: Yale University Press, 2014).
23. *Le Siege de la ville de Vienne en Ostrice tenu par l'empereur de Turquie* (Antwerp: Michel de Hoochstraten, 1529) (USTC 13012).
24. For a bibliography of these imprints, see Carl Göllner, *Turcica: Die europäischen Türkendrucke des XVI. Jahrhunderts. I. Band MDI–MDL* (Berlin: Akademie-Verlag, 1961).
25. For the wider context see Margarete Lindemann, *Die französischen Wörterbücher von den Anfängen bis 1600: Entstehung und typologische Beschreibung* (Tübingen: Niemeyer, 1994), esp. pp. 389–449; Frans Claes, *Lijst van Nederlandse woordenlijsten en woordenboeken gedrukt tot 1600* (Nieuwkoop: De Graaf, 1974).
26. Guicciardini, *Description de tout le Païs Bas*, p. 115.
27. On these handbooks see Jochen Hoock, 'Les Berlaimonts: manuels plurilingues à l'usage des marchands (XVIe–XVIIIe siècle)', *Revue de synthèse*, 133 (2012), 273–88.
28. Noël de Berlaimont, *Vocabulare van nieus ge-ordineert / Vocabulaire de nouveau donné et de rechief recorrigé* (Antwerp: Jacob van Liesveldt, 1527) (USTC 78045).
29. On early modern editions of Calepino's dictionary see Albert Labarre, *Bibliographie du dictionarium d'Ambrogio Calepino: 1502–1779* (Baden-Baden: Valentin Koerner, 1975).
30. Ambrogio Calepino, *Pentaglottos. Hoc est, quinque linguis, nempe latina, graeca, germanica, flandrica et gallica constans* (Antwerp: Gilles Coppenius, 1546) (USTC 66466), contains 732 unnumbered folios signed a^4 b-d^8 A-Z^8 AA-ZZ^8 Aa-Zz^8 Aaa-Ttt^8 (Ttt7–8 blank); the Berlaimont volume contains 40 unnumbered folios signed A-K4. Both were published in quarto.
31. See, for instance, *Coninck Karel ende Elegast een schone ghenuechlijcke historie* ([Antwerp: Jan van Doesborch?, n.d.]) (USTC 424759).
32. *Historie van Floris ende Blancefleur* ([Antwerp]: Jan van Doesborch, [1517]) (USTC 436979), and *Die historie van Peeter van Provencen* (Antwerp: Willem Vorsterman, ca. 1517) (USTC 436967).
33. Jean Bouchet, *De loose vossen der werelt* (Brussels: [Thomas van der Noot], 1517) (USTC 436964).
34. Jacob van Maerlant, *Harau Martin* ([Bruges: Johannes Brito, 1477]) (USTC 71288).
35. Jean Boutillier, *La Somme rurale*, published in Bruges by Colard Mansion in 1479 (USTC 70933) and in Delft by Jacob Jacobszoon van der Meer in 1483 (USTC 435578).
36. For a list of these French and Dutch editions, see respectively: Andrew Pettegree, Malcolm Walsby, and Alexander Wilkinson, *FB: French Vernacular Books. A Bibliography of Books Published in the French Language before 1601*, 2 vols (Leiden: Brill, 2007), I, 213; Andrew Pettegree and Malcolm Walsby, *NB: Netherlandish Books. Books Published in the Low Countries and in the Dutch Language Abroad before 1601*, 2 vols (Leiden: Brill, 2011), I, 249–50.
37. Olga van Marion, 'The Reception of Plutarch in the Netherlands: Octavia and Cleopatra in the Heroic Epistles of J. B. Wellekens (1710)', in *Recreating Ancient History: Episodes from the Greek and Roman Past in the Arts and Literature of the Early Modern Period*, ed. by Karl A. E. Enenkel, Jan L. de Jong and Jeanine De Landtsheer (Leiden: Brill, 2001), pp. 213–34 (p. 224).
38. For the French, Spanish, Italian, and English quadrilingual text, see Juan de Flores, *Histoire d'Aurelio et d'Isabelle, nouvellement traduits en quattre langues italien, espagnol, françois et anglois* (Antwerp: Joannes Steelsius, 1556) (USTC 440651). For the Dutch and French, see *Die historie van den ouden Tobias ende van sijnen sone den jongen Tobias | L'Historie de l'ancien Tobie et de son filz le jeune Tobie* (Antwerp: Jan van der Loe, 1551) (USTC 8864).
39. On this type of imprint as a genre, see Christian Dekesel, *Bibliotheca nummaria. Bibliography of 16th-Century Numismatic Books: Illustrated and Annotated Catalogue* (Crestline: Kolbe; London: Spink, 1997).

40. *De onghevaluweirde gauden ende zelven munten van veyl dyverschen conijncryken landen en steden* | *Les Monnoyes d'or et d'argent non valuées de plusieurs royaulmes pais et villes* (Ghent: Josse Lambert, for Symon Vanden Muelien in Bruges, Jaspar Vanden Steene in Ypres, Henric Goysle and Cornelis Vanden Kerckhove in Antwerp, Pieter Hasselt in Brussels, Bartholomeus Jacobszoon in Amsterdam, Pierre Haschart in Lille, and Alexandre Huaul in Tournai, 1544) (USTC 76302).
41. This was true in the context of a single city such as Paris (see the remarks made by Mullins in her 'Latin Books Published in Paris, 1501–1540', especially pp. 46–47), and for partnerships between booksellers in different towns; see the case of Caen, Rennes, and Rouen described in Léopold Delisle, *Catalogue des livres imprimés ou publiés à Caen avant le milieu du XVIe siècle, suivi de recherches sur les imprimeurs et les libraires de la même ville* (Caen: H. Delesques, 1903–04), and Malcolm Walsby, *The Printed Book in Brittany, 1484–1600* (Leiden: Brill, 2011), pp. 45–54.
42. In this case *La Couronnation de l'empereur Charles cinquiesme de ce nom faicte a Boloingne la grasse* (Antwerp: Willem Vorsterman, 1530 (=1531 n.s.)) (USTC 77906) for the French text, and *Die crooninghe van den keyser, gheschiet te Boloigne la grasse* (Antwerp: Willem Vorsterman, 1530) (USTC 400487) for the Dutch.
43. *Nyuewe sekere ende warachtighe tijdinghen, hoe dat dye hooch gheboren Vorst Ferdinandus tot eenen Roomschen keyser gecoren [sic] is, uutghegeven tot Franckfoort* (Antwerp: Jan II van Ghelen, 1558) (USTC 409072); *Vraye et nouvelle election imperialle du tresillustre tresredoubte et tresmagnanime don Fernande roy des Romains de Boheme* (Antwerp: Jan van Ghelen, 1558) (USTC 56045).

CHAPTER 4

❖

Rhetorical Encounters: *Puys*, Chambers of Rhetoric, and the Urban Literary Culture of the Burgundian Low Countries and Northern France

Anne-Laure Van Bruaene

In August 1455 the episcopal city of Tournai, at that time in French possession, organized a large shooting contest with fifty-nine participating companies from the kingdom of France, the Burgundian Netherlands, and the prince-bishopric of Liège. The competition of the crossbowmen was coupled with a poetry festival called *pui de amours* or *feste du roi* [feast of the king [of France]]. The innkeeper Jehan de Courolles presided as 'prince' over both the shooting contest and the *pui*. One evening, individual poets or 'réthoriciens' from outside the city competed for the best *chants roiaulx* and *amoureuses* — poems in praise of the king of France. There was also a drama contest open to visiting groups: this was won by Lille and Ypres, 'les ungs en langue franchoise, et les aultres en flamenghe' [the former in French, the latter in Flemish]. Tournai's parishes and local companies had their own theatre competition: the prize was awarded to 'la compagnie du Prince de Amours, qui estoit celle des réthoriciens' [the company of the Prince of Love, which was that of the rhetoricians].[1]

The Tournai festival can be seen as paradigmatic, as it brought together several key elements of fifteenth-century urban literary culture in the Burgundian Netherlands and its neighbouring territories. As the essay by Laura Crombie in this volume (Chapter 5) demonstrates, competitions of the guilds of archers and crossbowmen in this period often included theatrical performances. Moreover, the Tournai festival presented its visitors with an important public poetry contest, the *pui*. One of its prizewinners was Willem de Zomere from Flemish Oudenaarde, who probably competed in French.[2] But more remarkable is the bilingual character of the theatre competition. This was not unique: other bilingual drama contests took place on the occasion of shooting festivals or of civic processions, or independently as in Bruges in 1442 (see below), or in Brabantine Brussels and in Flemish Wervik in 1493.[3] This suggests that people in this region may not have been fluent in both languages but could quite easily understand each other.

The bilingual nature of (at least a part of) the Tournai event also invites us in our quest for cross-linguistic parallels to take a closer look at the terminology used in the contemporary chronicle description. The source distinguishes between different types of literary producers: individual 'réthoriciens' or poets coming from other towns, local parish groups, and a local company that performed theatre but also claimed the epithet 'réthoriciens' and acted under the authority of a 'prince'. In a remarkably similar vein, when the Dutch-speaking company from Ypres that won first prize returned from the festival, it was dubbed 'den prince ende ghildebroers van den Heilighen Gheest die men nomt de retorisiene' [the prince and the guild brothers of the Holy Ghost who are called the rhetoricians] in its hometown's city accounts.[4] This was Ypres's first full-blown chamber of rhetoric.

In this essay I want to discuss the early development of the chambers of rhetoric — both Dutch-language and French-language — within the context of the bilingual urban literary culture briefly outlined above. By the 1470s, the chambers of rhetoric had developed into guilds or confraternities of laymen devoted to the practice of vernacular theatre and poetry.[5] They had gained their first momentum during the reign of the Burgundian duke Philip the Good (1419–67), which was marked from around 1440 by relative political peace, strong state formation, fast economic growth, and dazzling cultural achievements in the fields of the visual arts, material culture, and music.[6] In recent years, much work has been done on the cultural mediation between the French-speaking Burgundian court and the Dutch- and French-speaking urban elites.[7] Less attention has been paid to cross-cultural contacts between Dutch-language and French-language towns. A notable exception for the field of literature and drama is Katell Lavéant's 2011 book *Un théâtre des frontières*, which pays ample attention to contacts and influences across the linguistic border. This essay can be read as a complement to Lavéant's insightful conclusions. My main argument is that cultural translations in this region were never a one-way process, since the early chambers of rhetoric both borrowed from and influenced wider developments. Therefore, rather than looking for origins, we must study literary phenomena in their often complex contemporary contexts.

Because of the elusiveness of the source material — for this period there are very few drama texts or poems that can be directly linked to a competition or other public event — it remains very difficult to form a clear idea of actual theatrical and poetical activities.[8] The main sources are the city accounts, which are notoriously dry and succinct. In addition, working in distinct historiographical traditions has not helped our understanding of literary practices that easily crossed linguistic borders. Ironically, French influences on the chambers of rhetoric are a long-standing theme in Flemish-Dutch scholarship, but in an overwhelmingly pejorative sense. In the nineteenth century literary historians disapproved of the rhetoricians because they had borrowed too much from the French language and in doing so had 'corrupted' the pure Dutch mother tongue.[9] Such negative appreciations have slowly disappeared, but the idea has remained that developments in the Dutch-speaking area were tributary to French developments. An argument in favour of this hypothesis is the importance of French loan-words such as *retorike*, *retorisien*, *prince*,

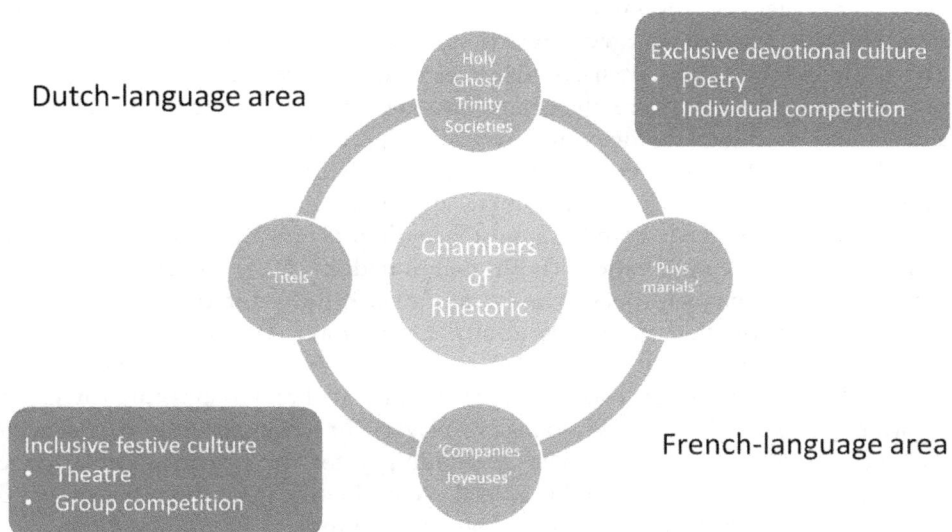

FIG. 4.1. The Structure of Urban Literary Culture in the Burgundian Low Countries

facteur, *ballade*, and *refrein* in the literary practice of the chambers of rhetoric.[10] Yet, as I will argue, the introduction of this new terminology into the Dutch-speaking Netherlands, which we can date fairly accurately, does not evidence an uncreative borrowing of existing models.

I will begin by adopting a rather structuralist approach, not to suggest that people in the past ever adjusted themselves to rigid models, but in a quest for parallels and meeting points (see Figure 4.1). Urban literary culture in the Burgundian Low Countries had two major cultural sources, neither one restricted by linguistic frontiers. On the one hand, there was a public and largely inclusive festive culture, which followed the ecclesiastical calendar and is most famous for its civic processions and Shrove Tuesday celebrations. Cities such as Lille, Tournai, Valenciennes, Ypres, Oudenaarde, Nieuwpoort, and Bruges had important processions devoted to the Holy Sacrament (Corpus Christi), Our Lady, or an important reliquary such as the Holy Blood of Christ.[11] From the late fourteenth century onwards theatre (both religious and comic), and in some cases full-blown theatrical contests, became a major feature of these public events.[12] On the other hand, there was a more exclusive devotional culture that also made extensive use of literary means of expression. Here, the focus lay on poetry. Competition was also a key element, not between groups but between individual poets.

The public festive culture of our first cluster, which I will discuss only briefly in this essay, is best documented by the city accounts. From the late fourteenth century onwards, these sources mention all kinds of groups and individuals that portrayed Old and New Testament figures, staged *tableaux vivants*, and performed passion plays during and after the annual processions, but also made merry and staged comic plays on the same occasions or during Shrove Tuesday celebrations. From the early fifteenth century onwards, more tightly organized groups developed in both the French- and Dutch-language areas. In the French-speaking region the most important groups were the *compagnies joyeuses*, associations with burlesque names and a predilection for comic and other profane plays. A famous example is the Abbaye de Lescache Pourfit from Cambrai, which is first mentioned in the city accounts of 1426. Very similar Dutch-language groups, called *titels*, performed in the towns of Western Flanders, most prominently in Ypres, for example the Royaerts and the Crancbestiers (both mentioned in 1427). There were direct contacts between the *compagnies joyeuses* and the *titels*: they visited each other's cities on the occasion of their respective annual processions. This is documented, for example, for early fifteenth-century Lille and Ypres. Yet, as the fifteenth century progressed, these companies evolved differently. In the French-speaking towns, the *compagnies joyeuses* became more dominant players. In some places, one association was given prominence and assumed responsibility for the organization of civic-wide festivals, as was the case in Arras (Abbaye de Liesse) and Cambrai (Abbaye de Lescache Pourfit). In Western Flanders, the opposite took place: as noted below, the *titels* lost out to the chambers of rhetoric. Many disappeared, but others survived by taking over the institutional forms of the chambers, becoming firmly organized guilds with a patron saint, regular cultic activities, and weekly meetings where the members were trained in the writing and reciting of texts in verse.[13]

The more exclusive devotional, literary culture of our second cluster was not necessarily the prerogative of tightly organized groups. For example, there are many indications that the famous Gruuthuse manuscript from Bruges (The Hague, Koninklijke Bibliotheek, MS 79 K 10, around 1400), with its large collection of songs, poems, and verse prayers, was produced within a circle of active poets; but it has proved difficult to identify an established literary confraternity.[14] In the French-language regions of Artois, Hainaut, Picardy, Normandy, and Walloon Flanders, however, *puys marials* developed, literary confraternities organizing annual poetry contests — also called *puys* — in honour of the Virgin Mary. Unfortunately, even today the *puys* remain something of a historical problem. Despite the important scholarship of Gérard Gros, Denis Hüe, and Dylan Reid, which has given us insights into the use of literary forms and the workings of particular *puys*, we are still waiting for a broader historical analysis of their origins and developments.[15] This may prove difficult because of a general lack of sources and a great deal of mystification in later accounts. The main problem with the *puys marials* is indeed their historical dating: according to some, the oldest *puy* was that of Arras, instituted in the thirteenth century, but this is disputed by other literary historians, who consider this a myth created in the fifteenth century.[16]

The oldest extant statutes are those of the Confrérie Notre Dame du Puy in Amiens (Picardy), registered in 1452. These tell us that this confraternity's main feast was the Marian feast of Candlemas. On this day a new *maistre* [master] was elected and a large poetry contest was held. For this occasion, the resigning *maistre* had to propose a refrain on an aspect of the Virgin on which the competing poets — all 'rhétoriciens expers en rhétorique' [rhetoricians expert in [the art of] rhetoric] — were expected to write *chants royaulx*.[17] The presentation and judging of the *chants royaulx* were accompanied by a large banquet and the performance of a *jeu de mistère* [mystery play]. The next day a mass for the deceased was sung, followed by the proclamation of the winner of the competition. The confraternity also celebrated the other Marian feasts, All Saints and Christmas, with more modest contests.[18] The Puy de la Conception in Rouen (Normandy), instituted in 1486, followed approximately the same model. The confraternity was presided over by a *prince* and the public contest was explicitly open to both poets from Rouen and outsiders.[19] The membership of the *puys* of Amiens and Rouen was manifestly elite: noblemen, prelates, rich merchants, influential guild masters, and — in the case of Rouen — royal magistrates.[20] Reid has convincingly argued that these elite members acted as 'patrons of poetry', rather than as poets in their own right. In imitation of courtly patronage, the *puy* offered a venue for rich townsmen to support lower-status poets and, at the same time, express their devotion to the Virgin Mary.[21]

The information on the *puys* of Artois, Hainaut, and Walloon Flanders is much sketchier. According to a seventeenth-century chronicle, the *puy* of Valenciennes was formalized in 1426.[22] The 1381 city accounts of Lille already mention a 'prince et compaignons dou puy' [prince and compagnons of the *puy*], but it is uncertain whether this association was a full-blown literary confraternity or a neighbourhood company.[23] The poetry of the court writer Jean Froissart suggests that in the final quarter of the fourteenth century he participated in *puy* contests in his home town Valenciennes, and in Lille and Tournai.[24] With the current state of research it seems safe to conclude that as institutions the *puy* confraternities were established at the earliest in the late fourteenth century, which accords with the European-wide acceleration in the formation of religiously inspired lay urban corporations in this period.[25] This does not mean that the practice of *puy* competitions with the genre of the *chant royal* cannot have been older.[26] Maybe a Dutch-language variant of the *puy* contest existed in Flanders: in Ypres, shortly after 1400 — there are no older city accounts extant — prizes were awarded for the best poems praising the Virgin Mary on the day of the annual Our Lady procession.[27]

Puy confraternities do not seem to have existed outside the French-language area. Yet some scholars have pointed out their similarities with the chambers of rhetoric.[28] Dirk Coigneau made the useful distinction between 'old style' and 'new style' chambers: while the second type was focused on theatrical performances, the first type lent much more weight to the production of poetry and, inspired by the model of the *puys*, considered the poetry contest as its defining activity.[29] More extensive archival research has rejected the chronology presented by Coigneau, but the idea of two different types of chambers of rhetoric has proved fruitful. Indeed, a number of early Dutch-language chambers of rhetoric seem to have had no direct roots in the public festive culture of their towns, since in the contemporary sources they were never mentioned in the context of annual processions or Shrove Tuesday celebrations. These chambers were active in the three leading cities of Flanders: Bruges, Ghent, and Ypres. Interestingly, these three chambers venerated the Holy

Ghost or Holy Trinity as their patron saint. As these societies did not receive regular payments or gifts of wine, their early history is not easy to reconstruct, but when we put the small pieces of information together a fairly coherent and intriguing picture emerges.

De Heilige Geest [The Holy Ghost] in Bruges was instituted in 1428. This date is provided by a much later — seventeenth-century — source, but on close scrutiny has proved reliable. The seventeenth-century description also names fourteen constituting members. In a conflation of the narratives of the Last Supper and Pentecost, the narration claims that on Maundy Thursday 1428, like the Apostles, the constituting members were inspired by a divine dove to commence their confraternity, hence also the chamber's name. The first members belonged to Bruges's local elite and higher middling groups: they were professionally active as brokers, highly skilled artisans, and visual artists. For example, two constituting members belonged to the craft of paternoster makers who had a vested interest in the promotion of devotion. Another member, Lodewijk Halyncbrood, was a painter who later left for Spain where he introduced the style of Jan van Eyck. In the vibrant cosmopolitan milieu of fifteenth-century Bruges, the young confraternity seems to have participated more widely in processes of cultural translation: in 1429, in the Hanseatic city of Lübeck, one of Bruges's most important commercial partners, the prestigious Zirkelgesellschaft reorganized from a devotional to a literary confraternity and introduced practices very similar to those of De Heilige Geest. Importantly, in this early phase, poetry seems to have taken a central place: several members of De Heilige Geest can be identified as Middle Dutch poets.[30]

In 1442, De Heilige Geest was mentioned for the first time in a contemporary source, namely the city accounts of Bruges. The city magistracy did not offer a subsidy of either wine or money, but paid for its own lodge on the Burg (the city's political square) in order to see the plays performed on the feast day of the Visitation of Our Lady. In fact, as we learn from the city accounts of many other cities, De Heilige Geest had organized a theatre competition in praise of its patron saint and had sent invitations to both Dutch-language (Ghent, Ypres, Oudenaarde, Damme, Dendermonde, Oudenburg, Mechelen) and French-language cities (Lille, Tournai, Saint-Omer). How many theatre groups actually participated is unknown, but since the 'ouvriers de retorique' [workers of rhetoric] of Tournai sought civic support for their attendance, this was no doubt a bilingual contest.[31]

We are better informed about Ghent's first chamber of rhetoric, De Fonteine [the Fountain]. In 1448 this confraternity asked the city magistracy for the ratification of its statutes. It had instituted a chapel in one of Ghent's parish churches shortly before 1446, so this was probably a fairly recent initiative.[32] The statutes of De Fonteine are the oldest extant for a chamber of rhetoric, which makes them a very valuable source; but, at the same time, it is dangerous to generalize from them.[33] In an interesting parallel with De Heilige Geest in Bruges, De Fonteine claimed divine inspiration with an elaborate reference to its patron saint, the Holy Trinity. De Fonteine also carefully positioned itself in relation to other literary companies. Its statutes complained that in most other notable cities in Flanders and other principalities there was a 'broedelic ende eerbaer gheselscip [...] van ghenouchten' [fraternal and honourable company of joy], but not in Ghent, the capital of Flanders. 'Gheselscip van ghenouchten' can be translated quite literally as *compagnie joyeuse*, so this seems to be a reference to the practices of the *titels* and *compagnies joyeuses* in both the Dutch- and French-language areas. Yet De Fonteine was also careful to distance itself by claiming the higher status of a 'gheselscepe van der const ende broederscip van der rethorique' [a company of art and confraternity of rhetoric].[34] This is the first attested use of the term 'rhetoric' by a fully established literary society in the Dutch-speaking Netherlands, and points to an understanding by contemporaries of the divergence between the more inclusive and exclusive strands of urban literary culture.

As De Fonteine was organized as a religious confraternity, its statutes pay considerable attention to the organization of masses and other cultic activities. The corporation was presided over by a vaguely circumscribed *upperste* [highest in charge] and four counsellors, who were assisted by a clerk and a messenger. De Fonteine engaged in theatre, but there were no strict rules for dramatic activities. An individual member could take the initiative to engage in the staging of public plays: he had to offer the roles to his brethren in the first instance, but if they refused he could engage outsiders. Every member was free to perform with his own neighbourhood if the city held a competition. Members did not have to join if De Fonteine went out of town to participate in a competition, but they were expected to contribute financially.[35] The statutes give much more prominence to the regular internal poetry contests. Every three weeks on Sunday afternoon a member was named who had to propose a *refrain* on which the members were required to write a poem. He also had to award a prize, appoint the jury, and pay for the expenses incurred.[36]

We do not know the names of the constituting members of De Fonteine, but for the following years there is some information. From 1452 to 1454 the chamber's *upperste* was Claeys vander Meersch, a master-painter who had been dean of the painters' guild in 1448. Vander Meersch was an influential artist-entrepreneur who secured many urban contracts for artistic decoration, for example of the city's belfry. His most prestigious commission was the painting of the canopy for the statue of Our Lady of Tournai, which a delegation from Ghent carried in the annual procession. Ghent had no important procession of its own, and therefore participated with maximum splendour in the Tournai procession: the city of Ghent was subject to the bishop of Tournai, and the two Scheldt cities maintained strong economic relations with each other.[37] The importance of the annual commission of the painted canopy is underscored by the fact that the artists were not only generously remunerated but also, as guests of honour, were conveyed by wagon to Tournai to attend the procession. Vander Meersch received the commission twenty-five times, which was an absolute record. He was assisted during many years by the sculptor Cornelis Boone, who was also a prominent member of De Fonteine. Other data corroborate the fact that the corporation recruited strongly from the milieu of Ghent artists.[38]

Due to the loss of the city archives in World War I, much less is known about the early development of De Heilige Geest in Ypres, although in the sixteenth century it prided itself on being the oldest chamber of rhetoric in Flanders.[39] As mentioned above, in the early fifteenth century a great number of *titels*, comparable to the French *compagnies joyeuses*, staged plays around the time of the annual procession of Our Lady. For this they received gifts of wine from the city magistracy. Yet in 1455 a considerable sum of money was offered to another group, which had never previously been mentioned in the city accounts. This was the association of 'den prince ende ghildebroers van den Heilighen Gheest die men nomt de retorisiene', who had won first prize at the drama contest in Tournai mentioned above. From then on, De Heilige Geest claimed a dominant position in its home town. Only this association attended the *landjuwelen* (prestigious Brabantine theatre competitions) in Leuven in 1478 and in Antwerp in 1496. For this it received substantial financial support from the city magistracy. In 1496, the aldermen of Ypres came to the home of one of the members to see their new play and to hear laudatory poems (*loven*).[40] All this indicates that the members of De Heilige Geest enjoyed a high status in local society, in all probability higher than the members of the *titels*. Although we lack further information, their choice of the Holy Ghost as their patron saint suggests an interesting parallel with the chambers of rhetoric of Bruges and Ghent.

The choice of the Holy Ghost or the Holy Trinity as patron saints was undoubtedly a self-conscious act. The statutes of De Fonteine from 1448 stress that the company depended on the Holy Trinity 'sonder wiens inspiratie niemen ter goeder perfectie commen sal' [without whose inspiration no one will come to full perfection].[41] The seventeenth-century myth of the institution of De Heilige Geest in Bruges stressed the importance of divine inspiration and equated the constituting members with the Apostles. This identification of rhetoricians with the Apostles was also a theme in early Dutch-language rhetorician literature. The idea was that through divine inspiration unlearned men could gain access to the Revelation.[42] An example is the famous *Refereyn van rethorica* (c. 1460–c. 1480), the oldest Dutch-language hymn on the art of rhetoric. Its author, Anthonis de Roovere, probably a member of De Heilige Geest in Bruges, skilfully compares the art of rhetoric to a plant that is fertilized by the Holy Ghost.[43]

The self-consciousness of the early chambers of rhetoric in Bruges, Ghent, and Ypres raises the question of their direct or indirect connections with the French-language *puys*. There are some interesting parallels but also significant differences. The members of the Holy Ghost/Trinity chambers enjoyed relatively high status, although those we have been able to identify were highly skilled and wealthy artists and artisans, not nobles or magistrates. The statutes of De Fonteine suggest that the poetry contest was its defining literary activity. De Heilige Geest in both Bruges and Ypres also engaged in the performance of poetry. Yet, for this period, we do not know of open poetry contests, similar to the *puy* contests, with participants from outside the corporations or even from out of town. Moreover, everything suggests that during their closed poetry meetings the members acted as poets in their own right rather than as patrons of poetry. At least from the 1440s onwards, the Holy

Ghost/Trinity chambers also fully engaged in theatre, a genre that was secondary in the *puys*. The chambers staged plays and participated in (Ypres) or organized (Bruges) drama contests. In doing so, they quickly integrated into region-wide networks.

By venerating the Holy Ghost or the Holy Trinity as their patron saints, the emerging chambers of Bruges, Ghent, and Ypres not only made a statement about their own self-definition as divinely inspired poets, but also created distance with respect to the *puys*, which were almost all devoted to the Virgin Mary. So the chambers' constituting members certainly did not aim to imitate the *puys* uncritically.[44] If we adopt a more conservative reading of the history of the *puys* and assume that the first confraternities were instituted at the earliest in the time span between 1375 and 1425, the development of the chambers of rhetoric (first Ypres, followed by Bruges and Ghent?) even runs almost parallel. Nevertheless, influences cannot be ignored, especially when the French poetic vocabulary was introduced into the practice of the chambers of rhetoric. Significantly, this happened at a later stage, from the 1440s onwards, in a period when peace and political stability created greater opportunities for interregional contacts and an atmosphere of cultural openness. The central concept of the *(seconde) rhétorique* had already been used in French-language regions from the fourteenth century onwards to refer to the vernacular art of poetry.[45] Around the middle of the fifteenth century it was appropriated in the Dutch-language region to designate an institutionalized literary practice. The first known mention of 'ghesellen van der retorike' [companions of rhetoric] is in the city accounts of Oudenaarde in 1441. These 'ghesellen' formed a rather loose group of players that performed theatre in the context of shooting contests.[46] As previously mentioned, in its 1448 statutes De Fonteine named itself a 'broederscip van der rethorique'; it also used the notion of *refrain* to refer to its preferred poetic genre for the first time in the Dutch-language region.[47] De Fonteine introduced the notion of *prince* in 1456 to replace the vague *upperste*.[48] De Heilige Geest, on the occasion of the Tournai festival in 1455, already used *prince* to refer to its leader and also — attested for the first time — *retorisienen*, as equivalent to the French *rhétoriciens*.[49]

Interestingly, in all cases, there was a Tournai connection. Oudenaarde and Tournai were two nearby towns on the river Scheldt. The early members of De Fonteine were closely involved with the annual procession of Our Lady of Tournai, while De Heilige Geest from Ypres triumphed in the lavish 1455 festival. In addition, 'ouvriers de retorique' from Tournai had participated in the contest organized by De Heilige Geest in Bruges in 1442. This raises the question of the organization of literary life in Tournai itself, but unfortunately a great deal of material was lost due to destruction during World War II.[50] We have, however, a nineteenth-century edition of a manuscript begun in 1477 with poetry and the statutes of 'la compaignie de l'escole de rhétorique' [the company of the school of rhetoric]. This source offers an intriguing puzzle, since the statutes stress that the members of this company wanted to revive an older practice.[51] Lavéant has suggested that this 'escole de rhétorique' was the heir of a *puy* confraternity that would have existed in the late fourteenth century. Indeed, in a poem from 1491 the confraternity was named 'Puy d'Escole de rhétorique'.[52] However, a close reading of the statutes reveals more similarities with the Holy Ghost/Trinity chambers in Flanders. Although no patron saint is mentioned, the text underlines that membership was restricted to thirteen men 'en commémoracion de nostre Saulveur Jhésuchrist et de ses douze apostles' [in commemoration of our Saviour Jesus Christ and his twelve apostles].[53] This is reminiscent of the conception of De Heilige Geest in Bruges, and suggests a cultivation of the same theory of divine inspiration. What is more, a large part of the statutes is devoted to the rules of a monthly closed poetry contest that is comparable to the practice in De Fonteine. Finally, the use of the concept of *escole* suggests a parallel with the practices in nearby Oudenaarde, where the chambers of rhetoric, which were instituted around 1470, were designated as *scole*.[54]

The 'escole de rhétorique' of Tournai at least partly followed the model of the Dutch-language chambers of rhetoric. This example indicates that cultural translation in the Burgundian Low Countries and its neighbouring territories was never a one-way process. Both French- and Dutch-language literary corporations borrowed from and influenced cross-linguistic models, and always did so creatively. In fact, in the sixteenth century a limited number of French-speaking chambers of rhetoric existed in cities such as Tournai, Mons (Hainaut), and Nivelles (Brabant).[55] Paradoxically, in the same period, due to a combination of political, economic and cultural factors — not least a growing consciousness of the distinctness of the Dutch language — bilingual contacts became much rarer than in the fifteenth century, creating two separate literary cultures.[56] But we should not project these later developments back onto the fifteenth century. For the 'golden age of Burgundy' it is more appropriate to think of only one urban literary culture that was bilingual in nature. This is true in a general sense, if we take both the more inclusive public festive culture and the more exclusive literary devotional culture as two ends of one spectrum. If so, we can include the *compagnies joyeuses* and the *titels* on the one hand and the *puys* and Holy Ghost/Trinity chambers on the other hand. But it is also true in a more particular, human sense, if we think of the many physical encounters of Dutch- and French-speaking poets and players during civic processions, Shrove Tuesday celebrations, *puy* contests, and theatre competitions in bustling cities such as Lille and Ypres, Bruges and Tournai.

Notes to Chapter 4

1. Frédéric, baron de Reiffenberg, 'La Fête de l'arbalète et du prince d'amour à Tournai en 1455', *Bulletin de la Commission Royale d'Histoire*, 10 (1845), 255–66 (pp. 265, 266).
2. Willem de Zomere won a silver mermaid 'met dichtene en met spele' [with poetry and play]; Bart Ramakers, *Spelen en figuren: Toneelkunst en processiecultuur in Oudenaarde tussen middeleeuwen en moderne tijd* (Amsterdam: Amsterdam University Press, 1996), p. 110.
3. Anne-Laure Van Bruaene, *Om beters wille: Rederijkerskamers en de stedelijke cultuur in de zuidelijke Nederlanden (1400–1650)* (Amsterdam: Amsterdam University Press, 2008), pp. 43, 69, 217; Lavéant, *Un théâtre des frontières*, pp. 166–69.
4. Van Bruaene, *Om beters wille*, p. 46.
5. Anne-Laure Van Bruaene, '"A wonderfull tryumfe, for the wynning of a pryse": Guilds, Ritual,

Theater, and the Urban Network in the Southern Low Countries, ca. 1450–1650', *Renaissance Quarterly*, 59 (2006), 374–405.

6. Wim Blockmans and Walter Prevenier, *De Bourgondiërs: De Nederlanden op weg naar eenheid, 1384–1530* (Amsterdam; Meulenhoff; Leuven: Kritak, 1997), pp. 122–24, 193; Andrew Brown, 'Civic Ritual: Bruges and the Counts of Flanders in the Later Middle Ages', *English Historical Review*, 122 (1997), 277–99 (pp. 288–89).

7. Jelle Koopmans, 'Rhétorique de cour et rhétorique de ville', in *Rhetoric — Rhétoriqueurs — Rederijkers*, ed. by Jelle Koopmans and others (Amsterdam: North-Holland, 1995), pp. 67–81; Peter Arnade, *Realms of Ritual: Burgundian Ceremony and Civic Life in Late Medieval Ghent* (Ithaca, NY: Cornell University Press, 1996); Susie Speakman Sutch, 'Dichters van de stad: De Brusselse rederijkers en hun verhouding tot de Franstalige hofliteratuur en het geleerde humanisme (1475–1522)', in *De macht van het schone woord: Literatuur in Brussel van de 14de tot de 18de eeuw*, ed. by Jozef Janssens and Remco Sleiderink (Louvain: Davidsfonds/Literair, 2003), pp. 141–59; Élodie Lecuppre-Desjardin, *La Ville des cérémonies: essai sur la communication politique dans les anciens Pays-Bas bourguignons* (Turnhout: Brepols, 2004); Graeme Small, 'When Indiciaires Meet Rederijkers'; Samuel Mareel, *Voor vorst en stad: Rederijkersliteratuur en vorstenfeest in Vlaanderen en Brabant (1432–1561)* (Amsterdam: Amsterdam University Press, 2010); Marie Bouhaïk-Gironès and Katell Lavéant, 'Le *Mandement de froidure de Jean Molinet*: la culture joyeuse, un pont entre la cour de Bourgogne et les milieux urbains', in *Jean Molinet et son temps: Actes des rencontres internationales de Dunkerque, Lille et Gand (8–10 novembre 2007)*, ed. by Jean Devaux, Estelle Doudet, and Élodie Lecuppre-Desjardin (Turnhout: Brepols, 2013), pp. 67–82.

8. Unique is the corpus of play texts performed in the context of the procession of Lille, around the middle of the fifteenth century; Alan E. Knight, 'Processional Theater in Lille in the Fifteenth Century', in *Le Théâtre et la cité dans l'Europe médiévale: Actes du Vème colloque internationale de la Société international pour l'étude du théâtre médiévale*, ed. by Jean-Claude Aubailly and Edelgard E. Dubruck (Stuttgart: Heinz, 1988), pp. 347–58; *Les Mystères de la procession de Lille*, ed. by Alan E. Knight, 5 vols (Geneva: Droz, 2001–11).

9. See, for example, Prudens Van Duyse, *Verhandeling over den drievoudigen invloed der rederijkkameren, voorafgegaan door een overzicht harer geschiedenis, tot antwoord op de volgende prijsvraag: quelle a été l'influence littéraire, morale et politique des sociétés et des chambres de rhétorique dans les dix-sept provinces des Pays-Bas et le pays de Liége* (Brussels: Hayez, 1861).

10. Dirk Coigneau, 'De const van rhetoriken: Drama and Delivery', in *Rhetoric — Rhétoriqueurs — Rederijkers*, ed. by Koopmans and others, pp. 123–40.

11. *Ieper tuindag. Zesde eeuwfeest. Een bundel historische opstellen*, ed. by Romain Vinckier (Ypres: Stedelijke culturele raad, 1983); Ramakers, *Spelen en figuren*; *La Grande Procession de Tournai (1090–1992)*, ed. by Jean Dumoulin and Jacques Pycke (Tournai: Fabrique de l'Eglise Cathédrale de Tournai, 1992); *Les Mystères de la procession de Lille*, ed. by Knight; Andrew Brown, *Civic Ceremony and Religion in Medieval Bruges, c.1300–1520* (Cambridge: Cambridge University Press, 2011).

12. Ramakers, *Spelen en figuren*, pp. 93–166.

13. Dylan Reid, 'Carnival in Rouen: A History of the Abbaye des Conards', *The Sixteenth Century Journal*, 32 (2001), 1027–55; Van Bruaene, *Om beters wille*, pp. 29–41; Katell Lavéant, 'The Joyful Companies of the French-speaking Cities and Towns of the Southern Netherlands and their Dramatic Culture (Fifteenth-Sixteenth Centuries)', in *The Reach of the Republic of Letters*, ed. by Van Dixhoorn and Sutch, I, 79–118; Anne-Laure Van Bruaene, 'Princes, Emperors, Kings and Investiture in the Festive Culture of Flanders (Fifteenth-Sixteenth Century)', in *Les 'Autres' Rois: études sur la royauté comme notion hiérarchique dans la société au bas Moyen Âge et au début de l'époque moderne*, ed. by Torsten Hiltmann (Munich: Oldenbourg, 2010), pp. 131–44; Lavéant, *Un théâtre des frontières*, pp. 42–74.

14. Joris Reynaert, 'Literatuur in de stad? Op zoek naar een voorgeschiedenis van het Gruuthuse-liedboek', in *De studie van de Middelnederlandse letterkunde: stand en toekomst: Symposium Antwerpen 22–24 september 1988*, ed. by Frits van Oostrom and Frank Willaert (Hilversum: Verloren, 1989), pp. 93–108; Herman Brinkman, 'De Brugse pelgrims in het Gruuthuse-handschrift', in *Stad van koopmanschap en vrede*, pp. 9–39; Jan Dumolyn, 'Une idéologie urbaine "bricolée" en Flandre

médiévale: les *Sept portes de Bruges* dans le manuscrit Gruuthuse (début du XVe siècle)', *Revue Belge de Philologie et d'Histoire*, 88 (2010), 1039–84.

15. Gros, *Le Poète, la vierge et le prince du Puy*; Hüe, *La Poésie palinodique à Rouen (1486–1550)*; Dylan Reid, 'Moderate Devotion, Mediocre Poetry and Magnificent Food: The Confraternity of the Immaculate Conception of Rouen', *Confraternitas*, 7 (1996), 3–10; Dylan Reid, 'Patrons of Poetry: Rouen's Confraternity of the Immaculate Conception of Our Lady', in *The Reach of the Republic of Letters*, ed. by Van Dixhoorn and Sutch, I, 33–78.
16. Ursula Peters, *Literatur in der Stadt: Studien zu den sozialen Voraussetzungen und kulturellen Organisationsformen städtischer Literatur im 13. und 14. Jahrhundert* (Tübingen: Niemeyer, 1983), pp. 214–19.
17. A. Breuil, 'La Confrérie de Notre-Dame du Puy, d'Amiens', *Mémoires de la société des antiquaires de Picardie*, 13 (1854), 485–662 (p. 609). 'Rhetoric' should be understood as *seconde rhétorique*, i.e. verse; see below on the use of this expression. On the lyric genre of the *chant royal*, see Marie-Claude de Crécy, *Vocabulaire de la littérature du Moyen Âge* (Paris: Minerve, 1997), pp. 59–61.
18. Breuil, 'La Confrérie de Notre-Dame du Puy, d'Amiens'; Maurice Duvanel, Pierre Leroy, and Matthieu Pinette, *La Confrérie Notre Dame du Puy d'Amiens* (Amiens: Mabire, 1997), pp. 2–4.
19. Reid, 'Moderate Devotion, Mediocre Poetry and Magnificent Food', p. 4.
20. Ibid., p. 6; Duvanel, Leroy, and Pinette, *La Confrérie Notre Dame du Puy d'Amiens*, pp. 4, 6–8.
21. Reid, 'Patrons of Poetry', pp. 43–46.
22. Gros, *Le Poète, la vierge et le prince du Puy*, pp. 40–43.
23. Léon Lefebvre, *Le Puy Notre-Dame de Lille du XIVe au XVIe siècle* (Lille: Lefebvre-Ducrocq, 1902), pp. 1–15.
24. Gros, *Le Poète, la vierge et le prince du Puy*, pp. 41, 45–46.
25. Reid, 'Patrons of Poetry', p. 42.
26. See also Peters, *Literatur in der Stadt*, pp. 214–19.
27. Van Bruaene, *Om beters wille*, p. 48.
28. Coigneau, 'De const van rhetoriken'; Pleij, *Het gevleugelde woord*, pp. 296–98.
29. Dirk Coigneau, '"Den Boeck" van Brussel: Een geval apart?', *Jaarboek De Fonteine*, 49–50 (1999–2000), 31–44.
30. Laurence Derycke and Anne-Laure Van Bruaene, 'Sociale en literaire dynamiek in het vroeg vijftiende-eeuwse Brugge: De oprichting van de rederijkerskamer De Heilige Geest ca. 1428', in *Stad van koopmanschap en vrede*, ed. by Oosterman, pp. 59–87.
31. Van Bruaene, *Om beters wille*, p. 43; Lavéant, *Un théâtre des frontières*, pp. 167, 438–39.
32. Van Bruaene, *Om beters wille*, p. 275.
33. Dirk Coigneau, '9 december 1448: Het Gentse stadsbestuur keurt de statuten van de rederijkerskamer De Fonteine goed. Literaire bedrijvigheid in stads- en gildeverband', in *Nederlandse literatuur, een geschiedenis*, ed. by M. A. Schenkeveld-van der Dussen (Groningen: Contact, 1993), pp. 103–08; Coigneau, '9 december 1448: De statuten van de rederijkerskamer De Fonteine worden officieel erkend door de stad Gent. Rechten en plichten van spelende gezellen', in *Een theatergeschiedenis der Nederlanden: Tien eeuwen drama en theater in Nederland en Vlaanderen*, ed. by R. L. Erenstein (Amsterdam: Amsterdam University Press, 1996), pp. 50–55.
34. Antonin Van Elslander, 'De instelbrief van de rederijkerskamer "De Fonteine" te Gent (9 december 1448)', *Jaarboek De Fonteine*, 6–7 (1948–49), 15–22.
35. Ibid.; Coigneau, '9 december 1448: De statuten'.
36. Van Elslander, 'De instelbrief van de rederijkerskamer "De Fonteine" te Gent (9 december 1448)'. See the discussion in Coigneau, '9 december 1448: Het Gentse stadsbestuur', pp. 106–07.
37. Marc Boone, 'Les Gantois et la grande procession de Tournai: aspects d'une sociabilité urbaine au bas moyen âge', in *La Grande Procession de Tournai (1090–1992)*, ed. by Dumoulin and Pycke, pp. 51–58; Arnade, *Realms of Ritual*, pp. 51–67.
38. Anne-Laure Van Bruaene, '"Abel in eenighe const": Claeys vander Meersch, meester-schilder, en de jonge Fonteine (1448–1476)', *Jaarboek De Fonteine*, 49–50 (1999–2000), 77–94.
39. Frans de Potter, *Geschiedenis der stad Kortrijk*, 4 vols (Ghent: Annoot-Braeckman, 1873–76), II, 44–46.

40. Van Bruaene, *Om beters wille*, pp. 46–47.
41. Van Elslander, 'De instelbrief van de rederijkerskamer "De Fonteine" te Gent (9 december 1448)'.
42. Moser, *De strijd voor rhetorica*, p. 85.
43. Ibid., p. 69.
44. See also Coigneau, '*De const van rhetoriken*'.
45. Koopmans, 'Rhétorique de cour et rhétorique de ville', p. 71; Crécy, *Vocabulaire de la littérature du Moyen Âge*, pp. 18–19.
46. Ramakers, *Spelen en figuren*, pp. 109–10.
47. Van Elslander, 'De instelbrief van de rederijkerskamer "De Fonteine" te Gent (9 december 1448)'; Coigneau, '9 december 1448: Het Gentse stadsbestuur', p. 106.
48. Van Bruaene, *Om beters wille*, p. 49.
49. For the French *rhétoriciens*, see Lavéant, *Un théâtre des frontières*, pp. 79–81.
50. Agathon Delangre, *Le Théâtre et l'art dramatique à Tournai* (Tournai: Vasseur-Delmée, 1905), pp. 5–10; Paul Faider and Pierre Van Sint Jan, *Catalogue des manuscrits conservés à Tournai* (Gembloux: Duculot, 1950), pp. 112–13; Alan Hindley and Graeme Small, 'Le Ju du Grand Dominé et du Petit: une moralité tournaisienne inédite du Moyen Âge tardif (fin XVe–début XVIe siècle). Étude et édition', *Revue Belge de Philologie et d'Histoire*, 80 (2002), 413–56 (p. 425).
51. *Ritmes et refrains tournésiens, poésies couronnées par le puy d'escole de rhétorique de Tournay (1477–1491)*, ed. by Frédéric Hennebert (Mons: Hoyois-Derely, 1837), pp. xvii–xx.
52. Lavéant, *Un théâtre des frontières*, pp. 88–90.
53. *Ritmes et refrains tournésiens*, ed. by Hennebert, p. xvii.
54. Ramakers, *Spelen en figuren*, pp. 112–13. On the educational motives of the Dutch-language rhetoricians, see Arjan van Dixhoorn, 'Writing Poetry as Intellectual Training: Chambers of Rhetoric and the Development of Vernacular Intellectual Life in the Low Countries between 1480 and 1600', in *Education and Learning in the Netherlands, 1400–1600: Essays in Honour of Hilde de Ridder-Symoens*, ed. by Koen Goudriaan, Jaap van Moolenbroek, and Ad Tervoort (Leiden: Brill, 2004), pp. 201–22.
55. Van Bruaene, *Om beters wille*, pp. 92, 96; Lavéant, *Un théâtre des frontières*, pp. 84–90.
56. Van Bruaene, *Om beters wille*, pp. 95–96; Lavéant, *Un théâtre des frontières*, pp. 168–69.

CHAPTER 5

Target Languages: Multilingual Communication in Poetic Descriptions of Crossbow Competitions

Laura Crombie

In Tournai, in 1394, the Great Crossbow Guild of Saint George invited sworn guilds from walled towns and *bonnes villes* to attend their spectacular competition.[1] Guilds were encouraged to come to Tournai, a French episcopal city surrounded by lands held by the dukes of Burgundy,[2] to compete in 'l'excellense du très noble, amoureus, deduisant, gracieux, plaisant, delicieux, et très recommandable jeu et esbatement de la balestre' [the excellent, most noble, beloved, sweet, gracious, pleasant, delightful, and highly recommended game and entertainment of the crossbow].[3] The crossbow is, they add, the king of all other games, and cannot be conducted with blasphemy but must be conducted with 'humilité, carité, fraternele amour, larguesce, sobrieté, chasté et toutes vertus' [humility, charity, brotherly love, largesse, sobriety, chastity and all virtues] (fol. 85ʳ). The competition was staged to please the king, Charles VI, in keeping with Tournai's position as a loyal *bonne ville* and to record the friendly community and the notable displays that would take place. The guild had been motivated to hold a competition:

> Considerans que la saincte escripture dist et tesmoingne qui huiseuse soit est [*sic*] mere de tous vices et marastre de toutes vertus et que creature humayne ne doye fuir et lui occuper d'aucunes bonnes euvres, affin que l'annemi ne treuve l'omme huiseus et que l'occupation soit bonne aprandre de ce que aucun puet parfaire, et que ne puet peu ou riens nuire, mes vivement à tous plaire et que creature humayne soit enclinée à luy occuper selon la plaisance de un chascun diversement, les uns d'un fait, les autres d'autre. (fol. 85ʳ)

> [Considering that the holy scriptures say and testify that sloth is the mother of all vice and injurious to all virtues, and that all human creatures should flee it and occupy themselves in good works, so that Satan does not find mankind idle and that they are well occupied in doing what can be done properly and does little or no harm, but pleases everyone greatly, and so that humans may be inclined to occupy themselves as it pleases each of them differently, with some enjoying one activity and others another.]

As we shall see, however, virtuous industry was far from the only goal of such competitions. Rather, they were planned, staged, and remembered to celebrate civic status, to promote guild honour, and to enhance multilingual regional communities. The 1394 Tournai event was staged in a peaceful period, with a truce in the Hundred Years War and tranquillity in the Low Countries with the end of Ghent's rebellion in 1385.[4] The decades either side of 1400 saw numerous very large competitions, at Mons in 1387, Tournai in 1394, Ghent in 1400, Mechelen in 1404, and Oudenaarde in 1408, with John the Fearless himself taking part in the last of these. The splendour of these events allowed a sense of civic identity to be made public and traditions of competitions to develop.

The Tournai event was attended by 387 crossbowmen, from 50 guilds, and was impressive not only in size but also in geographical appeal, bringing together guilds from across northern France and the Low Countries. The guilds of Paris, Ypres, Brussels, and Diksmuide all won prizes, and guilds from as far north as Amsterdam had been invited to attend.[5] Though many of those in attendance were from Dutch-speaking towns, the invitation that Tournai issued was in French. Its elaborate and well-chosen language may have been translated by the messenger himself, but the organizers expected their audience to understand the instructions on how and when to attend, and to compete in a francophone environment.

In understanding the multilingual world of the Burgundian Low Countries and their neighbours, the organization and commemoration of such archery and crossbow competitions allow for an analysis of urban values and modes of memorialization. After a brief outline of the development of archery and crossbow guilds, and their competitions, the events themselves will be analyzed. Examination of the linguistic choices made in organizing the events, in respect of both which language to write in and what values to emphasize, enables the shared values of events to be appreciated. In analyzing the ways in which events were commemorated, two poems, describing shoots of 1394 and 1498, will be considered. The poem describing the shoot of 1394 is significant as it is the first of its kind to survive, and so the later and more elaborate poem describing the event of 1498 cannot be analyzed without an understanding of how this tradition developed. Both texts will be closely analyzed as expressions of the civic values and cultural aspirations of competitions and their organizers; prizes will also be briefly discussed, as manifestations of those values and as cultural memory.

The Development of Guilds

Archery and crossbow guilds appeared in towns and even villages across northern Europe in the fourteenth century, but they are best and first documented in Flanders.[6] Town accounts in Ghent, Bruges, and Lille all refer to socio-devotional groups of archers and/or crossbowmen before 1330, organizing shooting events for their guild-brothers, receiving wine, taking part in processions, and looking after chapels.[7] It would seem self-evident to say that the guilds began as military organizations, and then developed into social and cultural communities, but this cannot be proven from civic sources; indeed, it seems that guilds first appear not as civic defenders, but as civic representatives. They started to obtain civic liveries, to organize competitions, to receive civic wine, even civic land, in the same generation as the great towns of Flanders invested in great buildings, especially their belfries, to show their autonomy and authority.[8]

Guilds received significant support and privileges from the dukes of Burgundy and from the Flemish nobility; they were part of durable and mutually beneficial urban-aristocratic communities. Guilds received the right to bear arms across the region, the right to assemble together for shooting, and immunity from prosecution should anyone be accidentally injured, even killed, during shooting practice. Obtaining such rights, especially in towns where no one else was allowed to be armed, marked the guilds out as powerful and patronized groups. Their links to the dukes brought them status, as well as making it easier to travel across and beyond Flanders for competitions. Guilds received more prolonged, and more pragmatic, support from their civic authorities. Town governors granted their guilds similar rights — to bear arms and to assemble, as well as immunity from prosecution — but they also gave them land to practise on, and funds for the communal side of guild life. Guilds received annual funds for their meals, and weekly funds for training and drinking. In Lille from 1443 the aldermen promised the crossbowmen six shillings a week 'pour aler boire en recreation ensemble' [to go drinking in recreational assembly].[9] Towns also gave the guilds generous funds to attend and to host competitions, almost always noting that such funds were given 'for the honour of the town', showing the guild to be civic agents.[10]

Archery and crossbow guilds were social and devotional groups, and have much in common with confraternities. Across Flanders almost all archery guilds were dedicated to Saint Sebastian, martyred by his own archers, and almost all crossbow guilds to Saint George, a chivalric saint who killed a dragon and upheld Christian values. Both were famous, martial saints, Roman soldiers killed during the persecutions of Emperor Diocletian; both were often seen as knights, and enjoyed fame and prestige across Europe.[11] That the guilds chose to identify themselves with such saints reveals their wish to be seen as martial, as just, and as defenders. As studies of craft guilds have noted, the choice of a patron saint is revealing for an understanding of how groups saw themselves and perceived of their social positions, even if their choice was a standard one.[12] Numerous Flemish crossbow guild seals depict Saint George, on horseback killing a dragon, emphasizing his martial prowess and his strength, and by connection the guilds' strength and their ability to protect as well as to represent their towns. In letters of invitation, guilds describe themselves not just as the 'Crossbow Guild of Ghent', but as the 'Greater Crossbow Guild of Ghent dedicated to the Holy Martyr and Knight Saint George', showing that dedication to, and celebration of, their patron was an integral part of their identity.

Shooting Competitions

Within their own towns, guilds competed to see who was the best archer or crossbowman, with the winner of their annual *papegay* competition (which involved shooting at a wooden bird, a parrot or jay, atop a wooden pole) being 'king' for the year.[13] All gathered together every year, with the best shooters named as guild-kings, and, where records can be found, attendance at the shoots was far more regular than at other guild events.[14] Regional competitions are the next logical step, especially in the competitive urban networks of Flanders. The earliest competition for which I have found archival evidence was held in Oudenaarde in 1328, though this is unlikely to have been the first competition; others have claimed that a competition in Ypres in 1323, or an event in Bapaume in 1326, was the earliest.[15] The town accounts of Lille and Ghent both record payments for their crossbow guilds to attend the Oudenaarde event, the first time either town had funded guild attendance at a competition.[16] Once recognized by civic funders, competitions grew quickly as events that allowed for building communities, for winning honour, and for enabling guilds to perform their own identities. An archery event was held in Lille in 1330 and twenty-five guilds attended a crossbow shoot in Ghent in 1331.[17] In spectacular regional events, placed on a regional stage, guilds could represent their town and find ways to demonstrate civic identity and augment their reputation. Larger towns, with their more generous funds and ability to attract aristocratic competitors who could help them win, had an advantage; but most guilds put a great deal of effort into their dramatic performances, and as this was done with civic funds the towns too were concerned for their success.

Civic authorities quickly recognized the potential of shooting competitions to bring honour to their town. Competitions were more than an exercise in shooting skills and showing off; they had the potential to strengthen, even rebuild, bonds with other towns and so link festive and socio-economic networks. Competitions became more elaborate in the fifteenth century, lasting longer, giving more prizes, and offering more opportunities for oral, written, and performed communication.[18] Across the fourteenth and fifteenth centuries, shooting competitions of varying sizes took place, with several held each year. Events could last a few days, and involve a handful of teams, or could last months, drawing in guilds from across northern France and the Low Countries and dominating civic space with hundreds of shooters and thousands of supporters and observers.

Preparations

Invitations were sent out in advance of shoots, to set out the rules of the competition and to encourage attendance. The Tournai crossbowmen sent out their 'varlet' (presumably messenger), Pierre Biuyen, to neighbouring towns to carry their elaborate letter of invitation for the 1394 competition. In Lille the civic authorities awarded him four *lots* of wine for telling the guild about the competition, welcoming him as they would any distinguished visitor or messenger.[19] Each surviving letter of invitation contains a mix of elaborate language, with the preambles describing the loving communities that would be built and the lofty ideals behind holding events, and practicalities that all competitors would have to understand, from the number who should shoot from each guild, to shooting distance, to when and where to enter the host town.

Town accounts make clear that shooting contests were staged almost every year from the close of the fourteenth century to the early sixteenth century, with several years seeing multiple events and only years of prolonged warfare, such as 1477, seeing none. Accounts often note thanks to messengers who told them about a particularly grand shoot, so it is surprising how few invitations to crossbow competitions survive, with fewer than twenty and many of these in contemporary or slightly later copies; no invitations to archery contests survive. This is, partially at least, an accident of survival: Ypres held a huge number of spectacular archery contests, and may well have preserved invitations with seals, as Ghent, Mechelen, and Oudenaarde did for crossbow competitions, before the civic archives were destroyed. Yet German towns, where the damages of time would also be expected to have taken their toll, preserve several hundred invitations from the fifteenth and sixteenth centuries.[20] It is equally clear from accounts of competition that princely permission to hold them was vital, yet only three letters of consent from the dukes of Burgundy to allow competition to be held have survived, and only one in its original form.[21]

This may simply be because the invitations were not seen as worth keeping after an event, or indeed that later archivists saw no value in the invitations. Despite such challenges, the surviving letters of invitation are evidence of the multilingual culture, and shared values, of northern France and the Burgundian Low Countries.[22] French-speaking towns of the region, such as Tournai and Mons, sent out letters in French, precisely setting out when teams should enter, the number of competitors, and the different prizes to be won. These letters were received by guilds in Dutch-speaking areas, who attended the shoot and followed the rules. The guilds of Ypres, Diksmuide, Antwerp, Oudenaarde, and Sluis, to name a few, were able to perform and communicate in the francophone environment of Tournai in 1394. The pattern continued over the fifteenth century, with another great shoot in Tournai in 1455 attended by more Flemish and Brabant guilds than francophone ones, despite an equally elaborate letter of invitation in French, again emphasizing community and honour.[23]

Several Dutch-speaking towns, including Mechelen and Hulst, issued invitations simply in Dutch. For Hulst, a small town in the far north of Flanders, this is to be expected. It was likely to be able to attract only a small audience — especially as its event was held just a year after Mary of Burgundy's death, and during the crisis of regency in 1483 — and that audience would be able to read Dutch.[24] Indeed, all the guilds that attended in 1483 were either Dutch-speaking or, like Bailleul, so near the linguistic boundary that knowledge of Dutch would be assumed. The same is not true for Mechelen, and in particular the great competition it staged in 1404. Mechelen was geographically and politically central for the Burgundian Low Countries: even before the establishment of a parliament there, the town was a special lordship, ruled directly by the dukes of Burgundy.[25] Mechelen was able to wield a significant influence, and was clearly trying to use the crossbow competition of 1404 to enhance its cultural standing among near and distant towns.

In 1404 Mechelen sent out four messengers, each with a letter of invitation. This was not unique; Ghent even kept accounts of the towns that their four messengers visited in 1440 and the gifts they received from each place. The Mechelen Guild seems to be unique in keeping all four copies of the letter of invitation; Ghent has accounts of which places were visited, but only one letter of invitation.[26] Each letter sent out in 1404 has seals from the guilds that the messenger visited. While some have survived in a better condition than others, the four letters are, as far as can be discerned, identical, though two are damaged. The four letters to be carried around the region are copies, on parchment of the same size and in the same hand, of the same text. The seals show that one messenger went west, into Flanders, carrying the invitation first to Walloon towns, including Lille, and then to large and small Dutch-speaking ones including Ninove and Ghent. Another went south and east into Brabant, again visiting large and small towns, and at least as far as the bishopric of Liège, having guilds attach their seal to the invitation. The third went north into North Brabant and Holland: the Dordrecht seal is clear, though several other on the invitation are too damaged to identify. These three messengers show that an impressive geographical range of teams was invited, with a number of French- as well as Dutch-speaking towns included in the event, and that the fame and honour of Mechelen was spread to towns across the Low Countries. The fourth letter, the text of which is the most damaged but which has the best-preserved seals, is the most interesting for a consideration of multilingual communities and regional connections.

The fourth messenger, with the same Dutch text outlining the good community that would be built in Mechelen through the competition, went south through Hainault and into France. He visited Paris, Rouen, Laon, Amiens, Ath, Brain-le-Comte, and many more French-speaking towns. It is, of course, possible that the messenger himself spoke French, and so provided an oral translation of the written text, but Mechelen had made a considered choice to send their messenger to France with a Dutch invitation, evidence of a multilingual world that extended as far south as Paris and as far west as Rouen. The Mechelen crossbow guild felt themselves to be part of this world, and in communication with it, through competitions.

The literary style used in the letters of invitation is further evidence of shared values across the multilingual regional communities. For their 1408 competition the Great Crossbow Guild of Saint George in Oudenaarde drew on the same values as are expressed in the 1394 Tournai invitation. They invite guilds from suitable towns whose members are 'spelende en versolasende metten edelsten, mueghelijcsten, ghenoughelijcsten, ende minlijcsten spele ende voren allen andren spelen' [playing and taking pleasure in the most noble, enjoyable, pleasant, and friendly game that surpasses all other games'], the crossbow. They should not compete with 'sconfieringhe' [hostility], 'maar zonderlinghe alle broedelike minne, solaes, ende reynicheit' [but uniquely [in] brotherly love, joy, and purity]. The Oudenaarde letter emphasized the virtue of the shoot and the virtue of the duke, John the Fearless, who had granted permission for the shoot to take place.[27] John attended the competition in person, participating like a guild-brother and carrying his own bow.[28] It is possible that the invitation was made particularly elaborate in the hope of persuading John to attend, or because the guild knew in advance that he would be present.

Civic communities operating within a multilingual world of shared cultural values drew on the same norms and values in inviting other guilds to attend their competitions, whether writing in French or Dutch. Ghent seems to be unique in sending out, for its great crossbow competition of 1498, a very large bilingual invitation. This document, of which only one copy has survived, is in itself an impressive investment as it is a large piece of parchment, and was carried across the region. The surviving copy includes seals from Flemish guilds; presumably other copies were carried into other regions, as in 1440. The 1498 invitation encouraged all to attend, first in Dutch and then in French. The script used for the Dutch text is slightly larger, and hence slightly clearer: it seems the scribe underestimated how much space would be needed, and had to squeeze in some of the details in French, using a smaller script. The invitation emphasizes the same values as earlier ones, particularly friendship, community, and the piety and prestige of the guild. Guilds are invited to attend in 'joie, concorde, unanimité et fraternelle communication' [joy, concord, unity and fraternal exchange]; the game must be played in an 'honeste et reverente' [honest and reverent] manner. The competition is organized with 'la grace et ayde de Dieu de paradis, sa benoite mere, et du glorieux chevalier dessus nommé Monseigneur Saint Joorge [sic], et tous les saincts et sainctes de paradis' [the grace and aid of God in Heaven, of His blessed mother, of the glorious knight mentioned above — Saint George — and of all the saints in paradise].[29]

The large document, carried by messengers across France and the Low Countries, represents the Ghent guild's efforts to place themselves on the regional stage. They consciously drew on the great event of 1440, but the 1498 event was attended by fewer competitors, from a smaller area. Indeed, the need to send out a bilingual invitation shows that Ghent had to make far more of an effort to encourage attendance. For the most part, guilds and the civic authorities who supported them assumed a multilingual knowledge but organized events in one language, showing confidence in their own collective identity. That similar values and priorities, of brotherhood or unity and of honour, are shown in invitations in both languages for more than a century emphasizes how certain community values were shared by guilds across and beyond the Burgundian Low Countries.

Remembering Competitions in Rhyme

It is clear that many shoots were seen as successful, as having brought honour to their town, as being worthy of remembering and celebrating. Numerous urban chronicles mention shooting competitions, often adding notes that the guild of the chronicler's town had performed well or had won prizes. When mentioning the 1394 competition in Tournai, local writers add small details showing the pride attached to their guild and the power of urban identity. The sixteenth-century Bruges chronicler Nicolas Despars notes that Paris won the prize for travelling the furthest, Ypres for best shot, and Douai for best entry, with Diksmuide and Brussels also winning silver flasks; and he adds that the Bruges crossbowmen were the first to shoot and were led by Pieter van der Schelle, a weaver.[30] An Oudenaarde chronicle describing the shoot states that fifty guilds took part, and praises the greatness of the Oudenaarde guild-brothers.[31] In Liège the canon Jean Stavelot, writing a continuation of the chronicles of Jean d'Outremeuse, is most concerned with political matters of local, even European, importance including schisms and peace negotiations, yet he describes a crossbow competition in Liège in 1441, and proudly recounts the crossbowmen of Liège travelling to other competitions.[32] Even the blind abbot of Tournai, Gilles le Muisis, writing in the mid-fourteenth century, described favourably a crossbow competition held in Tournai in 1350.[33] Crossbow competitions are mentioned in numerous civic sources; they were powerful events for building communities and for showing status, were remembered long after they had been held, and were seen by numerous authors as worth recording.

Proud, but short, entries in numerous civic and regional chronicles reveal the ubiquitous nature of shooting competitions, and their ability to inspire pride in local writers. For at least two competitions, poems were written to celebrate the events, to ensure that the fame of the gatherings would be commemorated. Very little can be ascertained about where each poem came from, or why it was written, and thus far only one copy of each poem has been found. Yet their existence — in unexpected locations in each case, suggesting that more await discovery — is evidence of the power of these events, and shows that commemoration of the spectacular shoots went beyond relatively short notes in prose chronicles. As a more public and performative medium than prose, verse commemorates the events in ways that are appropriate to the shoots, which themselves were public performances.[34]

The first, written in French to commemorate the Tournai shoot of 1394, is entitled 'Rym reprendant la dicte feste et lez villez qui vinrent et ossi comment il furent loti à traire' [Rhyme representing the aforementioned feast and the towns who went there, and also how the order of shooting was determined by lot].[35] The second poem, in Dutch, describes the 1498 crossbow competition in Ghent. It is described as being 'gestelt in properter rethorijke' [expressed in distinctive verse] and is entitled 'Dits Tprohemium vander voorsiede intreye' [This is the Overture for the Aforesaid Entrance]; the Latin word in the title is the only non-Dutch word in the poem.[36] The poem is printed in the 1531 edition of the *Excellente cronike van Vlaanderen* [Excellent Chronicle of Flanders]. Both poems praise the competition as a whole, not just the host town or the entrances made by different guilds to the event, and praise them as ways of building brotherhood and community.

The absence of other witnesses, and of documentary evidence of similar poems, is striking, as the guilds themselves are very well attested. Several towns, especially Oudenaarde and Mechelen, have rich archives for their crossbow guilds, preserving a good number of charters, invitations, even lists of gifts given to visiting guilds and letters describing shoots in other towns, but no poems describing the shoots. Several of the more prosperous archery and crossbow guilds commissioned and performed dramatic pieces, many in verse, but about patron saints or mythical stories, not about guilds themselves or competitions.[37] The 1498 Ghent poem is even absent from the so-called *Book of Pieter Polet*, which describes in great detail the spectacular competitions held in the city in 1440 and 1498.[38] Pieter was a crossbowman, and one of the organizers of the 1498 competition; his book first records everything he could find out about the 1440 shoot, drawing on now lost sources including lists of all competitors, and then provides a detailed account of the 1498 event. He records the financial accounts for the planning of the 1498 competition, and transcribes both the letter of invitation and Philip the Handsome's letter allowing the 1498 event to be held. As a *stadsbode* [town messenger], Pieter would have had access to accounts for the 1440 shoot, and he took great care in meticulously recording details about the planning of the 1498 event. He ends the book by including a copy of a charter issued by Philip the Handsome in 1501 requiring the heirs of deceased guild-brothers to pay their death fees.[39] Pieter's work is a faithful transcription of the sources, to judge by those that still survive: in both French and Dutch he is a careful copyist, and gathers together a good deal of information. Hence it seems likely that, had he known about a poem composed in Ghent in praise of either shoot, he would have included it. As no crossbow guild sources preserve poems, it is possible that they were written by another observer, perhaps a member of a chamber of rhetoric, but no firm arguments can be made from gaps in archives.

Both poems offer fascinating evidence for the multilingual nature of the Burgundian Low Countries, and the uses of poetry, rather than prose, for remembering and celebrating urban events. The 1394 Tournai poem, along with a copy of the letter of invitation for the shoot, have been carefully copied into the sole manuscript witness: Ghent, Universiteitsbibliotheek, HS 434. Immediately after them is a copy of the 1408 Oudenaarde letter of invitation, first in French and then in Dutch. A large and significant volume, HS 434 was described by baron Jules de Saint-Genois, in his inventory of the library's collection, as one of the most important Ghent manuscripts. It is composed of a range of charters, bulls, and edicts, most but not all relative to the history of the Low Countries, in Latin, French, and Dutch; no information on the manuscript's origins or provenance is available.[40] The volume as a whole is neat and generously spaced, with margins and occasional blank folios indicating a good deal of care and a certain lavishness. It is the work of several skilled scribes, with a very few words or points of clarification added later. The poem is followed by three blank pages, then the Oudenaarde invitations, followed by five blank pages, then a peace treaty between the Grand Master of Prussia and the King of Poland in January 1411 (probably the Treaty of Thorn). The care with which the poem is laid out is striking; the piece is transcribed in a single column, leaving sizeable margins on the page. The scribe could easily have fitted the poem, which occupies three openings, into a much smaller space by adopting a two-column layout. There is no indication that images were to be added, and indeed no later scribal notes in the margin to show that the poem was used or enjoyed by later readers.

In the rest of the manuscript, the only other urban documents involve Hanseatic merchants and major trade privileges; there are no references to any other urban events, and the 1394 poem is the only verse piece in the collection. The inclusion of texts about crossbow competitions is even more significant in this context than it would be in an urban compilation. To my knowledge this is the only copy of this poem: any Tournai originals that existed in the civic archive would have been destroyed with the rest of its holdings during the bombing of May 1940, though it is possible that other versions are in large collections such as this and have not yet been noticed. There is no explanation within the manuscript as to why texts are included, but the compilers or their patron(s) saw the invitations to the events of 1394 and 1408 and the poem as being significant, as worthy of being copied as the charters granted by kings. The blank pages may have been left with the intention of adding a copy of the Mechelen 1404 invitation, which as noted above had been delivered to Ghent, or details about other crossbow competitions, including a Ghent event of 1400.

The Tournai poem comprises a continuous sequence of octosyllabic couplets. The first 100 lines are an eloquent description of Tournai, the shoot, the cloths hung all over the streets, the winners of the various prizes, and the event itself. The forty-eight teams who shot are then described, followed by another thirty-five lines of verse, describing winning teams and the prizes they won, praising the skill of the visitors and the splendour of the hosts. Two final couplets, detached from the main text, provide an oblique clue to the author's name, exemplifying the indirect signatures that authors often inserted into their works in this period:[41]

> De faire j'ay escript mon nom;
> Après j'ay escript mon sournom.
> Regardés bien et hault et bas,
> Et lisiez: vous ne faurés pas. (fol. 90^r)

[In composing, I've written my name, and my sobriquet afterwards. Look carefully high and low, and read: you will not fail.]

The first 100 lines of the poem are the most interesting. Here the author declares that the competition was to honour God and the King of France, and that it was set out in very fine ordinance. The event takes place in Tournai, a noble city, which is covered in cloth, especially the royal colours, with the prizes also on display, guarded by men of the town in good faith and for the love of the company. By adopting the standard form of French narrative verse, the poem takes on a memorializing quality that lends cultural prestige to the shoot, in spite of the occasional clumsiness resulting from attempts to fit dates and facts into the form. For instance, the year 1394 is expressed as 'L'an six mains de quatorse cens' [the year six less than 1400] (fol. 87^v).

The shooting is described, with two targets set up 'entre le pork et le belfroy' [between the church porch and the belfry] (fol. 87^v). The competition is in the heart of Tournai, taking over civic space, showing the prominence of the guilds and their central place in civic culture. The poem does not just describe a town covered in cloth; it shows the cloth industry of Tournai being utilized to glorify the town and king. The profusion of cloth within the description, and especially the link between cloth and royal arms, along with repeated references to public decorations of buildings, and the garments worn by officials, insistently emphasize the decorations that express civic and royal prestige. There are 'draps asurez, non doubtés mie' [azure cloths, do not doubt this]; each target is covered 'd'un bel fijn drap tout vert' [by a fine, delicate cloth all in green] (fol. 87ᵛ). The description continues:

> Trestout estoit tresbien parét
> Et de bons ouvriers ordonnét
> De draps de vermeille campagne;
> Sus, castiaux d'argent: c'est l'ensengne.
> Et si avoit trois biaux compas
> Du roy de France sur les draps. (fols 87ᵛ–88ʳ)

[Everything was decorated very well by skilled workers, and hung with cloths to show castles argent on a field of gules: these are the arms [of the city]. There were also three fine circles on the cloths, bearing the arms of the King of France.]

The poet adds descriptions of the winners, including Bruges — whose company was the best turned out, for which they won 'le biel godet dorét' [the fine gold dish] (fol. 88ʳ) — with other details of the entrances and the presentations of courtesies and silver and gold prizes. The fairness of the competition, and the pleasure for all watchers who would see this wonderful shoot, are made clear. The same values are set out here as in letters of invitation, emphasizing unity and honour as well as the prestige of the town, but the poem is a far more elaborate project and is carefully crafted to record all details of the shoot in rhyme.

The teams are noted in the order in which they shoot. Their names and ordering are incorporated into the verse and rhyme scheme, with one team per line; the number of participants in each of the first thirty-four teams has been added, apparently by the same scribe, to the right of the relevant lines. The author of the text is likely to have been based in Tournai, as he shows relatively detailed knowledge of local geography, including significant civic buildings. The poem appears to be an original French-language composition: it contains no loan-words or other traces of Dutch that might suggest otherwise. Its scribe was clearly competent in both languages, however (the hand is the same as for the Oudenaarde invitation); indeed, the graphy 'fijn' (for 'fin', fol. 87ᵛ) suggests that Dutch may have been his first language. While the text is at times unsophisticated, its very existence demonstrates that the event was considered important enough to fix in collective memory through verse.

The source of the second poem, a description of the Ghent crossbow competition of 1498, has a good deal in common with that of the first. The poem appears, along with a woodcut, a copy of the Dutch portion of the letter of invitation, and a detailed account of the entrances made to the competition and the winners, in the 1531 printing of the *Excellente cronike van Vlaanderen*. The *Excellente cronike*, part of a tradition of Flemish chronicle writings, is a massive work, covering Flemish history from a semi-mythical past to the sixteenth century.[42] It makes only sparing and usually brief reference to urban events, so the space given over to prose, poetry, and a unique woodcut for the 1498 shoot is significant. Unlike HS 434, however, the *Excellente cronike* does contain a number of other poems, recently analysed by

Samuel Mareel.⁴³ The details of the competitions are described in a substantial prose account; also included is the (Dutch) letter of invitation, and a woodcut of a figure, usually identified as Philip the Handsome, shooting the crossbow between two targets and two buildings that can be interpreted as the belfry and the Church of St John the Baptist (now St Bavo's Cathedral) in central Ghent.⁴⁴ In all, the description of the competitions fills almost thirteen folios, evidence of the shoot's impact on contemporaries, and presents a perfect opportunity to analyze the guilds' representation of civic values and their emphasis on community.

The poem is longer than that of 1394, covering four and a half folios in a two-column layout. It consists of a sequence of *balladen*, each of three stanzas (on a basically symmetrical rhyme scheme such as *ababbcbc*, as at the beginning of the poem) followed by a half-stanza. Stanza lengths vary both within and between *balladen*, and in some cases the versification appears to be confused, perhaps due to corrupt transmission. Varying amounts of space are devoted to each town's entrance: some towns have a full stanza or multiple stanzas, others only partial stanzas. These poetic descriptions are then followed by prose descriptions of the entrances made by water, taking up thirty-eight lines. The chronicle goes on to describe the winners of the various prizes, again in straightforward prose, and then different events of 1501.The first part of the text emphasizes that the competitions will be pleasing to God, just as the 1394 poem did, and that great honour will come to all the teams who take part. God's saints have helped to establish the 'schietspele' [shooting-game] which is 'rijckelic' [elaborate]. As in the Tournai poem, a good deal of local geography is adduced, strongly implying a local Ghent writer, who describes an avenue between the town hall (*stadthuyse*) and belfry (*beelfroot*), with two lanes and lodges for shooting. The spectacle of this cosmopolitan assembly is described as 'een paradijs vol vramen' [a privileged paradise] (fol. Aa1ʳ), celebrating the town and the honour available in shoots. As in 1394, having a poem to describe the event is valuable in itself, possessing a greater cultural value and expressing more honour than a prose description would have.

The woodcut accompanying the description of the shoot, two folios before the poem (fol. Z4ʳ), further contributes to memorializing the event. Large and detailed, it closely mirrors the description in the chronicle, notably in depicting the two lodges, which are topped by the lion of Flanders and the Hapsburg eagle. Hence it would not readily lend itself to re-use, and as such indicates a high degree of commercial confidence on the part of Willem Vorsterman, whose commercial instincts were finely tuned by this point in his long career.⁴⁵

The ambition in the poem's form and scope is significant, especially by comparison with the poem on the 1394 Tournai shoot, which supplies much less detail on the participating teams and devotes more space to the host, Tournai, and to pleasing the king and to honouring God than to the competitors. In 1498 the opening *ballade* alludes to God and the saints, and to Ghent, but the poem does little to praise Philip the Handsome. He was present, his entrance with Bruges is mentioned (fol. Aa1ᵛ), but no extra praise is given to him. The mention of, but the absence of praise for, Philip the Handsome is comparable to the treatment of his great-grandfather Philip the Good in the book of Pieter Polet. Philip the Good took part in the Ghent shoot of 1440, even bringing his own team of nobles, yet his team is listed in its place in the shooting order, just like other teams. Philip is called 'our lord' the duke of Burgundy and count of Flanders, but there is no effort to praise him above any other competitor and no emphasis that the shoot was to please him.[46] In 1394 the Tournai shoot was to 'please the king', and the city's great shoot of 1455 was to 'praise and give thanks for the king's recent victories in Normandy'.[47] Ghent, and the author of the poem in the *Excellente cronike*, do not seem to place the same values on ducal participation, or praise for the duke.

The Ghent poem was published three decades after the event, whereas the Tournai poem is close to contemporary with the event it describes, which may have influenced their respective portrayals of the prince. The Tournai poem emphazises that the competition praised the living monarch, Charles VI (d. 1422), and was written in the same political environment in which the competition was held. The same is not true of the Ghent poem: Philip the Handsome had died in 1506, and he does not seem to have left such an impression on the town. The political landscape had changed dramatically by 1531, with the Hapsburg empire stretching from eastern Europe to Spain and incorporating South America, but Charles V had been born in Ghent. The relationship between the emperor and the town of his birth changed after 1540, but in the 1530s the bonds, begun with the 'innovative' spectacle of his 1500 baptism, were still significant, the Low Countries still valued by the Emperor.[48] In 1531, for instance, the Emperor held a chapter of the Order of the Golden Fleece in Tournai, a Hapsburg city since 1521. The 1530s also saw the creation of the first surviving panoramic view of Ghent, now in the city's Stadsmuseum, showing the town in its glory and celebrating civic values, with visitors including Erasmus and Dürer praising the town's wealth and splendour.[49] The 1530s was, then, a moment to reflect on the prestige and past of the towns and to hope for a continuation and expansion of that prestige, not necessarily linked to the emperor's father, but not in opposition to his legacy either.

In the poem details are given about every town that entered Ghent by land in 1498, with details of prestigious elements, linked to civic representation. The elaborate details provided about each team are far more developed than those for 1394. Oudenaarde had built up a tradition of impressive entrance ceremonies; during the 1440 competitions in Ghent they were so keen to hear whether they had won the prize for best entrance that they despatched two messengers on the same day.[50] The description of their entrance into Ghent in 1498 shows the guild keeping up this tradition:

> Oudenaerde quam inne met vuolge groot:
> Eerst twee wagens, daer inne drie lieden:
> Een trompet, tabijt wit, die hoeden root,
> Doen C ende XXX wagens. (fol. Aa2ʳ)

[Oudenaarde came in with a great entourage. First came two wagons with three people in them: a trumpeter in white robes and a red hood; then 130 wagons.]

The Oudenaarde entrance seems to have been one of the largest, but the prize for best entrance went not to Oudenaarde, but to Bruges. The Bruges crossbow guild entered in 'rijckelicke maniere' [rich manner] with five wagons and 'haer rethorijke' [her [Bruges's] rhetoric], probably a reference to one of the chambers of rhetoric in Bruges (fol. Aa1^v), followed by horsemen, wagons, trumpeters, pipers, and a jester:

> Doen XXIIII paer peerden, elc scheen een heer,
> Van Lombaerdyen ende huyter spaenscher wone
> Ende ooc duytschen huyter keyserlicke crone. (fol. Aa1^v)

> [Then 24 pairs of horses — each looked like a lord — from Lombardy and Spain, and also from the German lands under the imperial crown.]

The horses and their riders are an indication of the international standing of Bruges, or at least the international standing the town still wished to project, despite its waning commercial significance. The entrance also included Duke Philip the Handsome as the king of the Saint George guild, carrying their *papegay*. It is possible that this noble participant helped ensure victory, though the Bruges entrance is a sophisticated demonstration of status and international standing.

The descriptions of both Bruges and Oudenaarde provide far more details than any other description of entrances into competitions. Though smaller towns are described in less detail, with Oostende given four lines and Damme three, all are recorded in rhyme and all are described with care and details specific to each guild entered. Even small towns are noted as being part of the honourable displays: guilds are not equal, but they are all part of the prestigious regional community, and all are worthy of remembrance.

The guilds are described in the order in which they entered Ghent, with those from within Flanders entering on Sunday 20 May, and those from outside Flanders entering on Monday 21 May. Several, in particular 's-Hertogenbosch, Antwerp, and Brussels, three powerful Brabant towns growing in commercial importance, were far more lavish than any of the Flemish entrances; equally, they received far more attention in the poem. 's-Hertogenbosch's entrance was a carefully managed expression of status and of identity; they entered with 'vier waghens vol kisten' [four wagons full of chests] (fol. Aa3^r) as well as the guild-brothers in fine robes showing their prowess and status. The entrance featured numerous wagons, one of which was particularly elaborate and described in correspondingly exhaustive detail: it featured a lion in each corner, a wild man, and a maiden in white damask. The guild-brothers also used the name of their town, 's-Hertogenbosch, meaning literally 'ducal forest', within their entrance to ensure all observers would remember their entrance and identify it securely as theirs. The entrance also featured 'een silveren bosch' [a silver forest], again showing both wealth and urban pride. Moreover, the rhyme scheme for 's-Hertogenbosch is particularly intricate, with more frequent repetitions of rhymes than usual.

The Antwerp entrance is described in far more detail than any other, with thirty-two lines of verse describing the guild-brothers' entrance, and then seventeen lines of prose describing what they did the next day, before the poem returns to an account of Utrecht. Antwerp is the only guild to be described in both prose and rhyme; its entrance began with what appears to have been a play or *tableau vivant* about Julius Caesar, after which the guild-brothers are described in great detail, their costumes more colourful than those of other guilds. They are followed by trumpeters, jesters, rustics, men dressed half in arms, as well as more performances.

Antwerp was, in 1498, beginning its rise to power; with the decline of Bruges it was well on its way to becoming the trade gateway of the Low Countries, a position it had fully assumed by the time the poem was published in 1531.[51] The details of description may be influenced by Antwerp's sixteenth-century prominence, as much as its fifteenth-century spectacle, but the event was in any case impressive, with a huge amount of cloth and horsemen, and even an elephant, presumably a wooden festival elephant of the kind used in other civic and courtly performances.[52]

The thirty-two-line poem is a celebration of Antwerp's wealth and status. The prose account of what Antwerp did the next day is similarly interesting; as it is not in verse this may come from another source, but its inclusion implies that Vorsterman wanted this to be remembered as part of the entrance. The next day, Tuesday, all of the company went to church and mass, with their own singers and finery. In their procession from their hostelry to the church, the guild had 105 wagons covered in fine red cloth, which was subsequently distributed to the poor of Ghent. Antwerp showed not just its ability to put on a spectacular display, but made clear, through cloth, wealth, and devotion, that its guild far surpassed any of the Flemish guilds in wealth and generosity. Its entrance is a huge statement of strength and new wealth, encapsulated in the elephant and, more generally, in the length and detail of the account provided.

For all its finery, Antwerp did not win the prize for finest entry; this honour went to Brussels. Brussels would, six months later, host the baptism of Philip's first child, Eleanor,[53] and may have been using urban spectacles to prove itself a suitable court city; it was, after all, the birthplace of Philip's mother.[54] The entrance of the Brussels guilds included a wagon of jesters, fifty wagons full of flowers and pipers, wagons with towers, and the shooters themselves, well dressed and carrying torches (fol. Aa2ᵛ) with the arms of Saint Michael, patron saint of Brussels, and Saint George, patron of their shooting guild. Like Antwerp, Brussels demonstrated wealth and standing in its entrance, emphasizing its suitability as a ducal residence, perhaps even as a ducal capital. While Flemish guilds appealed to the 'public' and Antwerp showed strength and wealth, Brussels used its entrance into the 1498 competition to underline its prowess and nobility; indeed, its entry included the duke, as in Bruges, as the guild king.

Of course, not all of the entrances on the Sunday were so spectacular. Mons entered with just one wagon, covered in red cloth, and six pairs of horses, their king and four horsemen. Tournai were the only guild from the kingdom of France to take part, possibly reflecting the lasting damage the wars and violence from 1477 onwards had inflicted on cross-border festive networks. Their entrance was small, with just one wagon, their standard and guild-brothers; the size of their entrance, in relation to the size and wealth of Tournai, implies that the town no longer wished to invest in Flemish networks. The land entries from beyond Flanders are described in more depth, but what is striking about the poetic description of these events is the variety of displays, and that every entrance is recorded, though some are described in more depth than others.

After the land entries, a third day was set aside for entrances to be made by water. The water entrances are described in the chronicle, but in prose rather than verse. This formal variation may imply that the publisher was drawing on two or more pre-existing sources. The entrances made on the Scheldt by Diest, Menin, Bergen-op-Zoom, and Lierre are described with the same sorts of details mentioned, though accompanied by far less praise, than in the verse. Again, it is important that every team is mentioned and recorded, every member of the community remembered. Diest entered with a barge, burning torches, and a tree on which was a banner with the arms of the town, as well as eighteen culverineers. Menin, judged to have made the best entrance by water, entered with a ship covered in leaves, a target set up on their ship, perhaps a representation of the competition itself, and each member of the guild with 'an arrow in his neck' (fol. Aa4^{r-v}). These short descriptions ensured that all of the competition would be remembered, and that the event of 1498, like that of 1394, would be seen as a great spectacle showcasing the prestige of individual towns, and the prowess displayed in urban celebrations.

Material Remembrance

Remembrance was powerful, and perhaps most public, in verse, but material objects won during shooting contests show the same ideas of communication and community. Though variations existed, prizes can be broadly placed into three categories: wine, tableware, and impractical objects, all of which often became part of guild commemoration of identity. Wine is present from the earliest competitions onwards; it was a prestigious commodity in its own right, especially when paid for at civic expense. Competitions gave all guilds that attended gifts of wine, as they gave gifts of wine to all prestigious visitors, but not all guilds received the same amount. In 1399, for instance, the aldermen of Douai gave different quantities of wine not only as prizes, but also to different visitors to their crossbow shoot. As a drink it was valuable, but it also emphasized community: it is of course possible that the winner of the Douai shoot, a Lille man, could have consumed the prize of twelve *lots* (around twenty-five litres) himself, but it seems far more likely that this was a prize to be shared amongst the community, to strengthen brotherhood and commensality in commemorating their victory.[55]

Tableware, with a huge number of cups, jugs, ewers, and plates won by guilds, served a similar purpose. It was by far the most common prize given at competitions, showing the commensality and unity of guilds. Silver objects could be melted down or pawned, but inventories from Ghent, Bruges, and Oudenaarde show large quantities of silverware being kept in guild houses and chapels in the fifteenth and even the early sixteenth centuries.[56] Prizes available at the Oudenaarde 1408 competition were engraved with 'the arms of my lord Saint Georges', 'of our aforesaid very redoubtable lord and prince', and 'of this said town of Oudenaarde'.

In Tournai in 1455 all prizes 'bore the arms of Saint George, of the king and of the city'.[57] The same arrangement, of prizes honouring saint (and by connection guild), lord, and town, was seen in the prizes awarded across the fifteenth century. Hence in storing silver plates, jugs, and cups, the guild-brothers were remembering not only their own glory in winning, but the glory of the host in putting on such a fine spectacle, the objects lasting reminders not only of wealth, but of community and of honour.

Prizes in the third category, impractical objects, also emphasized the honour of competition, host, and winners, but by their construction and symbolism they did so to a greater degree. It was at the Oudenaarde shoot of 1408 that rather more impractical objects were first recorded. The team that made the best entry won a silver unicorn, those who travelled furthest won a silver crown, the best play won a silver monkey, and the best lights won jewels.[58] These prizes had no practical purpose: of course they could be melted down, but as with plates it is clear they were kept as symbolic valued objects. In 1408 Bruges won the unicorn, which is recorded in the guild inventory, among the first and most valued objects, as late as 1470.[59] The unicorn was noted as being from Oudenaarde, preserving the memory of Bruges's win and Oudenaarde's largesse, and so the honour of both, and ensuring that the spectacular shoot would be remembered. Silver animals also represent a conscious choice of symbolism, with great care taken to choose appropriate prizes.

The unicorn here is particularly striking. The famous myth of the unicorn is of a wild and ferocious animal, calmed by a virgin then killed, a pure creature, whose horn can repel poison; it is often linked to Christ's sacrifice on the cross, though it could carry negative connotations elsewhere.[60] There is a straightforward message here: the unicorn is a noble figure, adding to the nobility of Oudenaarde, their 'holy Knight' patron, Saint George, and the participation of John the Fearless. But the unicorn, rewarded for best entrance, must also be a tool to remember the beautiful entrance staged by Bruges, the potential for wildness and danger within the crossbowmen, and the potential sacrifice they might make for their cities. The Oudenaarde guild is not unique in giving prizes of mythical creatures: another Bruges inventory written before 1435 contains not just the town's unicorn, but also a dragon, won at Sluis, 'a Saint George', a pair of trumpets, an engraved *papegay*, 'two solid lilies', two engraved crowns, and an impressive collection of cups, plates, and crosses.[61]

Mythical creatures, especially unicorns, exploited established patterns of chivalric symbolism and status. The meaning of the monkey in Oudenaarde is less clear, and this is the only reference to a monkey. Monkeys had traditionally been seen as evil creatures, but by the late fourteenth century were also seen as playful, mimicking animals.[62] Oudenaarde rewarded the best play with a monkey, showing a conscious choice to reward an enjoyable play, presumably a comedy, with a prize fitting for mimicry. Though no pun seems to have been intended in Oudenaarde (the Dutch verb *na-apen*, 'to ape', is not attested until much later), Tournai did use prizes that played on words. In 1455 they wished to celebrate the recent victories of the French king and his eldest son, especially in Normandy. The best play won a silver royal *écu*, presumably a shield rather than a coin (prizes of money were very rare), and the second best a silver dolphin, a pun on the glory of the dauphin.[63] All prizes had a symbolic value and played a role in the exchange and enhancement of honour for hosts and guest, indicating the importance of performing in the shoots and commemorating these performances, even generations later.

Conclusions

The archery and crossbow guilds in and beyond the Burgundian Low Countries developed in a densely urbanized, competitive environment, and used their shooting events to build communities and to enhance their standing. In organizing competitions, guilds across the region emphasized brotherhood and honour; whether they wrote in French or Dutch or — exceptionally — both, they shared a culture and values, building multilingual networks. That invitations could be sent out across a bilingual region in just one language, and be understood and accepted by towns from Amsterdam to Paris, from Hulst to Tournai, shows the existence of a larger community bound together by shared values. Ghent's bilingual invitation of 1498 reflects the decline of such festive networks, and a greater need to publicize events and to encourage attendance after the troubles of Mary's reign and Maximilian's regency. The fact that two poems were written to describe crossbow competitions, both emphasizing display and entrances rather than the actual shooting, is significant for our understanding of how the events were commemorated.

Both poems show that different audiences wanted to remember the events. They make clear that competitions, and especially the entrances made to them, were about spectacle, symbolism, and communities. Such public manifestations of civic values were what made the events memorable; indeed, the later Ghent poem suggests that entrances became increasingly elaborate, attracting more attention than the prince, and serving more obviously as performances of collective identity. Prizes, especially elaborate silver objects such as unicorns and monkeys, added a material dimension to the commemoration of communities and helped to keep guilds active and to remind brothers of victors and of honour. The guilds drew on a range of traditions, shaping their own values and their own honour system to create and enhance networks across and beyond the Burgundian Low Countries and to communicate and commemorate both their distinctive local identities and their larger affinities in a competitive urban milieu by performing their shared multilingual culture.

Notes to Chapter 5

1. *Bonnes villes* were towns that were acknowledged political entities, recognized by and usually supporters of the crown. See Graeme Small, *Late Medieval France* (Basingstoke: Palgrave Macmillan, 2009), pp. 18–19.
2. Graeme Small, 'Centre and Periphery in Late Medieval France: Tournai', in *War, Government and Power in Later Medieval France*, ed. by Christopher Allmand (Liverpool: Liverpool University Press, 2000), pp. 145–74.
3. Ghent, Universiteitsbibliotheek (UBG), HS 434, fols 85^r–87^r (85^r). Further references are provided in the text. The document is edited in A. G. Chotin, *Histoire de Tournai et du Tournésis, depuis les temps les plus reculés jusqu'à nos jours*, 2 vols (Tournai: Massart et Janssens, 1840), I, 349–58.

The manuscript has been digitized, and is available on the Universiteit Gent website, under its title *Vredesverdragen*, <http://adore.ugent.be/OpenURL/app?id=archive.ugent.be:BB83AD24-4D58-11E3-8404-AE8B98481370&type=carousel> [accessed 13 June 2014].

4. For the political context see Christopher Allmand, *The Hundred Years War: France and England at War, c. 1300–1450* (Cambridge: Cambridge University Press, 1988), pp. 20–26; Anne Curry, *The Hundred Years War* (Basingstoke: Macmillan, 1993), pp. 74–87.

5. Laura Crombie, 'French and Flemish Urban Festive Networks: Archery and Crossbow Competitions Attended and Hosted by Tournai in the Fourteenth and Fifteenth Centuries', *French History*, 27 (2013), 157–75.

6. Theo Reintges, *Ursprung und Wesen der spätmittelalterlichen Schützengilden* (Bonn: Ludwig Röhrscheid Verlag, 1963), pp. 5–26; Andrew Brown and Graeme Small, *Court and Civic Society in the Burgundian Low Countries c.1420–c.1520* (Manchester: Manchester University Press, 2007), pp. 239–52; A. Janvier, 'Notice sur les anciennes corporations d'archers, d'arbalétriers, de couleuvriniers et d'arquebusiers des villes de Picardie', *Mémoires de la société des antiquaires de la Picardie*, 14 (1855), 5–380; Josee Moulin-Coppens, *De Geschiedenis van het oude Sint-Jorisgilde te Gent* (Ghent: Hoste Staelens, 1982); Eugeen Van Autenboer, *De kaarten van de schuttersgilden van het hertogdom Brabant (1300–1800)*, 2 vols (Tilburg: Stichting Zuidelijk historisch contact, 1993).

7. *Gentsche stads- en baljuwsrekeningen, 1280–1336*, ed. by Julius Vuylsteke and Alfons Van Werveke, 3 vols (Ghent: Meyer-van Loo, 1900–08), I, 86, 158; Bruges, Stadsarchief (SAB), 216, rekeningen 1336–37, fol. 100^r.; Lille, Archives municipales (AML), Comptes de la Ville (CV), 16016, fol. 21^v; 16020, fols 29^r–31^r.

8. Thomas Coomans, 'Belfries, Cloth Halls, Hospitals, and Mendicant Churches: A New Urban Architecture in the Low Countries around 1300', in *The Year 1300 and the Creation of a New European Architecture*, ed. by A. Gajewski and Z. Opačić (Turnhout: Brepols, 2007), pp. 185–202 (pp. 185–87); Peter Stabel, 'Markets in the Cities of the Late Medieval Low Countries: Retail, Commercial Exchange and Socio-cultural Display', in *Fiere e mercati nella integrazione delle economie europee, secc. XIII–XVII: atti della 'Trentaduesima settimana di studi', 8–12 maggio 2000*, ed. by Simonetta Cavaciocchi (Florence: Le Monnier, 2001), pp. 797–817 (pp. 802–05).

9. AML, 15883 (registre aux titres, M.) n. 61, fols 28^r–29^v.

10. Discussed in Laura Crombie, 'Defense, Honor and Community: The Military and Social Bonds of the Dukes of Burgundy and the Flemish Shooting Guilds', *Journal of Medieval Military History*, 9 (2011), 76–96; Jean-Marie Cauchies, '"Service" du prince, "sûreté" des villes: à propos de privilèges délivrés aux confréries ou serments d'archers et d'arbalétriers dans les Pays-Bas au XVe siècle', *Revue du Nord*, 94 (2012), 419–34. Several have been published, including John the Fearless's charter of rights to Lille in 1405 in *Ordonnances de Jean sans Peur, 1405–1419, Recueils des ordonnances des Pays-Bas, 1381–1506, Ordonnances de Philippe le Hardi, de Marguerite de Male et de Jean sans Peur, 1319–1419*, ed. by Jean-Marie Cauchies, 3 (Brussels: Commission royale pour la publication des anciennes lois et ordonnances de la Belgique, 2001), pp. 24–25; Philip the Good's charter to the archers of Lannoy in Georges Espinas, *Les Origines du droit d'association dans les villes de l'Artois et de la Flandre française jusqu'au début du XVIe siècle*, 2 vols (Lille: Raoust, 1941), II, 538–40; Laura Crombie, 'The First Ordnances of the Crossbow Confraternity of Douai, 1383–1393', *Journal of Archer Antiquarians*, 54 (2011), 21–28.

11. *Acta sanctorum — Aprilis tomus tertius*, ed. by Godfrey Henschen and Daniel van Papenbroeck (Paris Victor Palmé, 1866), pp. 100–58; David A. L. Morgan, 'The Cult of St George c. 1500: National and International Connotations', *Publications du Centre européen d'études bourguignonnes (XIVe–XVIe s.)*, 35 (1995), 151–62; *Acta sanctorum — Januarii tomus secundus*, ed. by Jean Bolland and Godfrey Henschen (Paris: Victor Palmé, 1863), pp. 265–85; Johanna Jacobs, *Sebastiaan, martelaar of mythe* (Zwolle: Waanders, 1993); Hugues Micha, 'Une rédaction en vers de la vie de Saint Sébastien', *Romania*, 92 (1971), 405–19.

12. Marc Boone, 'Réseaux urbaines', in *Le Prince et le peuple: images de la société du temps des ducs de Bourgogne, 1384–1530*, ed. by Walter Prevenier (Antwerp: Fonds Mercator, 1998), pp. 233–47; Anu Mänd, 'Saints' Cults in Medieval Livonia', in *The Clash of Cultures on the Medieval Baltic Frontier*, ed. by Alan V. Murray (Farnham: Ashgate, 2009), pp. 191–223; Paul Trio, 'The Emergence of New Devotions in Late Medieval Urban Flanders (Thirteenth-Fifteenth Centuries): Struggle

and Cooperation between Church/Clergy and Urban Government/Bourgeoisie', in *Städtische Kulte im Mittelalter*, ed. by S. Ehrich and J. Obserste (Regensburg: Schnell und Steiner, 2010), pp. 327–38; Andre Vauchez, 'Saint Homebon (†1197), patron des marchands et artisans drapiers à la fin du Moyen Age et à l'époque moderne', *Académie royale de Belgique. Bulletin de la classe des lettres et des sciences morales et politiques*, 6th ser., 15 (2004), 47–56.

13. Brown and Small, *Court and Civic Society in the Burgundian Low Countries c.1420–c.1520*, pp. 210–16.
14. Laura Crombie, 'Honour, Community and Hierarchy in the Feasts of the Archery and Crossbow Guilds of Bruges, 1445–81', *Journal of Medieval History*, 37 (2011), 102–13.
15. De Potter, *Jaarboeken der Sint-Jorisgilde van Gent*, pp. 10–16; Arnade, *Realms of Ritual*, p. 80; Marc de Schrijver and Christian Dothee, *Les Concours de tir à l'arbalète des gildes médiévales: un aperçu* (Antwerp: Antwerps Museum en Archief Den Crans, 1979), p. 2; E. van Cauwenberghe, 'Notice historique sur les confréries de Saint Georges', *Messager des sciences historiques, des arts et de la bibliographie de Belgique* (1853), 269–99 (p. 273).
16. AML, CV 16018, fol. 29^v; *Gentsche stads- en baljuwsrekeningen, 1280–1336*, ed. by Vuylsteke and Van Werveke, ii, 664.
17. AML, CV, 16019, fol. 54^r; *Gentsche stads- en baljuwsrekeningen, 1280–1336*, ed. by Vuylsteke and Van Werveke, ii, 765–66.
18. Crombie, 'French and Flemish Urban Festive Networks', pp. 158–61; Brown and Small, *Court and Civic Society in the Burgundian Low Countries c.1420–c.1520*, pp. 210–15; Arnade, *Realms of Ritual*, pp. 84–94.
19. AML, CV, 16125, fol. 34^v. 1 lot = 2.09 litres; see Monique Somme, 'Étude comparative des mesures à vin dans les états bourguignons au XVe siècle,' *Revue du Nord*, 58 (1976), 171–83.
20. The shooting guilds and their competitions in the Holy Roman Empire are the subject of Jean-Dominique Delle Luche, 'Le Plaisir des bourgeois et la gloire de la ville: sociétés et concours de tir dans les villes de l'Empire (XVe–XVIe siècles)' (unpublished doctoral thesis, École des Hautes Études en Sciences Sociales, 2015).
21. Other letters of consent must have existed. The invitation to the Mons shoot of 1387 stated that the event had been organized with the permission of Duke Albert of Bavaria; indeed, this type of formulation became standardized in letters. Philip the Good's letter of permission for the competition of 1440, and Philip the Handsome's permission for that of 1498, were both copied into the *Book of Pieter Polet* (see below). Philip the Good's letter allowing the 1462 compeititon in Oudenaarde is the only example I have found of a surviving original: Oudenaarde, Stadsarchief, Oude Archief (OSAOA), gilden 507/II/12 A.
22. This shared culture seems not to have extended to Lancastrian France. Though Norman towns attended competitions in Flanders while under French rule, they did not do so under English rule, and despite its proximity to Flanders and to Burgundian culture English Calais is never documented as attending or even being invited to any of these great competitions.
23. Crombie, 'French and Flemish Festive Networks', pp. 169–71.
24. Ghent, Stadsarchief (SAG), Sint Jorisgilde, niet genummerde reeks, Charters en diverse losse documenten, 30.
25. Jean-Paul Peeters, 'De financieel-economische situatie van de stad Mechelen in het midden van de 14de eeuw (1338–1359)', *Handelingen van de Koninklijke Kring voor Oudheidkunde, Letteren en Kunst van Mechelen*, 108 (2005), 29–60; Dirk Coigneau, '1 Februari 1404: De Mechelse voetboogschutters schrijven een wedstrijd uit. Stedelijke toneelwedstrijden in de vijftiende en zestiende eeuw', in *Een theatergeschiedenis der Nederlanden: Tien eeuwen drama en theater in Nederland en Vlaanderen*, ed. by R. L. Erenstein (Amsterdam: Amsterdam University Press, 1996), pp. 30–35. Mechelen and its various identities and civic groups, including the shooting guilds there, will be analyzed in a forthcoming collection to be edited by Peter Stabel.
26. Mechelen, Stadsarchief, titre IX, section 4, tirs et joutes, 1–4; the Ghent invitation is SAG, Fonds Sint Joris, 155, 2. Accounts of the messengers, and the gifts they received as the invited guilds, are in UBG, HS G 6112, fol. 16^{r-v}.
27. UBG, HS 434, fol. 95^r; OSAOA, gilden 241/2, fols 89^r–92^v; Van Cauwenberghe, 'Notice historique sur les confréries de Saint Georges', pp. 281–85.

28. Description from *Chronijke van Oudenaarde*, HS Quaemore (= OSAOA 241, unnumbered pages): 'graef Jan van Bourgognen en zijn geduchte Vrouw, waeren beyde ter schutterijen den graef schietende met de guldebroeders de stede van Audenaerde, maer den zelven heer moest dog zijnen bogen draegen op zijne schoutder gelijke de ander schutters' [Count John of Burgundy and his gentle wife were both at the shoot, where the count shot with the guild-brothers of the town of Oudenaarde, but that lord nevertheless had to carry his own bow on his shoulder, like the other shooters].
29. SAG, Fonds Sint Joris, 155, 2.
30. Nicolas Despars, *Cronijke van den lande ende graefscepe van Vlanderen van de jaeren 405 tot 1492*, ed. by J. de Jonghe, 4 vols (Bruges: Messchert, 1839–42), III, 169–70.
31. *Chronijke van Oudenaarde* (= OSAOA 241).
32. *Chronique de Jean de Stavelot*, ed. by A. Borgnet (Brussels: M. Hayez, 1861).
33. *Chronique et annales de Gilles le Muisit*, ed. by H. Lemaitre (Paris: Renouard, H. Laurens, 1906).
34. On these qualities of verse in the late Middle Ages, see Armstrong and Kay, *Knowing Poetry*, pp. 199–200.
35. UBG, HS 434, fols 87^v–90^r.
36. *Dits die excellente cronike van Vlaanderen, beghinnende van Liederik Buc tot keyser Carolus* (Antwerp: Willem Vorsterman, 1531; USTC 400512), fols Aa1^r–Aa3^v. Further references will be provided in the text. The edition has been digitized, and is available on the Universiteit Gent website, <http://search.ugent.be/meercat/x/bkt01?q=900000156054> [accessed 13 June 2014].
37. W. M. H. Hummelen, '*Pausa* and *Selete* in the *Bliscapen*', in *Urban Theatre in the Low Countries, 1400–1625*, ed. by Elsa Strietman and Peter Happé (Turnhout: Brepols, 2006), pp. 53–75.
38. UBG, HS G 6112.
39. The original charter also survives: SAG, Sint Jorisgilde, niet genummerde reeks.
40. Baron Jules de Saint-Genois, *Catalogue méthodique et raisonné des manuscrits de la bibliothèque de la ville et de l'université de Gand*, 3 vols (Ghent: Annoot-Braeckman, 1849–52), I, 98–105.
41. On such signatures, see especially Cynthia J. Brown, *Poets, Patrons, and Printers: Crisis of Authority in Late Medieval France* (Ithaca, NY: Cornell University Press, 1995), pp. 153–57.
42. See above, n. 36. For the longer tradition, see Johan Oosterman, 'De *Excellente cronike van Vlaenderen* en Anthonis de Roovere', *Tijdschrift voor Nederlandse Taal- en Letterkunde*, 11 (2002), 22–37; Jan Dumolyn and Elodie Lecuppre-Desjardin, 'Propagande et sensibilité: la fibre émotionnelle au cœur des luttes politiques et sociales dans les villes des anciens Pays-Bas bourguignons. L'Exemple de la révolte brugeoise de 1436–1438', in *Emotions in the Heart of the City (14th–16th century): Studies in European Urban History (1100–1800)*, ed. by Élodie Lecuppre-Desjardin and Anne-Laure Van Bruaene (Turnhout: Brepols, 2005), pp. 41–62 (pp. 44–46).
43. Samuel Mareel, 'Politics, Mnemonics, and the Verse Form: On the Function of the Poems in the *Excellente Cronike van Vlaenderen*', in *Staging the Court of Burgundy: Proceedings of the Conference 'The Splendour of Burgundy'*, ed. by Wim Blockmans and others (Turnhout: Brepols, 2013), pp. 249–54.
44. Arnade, *Realms of Ritual*, pp. 182–83.
45. See Yves G. Vermeulen, *Tot profijt en genoegen: Motiveringen voor de productie van Nederlandstalige gedrukte teksten 1477–1540* (Groningen: Wolters-Noordhoff/Forsten, 1986), pp. 128–53; Rita Schlusemann, 'De uitwisseling van houtsneden tussen Willem Vorsterman en Jan van Doesborch', *Queeste*, 1 (1994), 156–73; Rita Schlusemann, 'Buchmarkt in Antwerpen am Anfang des 16. Jahrhunderts', in *Laienlektüre und Buchmarkt im späten Mittelalter*, ed. by Thomas Kock and Rita Schlusemann (Frankfurt am Main: Peter Lang, 1997), pp. 33–39.
46. UBG, HS G 6112, fol. 41^r.
47. Brown and Small, *Court and Civic Society in the Burgundian Low Countries c.1420–c.1520*, pp. 222–25.
48. Rolf Strøm-Olsen, 'Dynastic Ritual and Politics in Early Modern Burgundy: The Baptism of Charles V', *Past and Present*, 175 (2002), 34–64.
49. Herman Balthasar and others, *Ghent: In Defence of a Rebellious City: History, Art, Culture* (Antwerp: Mercatorfonds, 1989), p. 107.
50. OSAOA, Stadsrekeningen, 1436–1448, fol. 202^r.

51. Wilfred Brulez, 'Bruges and Antwerp in the 15th and 16th Centuries, an Antithesis', *Acta Historica Nederlandicae*, 6 (1973), 1–26; J. Bolton and F. Bruscoli, 'When Did Antwerp Replace Bruges as the Commercial and Financial Centre of North-Western Europe? The Evidence of the Borromei Ledger for 1438', *Economic History Review*, 61 (2008), 360–79; Peter Stabel, 'Guilds in Late Medieval Flanders: Myths and Realities of Guild Life in an Export-Oriented Environment', *Journal of Medieval History*, 30 (2004), 187–212.
52. An elephant seems to have been present at Charles V's baptism in Ghent in 1500, and by the mid-sixteenth century Antwerp had an 'ommegang elephant'. See: Margrit Thøfner, *A Common Art: Urban Ceremonial in Antwerp and Brussels During and After the Dutch Revolt* (Zwolle: Waanders, 2007), pp. 59–71; Strøm-Olsen, 'Dynastic Ritual and Politics in Early Modern Burgundy', pp. 42–44. Elephants were also used in court spectacles, most famously when Olivier de La Marche entered the Feast of the Pheasant dressed as Holy Church (see Brown and Small, *Court and Civic Society in the Burgundian Low Countries c.1420–c.1520*, pp. 36–53), and were popular artistic symbols; see E. Dhanens, 'Literatuur en stadscultuur tussen middeleeuwen en nieuwe tijd', *BMGN, The Low Countries Historical Review*, 106 (1991), 421–25 (pp. 423–24). Real elephants were present in the Low Countries too, with one 'touring' Holland in the 1480s; see M. van Hasselt, 'A Burgundian Death: The Tournament in *Le Chevalier Délibéré*' (unpublished master's thesis, University of Utrecht, 2010), pp. 120–21, <http://www.knightorder.org.uk/history/A%20Burgundian%20Death.pdf> [accessed 20 June 2014].
53. Strøm-Olsen, 'Dynastic Ritual and Politics in Early Modern Burgundy', pp. 42–44.
54. Claire Billen, 'Brussel-hoofdstad', in *De grote mythen uit de geschiedenis van België, Vlaanderen en Wallonië*, ed. by Anne Morelli (Berchem: EPO, 1996), pp. 203–14.
55. Douai, Archives municipales, CC 204, pp. 189–90; Mario Damen, 'Giving by Pouring: The Functions of Gifts of Wine in the City of Leiden, 14th–16th Centuries', in *Symbolic Communication in Late Medieval Towns*, ed. by Jacoba Van Leeuwen (Leuven: Leuven University Press, 2006), pp. 83–100.
56. Two separate inventories, both in SAG, Sint Jorisgilde, niet genummerde reeks, 7; Louis Gilliodts-Van Severen, *Inventaire des archives de la ville de Bruges*, 9 vols (Bruges: Gailliard, 1871–85), IV, 542–49; OSAOA, gilden 507/II/2B.
57. Brown and Small, *Court and Civic Society in the Burgundian Low Countries c.1420–c.1520*, p. 220.
58. OSAOA, gilden 707/II/8A.
59. Gilliodts-Van Severen, *Inventaire des archives de la ville de Bruges*, IV, 542–49.
60. Debra Hassig, *Medieval Bestiaries: Text, Image, Ideology* (Cambridge: Cambridge University Press, 1995), pp. 70, 92–93; Lesley Kordecki, 'Losing the Monster and Recovering the Non-Human in Fable(d) Subjectivity', in *Animals and the Symbolic in Medieval Art and Literature*, ed. by L. A. J. R. Houwen (Groningen: Egbert Forsten, 1997), pp. 25–37; Margaret B. Freeman, *The Unicorn Tapestries, the Metropolitan Museum of Art* (New York: Dutton, 1976), pp. 11–32.
61. SAB, 385, Sint Jorisgilde, register met ledenlijst enz. 1321–1531, fols 76^r–82^r.
62. Horst Woldermar Janson, *Apes and Ape-lore in the Middle Ages* (London: Warburg Institute, University of London, 1952), pp. 29–54; Willene B. Clark, *A Medieval Book of Beasts* (Woodbridge: Boydell and Brewer, 2006), pp. 7–8, 42–44.
63. Brown and Small, *Court and Civic Society in the Burgundian Low Countries c.1420–c.1520*, p. 222.

CHAPTER 6

Wrapped in Rhetoric: The *Cent Nouvelles nouvelles* and Dutch *Rederijker* Literature

Dirk Coigneau

After finishing his (re-)translation of Boccaccio's *De casibus virorum illustrium* in dedication to Jean, duc de Berry, the French humanist and Latin poet Laurent de Premierfait also ventured, at the same Duke's request, upon a rendering of Boccaccio's *Decameron* into his mother tongue. The translator was not really versed in Tuscan but, thanks to the availability of a Latin version, managed to complete the work within three years and dedicated it to the Duke on 15 June 1414. Judging from the number of surviving manuscripts, the *Livre des cent nouvelles*, as Premierfait's translation came to be known, must have provided many an aristocratic company or individual with agreeable reading and entertainment.[1] Its success apparently inspired Jean de Berry's great-nephew, Philip the Good, Duke of Burgundy, to request a composition of his own 'Book of hundred novellas', which could then, logically, be called *Cent Nouvelles nouvelles*. A collection of one hundred short secular stories in prose, mostly humorous or frivolous, was duly produced under this title, and humbly dedicated by the anonymous author to his 'tresredoubté seigneur'.[2] The composition and dedication of the 'Burgundian' collection must be situated after 1456, and before the Duke's death in 1467.[3]

In both the *Decameron* and the *Cent Nouvelles nouvelles*, the stories are presented as being told by a variety of narrators. In Boccaccio's book the seven female and three male storytellers act within an all-embracing frame story: young and wealthy Florentines, they possess estates and servants which enable them to leave the city, afflicted by the Black Death, to indulge in a carefree pastime in an idyllic setting. The temporal organization of that pastime also structures the collection, presented as the outcome of ten sessions in which each of the ten participants tells a tale. The stories in eight of the sessions develop a specific theme, such as unhappy love (fourth day), tricks played by women on their husbands (seventh day), or tricks played by men on women (part of the eighth day). The frame story also states that the plague, and the ensuing struggle to survive, had made people less timid in physical matters; in so doing it partially explains the piquancy of some of the tales, particularly those told by female narrators. Such an 'excuse' was probably considered less necessary in the *Cent Nouvelles nouvelles*, whose thirty-seven different narrators are all male. They are identified as real people, though their names are mentioned only in the preliminary table of contents and in the headings that introduce the stories.[4] Indeed, for the original audience, which belonged to the same Burgundian court circle as the narrators, the compiler of the *Cent Nouvelles nouvelles* needed no frame story to bring their narrators together, since narrators and audience already formed a community.

Though the *Decameron* clearly established the number of stories to be collected, the *Cent Nouvelles nouvelles* did not follow Boccaccio's division into equal groups of ten and thematic units. Twenty-two of its narrators deliver only one story; six deliver two; six others deliver three, four, or five. By contrast, the remaining three narrators delivered the disproportionally high numbers of ten, fourteen, and fifteen stories, together making more than a third of the whole. These narrators are Philippe de Loan (ten stories); 'Monseigneur', i.e. Philip the Good (fourteen stories); and 'Monseigneur de la Roche', i.e. Philippe Pot (fifteen stories). As most contributions are distributed randomly across the collection, the recurrence of their narrators' names adds little to the book's formal structure. Nevertheless, in three places the collection shows a striking concentration of stories by one or two of the three main narrators. Among *nouvelles* 1–21, eight are attributed to Philip the Good (the first two *nouvelles* and six of the next fifteen), six to de la Roche, and three to Loan; among *nouvelles* 34–52, nine are by de la Roche; and among *nouvelles* 66–76, four are by Loan and three by Philip the Good. Most significant is the opening cluster, where the explicit ascriptions to 'Monseigneur' indicate to readers that the Duke's 'requeste' [request] (p. 22), mentioned in the dedication, not only elicited a response from his most important servants and acquaintances, but also implied the active collaboration of Philip the Good himself. Six more stories ascribed to Philip appear later in the collection. Hence the Duke's role in the project may be seen as a playful parallel to the temporary positions of the storytellers in the *Decameron*, who were each allotted the role of 'King' or 'Queen' over the company for the duration of a narrative session.

The *Cent Nouvelles nouvelles* does not exhibit thematic developments of the kind found in the *Decameron*. Nevertheless, the dedication calls attention to two general characteristics that may reflect some kind of advance stipulation. Whereas the stories in the *Decameron* take place mostly in Italy and sometimes in former days, the new stories are set 'es parties de France, d'Alemaigne, d'Angleterre, de Haynau, de Brabant et aultres lieux' [in places in France, Germany, England, Hainaut, Brabant, and elsewhere], and are 'd'assez fresche memoire' [very recent] (p. 22). Indeed, the recency of many stories is explicitly mentioned. In some cases the settings are presented as significant in themselves: narrators occasionally even express an 'ethnographic' interest in certain areas, ascribing to their population a natural aptitude for activities that are worth relating.[5] Most locations are situated within the Duke of Burgundy's territories or in the kingdom of France.[6]

The Duke's primary position among the narrators, and the spatial and temporal convergences among the stories, give the *Cent Nouvelles nouvelles* a degree of unity. The most explicit unifying factor, however, is the narrators' tendency to voice their awareness of how their activity can increase the number of tales being recorded.

Some present this activity as recitation, but most refer directly to the formation of a *numbered* collection of stories or, deictically, to '*this* book'. *Nouvelle* 32 is a case in point:

> Affin que ne soye seclus du treseureux et hault merite deu a ceulx qui traveillent et labourent a l'augmentacion et accroissement des histoires de ce present livre [...]. (p. 215)[7]
>
> [So as not to be deprived of the most felicitous and noble merit due to those who labour and toil to augment and increase the stories in this book [...].]

In the late fifteenth and early sixteenth centuries, 'this book' found a wider public through several printed editions. The first was published by Anthoine Vérard in Paris, and dated 24 December 1486; twelve subsequent editions are attested until *c*.1540, published in Paris, Lyon, or Rouen. In the Low Countries, however, editions are not recorded until 1732 (Amsterdam) and 1733 (The Hague).[8] Although some thirty stories are set in Flanders, Brabant, Holland, or Hainaut, the *Cent Nouvelles nouvelles* were apparently much less popular than other literary works emanating from the same court circle. In the last quarter of the fifteenth and the early sixteenth centuries, editions and/or Dutch translations of various works from the Burgundian court were produced in Bruges, Gouda, Haarlem, Schiedam, and Leiden: *L'Histoire de Jason* and *Le Receuil des histoires de Troyes* by Raoul Lefèvre, *La Dance aux aveugles* and *Le Doctrinal du temps present* by Pierre Michault, and *Le Chevalier délibéré* by Olivier de La Marche. In Brussels the proximity of the court and its literary figures inspired local rhetoricians and publishers to translate works such as Amé de Montgesoie's *Pas de la mort*, and La Marche's *Chevalier délibéré* and *Triumphe des dames*.[9] The *Cent Nouvelles nouvelles*, by contrast, was neither published nor translated in full.

Besides the collection's loose structure, which lent itself to selective readings of separate stories, two other factors may explain the absence of the *Cent Nouvelles nouvelles* from regional literary printing. Stories about Trojan heroes and chivalric deeds, or allegories and moralizing reflections on earthly and human transience, served lofty political ambitions and ascetic ideals; the light fiction of the *Nouvelles*, often erotic and ironic, was ill-equipped for such purposes.[10] Naïve admirers and fervent promoters of serious Burgundian literature may even have found the humorous novellas incompatible with their more earnest literary expectations and beliefs. Moreover, Anthoine Vérard 'frenchified' the first edition of the *Cent Nouvelles nouvelles* by systematically obliterating Picard elements and by shifting the reader's attention from the Duke of Burgundy towards the King of France. While Vérard retained the original dedication to Philip the Good, he also introduced a preceding woodcut, depicting the dauphin (later King Louis XI) as the central figure on a throne, surrounded by the Duke and other narrators. Furthermore, the dedication itself is enlarged by a note, attributing the stories delivered by 'Monseigneur' to 'Monseigneur le dauphin', who at the time of the collection's composition was indeed resident in Burgundy. Finally, the dedication is followed by a woodcut, depicting the offering of the book, printed in Paris, to King Charles VIII.[11] In a period that witnessed increasing animosity between the Burgundian

Netherlands and France, Vérard's interventions must have obscured the *Cent Nouvelles nouvelles*' status as genuine Burgundian court literature.

Nevertheless, the *Cent Nouvelles nouvelles* were of course read in the fifteenth- and sixteenth-century Netherlands. Five texts, of very different kinds, bear witness to the impact and effects of some of these readings. None refers explicitly to its source of inspiration, but in three cases textual evidence proves the stories to be taken directly from the *Cent Nouvelles nouvelles*. Though a direct verbal connection cannot be demonstrated in the two other texts, the likelihood of a thematic dependency is reinforced in one case (Colijn van Rijssele's *Spiegel der minnen*) by contextual elements, and in the other case (Everaert's *Esbatement van den visscher*) by the probable selection and combination of two *Nouvelles*. The five 'readings' are presented below in chronological order.

Colijn van Rijssele's *Spiegel der minnen*

In Haarlem in 1561 Dirck Coornhert published a serial, comprising six plays (altogether 6169 lines) by Colijn van Rijssele that represent an ultimately tragic love story, entitled *De Spiegel der minnen* [The Mirror of Love]. Coornhert's introduction elucidates the plays' pedagogical and aesthetic qualities, and explains that he had transcribed the text accurately and without emendations from an old, worn-out copy. Colijn van Rijssele is historically attested: a rhetorician who lived and worked in Brussels, he is thought to have died in 1503. The *Spiegel der minnen* was reprinted in 1577 and 1617; in the twentieth century it acquired the status of a *rederijker* 'classic', comparable with *Elckerlijc* [Everyman] and *Mariken van Nieumeghen* [Mary of Nemmegen]. Its modern editor, Margaretha Immink, compares the text with other amorous plays, and analyzes the characters' psychology and the plays' prosody.[12] Literary historians regarded the *Spiegel* as one of the earliest bourgeois dramas of European literature; modern adaptations were performed in the 1950s and 1960s.[13] Not until 1983, however, did scholars note the resemblance between the *Spiegel*'s plot and that of *nouvelle* 26 of the *Cent Nouvelles nouvelles*.[14] Johanna E. van Gijsen's 1989 study of the *Spiegel* compares *nouvelle* 26 with Colijn van Rijssele's text, and concludes that the novella exercised a clear but partial and limited influence. Considering it as the main source of the fourth play and of a few smaller scenes in the second, third and fifth plays, Van Gijsen notes contrasts as well as resemblances.[15]

A great contrast is certainly apparent between the ends of the respective stories. The *Spiegel* frequently indicates that its amorous protagonists, Dierick and Katherina, will both die (ll. 101–05, 127–30, 180–92, 201–05, 236–39, 358–60, 1734–36, 2160–65, 2526–27, 5019–25). This is not the case with Katherine and Gerard in *nouvelle* 26. After discovering that her beloved Gerard has begun a relationship with another girl, Katherine marries the man her parents had chosen for her; Gerard's subsequent feelings of guilt are intense but not fatal. The *Spiegel*'s tragic ending contrasts still more with the story of Margarieta van Lymboch and Etsijtes, which Van Gijsen signals as another of Colijn van Rijssele's 'main sources', but which ends with the lovers' splendid marriage.[16] The only tale among the possible sources listed by Van Gijsen to have a similar ending to that of the *Spiegel* is *Decameron* IV.8, in which Girolamo (Jherome in Premierfait's translation) dies after Salvestra (Silvestre in the French text) lets her beloved down — not by refusing to visit and comfort him during an illness, as in Katherina's case, but by marrying another man — as a result of his unintentionally delayed return from the town to which his mother and other relatives had sent him in the hope that he would forget the girl next door. Doctors cannot identify a physical cause for Jherome's death, as with Dierick's sickness in the *Spiegel*, and declare it to be brought about by his 'trop grande douleur' [excessive anguish].[17] Both stories explicitly state the fatal power of external forces that establish love in human hearts: in the *Decameron* the narrator claims that love had been sent and planted by 'les estelles du ciel' [the stars in the sky], while in the *Spiegel* Venus pours love onto Dierick and Katherina out of a watering can.[18] Similarly, both stories place responsibility for the tragic ending on the boy's relatives.[19] As Katherina dies after learning of Dierick's death, at the very moment of his funeral service, so Silvestre dies on seeing Jherome lying in state in the church; and each couple is buried in one grave.

Strangely, these resemblances did not impress Van Gijsen, who considers the most striking similarity to lie only in the stories' social settings.[20] Combined with the tragic ending, this is indeed compelling enough. In both stories, it is the same social difference which makes the mother and other relatives send their son away for business: each boy is the son of a wealthy merchant, who falls in love with a poor seamstress (Katherina) or tailor's daughter (Silvestre). Jherome is sent from Florence to Paris; Dierick from Middelburg, in Zeeland, to Dordrecht, in Holland. Hence, I consider the *Spiegel*'s plot to be based on an exemplary combination of two *nouvelles*: *Decameron* IV.8 (*nouvelle* 38 in Premierfait's *Cent Nouvelles*), which focuses mostly on the boy's position and fate; and *Cent Nouvelles nouvelles* 26, which primarily presents the girl's activities and feelings.

Colijn van Rijssele's use of the *Cent Nouvelles nouvelles*, which is more relevant to the present purpose, seems almost self-evident if we follow the scholarly consensus and identify the author with Colijn Caillieu.[21] The work of this Brussels rhetorician shows a great deal of familiarity with Burgundian themes and court literature. Caillieu wrote a short play on the birth of Margaret of Austria, and translated *Le Pas de la mort* by Amé de Montgesoie, who was the *varlet de chambre* [personal servant] of Margaret's mother, Mary of Burgundy.[22] Caillieu must have based his verse translation on a manuscript source, as no edition of Montgesoie's poem is known. Thus we may not rule out the possibility that Colijn Caillieu, alias 'van Rijssele', consulted a *Cent Nouvelles nouvelles* manuscript rather than waiting for Vérard's 1486 edition. The same goes for Premierfait's *Decameron* translation, which Vérard first printed in 1485.

Cent Nouvelles nouvelles 26 may well have captured Colijn's attention not only as one of two exceptionally long stories in the collection, but also because of its distinctive representation of love.[23] Contrasting with most *nouvelles*, which deal with frivolous encounters or adulterous escapades in a matrimonial context, *nouvelle*

26 is one of only two stories to recount a relationship between two young lovers in some psychological depth; the other is *nouvelle* 98 (pp. 545–53), which ends tragically with the death of both partners. It is also relatively unusual in having a moralizing conclusion, which exhorts disloyal lovers to 'se [...] mirer a cest exemple' [treat this exemplum as a warning mirror] (p. 181).

As previously mentioned, the *nouvelle*'s ending is less tragic than that of the *Spiegel*. Gerard, like Dierick, is pressed to leave the country — in his case Brabant, which he exchanged for the duchy of Bar — because of his affair with Katherine. In the play, Katherina follows Katherine's example in travelling, under the cover of a pilgrimage, accompanied by a male relative — an uncle in the novella, a cousin in the play — and disguised in man's clothes, to find her lover. In both cases, her lover fails to recognize her, despite dining or drinking with her and sleeping in the same bedroom. When speaking of love, both Gerard and Dierick deny the seriousness of their relationship with the girl they have left at home. In the course of her visit, Katherine discovers that Gerard broke his oath and started a relationship with another girl, to whom he even gave the ring she had given him as proof of their loyalty. Depressed, but not without 'virile vertu' [manly courage] (p. 178), Katherine returns to Brabant to marry a rich gentleman. In the play, Dierick, like Boccaccio's Jherome, remains faithful to the end; but Katherina's jealousy and pride, prompted by her taking at face value the words he spoke for fear of revealing his true feelings, prove fatal to him. Hence the genuine duplicity of the male lover in *nouvelle* 26 moves exclusively into Katherina's mind in the *Spiegel*.

In the *nouvelle*, the lovers' social environment affects their relationship only externally, by causing Gerard to leave the country. In the play, by contrast, both lovers internalize their parents' and friends' opinions, infecting their relationship with doubts and fears regarding their different social positions. Both lovers in *nouvelle* 26, in contrast with the *Spiegel* and *Decameron* IV.8, belong to the same aristocratic household, the richest partner being the girl. The narrator's only comment on this is his assertion that Katherine's friends were displeased by the affair, because Gerard 'n'estoit pas de si grand lieu ne de si grande richesse comme elle estoit' [was not so well-born or rich as she was] (p. 169). A marriage could not, therefore, be expected; but this is not really what makes Gerard leave. Rather, the affair is no longer secret: everyone comments on it, and only his departure can stop the rumours. This is more than an echo of the courtly love tradition; it reflects the way in which the *Cent Nouvelles nouvelles* pays frequent attention — often in initial or final remarks, and in an ironical or satirical way — to renown and reputations, honour, fame, secrecy, and the recounting of events considered 'dignes d'estre recitez et en audience et memoire perpetuelle amenez' [worth telling, hearing, and remembering forever] (p. 54).[24]

In the *Spiegel* honour and secrecy also play their part, but these are more closely connected with social and class difference. Such issues are certainly present elsewhere in the *Cent Nouvelles nouvelles*, where various knights fall in love with chambermaids or villagers. In most of these cases, however, male lust in the *nouvelles* is not reciprocated. In the play, by contrast, the love between the wealthy merchant's son Dierick and the poor seamstress Katherina is mutual; yet, for her friends, it is precisely the combination of Katherina's poor estate and Dierick's wealth, pride, and passion that makes her vulnerable to violation.[25] This is indeed the fate of several servant girls in the *Cent Nouvelles nouvelles*, who are importuned, pursued, assaulted, or raped by knights and even by the Count of Saint-Pol (*nouvelles* 9, 17, 18, 24). These stories, in contrast with two *nouvelles* (54, 57), where (as in *nouvelle* 26) female characters occupy the higher rank, do not explicitly reflect or moralize on class differences. The attitude of the townsman Dierick, the protagonist in a morally and psychologically complex *rederijker* play, is very different. Katherina's poor estate makes him not bold but unsure, full of doubts and fears, and even ashamed of his own natural temper that makes him love such a simple girl, not for a few moments of pleasure, but for eternity.[26]

Resulting from Dierick's failure to return on the appointed day — a motif deriving from *Decameron* IV.8 — Katherina's distrust arises at an earlier stage than Katherine's. Unlike the latter, Katherina undertakes her journey not only to meet her beloved but also, more specifically, to steal Dierick's girdle which contained the lock of hair she had given to him before he left Middelburg. The lock may be seen as a substitute for the ring Katherine gives to Gerard; it is in keeping with the situation, as Katherina cannot afford an expensive present for her lover. Whereas Gerard gives Katherine's ring away, Katherina's fears that Dierick might do the same with her lock are groundless. In the fourth play she succeeds in taking the girdle away from Dierick while he sleeps. In a subtle way, by putting it on her finger and feigning thoughtlessness, Katherine does the same with the ring, while talking with Gerard's mistress. Unlike Katherina, however, Katherine informs Gerard in a leave-taking letter about her visit in disguise, and declares that because he had given it to a third party, the ring, as a pledge, could be no longer considered his. Hence the ring, unlike the girdle, plays no part in the last of Katherine's actions that are paralleled in the *Spiegel*.

Reading the letter Katherine had written before returning to Brabant, Gerard realizes the truth. Devastated by the revelation of his disloyalty, he decides to follow Katherine, only to find her at her wedding-party, where she proudly turns her back on him when he approaches her. She also publicly refuses Gerard's invitation to lead her to the dance, ostentatiously accepting an invitation from another man a few minutes later. Much of this can be compared with events in the *Spiegel*'s fifth play (pp. 141–77). After Dierick's return to Middelburg, the protagonists see each other at a party, albeit only at a distance. To cheer up their son, whose health has deteriorated further since the loss of his girdle, Dierick's parents organize a dancing party in front of their house. Through his bedroom window, Dierick watches Katherina dancing amidst other young lovers. He is shocked to realize that she is wearing his girdle with her lock of hair, which strengthens his belief that she has deceived him with the 'man' who had come to steal the pledge from him. Thinking she has come with the girdle to denounce his failure to return on the appointed date and to demonstrate her engagement to the 'thief', Dierick asks his parents to bring her to him, but Katherina refuses their request. Besides the parallels with *nouvelle* 26, Dierick's perception of Katherina's appearance also seems to be inspired by *nouvelle* 33. Here, too, an expropriated piece of hair is used to reveal infidelity. The story, ascribed to Philip the Good himself, is about a lady who cuts off her hair for one of her two lovers as a proof of her exclusive loyalty. Knowing that she is continuing her double life, the recipient of the pledge gives it to the other man, who then denounces her dishonesty by showing her the hair during a public assembly. Roughly, then, the main plotline of the *Spiegel* is based on three novellas: *Decameron* IV.8 furnishes a frame for *Cent Nouvelles nouvelles* 26, into which *Cent Nouvelles nouvelles* 33 is in turn incorporated.

The prologue to the *Spiegel*'s first play states that, although the story could have been dramatized in two plays, such a short version would lack the 'sweetness' the author wants the audience to taste. Six plays, it claims, are needed for a right and complete unfolding of the love story's 'sin' [meaning] (l. 111) into dramatic action.[27] In the three tales that contribute most to the *Spiegel*'s plot, characters express themselves through direct speech in dialogues. In the plays, of course, this scenic technique, extended with monologues, replaces narrative entirely. Colijn van Rijssele also embellishes his text with fixed-form poems of various kinds, and enriches many emotional soliloquies through virtuoso feats of rhyming.[28] The prologue's reference to 'sin' echoes the genre to which the *Spiegel* belongs: the *spel van sinne* or morality play, an allegorical form that Colijn Caillieu/van Rijssele seems to have been the first to apply to amorous narrative material. It is perhaps this innovation that caused him to be dubbed 'den amorösen Colijn' [the amorous Colijn]. The oldest known example is his play *Van Narcissus ende Echo*, a play of unfulfilled love like the *Spiegel*, with a tragic ending for both protagonists.[29] Explaining the *Spiegel*'s high number of six plays by the need for a dramatic presentation of the story's meaning, Colijn van Rijssele put into practice a principle that Matthijs de Castelein later advocated explicitly in his manual on Dutch versification, *De Const van Rhetoriken* (completed 1548, published 1555): plays should not simply turn stories into rhymed texts. Such simply dramatized narratives are the kind of theatre that is staged by semi-professional actors as a 'camerspel' [play for money]. Rather, a real rhetorician should combine plot with 'conceptien' [conceptions], which means that he should interpret the story by explicating its psychological and social implications and its moral and pedagogical usefulness.[30] The technique of adding 'conceptions' generally involved introducing (usually two) demonic *sinnekens* and other characters, who could influence and comment on the 'historical' actors and actions from a level that is wider in time and space than the narrative facts.[31] So, in the *Spiegel*, four kinds of characters or levels of action can be distinguished: the central story, based on the novellas; the both fierce and funny plotting of (the exceptional number of) three *sinnekens* as representatives of and influences on the protagonists' psychological weaknesses; the planets and astrological figures Saturn, Phoebus, Venus, and Leo, stirring the protagonists' tempers and filling their hearts with love; and the all-embracing frame of the *outer* play, comprising the 'acted' prologues and conclusions that accompany each of the six *inner* plays.

Unlike 'read' prologues (and conclusions), focusing wholly and directly on the audience, 'acted' prologues are performed by figures who mainly address each other.[32] In the *Spiegel* these persons are Jonstighe Sin [Kindly/Favourably

Disposed Mind] and Natuerlijck Ghevoelen [Natural Feeling (i.e. a sense of what is natural)]. In their dialogues a combination of elements from the *Decameron* and the *Cent Nouvelles nouvelles* is also perceptible. The elements derive from the external narrator's preface to the *Decameron*, the introductory observations in *Decameron* IV.8, and the *Cent Nouvelles nouvelles*' dedication to the Duke. Just like Boccaccio's primary narrator, Jonstighe Sin, representing the poet, explains how his artistic project ensues from a personal love-affair, which had not (yet) been successful because of his beloved's higher position. Thanks to the kind consolations of friends, the *Decameron*'s narrator survived the heaviest pains, so much so that his love could abate, turning the former grief into a sweet pleasure. Now, just as conversation with his friends once helped him in his amorous distress, he wants to comfort those who suffer the same, by telling them happy and unhappy love stories and other adventures; and, in particular, to serve and 'seduce' sweet ladies in love. In the *Spiegel*, Jonstighe Sin has a similar comforting and seductive aim. With the play, presenting the sweetness and harshness of love with which he himself is familiar, Jonstighe Sin wants to favour all lovers, but primarily hopes to gain the sympathy of his beloved, despite her lack of responsiveness. In the final prologue he can express his joy at receiving comfort from the compassion that the play has inspired in his beloved. So, thanks to Dierick and Katherina's tragic story, his own grief is turned into sweet pleasure and relief.[33]

In her introduction to *Decameron* IV.8, which provides the *Spiegel*'s frame story, the internal narrator criticizes the conceit of those who think their advice to be better than the counsels of nature. Love, the most natural of all things, she states, follows its own immanent course, ignoring the presumptuous judgments or wishes of others. Jherome's mother tries to expel love from her son's heart — a love presumably sent by the stars — but succeeded only in expelling his soul from his body. The same views on the naturalness of love and the frustrating and fatal effects of short-sighted pride and materialism, dividing what nature wants to unite, are expressed in the *Spiegel*'s prologues and conclusions. Here the poet, Jonstighe Sin, explains that he is depicting the *natural* course of Dierick and Katherina's love, as in a mirror; he is inspired and supported by Natuerlijck Ghevoelen, who represents his own amorous and compassionate feelings, but also those of his beloved and of the young spectators.[34]

Two motifs link the play's prologue with the *Cent Nouvelles nouvelles*. As previously noted, the *nouvelles* are called 'new' in the dedication to the Duke (p. 22), because they are set not in Italy but in different countries, closer to and often within the Burgundian territories; because their contents are of recent date; and because their 'taille et fasson' [style and composition] are 'de myne beaucop nouvelle' [very new in their appearance]. Two of these arguments return in the *Spiegel*'s first prologue: Jonstighe Sin, seeking a suitable narrative, rejects antique subject-matter that lies beyond the reach of our memory, and also prefers something that could have happened 'hier te lande' [here in this country]. Natuerlijck Ghevoelen suggests the story of Katherina and Dierick, which happened only a few years before in Zeeland, in the town of Middelburg (ll. 74–89).[35]

Colijn's 'novelty', though much appreciated by later literary historians, was not imitated by his fellow rhetoricians. Rather, it was his older amorous play *Van Narcissus ende Echo* that set the example; it was followed by plays on Mars and Venus, Pyramus and Thisbe, Leander and Hero, Aeneas and Dido, Jupiter and Io, and others.[36] Novelty was regularly demanded in invitations to rhetoricians' contests, especially in respect of comic drama; but 'old', biblical and classical material was greatly appreciated in serious plays.[37] The Amsterdam rhetorician Egbert Meynderts, for instance, prioritized the lively evocation of the past. For him, the *rederijker*'s highest artistic ambition should be to strengthen people's moral conduct by moving their hearts and minds in showing living characters, who play out old stories in such a way that actions carried out long ago are presented as if they are happening on the spot.[38] Inspired by the *Cent Nouvelles nouvelles* and other *nouvelles*, Colijn van Rijssele did not attempt to bridge the gap between past and present, but created a wholly contemporary, exceptional case with the *Spiegel*.

Cornelis Everaert's *Esbatement van den Visscher*

The *Spiegel* and its two main narrative sources are concerned with a serious and chaste relationship between two young lovers that is hampered by social differences, parents, and the infidelity of one partner or the mutual suspicion of both. In most of the *Cent Nouvelles nouvelles*, however, amorous material is developed quite differently, presenting sexual appetite and/or gratification as characters' initial drive or main concern. Of around seventy amorous stories, a majority of forty-eight involve husbands, wives, priests, monks, or nuns pursuing illicit sex and the tricks they use to conceal their lustful designs or deeds. In some cases, these attempts are countered by duped or unwilling partners who equally use tricks to reveal, prevent, or avenge the acts. The collection is completed by eight *nouvelles* in which sexual naivety or ignorance is mocked (7, 12, 20, 22, 25, 29, 80, 82); eighteen tales of ignorance, bluntness, misunderstanding, or luck in other matters, mainly in the second half of the collection (5, 6, 11, 42, 52, 53, 70, 74, 75, 79, 83, 84, 86, 89, 94, 96, 97, 100); and four serious stories (26, 77, 98, 99). The dynamics of late medieval comic drama being stirred equally by trickeries, misapprehensions, and unforeseen emergences, the *Cent Nouvelles nouvelles* surely contained useful and inspiring matter for rhetoricians writing farces.[39]

Yet, apart from general themes of adultery and lecherous clerics, comparisons between the *Cent Nouvelles nouvelles* and Dutch rhetoricians' farces reveal few common elements.[40] Only in five *nouvelles* have I found some parallel or similarity. *Nouvelle* 27, for instance, relates how a man is trapped in a chest into which he stepped to show his adulterous wife it would be too small to contain her clothes. A similar event occurs in a contrasting context in the Dutch farce *Coster Johannes* [Sexton John], where Johannes wishes to prove that the trap his mistress's husband had set to catch a dog is too wide.[41] *Nouvelle* 29 concerns a bridegroom who, surprised that his wife gives birth during their wedding night, despairs of the huge family for which he will never be able to provide. Comparable is the peasant in the Dutch farce *Een boer en Meester Marten* [A Peasant and Doctor Martin] who, because his wife has a child after only four weeks of marriage, fears he will have to buy twelve cradles a year, or even thirteen if twins are born.[42] Such comic motifs surely led an itinerant life, separate from the fixed and written stories from which we know them. It would, therefore, be going too far to suggest a direct relationship between the *nouvelles* and the plays. The same goes for *nouvelle* 61 and the farce *Lichtekoij* [Light-o'-Love], though their *plots* are clearly related. In both texts, members of a family, scandalized at what a cousin has told them about a female relative's adulterous behaviour, seek revenge by scolding their relative and preparing to kill the lover. When he visits the woman, they lock him up in a bin or chest (in the *nouvelle* and the play respectively), but while they seek reinforcements she finds a key; the lover flees, and she replaces him with a donkey (in the *nouvelle*) or a dog (in the play). Confronted with the animal, the deceived husband decides to live in peace with his wife. Besides the details of the chest and dog, the play deviates from the *nouvelle* only in its social setting (the wife in the play is a poor spinner, the husband in the *nouvelle* a merchant), the type of lover (a priest in the play, a young man in the *nouvelle*), the way the lover is imprisoned (by force, while the husband is absent, in the play; through the husband's deception in the *nouvelle*), and the number of relatives seeking revenge (fewer in the play).[43] The Dutch play clearly presents a version of the same story, but its anonymous author need not have read the *Cent Nouvelles nouvelles*, nor *Dat bedroch der vrouwen* (discussed below) which contains a Dutch translation of *nouvelle* 61.

By contrast, it seems probable that Cornelis Everaert's *Esbatement van den visscher* [Farce of the Fisherman] is based on a personal reading and selection from the *Cent Nouvelles nouvelles*. Everaert (d. 1556) worked in Bruges as a fuller and dyer, and served the city's two chambers of rhetoric, De Heleghe Gheest [The Holy Spirit] and De Drie Santinnen [The Three Female Saints]. Both chambers are mentioned in the final two lines of *Van den Visscher*. The latter survives in the author's autograph manuscript, alongside thirty-four other plays of his; it is undated, though its first editors suggest the approximate dating 1530–31 on the basis of its position in the manuscript, and has been considered one of Everaert's best plays. An English translation appeared in 2012.[44]

In *Van den Visscher* a man and his wife, fishing out at sea, are caught in a storm. Fearing death and damnation, they agree to hear each other's confession in the absence of a priest. The woman speaks first, confessing that their second and third sons were fathered by her servant and her chaplain respectively. Respecting the sacramental character of his wife's declaration, the fisherman keeps his temper and, seeing the storm die down, refrains from confessing himself. Back home, however, he warmly greets the eldest son but curses, scolds, and beats the others. His wife reproaches him for this selectivity; it makes no sense, she maintains, since all three children are his. She then explains the 'real' meaning of what she had said at sea, to reconcile it with this claim. Her husband was her 'servant', as he had served her since their wedding, both sexually and by rowing and steering at sea; he was also her 'chaplain', as he had heard her confession. Wholly convinced, the man accepts his wife's reproaches and asks her forgiveness.

Without further investigation, Muller and Scharpé mention several narratives where a husband acts as his wife's confessor.[45] Only three predate Everaert's play:

the French fabliau *Le Chevalier qui fist sa femme confession*, *Decameron* VII.5, and *Cent Nouvelles nouvelles* 78. Of these, only the latter contains the combination found in the Dutch play: a *true* confession of adultery, and a *false* affirmation of innocence as the wife verbally identifies the lovers with her husband. In the *nouvelle* there are three lovers: a squire, a knight, and a priest. As in the Dutch play (ll. 186–98), it is the wife's adultery with the priest that elicits her husband's greatest anger.

The play deviates from *nouvelle* 78 in three respects: its setting at sea, the reason for the confession and the way the confessor presents himself, and the confession's contents. The second and third points are most important. In *nouvelle* 78 the husband hears his wife's confession disguised as a priest, out of suspicion; in the play the confession involves no deception. Moreover, the play pays significant attention to the children, during and after the confession. Unlike all the other stories mentioned above, the fisherman's wife refers to her adultery only indirectly, by describing her lovers as the fathers of her children. These elements, significantly, appear elsewhere in the *Cent Nouvelles nouvelles*: in *nouvelle* 51, the only other story in the collection where a wife 'confesses' her adultery. In this tale, a woman on her deathbed believes it would be wrong to leave all her children in her husband's charge, since several have other fathers. After sending her husband to doctors and chemists in town, she invites two former lovers and assigns them the children she had by them. As death approaches she confesses her adultery to her husband, explaining which children must be sent to which father after she dies; the husband duly carries out her wishes. In the play it is the fisherman who, ashore after the confession, suggests to his wife that the children be returned to their natural fathers. One by one the sons had come to welcome their 'father', strangely ignoring their mother who survived the storm as well. Maybe this selectivity can also be explained by *nouvelle* 51, where one of the sons runs to meet his 'father' on his return from town. Drawing on *nouvelle* 51, Everaert renounces the theatrical opportunity of the husband's disguise as a priest.[46] Hence the play's comic plot rests wholly on the wife's explanation. To make room for this, the threat of death that provokes the confession must only be temporary; a storm at sea afforded a straightforward solution.

In both *nouvelle* 78 and Everaert's play, the wife deceives and satisfies her husband by a 'rhetorical' performance of words and meanings. According to the *nouvelle*'s narrator, the wife had a 'subtil et percevant engin' [clever and cunning mind] (p. 466); she readily responds to her husband 'comme le saint Esperit l'inspira' [as if inspired by the Holy Spirit] (p. 465). As rhetoricians considered their own art a gift of the Holy Spirit, this formulation may have struck Everaert. His play expresses the power of words to override facts, not only in the wife's explanation of her confession but also, before the storm, by the fantastical way in which the fisherman and his wife describe what they see in the water. They point out to each other a codfish chased by a shrimp, a crab wearing a ray around its neck, an oyster that wants to poke out the eyes of a haddock, and a sole trying to reconcile them (ll. 50–67). The farce's moralizing conclusion also underlines the benefits of using words creatively: it combines pragmatism with irony, stating that it is better to lie and live in peace than to tell the truth and quarrel (ll. 280–81).

Dat bedroch der vrouwen

Though the *Cent Nouvelles nouvelles* was not translated in its entirety, its contents were not wholly inaccessible to the sixteenth-century Dutch reading public. At least eighteen *nouvelles* appear in two thematically related compilations of prose stories. The larger collection, containing twenty-three stories of which eleven are borrowed from the *Cent Nouvelles nouvelles*, is entitled *Dat bedroch der vrouwen* [The Deceit of Women]. It was clearly popular, appearing in several editions, and in an English translation entitled *The Deceyte of Women*. Only one complete copy of the Dutch editions survives: an undated quarto, containing thirty-nine different woodcuts including the printer's mark, printed by Jan Berntsz in Utrecht. Its form and content correspond closely to the reprints that Berntsz produced, from 1532 onwards, of texts initially published by Jan van Doesborch in Antwerp. Hence Van Doesborch is generally regarded as the original compiler, editor, and printer of *Dat bedroch der vrouwen*.[47] This attribution is reinforced by, and also explains, the existence of the English translation. From the beginning of his publishing career, Van Doesborch aimed at the English market by printing translations of Dutch fictional texts. However, no copy of *The Deceyte of Women* printed by Van Doesborch survives; the English text is preserved in London editions printed by William Copland for John Wight and for Abraham Vele, both dating from the late 1550s. The twenty woodcuts in these editions differ from those in Berntsz's *Bedroch*; neither English edition contains the Dutch version's preliminary list of twenty-four misogynistic quotations from biblical, ecclesiastical, and classical authorities, nor its twenty-third and last story, a translation of *Cent Nouvelles nouvelles* 62.[48] The English editions' contents probably reflect Van Doesborch's original ensemble.

The *Bedroch* makes no reference to the origin of the stories taken from the *Cent Nouvelles nouvelles*, which appear largely in the same order as in the Burgundian collection: *nouvelles* 1, 13, 16, 27, 28 (following *nouvelle* 34 in the *Bedroch*), 34, 35, 37 (following *nouvelle* 38 in the *Bedroch*), 38, 61, and 62. Looking for stories illustrating 'the deceitfulness of women', Van Doesborch seems to have stopped his reading of the *Cent Nouvelles nouvelles* around *nouvelle* 61. From this reading, however, he consistently and almost systematically chose the stories in which a woman not only cuckolds her husband (or, in *nouvelle* 28, misleads her female bedmate), but shows a particular creativity in lying to him (and, in *nouvelle* 34, to her lovers as well), or in finding or executing tricks to conquer his mistrust, vigilance, or revenge.[49] Only *nouvelle* 62, the last story in the *Bedroch*, sits uneasily in the series, and indeed with the book's general theme. The woman's deceit in this *nouvelle* is not creatively expressed or underlined by a confrontation with her husband, but by the beguiling of her two lovers, each of whom had believed himself to have no rival; publicly blamed by them both, she is ultimately more deceived by her lovers than her husband was by her.[50] This contrasts notably with the *Bedroch*'s version of *nouvelle* 34. Here the translator secured the woman's success by replacing the original open ending by an additional lie which makes the husband believe his wife's two fleeing lovers are her doctor and surgeon. The *Bedroch*'s version of the story was also versified in a song that survives in the famous *Antwerps liedboek* (1544).[51]

Besides supplying eleven — originally maybe ten — *nouvelles*, the *Cent Nouvelles nouvelles* also affected the *Bedroch*'s general structure and presentation. The titles of all the translated *nouvelles* describe them explicitly as tales of a recent act of deception. The insistence on their newness sharply contrasts them with eleven biblical or classical stories, with which they systematically alternate. In seven of these stories, the title refers explicitly to an ancient act of deception; the titles of the other four mention only the main characters' names, which themselves indicate the antiquity of their subject-matter (Adam and Eve, Lot and his daughters, Jael and Sisera, Judith and Holofernes). The *Bedroch*'s dual presentation surely originates in the dedication of the *Cent Nouvelles nouvelles*, but, in contrast with the latter's programmatic choice of new and recent acts over long-ago affairs, Van Doesborch creates a well-balanced ensemble in which the biblical and classical stories furnish authority and seriousness while the tales of recent events supply novelty and humour. As noted earlier, both thematic components reflect the taste and interests of rhetoricians.

As P. J. A. Franssen has shown, the 'old' stories were mostly recycled from texts that Van Doesborch had previously published.[52] The 'new' stories are fairly close translations of the *nouvelles*, with occasional abridgement and amplification. Abridgements mainly concern the respectability and virtues ironically ascribed to various characters, 'learned' references to literature, detailed descriptions of meals and luxury, and the presence of servants in aristocratic households.[53] The most drastic reduction affects *nouvelle* 27: the entire closing episode, where chattering and giggling maidservants mock their cuckolded master, is skipped.[54] Moreover, the translations omit almost all words and phrases that reveal the narrator's involvement, or suggest a direct communication with readers or listeners: these include affirmations of veracity, such as 'Dieu scet' [God knows]; short cuts, such as 'pour abreger' [to be brief]; and forms of address that attract attention or highlight necessary information, such as 'or devez vous savoir' [now you must know].[55] The direct speech of the characters, on the other hand, is followed fairly closely. Stripped of expressions that establish connections between narrator and audience, the 'new' stories are brought into harmony with the narrative style of the 'old' ones in the *Bedroch*.

With his selection of stories on the deceit of women, Van Doesborch seems to return to the thematic approach of the *Decameron*'s seventh day, when the narrators tell of tricks played by wives on their husbands. Most sixteenth-century readers, however, will have associated the *Bedroch*'s thematic series with actual *rederijker* practices. The creation of a set of texts (or *tableaux vivants*, so-called *punten* on wagons or scaffolds) that present variations on an imposed theme was indeed the main object of the chambers' lyrical and theatrical contests.[56] Of course, the rhetoricians answered the proposed questions in verse, not in prose. Nevertheless, symmetrical reiteration and accumulation being the main structuring techniques in *rederijker* poetry, Van Doesborch's series of twenty-two regularly alternating 'old' and 'new' stories — only the twenty-third, *nouvelle* 62, disturbs the equilibrium — is not devoid of poetic qualities. Within the stories, too, the Dutch translator shows himself a rhetorician in heightening the dramatic and 'rhythmic' aspects of the *nouvelles*' texts. In his rendering of *nouvelle* 1, for instance, the account of a wife's unpleasant welcoming of her husband is turned into a theatrical scene by adding 'ende si sette haer handen in haer zijde' (fol. B4ʳ) (*Deceyte*: 'and she set her hands on her side'), and by the conversion of indirect into lively direct speech.[57] Literary pleasure in the accumulation of words is perceptible in extensions of one word into several. Where the French text of *nouvelle* 13, for instance, only mentions going 'en aucun pelerinage' [on some pilgrimage] (p. 96) as an opportunity for a clerk and his master's wife to leave together, the *Bedroch* turns this into 'als die vrouwe reedt bevaert, oft tot kermissen oft tot jaermercten' (fol. C3ʳ) (*Deceyte*: 'whan that his wife rode out to pilgrimage or to weddings or to any other festes');[58] where in *nouvelle* 38 a single pike is bought for a dinner, the *Bedroch* creates a small still life by mentioning, along with the 'val' [pike], other fish such as 'carpers, braessemen, ende snoecken' (fol. G2ʳ) (*Deceyte*: 'carpes, bremes and pykerel, and other such small fishes').[59] The most impressive poetic extension, however, appears in the Dutch and English versions of *nouvelle* 37. Here the following passionate address — couched in terms that would perfectly suit a *rederijker* amorous *refrein* — is added to a lover's letter:

> O mijn schoon gracious lief mijnder herten confoort, troost mijnder sinnen, mijn leven, mijn vruecht, mijn verblijdinge die mijn herte so starckelic gevangen hebt metten strick uwer liefden, want ghi zijt boven alle vrouwen die graciooste, amoreuste, die volmaectste, daer die nature niet aen vergeten heeft. (fol. J2ᵛ)

> [O my most fairest and gracious lover and comfort of my heart, the hope of my intent and mynde, the whyche hath so strongly caught my heart in the snare of your love, for ye be among all women the most gracious the most comliest and one that nature hath not forgotten.] (*Deceyte*)[60]

The lovers' encounter, mentioned in the *nouvelle* only as 'ilz se deviserent' [they conversed] (p. 260), is subsequently amplified and poeticized as:

> Ende [...] ginc [...] bi haer soete lief daerse minlijc ontfangen was met minlike cuskens zeer amoreuslijck malcanderen omhelsende, daer lief by lief zeer lieflijc van haer liefde langen tijt spraken. (fol. J3ʳ)

> [And [...] went [...] to her swete hert, of the whiche she was lovingly receyved, and kissed her sweetly, and lovingly embraced eche other and there was love by love, and there love spake to love a longe tyme together.] (*Deceyte*)[61]

As for its 'meaning', the *Bedroch*'s moral message is rather complex. There is some similarity with opinions expressed during the *Decameron*'s seventh day, where Emilia tells her female listeners that the deceit she will recount may prove useful to them; Filostrato, for his part, points out the usefulness of stories that make men aware of women's deceit; and all narrators and listeners appear to side more with the wives and lovers in the stories than with the cuckolded husbands, especially those haunted by jealousy. All these elements appear in some form in the *Bedroch*. Men and women are urged at the outset to learn from the book, the former to know the deceit of women, the latter to know how to practise ingenious trickery.[62] The tolerance for sex and sympathy for adulterous lovers, also apparent in the selected *nouvelles*, are retained and occasionally amplified in the translations.[63] Particularly noteworthy is the twentieth story, *nouvelle* 37, in the *Bedroch*, where the husband is dismissed from the outset by being described as 'jalours' [jealous] (fol. J1ʳ) in the title.⁶⁴ In the *Bedroch* — but not in the *Deceyte* — this story is followed by a note claiming that it resembles what happened to a Lombard and a merchant's wife 'int corte zuytwerck' [in the short southern bulwark, i.e. in Southwark] (fol. J3ʳ) in London. The remark shows Van Doesborch's familiarity with the literary caricature of the bad, old, jealous husband; it may be interpreted, I would suggest, as a distorted echo of Chaucer's *Merchant's Tale*, of the Lombard knight Januarie and his wife May, told in Southwark's Tabbard Inn.⁶⁵

However, despite some similarities with the *Decameron*'s seventh day, the combination of the *nouvelles* with 'old' stories, within a specific moral frame, makes the *Bedroch* function in a different way. The contrast is expressed most clearly by the difference between Filostrato's and Van Doesborch's views of the usefulness of telling stories of women's deceit. Both are concerned with the importance of making men alert, but their starting points and aims are diametrically opposed. Filostrato basically assumes that men, particularly husbands, are inclined to play tricks on women. Consequently, stories of the reverse process may be very effective in restraining them from cozening their wives. Van Doesborch's perspective, by contrast, is rather one-sided. The *Bedroch* seeks to teach men to beware of women's deceitfulness. Whatever the moral underpinning of the tales — in the 'old' stories, for instance, God helped Judith to seduce and kill Holofernes by making her more attractive — they all position men as victims of women. For most *nouvelles* this entails a shift of perspective, comparable with the technique used in rhetoricians' theatre, switching from a central action to external comments and moral 'meanings'. As women have beguiled even the wisest and most powerful men, the surest means of protection is said to be total avoidance of their company. At the same time, however, the *Bedroch* maintains there can be no delectable conversation without a woman, the sight of her beautiful face being the most cheering thing for a man (fol. K4ʳ). The basic belief that virtuous women do exist offers a way out of the dilemma; therefore cautious men must not give up their hopes of a harmonious and peaceful marriage (fols A1ᵛ, B1ʳ, B2ʳ⁻ᵛ, D2ᵛ, H4ʳ, K4ʳ).⁶⁶ The *Bedroch*'s introductory list of quotations, however, has a very different effect: it foregrounds not women's conscious deceit, but fear, asceticism, and demonization of female beauty (fols A2ʳ–B1ʳ). The list reflects the tenor of Jan Berntsz's pious and ecclesiastical publications; it may well have been absent, as it is in the *Deceyte*, from Van Doesborch's edition(s) and added only by the later publisher, along with *nouvelle* 62 (fols K2ʳ–K4ʳ), borrowed at that point from the *Cent Nouvelles nouvelles* as the first *nouvelle* following the last story originally selected, in an ill-conceived attempt to fill up the book's final gathering.⁶⁷

Die ontrouwe der mannen

Towards the evening of the seventh day, to avoid giving the impression of taking revenge, the 'queen' of the next narrative session in the *Decameron* decides that her theme should not be solely the tricks that men play on their wives, but also those that women play on men and men play on one another. Hence only four of the tales told on the eighth day involve men deceiving women. No such fear of criticism seems to have troubled the compiler of a Dutch narrative collection, printed in 1543 by Marten Nuyts in Antwerp, which can be regarded as a reaction or counterpart to the *Bedroch*. Its introduction claims that the book will cover various men who were untrue to their promises; this is indeed what the eleven stories relate. The book must have contained a few more stories, but its only surviving copy lacks one gathering and three further leaves, including the first. In the absence of a title-page, scholars have proposed diverse titles; by analogy with *Dat bedroch der vrouwen*, I suggest *Die ontrouwe der mannen* [The Disloyalty of Men], as *ontrouwe* [disloyalty, infidelity] appears in the titles of all but the last of its stories, just as *bedriegen* or *bedroch* [to deceive/deceit] appears in the title of each story in the *Bedroch*.[68]

Franssen has identified the three 'old' stories in the *Ontrouwe* as deriving from books published by Van Doesborch. Because of this and the book's thematic relation with the *Bedroch*, Van Doesborch is also considered to be the *Ontrouwe*'s compiler and first printer.[69] Yet, unlike the *Bedroch*, the tales in the *Ontrouwe* are not entitled explicitly as 'old' or 'new', and only the final six present a regular alternation of one 'old' story with two 'new' ones. The general structure thus seems to elude the rhetoricians' passion for symmetry. Eight of the surviving stories are 'new'; the three 'old' narratives are respectively classical, biblical, and medieval in origin. Apart from one, which shows some verbal resemblances with *Decameron* VIII.2, the 'new' stories are drawn, without acknowledgement, from the *Cent Nouvelles nouvelles*.[70] They are presented in their original order, apart from the first and second in the sequence: they are *nouvelles* 9, 14, 18, 26, 39, 67, and 68 (*nouvelles* 26 and 14 are the first and second 'new' stories in the *Ontrouwe*).

Again, as in the *Bedroch*, the *Ontrouwe* offers a representative choice of *nouvelles*, in this case of stories in which women suffer from a man's disloyalty or abuse of confidence. The main topic is not male adultery, but dishonesty *within* an amorous relationship (adulterous in *nouvelles* 9, 39, and 67; the betrayal of a secret sexual encounter; or, in *nouvelle* 68, a husband's unfair treatment of his adulterous wife. Just like Colijn van Rijssele, the compiler seems to have been charmed by *nouvelle* 26. Although the translation leaves the young lady nameless, it is placed ahead of *nouvelles* 9, 14, and 18 as the first 'nouvelle' to follow the initial, classical story of Jason (fol. C1^r); the introduction seems to allude specifically to this first 'new' story, by mentioning men who are disloyal even though they are steadfastly loved by beautiful *rich* girls ('schoone rijcke lievekens', fol. A2^r). Unfortunately the end of the story, which may have been followed by interpretative remarks, is lost with the rest of gathering D.

The abridgements in the translation, as in the *Bedroch*, involve aristocratic preoccupations (nothing is said in the translation of *nouvelle* 26 about Gerard's interest in hunting), the luxury of meals, clothes, hotels, or the availability of servants, horses, or artillery (*nouvelles* 9, 18, 26). Military metaphors for sexual activities (*nouvelles* 9, 18) are removed.[71] Again as in the *Bedroch*, formulations expressing the narrator's involvement with his story or audience are omitted.[72] As for additions and amplifications, the translation of *nouvelle* 9 evinces the most creativity. A walk outside, during which a nobleman agrees with his friend to share the sexual services of the housemaid, is introduced (fol. E4^r); and the narrative is dramatized to a greater extent, with four passages of direct speech increased to ten. Investment in verbal creativity is reflected by the coinage 'pausmaker' [popemaker], used twice in the translation of *nouvelle* 14, which tells of a hermit who deceives a devout woman into believing her daughter is elected to beget his child, who is to become a pope (fol. E2^{r-v}); by the introduction of proverbs into *nouvelles* 9, 18, 39, and 67 (fols E3^v, F4^r, G2^r, H2^r); and by the extension of a list of five means of seduction in *nouvelle* 67 (p. 414) to seven (fol. H1^v).

In moral terms, the most important change of perspective, effected by a combination of omission and addition, appears at the end of *nouvelle* 18. The story concerns a Burgundian nobleman who, lodging in Paris, refuses to leave the room of a chambermaid he has pursued and slept with, even after she returns the money she had previously asked of him. Despairing of being detected by her master and his wife, she finally carries him out on her shoulders. As they pass her master's chamber, however, the nobleman wakes the host and his wife by breaking wind loudly. Reprimanded, betrayed, and humiliated, the girl leaves the household soon afterwards. In the last sentence of the *nouvelle* we are told that the guest returns to Burgundy, and 'joyeusement' [gleefully] (p. 125) recounts the episode to his companions. In the Dutch translation this light-hearted ending is replaced by a sentence evoking pathos through enumeration: 'Siet wat grooter ontrouwe ghebuerde dit schamel meysken, want si hadde voor haren arbeyt spotten, gecken, schade, grote schande, ende oneere' [See what great disloyalty befell this poor little girl, for in return for her efforts she was mocked, derided, disadvantaged, greatly shamed, and dishonoured] (fol. G1^v).

Thanks to the compiler's pragmatic concern with the vulnerable position of girls in love and female lovers in adulterous relations, the book's general tone is near to that of the *Decameron* and the *Cent Nouvelles nouvelles*, both of which are tolerant of love and sex. This spirit does not exclude moral or religious considerations, but these do not predominate, as is shown by the warning that follows the final story and thereby serves as the last word on the matter. Here, women who cheat on their husbands are urged to act carefully and with complete secrecy if their husband is cruel. If their husband is henpecked, however, there is no need to take major precautions; but it is best to fear God and obey his commandments (fol. H4^r).[73]

Jan Fruytiers's *refrein*

Interest in the *Cent Nouvelles nouvelles* as a collection appears to diminish after 1540. No editions were printed in the remainder of the sixteenth century. Yet, while the *nouvelles*' narrative style, prolixity, and vocabulary seem to have fallen from favour, the stories themselves did not lose their attractiveness. From 1549 onwards, many of the stories were included, in shortened and lexically updated versions, in compilations such as *Les Fascetieux Devitz des cent nouvelles nouvelles*, *Les Joyeuses Adventures et plaisant facetieux deviz*, and the *Recueil des plaisantes et facétieuses nouvelles* (which was also printed in Antwerp, by Gerard Spelman in 1555). A similar fate befell Premierfait's translation of the *Decameron*.[74] Yet history seems to repeat itself: a new French translation of the *Decameron*, by Antoine Le Maçon, appeared in 1545.[75] The book was dedicated to Marguerite de Navarre, who herself contributed significantly to the francophone short story tradition with her posthumously published collection *L'Heptaméron* (1559).

In July 1561 a *rederijker* contest was organized in Rotterdam, where the most important chambers in Holland could compete in serious and comic drama, and in the three categories — *in 't vroede* (moralizing, didactic, or religious poems), *in 't amoureus* (love poems), and *in 't sot* (comic or satirical poems) — of their main lyric genre, the *refrein*. The texts of the plays and poems were printed in 1564 by Willem Silvius in Antwerp. The only *refrein* category without an imposed theme was the *refrein in 't sot*; this freedom was exploited by Jan Fruytiers, the leading poet of the three-strong delegation from Rijnsburg near Leiden, each of whom presented a poem that told a story borrowed from a French *nouvelle*. While his colleagues selected *nouvelles* 5 and 38 from the recently-published *Heptaméron*, Fruytiers himself chose *nouvelle* 30 from the *Cent Nouvelles nouvelles*.[76]

Turning a novella into a *refrein* was not self-evident: narrative and lyric forms are not natural partners. The formal structure of the *refrein*, the *rederijker* variant of the French *ballade* with its recurring refrain, favours the composition of contemplative or exhortative texts, enumerative surveys, dramatic monologues, or dialogues comprising a single scene. Of the three competitive categories, the *refrein in 't sot* was certainly the most receptive to descriptions of short and simple processes, such as a sexual encounter or a grotesque event (for instance a poor and filthy wedding, or a farting contest between nuns). However, these scenes rarely form part of a sequence of events. In a corpus of 319 fifteenth- and sixteenth-century *refreinen in 't sot*, only six can be said to tell a story that leads its actors into different situations. One of these is Fruytiers's *refrein*.[77]

Rijnsburg's unique presentation of three versified novellas doubtless reflects the same eccentric approach that would later make Fruytiers exploit the genre of the song to its limits. In 1565 he published his *Ecclesiasticus*, comprising the complete book of Jesus Sirach's biblical proverbs in song form; he then began recasting all the Pauline epistles as songs, but completed only Romans before his death. It is hardly surprising that such a poet, who has been described as miscalculating the possibilities of the lyric, should have chosen a rather challenging *nouvelle* to convert into a *refrein*.[78] In any case, he needed five stanzas of seventeen lines, rather than the four stanzas of thirteen or fifteen lines (and one with sixteen) used in the other Rotterdam *refreinen in 't sot*.[79] I have examined elsewhere the way in which Fruytiers forced the story into the form of the *refrein*; here I shall focus on the peculiarity of his choice.[80]

Alexandra Velissariou has characterized *nouvelles* 30 and 60 as culminations of the adulterous triangles that account for a third of the hundred tales. Each presents three husbands, three wives, and three lovers. In *nouvelle* 30 three merchants and their wives decide, during a pilgrimage, to abstain from sex and sleep in different rooms; at one of their stopping places, three friars gain access to the women's room and take their husbands' places. In *nouvelle* 60 three married women, disguised as monks, regularly meet their clerical lovers in a monastery.[81] Three lascivious monks being better than one, both stories may have exerted a greater attraction on the reformist satirist Fruytiers — who declared himself a firm Calvinist — than other stories of clerics' sexual activities. Of the two, he understandably preferred *nouvelle* 30, where the blame for the adultery can be attached exclusively to the friars (whom the wives believe to be their husbands, who seem to have acquired an extraordinary new virility), and where the folly of vows and pilgrimages is revealed. Nevertheless, satire on monks was prohibited in the Netherlands by an edict of 1560, which forbade rhetoricians from disseminating songs, plays, or poems dealing with 'onse religie ofte gheestelicke luyden, 't zy aengaende heure persoonen oft staten' [our religion or clerics, whether as individuals or as an estate].[82] Fruytiers's provocative stance is apparent in his use of the very word *staat* [estate]: he describes the monks as 'drije wiens staet v hier sal zijn versweghen' [three of whom the estate will not be spoken of here] (l. 5), and subsequently refers to them as the 'onghenoemde' [non-mentioned] (ll. 26, 36). Most likely this ostentatious concealment raised questions in Rotterdam among Fruytiers's fellow rhetoricians, which may have been answered with reference to the original *nouvelle*.

Another issue in Rotterdam may have been the *refrein*'s very unusual number of five stanzas.[83] Here, a closer reading of the text makes clear that this number enabled Fruytiers to fit the story into a remarkable symmetrical structure. For the *stok* or *(stok)regel*, i.e. the refrain ending each stanza, he chose the proverb 'want tis te laet gheclaecht als een dinck ghedaen is' [for it is too late to complain when something has been done]. The line is successively put as direct speech into the mouth of a member of each of the three trios that are involved in the tale. This is done in such a way — the *stok* being pronounced by a husband in the first and fifth stanza; by a wife in the second and fourth stanza; and by an 'onghenoemde' in the third and 'central' stanza — that the text presents not only a funny story, wrapped in a *refrein*, but also a pleasing chiasmus, to be recognized and appreciated by *rederijker* connoisseurs.

Conclusion

No clarion call or triumphal entry welcomed the Burgundian *Cent Nouvelles nouvelles* into fifteenth- and sixteenth-century Dutch literature. The collection was not translated in its entirety, and authors who made use of it made no reference to their source. The Multilingual Muse worked in silence here. A few talented individuals — it is not mere chance we know their names: Colijn van Rijssele, Cornelis Everaert, Jan van Doesborch, and Jan Fruytiers — picked out their cherries from the big cake, integrating particular *nouvelles* with their own *rederijker* genres or editorial practices. The interplay of dependence and empowerment made Colijn van Rijssele and Fruytiers — the first and last authors in this chronological survey — write texts that take a unique or eccentric position towards the dominant thematic patterns of the genres involved. Colijn van Rijssele used the plots of two *nouvelles* and *Decameron* IV.8 as the basis for six *spelen van zinne*, which together present a drama that, with its formal complexity and verbal richness, will have been looked upon by many rhetoricians, including the author himself, as a work of art with which the novella as a simple story in prose could hardly be compared. Fruytiers, for his part, succeeded brilliantly in fitting a rather complex narrative into the tight form of a *refrein*. The three main *rederijker* genres are completed by Everaert's *esbatement*, a comic play in which the *Cent Nouvelles nouvelles* and rhetoricians' interest in ready wit and verbal tricks are effectively combined. Finally, albeit in prose rather than verse, rhetoricians' interests in thematic variation, classical and biblical material, theatre, and lyrical flows of words made Van Doesborch's translations of selected *nouvelles* into a constitutive part of genuine compilations whose structure, function, and character differ markedly from the Burgundian collection. To conclude with another metaphor: leaving their aristocratic home, some *Nouvelles nouvelles* met and married Dutch *rederijker* literature, the latter proving to be a self-assured partner, if not the stronger.

Notes to Chapter 6

1. A survey of the manuscripts of Laurent de Premierfait's translations of *De casibus* (version 1400 and version 1409) and the *Decameron* is available on the *Archives de littérature du Moyen Âge* (ARLIMA) website, <http://www.arlima.net/il/laurent_de_premierfait.html> [accessed 12 April 2017]. On Premierfait's translations of both works, see various studies in *Un traducteur et un humaniste de l'époque de Charles V, Laurent de Premierfait*, ed. by Carla Bozzolo (Paris: Publications de la Sorbonne, 2004): Carla Bozzolo, 'Introduction à la vie et à l'oeuvre d'un humaniste', pp. 17–30 (pp. 22–23); Carla Bozzolo, 'La Conception du pouvoir chez Laurent de Premierfait', pp. 53–68 (p. 59); and Anne D. Hedeman, 'Visual Translation: Illustrating Laurent de Premierfait's French Versions of Boccaccio's *De casibus*', pp. 83–113 (pp. 90–91). A manuscript of the *Decameron* translation (BnF, MS fr. 129), and a copy of an edition by Anthoine Vérard (*Des cent nouvelles*, USTC 61164), are accessible via the *Gallica* resource of the Bibliothèque nationale de France, <http://gallica.bnf.fr/ark:/12148/btv1b9009540b.r=cent%20nouvelles?rk=42918;4> and <http://gallica.bnf.fr/ark:/12148/btv1b73000330.r=premierfait%20verard?rk=42918;4> [accessed 11 April 2017] respectively.
2. The dedication is cited from *Les Cent Nouvelles nouvelles*, ed. by Franklin P. Sweetser (Geneva: Droz, 1966), p. 22. Subsequent references are to this edition (referred to as Sweetser), and are provided in the text.
3. Alexandra Velissariou, *Aspects dramatiques et écriture de l'oralité dans les 'Cent Nouvelles nouvelles'* (Paris: Honoré Champion, 2012), pp. 12, 14–16 ('author'), 27–29 (date).
4. Sweetser, pp. 648–49, lists the narrators and the stories they tell. Biographical information is supplied in *Les Cent Nouvelles nouvelles*, ed. by Pierre Champion (Paris: Droz, 1928), pp. ix–l.
5. See especially *nouvelles* 8 (Brussels), 10 and 19 (England), 14 (Burgundy), 20 (Champagne), 78 and 90 (Brabant).
6. See *Les Cent Nouvelles nouvelles*, ed. by Champion, p. lxix.
7. See also the various metadiscursive comments by the narrators of *nouvelles* 1, 5, 9, 10, 12, 24, 27, 28, 37, 40, 45, 57, 72, 81, 84, 85, 88, 90, 93, and 100; and Peter Koj, *Die frühe Rezeption der Fazetien Poggios in Frankreich* (Hamburg: Universität, Romanisches Seminar, 1969), pp. 66–73.
8. Velissariou, *Aspects dramatiques et écriture de l'oralité dans les 'Cent Nouvelles nouvelles'*, pp. 51–75.
9. Caillieu, *Dal sonder wederkeeren of pas der doot*, ed. by De Keyser; Michault, *Doctrinael des tijts*, ed. by Schuijt, pp. 40–55; Pertcheval, *Den camp vander doot*, ed. by Degroote; Gilbert Degroote, 'Diets-Bourgondische letteren te Brussel', *Dietsche Warande en Belfort*, 97 (1952), 402–21 (pp.

412–20); Michault, *Van den drie blinde danssen*, ed. by Schuijt, p. xxxv; Wilma Keesman, 'Troje in de middeleeuwse literatuur: Antiek verleden in dienst van eigen tijd', *Literatuur*, 4 (1987), 257–65 (pp. 262–63); Keesman, 'Jacob Bellaert en Haarlem'; Brinkman, 'De weerklank van de Bourgondische hofliteratuur in het Middelnederlands', pp. 127–30; Rineke Nieuwstraten, 'Vervaardigers en bezitters van Raoul Lefèvre's *Histoire de Jason*: Kanalen voor de verbreiding van een idee', *Millennium: Tijdschrift voor middeleeuwse geschiedenis*, 8 (1994), 134–47; Saskia Raue, 'Een nauwsluitend keurs: Aard en betekenis van *Den triumphe ende 't palleersel van den vrouwen* (1514)' (unpublished doctoral thesis, University of Amsterdam, 1996); Dirk Coigneau, 'Per haute-couture ten dodendans', *Queeste*, 4 (1997), 84–93; Sutch, 'De Gouda-editie van *Le Chevalier délibéré*', pp. 137–55; Jongenelen, 'Pieter Willemsz' vertaling van *Le chevalier délibéré*'. Shortened versions of the Dutch translations of both Lefèvre's works, edited between 1483 and 1485 by Jacob Bellaert in Haarlem, were printed in 1521 by Jan van Doesborch in Antwerp (USTC 410164). Van Doesborch also published Colijn Caillieu's translation of Montgesoie's *Le Pas de la mort* in 1528 [USTC 437415]: Peter J. A. Franssen, *Tussen tekst en publiek: Jan van Doesborch, drukker-uitgever en literator te Antwerpen en Utrecht in de eerste helft van de zestiende eeuw* (Amsterdam: Rodopi, 1990), pp. 74, 78–79, 127–29, 133–34, 224–25.

10. Besides the courtly works noted above, the 'penetration' of which was rather limited in time and space (Brinkman, 'De weerklank van de Bourgondische hofliteratuur in het Middelnederlands', pp. 130–32), there is a more general interest in crusading narratives, devoted to chivalric figures such as Godefroi de Bouillon, Gillion de Trazegnies, Olivier de Castille, Saladin, and Jean de Ponthieu. Cf. *Splendeurs de la cour de Bourgogne: récits et chroniques*, ed. by Danielle Régnier-Bohler (Paris: Robert Laffont, 1995), pp. xv–xxix, 111–13, 251–53, 371–74; Luc Debaene, *De Nederlandse volksboeken: Ontstaan en geschiedenis van de Nederlandse prozaromans gedrukt tussen 1475 en 1540* (Antwerp: De Vlijt, 1951), pp. 74–81, 125–33, 221–22, 228–29, 249, 263; Franssen, *Tussen tekst en publiek*, pp. 44–47, 60–61; Erwin Mantingh, '"... twelke al gheviel int Spel van Strasengijs": Naar aanleiding van een ongekend drama in Oudenaarde anno 1373', *Queeste*, 7 (2000), 38–50; Diewke E. van der Poel, 'De voorstelling is voorbij: Vermeldingen van wereldlijk toneel en de casus van *Strasengijs*', in *Spel en spektakel: Middeleeuws toneel in de Lage Landen*, ed. by Hans van Dijk and others (Amsterdam: Prometheus, 2001), pp. 111–32 (pp. 125–32); Werner Waterschoot, 'Arend de Keysere: Een voorzichtig experimentator', in *Geschreven en gedrukt*, ed. by Pleij and Reynaert, pp. 119–35 (pp. 123–25).
11. Velissariou, *Aspects dramatiques et écriture de l'oralité dans les 'Cent Nouvelles nouvelles'*, pp. 54–56.
12. Colijn van Rijssele, *De spiegel der minnen*, ed. by Immink, pp. xix–lxxv, 218–21. Subsequent references are to this edition (hereafter referred to as Van Rijssele), and are provided in the text.
13. J. Pop, *De spiegel der minnen* (Leiden: Spruyt, Van Mantgem & De Does, 1987), pp. 28–42.
14. Marc Boone, Thérèse de Hemptinne, and Walter Prevenier, 'Fictie en historische realiteit: Colijn van Rijsseles *De spiegel der minnen*, ook een spiegel van sociale spanningen in de Nederlanden der late middeleeuwen?', *Jaarboek De Fonteine*, 34 (1984), 9–33 (pp. 13–18). *Nouvelle* 26 (Sweetser, pp. 163–81) is the only story narrated by 'Monseigneur de Foquessoles, escuier de la chambre de Monseigneur' (p. 163) [Monseigneur de Foquessoles, squire of the Duke's chamber]; see *Les Cent Nouvelles nouvelles*, ed. by Champion, p. xxxvi.
15. J. E. van Gijsen, *Liefde, kosmos en verbeelding: Mens- en wereldbeeld in Colijn van Rijsseles 'Spiegel der minnen'* (Groningen: Wolters-Noordhoff/Forsten, 1989), pp. 43–45, 251–52.
16. Van Gijsen, *Liefde, kosmos en verbeelding*, pp. 37–41, 242–47. See also Annelies van Gijsen, 'Katherina Sheermertens, Margarieta van Lymborch, and Margaret of Austria: Literary and Historical Backgrounds in Colijn van Rijssele's *Spiegel der minnen*', *Publications du Centre européen d'études bourguignonnes (XIVe–XVIe s.)*, 31 (1991), 165–74 (pp. 170–74).
17. Paris, Bibliothèque de l'Arsenal, MS 5070 (*Le Livre appellée Decameron*), fol. 172^v; see also 'par excessive amour il mouru' [he died of a surfeit of love] (MS 5070, fol. 170^r); and Van Rijssele, ll. 2306–50, 4129–47. An interesting parallel may be drawn between Jherome's death, resulting from the real presence of Silvestre's husband in bed, and Dierick's fainting while visualizing Katherina making love with another man (Van Rijssele, ll. 4702–27).
18. Paris, Bibliothèque de l'Arsenal, MS 5070, fol. 170^r; and Van Rijssele, ll. 226–35, 248–54, 349–57.

19. In *nouvelle* 26 this is especially clear in the narrator's introduction. For the *Spiegel*, see ll. 101–04, 131, 2166–76, 4005–11, 4157–61.
20. Van Gijsen, *Liefde, kosmos en verbeelding*, pp. 45–46, 252.
21. Ibid., pp. 13–21; see also Sutch, 'Dichters van de stad: De Brusselse rederijkers en hun verhouding tot de Franstalige hofliteratuur en het geleerde humanisme (1475–1522)', pp. 142–46; and Dirk Coigneau, 'Van de *Bliscappen* tot Cammaert: Vier eeuwen toneelliteratuur in Brussel', in *De macht van het schone woord: Literatuur in Brussel van de 14de tot de 18de eeuw*, ed. by Jozef Janssens and Remco Sleiderink (Louvain: Davidsfonds/Literair, 2003), pp. 213–33 (pp. 217–23).
22. See note 8 above, and Mareel, *Voor vorst en stad*, pp. 156–65. Colijn van Rijssele also knew Michault Taillevent's *Debat du cuer et de l'ueil*: Van Gijsen, *Liefde, kosmos en verbeelding*, pp. 16, 45–46, 229; Annelies van Gijsen, 'De tussenspelen uit de twee *Handels der Amo(u)reusheyt*', in *Spel in de verte: Tekst, structuur en opvoeringspraktijk van het rederijkerstoneel*, ed. by B. A. M. Ramakers (Ghent: De Fonteine, 1994), pp. 59–86 (pp. 77–82).
23. Ninety-seven of the hundred *nouvelles* take up fewer than twelve pages in Sweetser's edition (fifty-three of these comprise five pages or fewer). *Nouvelle* 33, briefly discussed below, occupies fourteen pages; *nouvelles* 26 and 99 comprise nineteen and twenty-five pages respectively. *Nouvelle* 99 is a version of the famous pseudo-Petrarchan *Historia Aroni et Marinae*, an exemplum of conjugal fidelity; it is reduced to around two-thirds of its original length in Vérard's edition (USTC 61164, fols D6^v–E4^v) (Velissariou, *Aspects dramatiques et écriture de l'oralité dans les 'Cent Nouvelles nouvelles'*, pp. 48, 56). Its Dutch version, *Teghen die strael der minnen* (USTC 435703), printed about 1484, is adapted from a Latin text which may have been the original *nouvelle*'s model: *Twee uit het Latijn vertaalde Middelnederlandse novellen*, ed. by R. Pennink (Zwolle: Tjeenk Willink, 1965), pp. 9, 11–16, 29–30. The relation is misrepresented by Braekman, who maintains the Dutch text is based on *nouvelle* 99: *Dat bedroch der vrouwen*, ed. by W. L. Braekman (Bruges: Marc Van de Wiele, 1983), p. 8. Subsequent references are to this edition (referred to as Braekman), and are provided in the text.
24. Further examples among the first forty *nouvelles* include pp. 30, 37, 72, 78, 104, 114, 125, 154, 182, 190, 191, 206, 207, 227, 240, 241, 246, 272, and 277.
25. Van Rijssele, ll. 1188–1203 (esp. 1196–99), 1256–61, 1351–1411 (esp. 1396–99).
26. See Dirk Coigneau, 'Liefde en lichaamsbeleving op het rederijkerstoneel', *Jaarboek De Fonteine*, 34 (1984), 115–32 (pp. 124–26). On class-consciousness in the *Spiegel*, see Boone, De Hemptinne, and Prevenier, 'Fictie en historische realiteit', p. 27; Van Gijsen, *Liefde, kosmos en verbeelding*, pp. 131–32, 135–45; Annelies van Gijsen, 'Love and Marriage: Fictional Perspectives', in *Showing Status: Representation of Social Positions in the Late Middle Ages*, ed. by Wim Blockmans and Antheun Janse (Turnhout: Brepols, 1999), pp. 227–63 (pp. 257–61).
27. I read 'den sin [...] beweghen' (l. 111) as 'lead/direct the story's sense'. Van Gijsen, by contrast, suggests 'move the spectator's mind': Van Gijsen, *Liefde, kosmos en verbeelding*, pp. 173–76.
28. Van Gijsen, *Liefde, kosmos en verbeelding*, pp. 24–25, 200–01; Dirk Coigneau, 'Strofische vormen in het rederijkerstoneel', in *Spel in de verte*, ed. by Ramakers, pp. 17–44 (pp. 20–22).
29. 'Den amorösen Colijn' figures in the sixteenth-century manuscript of *Van Narcissus ende Echo* (Ghent, Universiteitsbibliotheek, HS 900); Annelies van Gijsen, 'De amoureuze spelen: De herschepping van klassieke stof op het rederijkerstoneel', in *Spel en spektakel*, ed. by Van Dijk and others, pp. 215–27 (pp. 217, 220–23); Coigneau, 'Van de *Bliscappen* tot Cammaert', pp. 217–23; Anke van Herk, *Fabels van liefde: Het mythologisch-amoureuze toneel van de rederijkers (1475–1621)* (Amsterdam: Amsterdam University Press, 2012), pp. 18–19, 41–44.
30. Matthijs de Castelein, *De const van rhetoriken* (Ghent: Jan Cauweel, 1555; USTC 400939), p. 21; Dirk Coigneau, 'Drama in druk, tot circa 1540', in *Spel en spektakel*, ed. by Van Dijk and others, pp. 201–14 (p. 205); Herk, *Fabels van liefde*, pp. 64–65.
31. On the rhetoricians' technique of framing and shifting perspectives, see W. M. H. Hummelen, 'The Dramatic Structure of the Dutch Morality', *Dutch Crossing*, 22 (1984), 17–26, and 'The Boundaries of the Rhetoricians' Stage', *Comparative Drama*, 28 (1994), 235–51; Herk, *Fabels van liefde*, pp. 61–83.
32. On the distinction between 'read' and 'acted' prologues, see Hummelen, 'The Boundaries of the Rhetoricians' Stage', pp. 239–40.

33. Van Rijssele, ll. 10–13, 22–37, 56, 66–69, 107–10, 120–21; ll. 1109–16, 1142–57 (l. 1154: 'Al minne ick lacen mijn overhoot' [Though, alas, I love my superior]), 1179–87; ll. 2127–32, 2137–42; ll. 3092–3103, 3144–45, 3150–51; ll. 3968–69, 4025–32, 4077–85; ll. 5035–73, 5119–23; ll. 6108–19, 6148–49, 6158–69.
34. Van Rijssele, ll. 38–41, 49, 66–69 (the natural course of love), 99–104, 117–19; ll. 1097–1104, 1111–13, 1142–45, 1155–57, 1164–65; ll. 2120–21, 2135–53 (the play as the mirror of natural love), 2197–98; ll. 3120–21; ll. 3963–67, 3994–97, 4025–32, 4077–80, 4090–92; ll. 5026–31; ll. 6131–49 ('goods' as the devil, dividing lovers), 6161–68. Van Gijsen interprets 'natuerlijck ghevoelen' in an exclusively poetic sense, as the poet's inborn nature: *Liefde, kosmos en verbeelding*, p. 165; 'Katherina Sheermertens, Margarieta van Lymborch, and Margaret of Austria', p. 167.
35. The first and final sentences of *Cent Nouvelles nouvelles* 26 point out that the story happened recently, in Brabant: Sweetser, pp. 163, 181.
36. Van Gijsen, 'De amoureuze spelen', pp. 216–23; Herk, *Fabels van liefde*, pp. 12–58.
37. Dirk Coigneau, 'Bedongen creativiteit: Over retoricale productieregeling' , in *Medioneerlandistiek: Een inleiding tot de Middelnederlandse letterkunde*, ed. by Ria Jansen-Sieben, Jozef Janssens, and Frank Willaert (Hilversum: Verloren, 2000), pp. 129–37 (p. 131).
38. Moser, *De strijd voor rhetorica*, p. 260 (ll. 44–49).
39. See Bernadette Rey-Flaud, *La Farce ou la machine à rire, théorie d'un genre dramatique 1450–1550* (Geneva: Droz, 1984), pp. 237–44.
40. Femke Kramer, *Mooi vies, knap lelijk: Grotesk realisme in rederijkerskluchten* (Hilversum: Verloren, 2009), pp. 267–303, surveys seventy-seven rhetoricians' farces.
41. C. Kruyskamp, 'De klucht van koster Johannes', *Jaarboek De Fonteine*, 8 (1950), 25–41 (pp. 38–39); *Trou Moet Blijcken. Deel 7: Boek G, bronnenuitgave van de boeken der Haarlemse rederijkerskamer 'de Pellicanisten'*, ed. by W. N. M. Hüsken, B. A. M. Ramakers, and F. A. M. Schaars (Assen: Quarto, 1997), fols 123^v–128^r (fol. 127^{r-v}); Kramer, *Mooi vies, knap lelijk*, p. 289.
42. *Trou Moet Blijcken*, fols 29^v–36^v (fol. 30^r); Kramer, *Mooi vies, knap lelijk*, pp. 282–83.
43. *Trou Moet Blijcken*, fols 37^r–43^v; Kramer, *Mooi vies, knap lelijk*, p. 283.
44. On dating, see Cornelis Everaert, *Spelen*, ed. by J. W. Muller and L. Scharpé (Leiden: Brill, 1920), pp. xxxv–xxxvi. References are to Everaert, *De Spelen*, ed. by Hüsken, II, 628–44, and are provided in the text. Dutch text with English translation in Ben Parsons and Bas Jongenelen, *Comic Drama in the Low Countries, c.1450-1560: A Critical Anthology* (Cambridge: D. S. Brewer, 2012), pp. 184–205.
45. Everaert, *Spelen*, ed. by Muller and Scharpé, p. 615.
46. Velissariou, *Aspects dramatiques et écriture de l'oralité dans les 'Cent Nouvelles nouvelles'*, pp. 554–60, discusses the 'dramatic' character of the disguise and false confession in *nouvelle* 78, and the use of the motif in three French farces.
47. USTC 421111. On Berntsz and Van Doesborch and the book's content, see: Herman Pleij, 'Een fragment van de oudste Nederlandse novellenbundel te Cambridge', in *Opstellen door vrienden en vakgenoten aangeboden aan C. H. A. Kruyskamp*, ed. by Hans Heestermans (The Hague: Martinus Nijhoff, 1977), pp. 142–55 (pp. 150–53); Braekman, pp. 8–17; W. Waterschoot, '*Dat bedroch der vrouwen* [review]', *Spiegel der Letteren*, 26 (1984), 93–100; P. J. A. Franssen, '*Dat bedroch der vrouwen*, een onderzoek naar de functie van een 16e eeuwse verhalenbundel I', *Spektator*, 12 (1982–83), 270–89 (pp. 270–77); Franssen, *Tussen tekst en publiek*, pp. 27–31. Apart from Berntsz's edition, a 1555 Antwerp edition by Jan Roelants is recorded, and three out of nine gatherings survive of an undated edition by Jan van Ghelen (Antwerp, *c.*1560): Pleij, 'Een fragment van de oudste Nederlandse novellenbundel te Cambridge', pp. 146–48; Braekman, pp. 10–11. The book's popularity is also indicated by a dialogue between the printer and a woman — whom contemporaries would, according to Pleij, have recognized as the poet Anna Bijns — that serves as a promotional prologue in *Tprofijt der vrouwen*, a herbal and prescription-book aimed especially at women, of which the oldest surviving edition dates from 1561. The dialogue describes *Dat bedroch der vrouwen* as a book by which women are scandalized. See *Dat bedroch der vrouwen*, ed. by Braekman, p. 11; P. J. A. Franssen, '*Dat bedroch der vrouwen*, een onderzoek naar de functie van een 16e eeuwse verhalenbundel II', *Spektator*, 13 (1983–84), 167–81 (pp. 168–71); Franssen, *Tussen tekst en publiek*, pp. 33–34; Herman Pleij, *Komt een vrouwtje bij de drukker... Over*

gezichtsveranderingen van de literatuur uit de late middeleeuwen (Amsterdam: Bert Bakker, 2008), pp. 33–39, 51–55, 'Over Anna Bijns als persoon', in *Met eigen ogen: De rederijker als dichtend individu (1450–1600)*, ed. by Dirk Coigneau and Samuel Mareel, special issue of *Jaarboek De Fonteine*, 58 (2008), pp. 21–44 (pp. 25–33), and *Anna Bijns, van Antwerpen* (Amsterdam: Bert Bakker, 2011), pp. 213–19, 227–36.

48. Vele's edition is edited by Friedrich Brie, as 'The Deceyte of Women: älteste englische Novellensammlung (1547)', *Archiv für das Studium der neueren Sprachen und Literaturen*, 84 (1929), 17–52. Subsequent references are to this edition (referred to as Brie), and are provided in the text. See Braekman, p. 12; Franssen, *Tussen tekst en publiek*, p. 81; Robert W. Maslen, 'The Early English Novel in Antwerp: The Impact of Jan van Doesborch', in *Narrative Developments from Chaucer to Defoe*, ed. by Gerd Bayer and Ebbe Klitgard (New York: Routledge, 2011), pp. 137–57 (pp. 141–44).
49. Other examples of this type of story, albeit not present in the *Bedroch*, are *nouvelles* 72, 78, and 88.
50. Because of the beguiled lovers' revenge, *nouvelle* 62 represents rather another type of story, such as *nouvelles* 45, 47, 56, 60, 73, 85, and 93. In these, cuckolded husbands find satisfaction in a fierce or cruel punishment of their wives and/or the lovers.
51. Sweetser, p. 245; Braekman, fol. E1^v; Brie, p. 34. On song 188 in the *Antwerps liedboek*, see Franssen, 'Dat bedroch der vrouwen II', pp. 169, 172, and n. 17; and *Het Antwerps liedboek*, ed. by Dieuwke E. van der Poel, 2 vols (Tielt: Lannoo, 2004), I, 421–23; II, 422–25.
52. Franssen, *Tussen tekst en publiek*, pp. 79–81.
53. References to literature specifically in *nouvelles* 28 and 37 to Boccaccio's *De casus virorum illustrium* and to Matheolus, Juvenal, and the *Quinze Joyes de mariage* (Sweetser, pp. 191, 254).
54. Sweetser, pp. 188–90; compare Braekman, fol. D3^v, and Brie, p. 32.
55. On these expressions, see Velissariou, *Aspects dramatiques et écriture de l'oralité dans les 'Cent Nouvelles nouvelles'*, pp. 254–75. The only exception is 'dont je vous parle' [of whom I'll tell] in *nouvelle* 28 (p. 191), rendered as 'daer ick af spreken sal' in the *Bedroch* (Braekman, fol. E3^v), but absent from the *Deceyte* (Brie, pp. 35–36).
56. Cf. Coigneau, 'Bedongen creativiteit', pp. 130–35.
57. Sweetser, pp. 28–29; Brie, p. 25.
58. Sweetser, p. 96; Brie, p. 28.
59. Sweetser, p. 261; Brie, p. 41.
60. Brie, p. 49.
61. Sweetser, pp. 258, 260; Brie, p. 49.
62. Braekman, fol. A1^v. This does not appear in the *Deceyte* (of which the title-page says it is 'newly corrected'): Brie, pp. 22–23.
63. Sexual activity is described more concretely in the translations of *nouvelles* 27 and 62. Compare, for instance, 'et firent ce pourquoy ilz estoient assemblez, qui mieulx vault estre pensé des lysans qu'estre noté de l'escripvant' [and they did the thing for which they had come together, which it is better for readers to imagine than for the writer to describe] (Sweetser, p. 186) with 'And thus ben these two lovers gon to bed together and lovynglye have helsed and kissed eche other laborynge so sore that they both did swete in obtaining theyr lovely purpose' (Brie, p. 32; cf. Braekman, fol. D3^v). See also Sweetser, pp. 390, 391; Braekman, fol. K3^r.
64. Cf. Brie, p. 48.
65. A further association between this story (*nouvelle* 37) and the *Canterbury Tales* lies in its description of a man who 'had for the moste parte red all the practyces of the women how that they were wont to deceive their husbandes' (Brie, p. 48; cf. Braekman, fol. J1^r). This reading reminded Franssen of 'the boke of wikked wyves' in the *Wife of Bath's Prologue* (Franssen, 'Dat bedroch der vrouwen I', pp. 273–75; *Tussen tekst en publiek*, pp. 156–58).
66. Cf. Brie, pp. 24, 31, 47, 52.
67. Franssen, *Tussen tekst en publiek*, pp. 29–32, surveys Berntsz's publications. Pleij, 'Een fragment van de oudste Nederlandse novellenbundel te Cambridge', pp. 151–52; Braekman, p. 12; and Franssen, *Tussen tekst en publiek*, p. 81, consider Berntsz's combination to be the original one. The *Deceyte* would have dropped the last story, because of its warning against loose-lipped Englishmen.

68. A facsimile is available at <http://cf.hum.uva.nl/dsp/scriptamanent/bml/Bedroch_der_mannen/Bedroch_der_mannen.pdf> [accessed 23 June 2017]. The collection has been designated *Historie van Jason*, after its first story; *Het bedrog der mannen* (Pleij, 'Een fragment van de oudste Nederlandse novellenbundel te Cambridge', p. 148; Franssen, 'Dat bedroch der vrouwen I', pp. 280–81, and *Tussen tekst en publiek*, pp. 81–82); and *Van die groote ontrouwicheyt des mans*, on the basis of a phrase in the book's introduction (fol. A2^r; W. Nijhoff and M. E. Kronenberg, *Nederlandsche bibliographie van 1500 tot 1540*, 3 vols (The Hague: Nijhoff, 1923–61), no. 0939). See also Braekman, p. 9. Apart from the stories' titles, *ontrouwe* appears fourteen times in the texts, and *ontrouwicheyt* three times (fols A2^r, B3^r, F3^v), while *bedroch* figures only once (fol. F2^v).
69. Franssen, *Tussen tekst en publiek*, pp. 31, 81–82, 130–31, 185.
70. C. Kruyskamp, 'Een onbekende verhalenbundel van 1543', *Tijdschrift voor Nederlandse Taal- en Letterkunde*, 78 (1961), 161–67.
71. Sweetser, pp. 76, 122; compare *Ontrouwe* (see n. 67 above), fols E4^v, F4^v.
72. The only exception appears in the translation of *nouvelle* 26, where 'Pour abreger' [to be brief] (p. 173) is rendered as 'Ende opt cortste gheseyt' [and, to put it as briefly as possible] (fol. C3^v).
73. See also Pleij, *Het gevleugelde woord*, pp. 497–98, 593–94.
74. Koj, *Die frühe Rezeption der Fazetien Poggios in Frankreich*, pp. 108–10, 191–94; Dirk Coigneau, 'Drie Rijnsburgse refreinen te Rotterdam (1561) en hun Franse bron', *Verslagen en Mededelingen van de Koninklijke Academie voor Nederlandse Taal- en Letterkunde* (1977), 239–90 (pp. 249–50); Rey-Flaud, *La Farce ou la machine à rire, théorie d'un genre dramatique 1450–1550*, pp. 59–60.
75. Le Maçon's translation was the source of Dirck Coornhert's 1564 edition of fifty novellas from the *Decameron*, *Vijftich lustige historien ofte nyeuwicheden* (USTC 411275).
76. Silvius's editions are USTC 402938 and 407604. Textual evidence indicates that Fruytiers's source was the original Burgundian collection, rather than later sixteenth-century anthologies that also include the *nouvelle*: Coigneau, 'Drie Rijnsburgse refreinen te Rotterdam (1561) en hun Franse bron', pp. 246–53. The poem appears on pp. 246–48, and in *Spelen van sinne vol schoone allegatien: Drijderley refereynen (De Rotterdamse spelen van 1561)*, ed. by Henk J. Hollaar (Delft: Eburon, 2006), pp. 321–23; further references are provided in the text.
77. Dirk Coigneau, *Refreinen in het zotte bij de rederijkers*, 3 vols (Gent: Koninklijke Academie voor Nederlandse Taal- en Letterkunde, 1980–83), II, 370–74.
78. W. A. P. Smit, *Dichters der reformatie in de zestiende eeuw: Een overzicht met bloemlezing* (Groningen: Wolters, 1939), p. 111.
79. Coigneau, *Refreinen in het zotte bij de rederijkers*, I, 52–54.
80. Coigneau, 'Drie Rijnsburgse refreinen te Rotterdam (1561) en hun Franse bron', pp. 253–64.
81. Velissariou, *Aspects dramatiques et écriture de l'oralité dans les 'Cent Nouvelles nouvelles'*, pp. 430–31.
82. Quoted from F. C. van Boheemen and Th. C. J. van der Heijden, *Retoricaal memoriaal: Bronnen voor de geschiedenis van de Hollandse rederijkerskamers van de middeleeuwen tot het begin van de achttiende eeuw* (Delft: Eburon, 1999), p. 14; see Coigneau, 'Drie Rijnsburgse refreinen te Rotterdam (1561) en hun Franse bron', pp. 255–56.
83. Except for Fruytiers's *refrein in 't sot* and one *refrein in 't vroed* (by an Amsterdam poet) from the same Rotterdam festival, all *refreinen* presented at *rederijker* contests had four stanzas: Coigneau, *Refreinen in het zotte bij de rederijkers*, I, 202.

CHAPTER 7

❖

Cross-Cultural Intersections in the Middle Dutch Translations of *Le Chevalier délibéré* by Olivier de La Marche

Susie Speakman Sutch

In April 1483, a year after the death of Duchess Mary of Burgundy, Olivier de La Marche completed *Le Chevalier délibéré*, an allegorical poem that narrates the pseudo-autobiographical quest of the Author, figured as Chevalier. Comprising 338 octaves of octosyllabic verse, this poem circulated in numerous manuscripts between *c.* 1484 and the end of the sixteenth century, the vast majority produced in France, and in fourteen printed editions between 1488 and 1540.[1] Of the printed editions, ten appeared in France (eight in Paris, two in Lyon) and four in the northern Low Countries. Of these four, two were editions of the original poem in French — by the Collaciebroeders in Gouda after 31 October 1489, and by the priest Otgier Pietersz Nachtegael in Schiedam *c.* 1498 — and two were editions of two different translations of this poem into Middle Dutch that were made respectively in Haarlem and in Brussels. The first translation, completed by Pieter Willemsz in Haarlem (1492), was commissioned by Klaas van Ruyven, the city's *schout* [sheriff] who was killed during the *Kaas- en Broodvolk* uprising (Bread and Cheese Revolt) in 1492. Johannes Steemaer, alias Pertcheval, a prominent member of the Brussels chamber of rhetoric, De Lelie [The Lily], completed his translation in 1493. Neither translation was immediately printed, however. Ten years would pass before the Schiedam printer Nachtegael issued Pertcheval's translation, entitled *Den camp vander doot,* on 27 June 1503. For this edition he re-used the type and the woodblocks for the illustrations that had served the Collaciebroeders for their printing of *Le Chevalier délibéré*; he did this as well when he reprinted the French original mentioned above. Another five years would lapse before Jan Seversz printed Willemsz's translation in Leiden with the title *Vanden ridder welghemoet*, using both the type and the woodblocks that Nachtegael had used to produce his two editions. All four of these editions, therefore, have the same format, are printed using the same type, and share the same woodcuts.

It was indeed the woodcuts that initially generated the greatest interest in *Le Chevalier délibéré* on the part of modern scholars. The Schiedam reissue of the Collaciebroeders' edition of La Marche's French original received scholarly attention in the late nineteenth and early twentieth centuries, especially among bibliophiles, who were very impressed by the high technical level of the woodcuts illustrating the narrative, leading to the publication in London of a transcription of this edition containing reproductions of the illustrations in 1898 and then to the publication in Paris of a facsimile edition in 1923.[2] Meanwhile, the only extant copy of the Gouda edition remained in private hands and was not accessible for consultation by the wider public until the recent publication of a photographic reproduction of this incunabulum, now housed in the library of Jean Bonna in Geneva.[3] The Middle Dutch translations, in the meantime, received notice only belatedly; more information about these two editions slowly began to emerge in the 1930s thanks to bibliographers, literary scholars, and art historians. In the middle of the twentieth century a photographic reproduction of *Den camp vander doot* was issued at Antwerp.[4] Only fragments of Pieter Willemsz's *Vanden ridder welghemoet* were known, however, until Herman Pleij's discovery in the late 1980s of a complete copy of this work in the Österreichische Nationalbibliothek in Vienna.[5] Although, unfortunately, this last text is not yet available in a modern edition, work by Bas Jongenelen sheds important light on instances where *Vanden ridder* diverges from La Marche's source text, based on a close reading of both poems, and he also presents a thorough treatment of the extra stanzas interpolated into Willemsz's poem that expanded it to 365 stanzas.[6] Jongenelen further analyzes the translation techniques used by Pieter Willemsz in rendering the French source text, building on the same criteria he used in his earlier study of Johannes Pertcheval's *Den camp vander doot*, in which he engages in a systematic dissection of the discrepancies between the source and the target texts and wrestles with the issue of audience.[7] Jongenelen's penetrating analysis of these two translations contributes to our better understanding of the relationship between both Middle Dutch poems and their French source with regard to their content.[8]

Taken together, these four editions offer a unique opportunity to examine cross-cultural interactions between French- and Dutch-speakers at the end of the fifteenth century from two different perspectives, the one textual, the other paratextual. That two distinct but contemporary translations were made of the French source text, namely the edition of *Le Chevalier délibéré* printed by the Collaciebroeders in Gouda, means that it is possible to measure the influence of the French original on two separate authors writing at the same moment in and for two different Dutch-speaking communities, one in Brussels, the other in Haarlem, and to evaluate the extent to which French is embedded in Middle Dutch literature of these two language groups. Furthermore, the nearly concurrent printing of a French original and a Middle Dutch version of the same text by the same printer makes it possible to assess the adjustments the printer brought to this aspect of the reproduction process, and to consider what his motivations might have been for making them. In the discussion that follows I shall address these issues in turn, first comparing the two editions produced in Schiedam, then analyzing the impact of the lexical features of the French source text on the two Middle Dutch translations.[9] The key player in the former investigation is the printer Otgier Nachtegael; the key player in the latter is the translator, be he Johannes Pertcheval or Pieter Willemsz.

Paratext as Site of Cross-cultural Interaction: The Printer Otgier Nachtegael at Work

When Otgier Nachtegael printed *Le Chevalier délibéré* in Schiedam, he re-used the woodblocks and the type he had procured from the Collaciebroeders. He reset the text scrupulously, respecting the layout of the Gouda exemplar, the disposition of stanzas (whether five, six, seven, or eight per page), and the placement of the woodcuts. The only alteration he made was to substitute his printer's mark for the Gouda patron's mark (fol. f3^v). When he later printed Johannes Pertcheval's translation using the same typographic material, however, his task became more difficult as he was re-using woodblocks in which were embedded French legends and labels that his readers might not immediately understand. His first solution was to cut out the original captions to all sixteen woodcuts and substitute legends in Dutch. Immediately above the title illustration, he declares that the title of his book is 'den Camp vander doot' in a couplet that better conforms to the content of that illustration, figuring as it does the knight Chevalier's final battle against Death (fol. a1^r). The new legend, furthermore, beckons to the reader by announcing that he should study the contents of this book 'want het is u noot' [for it is necessary for you (to do so)].[10] Nachtegael further reinforces the moral import of this book by inserting a prologue that explains its usefulness for the general reader (fol. a2^r): as the prophet Job has taught us, life on earth is a struggle and everyone must learn to conduct himself in this struggle in such a way as to gain the immortality of his soul. This book, the prologue asserts, is full of useful examples to help the reader achieve this goal.[11] The title image depicting the knight Chevalier in combat against Death is the perfect visual representation of the final moment in man's earthly struggle and thus truly reproduces visually the title of the book — 'den Camp vander doot' — which is reasserted in the rubrics of the prologue, above and below (fol. a2^r). The substituted legend for the woodcut showing the author-Chevalier before he embarks on his quest translates in part the original French caption, 'Cy commence le premier chappitre du traictié Le chevalier deliberé' [Here begins the first chapter of the treatise entitled *The Resolute Knight*] (fol. a1^v), as follows: 'Hier beghint een bouck oft een tractaet [...] Deerste [kapittel] vanden Ridder gedelibereert' [Here begins a book or a treatise [...] the first [chapter] of *The Resolute Knight*] (fol. a1^v), thus referring to the title of the original French poem *Le Chevalier délibéré*.[12]

Nachtegael's second response to the cross-cultural interaction introduced into his edition of *Den camp vander doot* by the re-use of the Gouda woodblocks, which contained French names and terms with which his readers might not be familiar, was to append to the very end of his edition a *tafel* or short glossary, in which a translation of each French expression is provided (fols f3^v–f4^r). He calls attention to this addition twice: immediately below the Amen of the Prologue (fol. a2^r), and again in a final stanza explicitly composed to introduce it and to certify its usefulness to the reader (ll. 2657–64).[13] The printer's interventions in all likelihood had everything to do with marketing strategies aiming to attract as wide a range of Dutch-speaking customers as possible. Nachtegael provides his target audience with a means to decode the French words and names occurring in the illustrations, and puts his readers at ease by promising them that this glossary gives a translation of 'die walsche namen' [the French names] embedded in those images. He assures his readers of the usefulness of the book they are about to purchase in the recast caption to the title illustration and in the colophon: 'Hier eyndet een profitelijc boeck gehieten *den Camp vander doot*' [Here ends a profitable book called *The Joust of Death*]. Finally he reassures any potential buyer of the high quality of his printing job: 'Welcke boec constelijc ende wel gheset is, ende mit naersticheit ghecorrigeert' [This book has been artfully and well (type)set and corrected with care].

Translation as Site of Cross-cultural Linguistic Interactions: Johannes Pertcheval and Pieter Willemsz at Work

We are fortunate to know the identity of both the translators of La Marche's poem. In addition to translating La Marche's *Chevalier délibéré*, Johannes Steemaer alias Pertcheval was a respected member of the chamber of rhetoric De Lelie.[14] With the chamber's *factor* or principal author, Jan de Baertmaker alias Smeken, who was also the official poet of the city of Brussels from 1485 until his death in 1517, Pertcheval organized public literary competitions, urban festivities on the occasion of entry ceremonies for Maximilian of Austria and Philip the Handsome, as well as civic celebrations of peace treaties, ducal births and baptisms, and so forth.[15] De Lelie organized a rhetoricians' competition, to begin on 12 May 1493, that was to bring together both French-speaking and Dutch-speaking chambers from the whole of the Low Countries.[16] With three of his peers in the chamber, including Jan Smeken, Pertcheval established a chapter of the very popular devotion to Our Lady of the Seven Sorrows in the church of St Gaugericus (Sint-Gorik) in 1499. Furthermore, not only was he one of this brotherhood's first heads or provosts, he was likewise the first keeper of its accounts as well as the first recorder of the confraternity's membership register.[17] As for biographical information regarding Pertcheval's counterpart in Haarlem, we are not so lucky. Other than three references to a Pieter Willemsz 'schilder' [painter] in entries from the accounts of the guild of St Luke in Haarlem — and it is not certain that this is the same Pieter Willemsz — no biographical information about him has emerged.[18]

That the translations were produced almost simultaneously, in 1492 and 1493 respectively, can be explained by contemporary circumstances. Because the Gouda edition of *Le Chevalier délibéré* was the source text for Pieter Willemsz's translation project, he cannot have undertaken this task until after 31 October 1489, the earliest possible date ascribed to this publication.[19] This same reasoning likely holds as well for the timing of Johannes Pertcheval's assuming the task of making a translation of the same French edition. But as regards the situation of the city of Brussels, we must also consider political circumstances, namely the Flemish revolt against Maximilian of Austria that had flared up off and on for ten years after the death of Mary of Burgundy on 27 March 1482 and had spilled over into Hainaut, Brabant, Zeeland, and Holland. By the end of August 1489 Brussels had capitulated to Maximilian's troops under the command of his lieutenant-general Albert of

Saxony.[20] But the military conflict did not truly come to an end until peace treaties in 1492–93 officially terminated the Flemish revolt, thus setting the stage for Philip the Handsome's emancipation to be declared.[21] By the summer of 1493 Philip was poised to assume personal rulership over the provinces over which Maximilian had heretofore governed as regent on his behalf.[22] The completion by Pertcheval of the translation of an important and well-known literary work by Philip's 'conseiller, grant et premier maistre d'ostel' [counsellor, grand and first chief steward of the household], at whose centre is an encomium to that prince's mother and forebears, could not come at a more auspicious moment, one that can perhaps be coupled with the bilingual rhetoricians' competition that De Lelie hosted in May 1493 with the full support of the Hapsburg ruler, as mentioned above.[23]

The overarching goal of this section is to assess the translation practices of Pieter Willemsz and Johannes Pertcheval by comparing their poems both to La Marche's and to each other's, and to determine the extent of the linguistic influence of the French source poem on their Middle Dutch products. Juxtaposing these two concurrent translations makes it possible to glimpse two writers, confronted with the same French source, wrestling with cross-cultural interactions on the lexical and cultural level. Having access to two completely independent and contemporary renderings of *Le Chevalier délibéré*, furthermore, provides us with a unique chance to assess the extent to which French loans were prevalent in the literary idiom at their disposal. In both translations the presence of words of French origin is imposing, and especially dense in the case of *Den camp vander doot* where there are over 300 borrowings from the French source (see below). This leads me to suspect that both translators were quite confident that their readership was conversant with the appropriated vocabulary; indeed, the vast majority can be found in the *Middelnederlandsch woordenboek*, indicating that their usage was probably well integrated in the literary language of the Dutch-speaking northern and southern Netherlands by the end of the fifteenth century.[24] In what follows I first discuss the role of doublets in these translations in order to assess what they reveal about the relationship between the source and target languages, before addressing the presence of French loans themselves in the two poems.

Johannes Pertcheval and *Den camp vander doot*

The presence of doublets in Pertcheval's translation, which in other literary circumstances might serve as indicators of tension between a French source and a Dutch rendering, occurs very rarely. These doublets are of two sorts: either a pair of synonyms in Middle Dutch to capture the sense of the original French word or a bilingual pair, one word mirroring the usage in the original coupled with its translation. The first style, doublets in Middle Dutch, is very infrequent. In a chapel in Understanding's cloister the Author is amazed to have seen relics of the cruel deeds of Accident but none of proud Debility's: 'riens veü n'avoies [...] | Des fais de Debille le Fier' [I had seen nothing [...] | of the deeds of cruel Debility] (*Chevalier* 74.5, 74.7); 'Aengaende Crancheyt oft der outheyt fier' [Pertaining to Debility or fierce Old Age] (l. 543). Likewise the number of tombs of empresses, queens, ladies, duchesses, countesses, and wives he sees in Fresh Memory's cemetery are incalculable: 'Par nombre non a extimer' [In countless number] (*Chevalier* 207.2); 'Sonder nommere oft enich ghetal' [Countless or without number] (l. 1602). Or again, when Accident sees Mary of Burgundy enter Atropos's closed lists ready to do battle against him, he needs encouragement from 'Foursenez son conseillier' [Madness, his counselor] (*Chevalier* 261.1); 'Dwaes of Dul zijn cancellier [*sic*]' [Fool or Numskull his chancellor] (l. 2033).

More numerous, as might be expected, are the bilingual doublets in which Pertcheval pairs the French loan taken over from La Marche's original with a Middle Dutch word that serves to explain its meaning. Immediately on the verso of the title-page of *Den camp vander doot* the caption to the woodcut illustration gives us the first doublet: 'Hier beghint een bouck oft een tractaet' (fol. a1ᵛ), the caption to the first illustration in the French edition naming this work simply a 'traictié' (fol. a1ᵛ). In Fresh Memory's cemetery the Author sees and describes the graves of noble and heroic men, among whom is Duke Louis of Bourbon, who 'Jut la par Debile maté' [Lay there, laid low by Debility] (*Chevalier* 198.2);[25] 'de hertoge Loys | Lach daer bij Crancheit plat ende mat' [duke Louis | lay there flat and struck down by Debility] (ll. 1529–30). We have to wait until the very last stanzas of Pertcheval's text to discover three more bilingual doublets. In his teachings to help the Author prepare for his own single combat against Death, Understanding names certain accessories that he must have in hand:

> Et pour entrer en telz destrois
> Il te fault une banerolle
> Qui sera faite de la croix. (*Chevalier* 315.1–3)

> [And to enter into such straits
> You must have a pennon
> Which will be made of the cross.]

> Als ghij dusdanighe wech in slaen sult
> Hebt inde hant een baniere oft vane
> Als dat heylich cruys dat den viant verdult. (*Den camp*, ll. 2465–67)

> [When you enter such a path
> Have in your hand a banner or pennon
> As that holy cross that confounds the enemy.]

And during the final combat itself the Author is instructed that he must honour the judge: 'Le Juge tu honnoureras | Et luy seras obedïent' [You will honor the Judge | And be obedient to Him] (*Chevalier* 322.1–2); 'Een rechter oft iugie suldi moeten eeren | En gij moet hem onderdanich wesen' [You must honour an arbiter or judge | and you must be obedient to him] (ll. 2521–22). Once Understanding has departed, his teachings complete, the Author reflects on the quest he has just completed:

> En la marche de ma pensee
> Et ou paÿs d'Avise Toy
> Est ceste queste commencee. (*Chevalier* 337.1–3)

> [This quest was begun
> In the marches of my mind
> And in the land of Look To Yourself.]
>
> [I]nde maertsche van mijnen ghepeyse
> En int lant van Wilt u aviseren
> Es begost dese queste oft reyse. (*Den camp*, ll. 2641–43)
>
> [In the marches of my thought
> And in the land of Take Your Own Counsel
> Was this quest or voyage begun.]

This handful of examples might indicate Pertcheval's hesitancy with regard to his audience's familiarity with these few French words, yet I strongly doubt that this was the case. Certainly Crancheit has played a decisive role in his poem from the very beginning, indeed from the moment when Ghepeyse informs the Author who Atropos's two champions are, namely 'de oude Crancheit oft Accident' [Old Debility or Accident] (l. 40). The other loan-words occur at least once elsewhere in his text, and 'ban(n)iere(n)' four times. And although 'queste' occurs in this one instance alone, I conjecture that it would have been quite current in literary circles given the popularity of chivalric romances. The only exception might possibly be 'Foursenez', as 'Dwaes of Dul' (l. 2033) does not do justice to this embodiment of a most drastic mental state.[26]

One final bilingual doublet confirms my sense of the translator's confidence in the linguistic competence of his urban readership. It appears twice at the very end of *Den camp vander doot* and occurs completely independently of the French original: the moment when Johannes Steemaer addresses his audience, names himself, and identifies the role he has played in the translation that the reader has just finished. In the former he links his name, via his alias, with its two terms reversed, to the French author by citing La Marche's motto, demonstrating his familiarity with the Burgundian poet's device; in the latter he proclaims his authorship of the translation:

> Dus wilt al u stucken wel ordineren.
> Tes den raet van *Cheval pert*
> En van hem *Qui tant a souffert*. (*Den camp*, ll. 2646–48)
>
> [Thus get all your ducks in a row.
> This is the advice of *Cheval pert*
> And of him who has suffered so much.]
>
> *Den campe vander doot* tot alle tye
> Sal dit boeck hieten al boven al,
> Ghetranslateert bij eenen Pertcheval. (*Den camp*, ll. 2654–56)
>
> [*The Joust of Death* for all time
> Will this book be called, above all else,
> Translated by one Pertcheval.]

The limited number of doublets in this Middle Dutch translation betrays, in my view, an absence of tension between French and Dutch in this text and the translator's confidence in the linguistic abilities of his target audience.[27] This conclusion is reinforced by the fact that, as indicated above, there are well over 300 instances, counting innumerable repetitions, where the translator has taken over a word present in the French source and made the necessary orthographic adjustments to adapt these lexical items to Middle Dutch. The adoptions include the names of allegorical agents, allegorized attributes of objects, and terms for some weapons and armour used by the combatants in the armed clashes recounted in the poem. They also encompass verbs depicting numerous actions, descriptive adjectives, nouns designating objects, emotions, virtues, political and military offices, religious functions, states of mind, intellectual disciplines, tournament decorations, participants and practices, and many more. Furthermore, Pertcheval spontaneously uses French loan-words that have no antecedent at that particular point in *Le Chevalier délibéré*.[28] The impact of the French source is, thus, very palpable throughout *Den camp vander doot*.

Two small examples are emblematic of the very pronounced imprint of *Le Chevalier délibéré* on Pertcheval's poem. The first demonstrates how literally the Brussels poet translated the French source at times. Among the pieces of advice that Understanding gives the Author is that he is to rely on no one else: 'Il s'entent que nulle personne [...] | Ne doit prendre en autruy fiance' [It is understood that no one [...] |Should rely on another] (*Chevalier* 295.3, 5), an admonition that Pertcheval translates as follows: 'Zo verstaetmen dat geen persoon int leven [...] | Enich betrouwe in anderen houwe' [So it is understood that no person alive [...] | Should have any confidence in others] (ll. 2307, 2309). It is the locution 'geen persoon' that is so telling with regard to how closely Pertcheval is following the thought expressed in the source text. Certainly 'geen persoon' literally renders 'nulle personne', but Dutch-speakers would not say this; they would use the pronoun *niemand*, just as Willemsz does (*Vanden ridder* 320.3). The second reflects the linguistic gymnastics that Pertcheval occasionally performs. The Author sees the grave of Pierre de Brezé in Fresh Memory's cemetery and laments that 'La fut sa vaillance faillye' [His valour was of no use there] (*Chevalier* 183.6). Where a contemporary Dutch-speaker would simply have relied on the expression *sijn vroemheit* to render 'sa vaillance', as Willemsz does (*Vanden ridder* 187.6), Pertcheval constructs a neologism based on the adjective *vaillant*: 'Sijn vaillandicheit was daer smal' [His valour was of little value there] (l. 1414).

Pieter Willemsz and *Vanden ridder welghemoet*

So far as I have been able to determine, there is only one doublet in Pieter Willemsz's poem. Among the relics betokening Accident's deeds that Understanding shows the Author are the bow and arrows that Paris used to slay Achilles, whom La Marche describes as 'Le plus vaillant que fust en Grece' [The most courageous of the Greeks] (*Chevalier* 58.8). For Willemsz Achilles is 'den vroemsten vaeliant | van alle den heren wt Gryeckerlant' [The most courageous valiant | of all the lords of Greece] (61.7–8), a doublet that nicely captures the superlative of the French source. A further doublet appearing in the edition printed by Jan Seversz owes its existence to the compositor rather than the poet/translator, as Jan Seversz simply had the captions for the woodcut illustrations reset copying those Otgier Nachtegael had used in *Den camp vander doot*. Hence the doublet 'een boec oft een tractaet' occurs in the caption for the first illustration of his edition as well (fol. a1ᵛ).

As in the case of Pertcheval's translation, borrowings of words from the French source are quite abundant in that by Willemsz, and all are appropriately modified to reflect Middle Dutch usage and spelling. These lexical items serve the same functions as well: they name and describe allegorical personifications and the allegorized attributes of objects the French source has put forward; they designate certain weapons wielded by the adversaries and armour protecting their bodies. Verbs describe manifold actions and nouns specify emotional qualities and states of mind, the attributes and protocol of tournament practice, intellectual branches, military titles, political and religious functions, and much more. Moreover, a comparison of Willemsz's poem with Pertcheval's text reveals that in around 200 instances these borrowed terms in fact overlap with lexical items Pertcheval had used in *Den camp vander doot* in his rendering of the same lines. Furthermore, as was Pertcheval's practice, Willemsz employs French loan-words spontaneously where the French source offers no antecedent to prompt the insertion of such terms.[29] Therefore, it seems that Willemsz too had confidence in the linguistic proficiency of the audience for whom he translated La Marche's poem.

What we have seen so far are instances where the cross-cultural interaction between French and Middle Dutch rests on the two Dutch-speaking poet/translators borrowing from and mirroring the French source. Very telling as well are the instances where the translators eschew taking over vocabulary from the French text and instead render the words in Middle Dutch, as this practice likewise reveals the level of these writers' mastery of the lexicon in and the culture evoked by La Marche's poem. There are relatively few such cases in Pertcheval's work, and these run counter to what readers might expect, as his habits in respect of loan-words are regular, frequent, and predictable.[30] More striking and vastly more numerous are the cases where Willemsz demonstrates more flexibility in his translation practices, adopting a term from the French source in one instance and preferring to translate it into Middle Dutch in another. I will explore three representative clusters of such word usage in turn.

The first cluster that merits our attention concerns the word *emprise*. The first usage of this word occurs very near the beginning of the poem, when Thought advises the Author to heed the summons of the herald Excess to face Accident. Willemsz's translation retains *emprise*, as Kronenberg was quick to observe:[31]

> Il est temps que tu te chappitres,
> Car tu as touchié a l'emprise
> Depuis ta premiere chemise. (*Chevalier* 8.6–8)
>
> [It is time that you take yourself to task,
> For you have been approaching this undertaking
> Since you were first born.][32]
>
> Ende Accident de di besprongen mits desen heeft
> Angetast sijn emprise, den camp an genomen
> Van dat u deerste hemde ant lijf was gecomen. (*Vanden ridder* 9.6–8)

[And Accident, who attacked you with these [dispatches],
Touched on his undertaking, the battle accepted
From the moment that a shirt was first put on your body.]

What Kronenberg cannot have known, however, given the fragmentary nature of the stanzas she had to work with, is that there are six other occurrences of the word *emprise* in *Le Chevalier délibéré*, in each of which Willemsz eschews adopting the French word and selects various Dutch synonyms: *voernemen* (39.1, 157.6), *opset(te)* (245.1, 266.4), *opsettingen* (334.3), and even *campe* (42.4) instead.

A second cluster revolves around the word *propos* and demonstrates precisely the opposite inclination. The first time we encounter the term is when Thought 'Prist ung propos de verité' [Began to talk about truth] (*Chevalier* 2.2), which Willemsz translates: 'Onderwees mi menige warachtige leere' [Instructed me in many a true lesson] (2.2). Later the Author comments on his host Understanding: 'Et trouvay mon hoste notable | En son propos tant agrëable' [And I found my host excellent | In his most agreeable conversation] (*Chevalier* 42.3–4); Willemsz's rendering is 'Wiens leringe mi seer bequaem docht wesen' [Whose instruction seemed to me very pleasant] (45.4). But elsewhere Willemsz uses *propoost*, not only to translate its French cognate — hence 'Rentrant en mon premier propos' [Returning to my first intent] (*Chevalier* 120.3) becomes 'In mijn eerste propoest weder tredende mi stelde' [I returned to my first intention] (124.3) — but also independently of the source, to refer to Understanding's teachings: 'Mer nu comt dalder starcste na u propoost' [But now comes the most difficult part] (337.3) renders 'Mais au primes vient le plus fort' [But the most painful thing comes first] (*Chevalier* 312.3).

The third cluster involves the primary chivalric virtue that a knight, duke, prince, or king must embody, namely *vaillance* [courage or valour]. Of the fourteen times a hero or prince is praised for being *vaillant* in the French source, or is renowned for his *vaillance* or has performed *vaillamment*, in only three cases does Willemsz use *vaeliant* (21.1) or *vailiant* (173.3), including the doublet characterizing Achilles cited above (61.7). In all other instances he employs some form of the synonyms *vroem*, *stout*, and *coen*; in this respect he shows himself to be linguistically more adaptable than his Brussels peer, who in nine cases uses a French loan based on the adjective *vaillant* and in two others inserts *vaillant* (ll. 1354, 1438) to capture the meaning of 'a prisier' (*Chevalier* 176.2) and 'de nom' (*Chevalier* 186.6).[33]

These three clusters of examples exhibit Willemsz's versatility as a translator, inclined in one instance to select a French word from the source poem and in another to resist doing so. There is one important semantic field, however, where he emphatically abstains from appropriating a French term from his source, namely vocabulary relating to armed battles (*bataille*), the lists (*lices*) where the fatal single passages at arms (*pas*) occur, and the shield (*targe/tergon* or *escu*) with which the combatants protect themselves from the blows of their adversary. In all these cases he resolutely translates these words rather than borrowing a French term from La Marche's poem.

The noun *bataille* occurs ten times in *Le Chevalier délibéré*; seven of these ten refer to the mortal battle that Thought tells the Author he will have to face and for which

Understanding prepares him, and to the single combats that he and Fresh Memory witness in Atropos's lists. In contrast to Pertcheval, who retains the French term in all seven instances, Willemsz uses the nouns *camp* or *strijd*, or in one instance the verb *vechten*.[34] To translate the lists, *lices* or *en lice* (mentioned five times in the source text), Willemsz oscillates between vocabulary that refers to the closed spaces where such armed struggles occur, namely *parcke* and *baelgen*, and vocabulary that refers to the armed conflicts themselves: *camp*, *camp besloten*, and *battaelgen*, the only time he selects a word closely related to *bataille*.[35] The word *pas*, in the sense of *pas d'armes*, occurs in the French source some nine times, in reference to Amé de Montgesoie's poem *Le Pas de la mort*, to the deadly contests overseen by Atropos, and to the three single combats that the Author and Fresh Memory watch in Atropos's lists. While Pertcheval consistently takes over this word in eight cases, and spontaneously translates 'en lice' by 'in desen pas' (l. 1997), Willemsz never does. Where *pas* means the place where the single combats take place, he renders it as *parc(k)*, *ter plaetsen*, or *wech*; where it means the clash between the two armed adversaries, it is translated as *camp* or *te campen*.[36] Finally, in all fourteen instances where the words *targe*, *tergon*, and *escu* occur in *Le Chevalier délibéré*, Willemsz uses *sc(h)ilt* or *scilde*.[37] Interestingly Pertcheval, who repeats *taerg(i)e* or *taerdge* in three places and chooses *schilt* in two others, consistently translates all eight occurrences of *escu* by *sc(h)ilt*.[38]

Conclusion

In the preceding discussion my aim has been to elucidate how Johannes Pertcheval and his Haarlem colleague Pieter Willemsz contended with and resolved the linguistic challenges imposed by and inherent in rendering La Marche's *Chevalier délibéré* into Middle Dutch. As we have seen, the impact of the source language on the target language of the two translations diverges. The idiom of the Brussels text reflects a much denser presence of French than the Haarlem version, because Pertcheval consistently relies on and prolifically adopts loan-words from the French source, literally embedding French-Dutch linguistic transcultural interactions in his poem. Meanwhile, by being less systematically reliant on the French source for loan-words to appropriate — there are a third fewer borrowings in his text than in Pertcheval's, as indicated above — and by being flexible and selective in his choice of Middle Dutch vocabulary to translate the French original, Pieter Willemsz has produced a more autonomous translation, with the result that the influence of the French source appears much less pronounced in his poem.

At the same time, however, while vastly divergent from each other and testifying to the lexical imprint of the French source to different degrees, both translations faithfully reproduce the content of the French original.[39] Indeed, neither is interventionist.[40] Johannes Pertcheval's translation is more literal, as both Jongenelen and Kronenberg point out.[41] This is in part because of his very extensive adoption of the lexicon of the French source, which creates the impression that he is possibly more accurate than his Haarlem peer. Willemsz's translation, meanwhile, is wordier and more circuitous, but it often comes closer to capturing subtleties of sentiment or meaning than the Brussels version.⁴² Willemsz, in fact, often apprehends a sentiment intimated in the French, and makes the implied emotion explicit in his poem. For example, after Mary of Burgundy has succumbed to Accident, bringing to an end the era of Valois Burgundy, the author addresses a two-stanza apostrophe to his readers that begins: 'O vous qui ce livre lisés, | Assavourez ceste adventure' [O you who read this book | Take well into account this adventure] (*Chevalier* 265.1–2). Willemsz's rendering is more emphatic and closer to the emotion evoked in the French lines than Pertcheval's more distant interpretation: 'O ghi alle die dit boucxken sult overlesen | Smaect doch dese bittere avonturen' [O you all who will read this book | Just taste this bitter adventure] (*Vanden ridder* 271.1–2); '[O] lesers lesende hier af den reghele | Wilt dees aventuere wel overdincken' [O readers reading here these lines | Reflect carefully on this adventure] (*Den camp*, ll. 2065–66). Or again, in outrage at having witnessed the unjust deaths of his three Burgundian benefactors, the Author determines to take vengeance, readying himself to do battle with Accident, Debility, or both at once: 'J'ay toute crainte despitee | Sy ay ma visiere baissee' [I scorned all fear | And lowered my visor] (*Chevalier* 267.3–4). While Pertcheval's protagonist merely lowers his head (*Den camp*, l. 2084), Willemsz's does not simply lower his visor but, holding his fears to be of no account, slams it down, betraying the strong emotion of the moment that this gesture makes manifest: 'Hebbe ic alle vresen voir spijse geacht | Mijn visiere ter aerden geslegen met cracht' [I stared down all my fears | [And] slammed my visor down with force] (*Vanden ridder* 273.3–4).

Willemsz likewise seizes subtleties of meaning that seem possibly to have escaped Pertcheval's notice because he has simply adopted the French term from the source. For example, stopped before the Palace of Love, the Author wonders at the beautifully dressed ladies and damsels: 'Et pour entretenir icelles | Mains gorgias et bien en point' [And to complement them | many galants, finely turned out] (*Chevalier* 111.6–7). In his rendering Pertcheval repeats the word *gorgias*: 'Menighen gorgias menich edel diet' [Many gallants, many noble folk] (*Den camp*, l. 839). Willemsz, on the other hand, perfectly decodes *mains gorgias*: 'Ende om dese ioncfrouwen wel tonderhouwen | Menich frisch iongman die daer bi lagen' [And to cater to these young ladies | Many a dapper young man lounging there] (*Vanden ridder* 115.6–7). Elsewhere, Understanding explains to the Author how Agamemnon's wife had him traitorously slain through a ruse of her lover: 'De son paillart par subtillesse' [Through a ruse of her lover] (*Chevalier* 62.5); in Pertcheval's wording this is 'By hueren paellairt die ter quader fame stoet' [By her lover, who had a bad reputation] (*Den camp*, l. 444).⁴³ Willemsz's phrase 'Doer haer roffyaen mit valscher subtijlhede' [By her panderer with a false ruse] (*Vanden ridder* 65.5) casts Clytemnestra's lover Aegisthus in an even blacker light than does the more generally pejorative *paillart*, as the first meaning of *roffyaen* in the *Middelnederlandsch woordenboek* is *koppelaar* ('panderer', 'pimp'), which in fact is one of the meanings of the English *ruffian* according to the *Oxford English Dictionary* ('prostitute's pimp').

One final example strikingly attests to Willemsz's mastery of nuances in French. Accident and Mary of Burgundy are on the point of engaging in battle; her beauty, worth, courage, and youth give him pause, and make him doubt the outcome of their contest. His counsellor steps up to give him advice: 'Mais Foursenez son conseillier | Luy dist: "Te fauldra le courage"' [But Madness, his counselor, said to him | "You will need to have heart"] (*Chevalier* 261.1–2). Pertcheval's translation of this counsellor's name shows hesitancy and occasions the use of a doublet, as we have seen above: '[M]er Dwaes of Dul zijn cancellier [*sic*]' [But Fool or Numskull his chancellor] (*Den camp*, l. 2033). Willemsz's rendering of this name, by contrast, is spot on, demonstrating a keen understanding of the idiom of the source text: 'Maer Raserye was genaemt sijn raet' [But Rage was the name of his counsellor] (*Vanden ridder* 267.1).

This exploration of the cross-cultural interactions of French and Middle Dutch in the contemporary translations of *Le Chevalier délibéré* by Olivier de La Marche, while not exhaustive, has sought to reveal that French and Middle Dutch sit easily side by side in both target texts, and especially in Johannes Pertcheval's *Den camp vander doot*. The abundance of French words in his poem probably ought not to be that surprising given that Brussels was one of the principal residences of the French-speaking court, and hence it is not unreasonable to anticipate a higher density of words of French origin in the literary idiom at his disposal. What is perhaps more unexpected is the proficiency as a translator that the Haarlemer Pieter Willemsz often shows in *Vanden ridder welghemoet*, and that my sampling of his rendering of particular clusters of words has brought to light. But here too we ought not to be so surprised by his keen knowledge of French culture as represented in the aristocratic allegorical source text once we recall that the printer Jacob Bellaert had printed in Haarlem concurrent Middle Dutch/French editions (*c.* 1485–86) of two of the masterpieces of Burgundian court literature by Raoul Lefèvre: the stories of Jason and of Troy.[44] Both translators, thus, have a highly developed linguistic awareness of cultural productions in French and skilfully illustrate, each in his own way — Pertcheval by cleaving to the French original and Willemsz by proceeding more spontaneously — the processes of cross-cultural interaction in their Middle Dutch versions of *Le Chevalier délibéré*.

Notes to Chapter 7

1. There are currently eighteen known manuscripts of *Le Chevalier délibéré*. Carleton W. Carroll provides essential information on sixteen of these; see Olivier de La Marche, *Le Chevalier deliberé (The Resolute Knight)*, ed. by Carleton W. Carroll, trans. by Lois Hawley Wilson and Carleton W. Carroll (Tempe: Arizona Center for Medieval and Renaissance Studies, 1999), pp. 14–26. References below are to stanza and line number, in the form '*Chevalier* 261.1'. When referring to personifications in La Marche's poem, I use the English names from this edition unless specifically discussing French or Dutch terminology. On the manuscript now in the Bibliothèque Jean Bonna in Geneva, see Olivier de La Marche, *Le Chevalier délibéré: édition originale, Paris, par Antoine Vérard, 1488; seconde édition, Gouda, Collaciebroeders (?), 1489; manuscrit, Flandres, env. 1484*, ed. and trans. by Sylviane Messerli (Geneva: Fondation Martin Bodmer, 2010), p. 54. On the manuscript produced in Brussels in 1547 modeled on the Gouda edition, see Christie's, *Valuable Manuscripts and Printed Books: Auction, London, King Street, Tuesday 24 November 2009*, Sale 7760, lot 7.

2. Olivier de La Marche, *Le Chevalier délibéré*, pref. by F. Lippmann (London: for the Bibliographical

Society at the Chiswick Press, 1898); La Marche, 'Le Chevalier délibéré par Olivier de La Marche, Schiedam vers 1498', in Recueil de pièces historiques imprimées sous le règne de Louis XI reproduites en fac-similé, ed. by Émile Picot and Henri Stein (Paris: pour la Société des Bibliophiles François [Francisque Lefrançois, Libraire], 1923), pp. 241–306.
3. See La Marche, Le Chevalier délibéré, ed. and trans. by Messerli.
4. Pertcheval, Den camp vander doot, ed. by Degroote.
5. M. E. Kronenberg, 'Een onbekende Nederlandsche vertaling van Le Chevalier délibéré, door Pieter Willemsz. gemaakt', Tijdschrift voor Nederlandsche Taal- en Letterkunde, 51 (1932), 178–96; M. E. Kronenberg, 'Fragmenten der Nederlandse vertaling van Le Chevalier délibéré door Pieter Willemsz.', Tijdschrift voor Nederlandse Taal- en Letterkunde, 69 (1951), 169–79; Herman Pleij, 'Ridder Welghemoet in Wenen', Literatuur, 4 (1987), 97–98.
6. Jongenelen, 'Pieter Willemsz' vertaling van Le Chevalier délibéré'. Four stanzas of the source poem have each been expanded into two; stanza 338 is replaced by three final stanzas (363–65) that serve as a colophon in which Pieter Willemsz declares he completed the translation of this poem from the French in 1492 and laments the recent death of his patron Klaas van Ruyven, at whose behest he undertook this project. Twenty-one additional stanzas lauding recently deceased prominent figures have been inserted, mainly between stanzas 278 and 279 of La Marche's poem; I have left these interpolated stanzas aside in the analysis of Willemsz's translation as his authorship of these stanzas is uncertain. References to the Seversz edition below are to stanza and line number. The quotations from the Seversz edition, and all other pre-modern sources, are normalized in accordance with standard editorial practices.
7. Jongenelen, 'Jan Pertcheval's Translation of Le Chevalier délibéré'. Jongenelen argues in this article that the target audience for Johannes Pertcheval's translation was the Dutch-speaking urban middle classes (pp. 207, 212).
8. Jongenelen is also particularly adept at identifying translation errors in each work: see 'Jan Pertcheval's Translation of Le Chevalier délibéré', pp. 201–02; 'Pieter Willemsz' vertaling van Le Chevalier délibéré', pp. 248–49. A few more translation errors can be added to those cited by Jongenelen and by Kronenberg in 'Een onbekende Nederlandsche vertaling', pp. 194–95. For Den camp vander doot: 'cancellier' (l. 2033) for 'conseillier' (Chevalier 261.1); Pliny's name is omitted (l. 1934) as is the name of the French king (l. 2224), but the name 'Chato' is added (l. 1097) where the French source mentions Plato and Socrates (Chevalier 144.1); 'ioden' are added (l. 512) where the French source only mentions 'Catholicques et payens' (Chevalier 70.8), and 'menige iode' is included among the mighty peoples buried in Fresh Memory's cemetery (l. 1516), though absent from the French source (Chevalier 196). At l. 1483 Cosimo de Medici (Chevalier 192.3) is given as 'Cosmas de medicus', but this might simply be the fault of the compositor. There are likewise occasional missettings of 'u' for 'n' and vice versa, such as 'indas' rather than 'iudas' (l. 501) and 'Teruant' instead of 'Ternant' (l. 1438). At l. 1910 'consoort' is given for 'confoort', at l. 2200 'consort' for 'confort', and at l. 1777 'defendeelde' for 'defendeerde'. Such typesetting errors are likewise relatively few in number in Vanden ridder welghemoet. Of more consequence are 'Sijn harnas' (226.3) for 'Son herault' (Chevalier 220.3), 'mijn paert' for 'mijn baert' (119.7), and 'abijsen' for 'avijsen' (122.7). Willemsz's ignorance of the identity of Amé de Montgesoie (Chevalier 5.3) and Francesco Sforza (Chevalier 184.7) is evident in his translation of these names (6.1, 188.7). See, for the former, Kronenberg, 'Een onbekende Nederlandsche vertaling van Le Chevalier délibéré', pp. 194–95 and, for the latter, Jongenelen, 'Pieter Willemsz' vertaling van Le Chevalier délibéré', p. 249.
9. As Jan Seversz's edition of Vanden ridder welghemoet was not part of a project of parallel reproductions of a French original and a Middle Dutch translation of Le Chevalier délibéré, it does not figure in this part of my discussion.
10. The translations of lines from Den camp vander doot and Vanden ridder welghemoet are my own.
11. The dislocation to the layout of the poetic text caused by the insertion of the Prologue at the outset of the translation is immediately rectified on the verso of the first text leaf (fol. a2^v). From this point on the layout of Den camp vander doot mirrors that of Nachtegael's edition of the French original.
12. Unless indicated otherwise, the translations of lines from Le Chevalier délibéré are those by

Wilson and Carroll (*Le Chevalier délibéré* , ed. by Carroll) with occasional alterations which are signalled in the notes.

13. The rhyme scheme in this octave does not follow that of the rest of the poem; it is rather in rhyming couplets.
14. For the most recent and complete biographical information about Johannes Pertcheval, see Remco Sleiderink, 'Johannes Steemaer alias Pertcheval: De naam en faam van een Brusselse rederijker', in *'Want hi verkende dien name wale': Opstellen voor Willem Kuiper*, ed. by Marjolein Hogenbirk and Roel Zemel (Amsterdam: Stichting Neerlandistiek VU; Münster: Nodus Publikationen, 2014), pp. 149–54.
15. Jozef Duverger, *Brussel als kunstcentrum in de XIVe en de XVe eeuw* (Antwerp: De Sikkel; Ghent: Vyncke, 1935), pp. 86–95. The city also paid Pertcheval for making an almanac (1497–1507) intended for surgeon-barbers (Duverger, p. 86); no copies of these yearly almanacs survive so far as I know.
16. Van Bruaene, *Om beters wille*, p. 64.
17. 'Rekeninghe vander broerscap van Onser Vrouwen Seven Ween', Brussels, Archives de la ville de Bruxelles, Archives historiques, registre 3837 (10 March 1499–21 May 1506), pp. 1–114; 'Liber authenticus sacratissimae utriusque sexus christifidelium confraternitatis septem dolorum beatae Mariae virginis nuncupatae', Brussels, Archives de la ville de Bruxelles, Archives historiques, registre 3413 (10 March 1499–1522(?)), fols 161^r–274^r.
18. Adriaan van der Willigen, *Les Artistes de Harlem: notices historiques avec un précis sur la gilde de St. Luc* (Haarlem: Les Héritiers F. Bohn; The Hague: Martinus Nijhoff, 1870), pp. 53 [1497], 41 [1504]; Hessel Miedema, *De archiefbescheiden van het St. Lukasgilde te Haarlem: 1497–1798*, 2 vols (Alphen aan den Rijn: Canaletto, 1980), II, 395 [1502].
19. *Incunabula Printed in the Low Countries: A Census*, ed. by Gerard van Thienen and John Goldfinch (Nieuwkoop: De Graaf, 1999), p. 259 (no. 1403). Elsewhere I argue that Klaas van Ruyven's brother-in-law Jan van Cats may have sponsored the printing of this edition; see Susie Speakman Sutch, 'De Gouda-editie van *Le Chevalier délibéré*'. Van Cats died in 1488 or 1489, which might explain why his brother-in-law Van Ruyven commissioned Pieter Willemsz's translation.
20. Jelle Haemers, 'Philippe de Clèves et la Flandre: la position d'un aristocrate au coeur d'une révolte urbaine (1477–1492)', in *Entre la ville, la noblesse et l'état: Philippe de Clèves (1456–1528) homme politique et bibliophile*, ed. by Jelle Haemers, Céline Van Hoorebeeck, and Hanno Wijsman (Turnhout: Brepols, 2007), pp. 21–99 (p. 66).
21. The treaty of Cadzand between Ghent and Albert of Saxony, 29 July 1492; the treaty of Sluis between the military leader of the Flemish rebels, Philip of Cleves, and Maximilian's lieutenant-general, 12 October 1492; the treaty of Senlis, between Maximilian and the French king Charles VIII, 23 May 1493. See Jean-Marie Cauchies, *Philippe le Beau, le dernier duc de Bourgogne* (Turnhout: Brepols, 2003), pp. 19–23.
22. Van Bruaene, *Om beters wille*, pp. 63–66; Cauchies, *Philippe le Beau, le dernier duc de Bourgogne*, pp. 30, 32.
23. Henri Stein, *Étude biographique, littéraire et bibliographique sur Olivier de La Marche* (Brussels: Hayez, 1888), p. 189 (*pièces justificatives*, XLV, dated 12 November 1493).
24. Eelco Verwijs and others, *Het Middelnederlandsch woordenboek*, 10 vols (The Hague: Martinus Nijhoff, 1882–1952).
25. 'Lay there, foiled by Debility' in Wilson and Carroll's translation.
26. Godefroy, *Dictionnaire de l'ancienne langue française et de tous ses dialectes du IXe au XVe siècle*, IV, 97: '*forsené*, part. passé, jeté hors du sens, furieux, enragé'. The *tafel* in Nachtegael's edition offers 'sot of dul' as the translation for 'Foursené' (fol. f3^v). Wilson and Carroll opt for 'Madness', rather than the stronger 'Rage' or 'Fury', which both come closer to the meaning of the original French.
27. The presence of the French expressions in ll. 2647–48 points in the same direction.
28. For example: *orisoen* (l. 177), *geordineert* (l. 322), *ghecontinueert* (l. 325), *fantasien* (l. 357), *fantaseren* (l. 526), *declareren* (l. 692), *gheordineert* (l. 737), *in contrarien* (l. 740), *contrarieert* (l. 740), *fantasye* (l. 790), *occupeerne* (l. 1051), *gepointratuert* (l. 1143), *gheborduert* (l. 1146), *presenteren* (l. 1205), *gheexalteert* (l. 1228), *aventurende* (l. 1309), *ghebourdeert* (l. 1699), *instancie* (l. 1709), *chierheit* (l. 1993, deriving

from the French *cher* to render 'magnificence'), *querelen* (l. 2500), *opinioen* (l. 2587), as well as at least two of Latin origin: *gheincorporeert* (l. 234) and *expedieert* (l. 1262), *g(h)eexpedieert* (ll. 1512, 1567).
29. For example: *portraturen* (54.5), *narreert* (60.7), *ymagineren* (75.8), *dissimuleren* (133.3), *chierlic* (163.2, in the sense of 'costly', deriving from the French *cher*), *intencie* (166.4), *domineren* (175.5), *regeren* (175.6), *apperencye* (197.2), *mencie* (197.5), *assistencie* (197.6), *substancy* (221.8), *ordinancie* (274.6), *ordinere* (327.6), *geordineert* (333.6), *geaprobeert* (335.5), *geiugeert* (335.6), *gefaetsoneert* (339.3), *gefigureert* (339.4), *gelimiteerden* (353.7), and at least one of Latin origin: *resolverende* ('Int besluiten mi selven resolverende', 219.3).
30. For example, his usage of a past participle built on the Latin *expedio*, 'to dispatch', at l. 1567 for 'definé' (*Chevalier* 202.7) and l. 1512 for 'despeschié' (*Chevalier* 195.8). On the other hand, when Mary of Burgundy arrives at Atropos's lists, she is seated on a litter, 'une lictiere' (*Chevalier* 253.1), supported by two unicorns. Interestingly Pertcheval does not use the word *litiere*, as might be expected given its Latin root, but rather the Dutch term *rosbaer* in all three instances where *lictiere* occurs in the source. Willemsz, on the contrary, takes over the term from the source in all three cases. These are among a couple of dozen occasions at most where Willemsz has retained a term from the French source and Pertcheval has translated it into Middle Dutch.
31. Kronenberg, 'Fragmenten der Nederlandse vertaling van *Le Chevalier délibéré* door Pieter Willemsz.', p. 175, n. 14: '*emprise*. Overgenomen uit het origineel'.
32. Literally, 'from your first shirt'.
33. *Vroem* (57.5, 60.5, 63.7, 174.3, 184.7 where *vroem* is coupled with *stout*, 187.6, 190.3, 201.5); *stout* (86.6, 249.1); *coen* (173.4), *coene* (190.2 inserted spontaneously).
34. *Camp* (11.8), *campe* (273.1); *strijt* (220.8, 236.8, 310.2), *strijde* (235.8); *vechten* (308.2).
35. *Parcke* (226.2); *baelgen* (227.1); *camp* (308.1), *camp besloten* (310.3), *battaelgen* (224.2).
36. *Parc(k)* (174.7, 255.8); *ter plaetsen* (262.5); *wech* (222.3); *camp* (6.5, 18.3), *te campen* (7.6).
37. *Sc(h)ilt* (13.5, 19.3, 22.3, 83.3, 86.1, 93.7, 94.2, 232.4, 264.3, 323.3, 339.3); *scilde* (88.3, 186.6, 234.8).
38. *Taerge* (l. 139), *taerdge* (l. 1756), *taergie* (l. 1775); *schilt* (ll. 2011, 2331); *sc(h)ilt* to translate *escu* (ll. 92, 587, 609, 627, 671, 674, 1406, 2459).
39. Kronenberg, 'Fragmenten der Nederlandse vertaling van *Le Chevalier délibéré* door Pieter Willemsz.', p. 170, remarks that '[d]e twee vertalingen [...] hemelsbreed verschillen'.
40. Although it is feasible that Willemsz could have penned some of the interpolated stanzas, this cannot be conclusively proven.
41. Kronenberg, 'Een onbekende Nederlandsche vertaling van *Le Chevalier délibéré*, door Pieter Willemsz. gemaakt', p. 182, remarks that Pertcheval's translation 'zich vrijwel slaafs aan het Fransche voorbeeld houdt' [adheres almost slavishly to its French source]; Jongenelen judges Pertcheval to be 'indeed a very accurate translator who translated the original text almost 1-to-1' ('Jan Pertcheval's Translation of *Le Chevalier délibéré*', p. 212), and *Den camp vander doot* to be 'een heel strikte en adequate vertaling' [a highly rigorous and appropriate translation] ('Pieter Willemsz' vertaling van *Le Chevalier délibéré*', p. 233). For his part, Degroote, in the introduction to his edition of Pertcheval's poem, praises 'hoe nauwkeurig over het algemeen onze Vlaamsche dichter zijn model heeft weten na te bootsen' [how accurately, in general terms, our Flemish poet managed to replicate his source] (p. xxxi) and concludes, regarding his translation, 'Zoo hebben we hier in "den Camp vander doot" een vertaling, die vrij zuiver kan genoemd worden' [Hence we have here, in *Den camp vander doot* [The Joust of Death], a translation that can be called quite pure] (p. xxxiii).
42. Kronenberg, 'Fragmenten der Nederlandse vertaling van *Le Chevalier délibéré* door Pieter Willemsz.', p. 170; Jongenelen, 'Pieter Willemsz' vertaling van *Le Chevalier délibéré*', p. 249.
43. Pertcheval, *Den camp vander doot*, ed. by Degroote, p. 74, takes *stoet* to be *staet* and thus translates 'ter quader fame staen' as 'een slechte reputatie hebben'.
44. See *Incunabula Printed in the Low Countries*, ed. by Thienen and Goldfinch, nos. 1416, 1417, 1420, and 1421: Raoul Lefèvre, *Fais et prouesses du chevalier Jason* ([Haarlem: Jacob Bellaert, c. 1486–1488]) (USTC 71245); Raoul Lefèvre, *Historie van den vromen ridder Jason* (Haarlem: Jacob Bellaert, [c. 1483–1485]) (USTC 435612); Raoul Lefèvre, *Le Recueil des histoires de Troyes* ([Haarlem: Jacob Bellaert, c. 1485–1486]) (USTC 71249); Raoul Lefèvre, *Vergaderinge der historien*

van Troyen (Haarlem: Jacob Bellaert, 1485) (USTC 435730). Among the seventeen or so works Bellaert printed at Haarlem between 1483 and 1486, *Fais et prouesses du chevalier Jason* and *Le Recueil des histoires de Troyes* were the only works in French.

CHAPTER 8

The Blind Leading the Blind? Choreographing the Transcultural in Pierre Michault's *La Dance aux aveugles* and Gheraert Leeu's *Van den drie blinde danssen*

Rebecca Dixon

On 9 August 1482 the Gouda printer Gheraert Leeu published *Van den drie blinde danssen*, a translation of the Burgundian Pierre Michault's *La Dance aux aveugles* (1464), a *prosimetrum* allegory in which a first-person narrator or *acteur*, accompanied by Understanding, visits three parks, each governed by a blind figure who presides over the world's allegorical dances: love, fortune, and death. The translator, though broadly following closely the structure and content of Michault's original, does things differently with verse as he reworks the courtly original for the new urban context of the *rederijkerskamers*, the chambers of rhetoric. In so doing, he contributes to the transcultural traffic of texts from French to Dutch gaining momentum in the Burgundian Netherlands in the later fifteenth century. Both these poetic traditions — the courtly and the urban, the French- and the Dutch-speaking — have at their heart technical virtuosity, but this functions in distinct ways which are specific to the context in and for which the works were produced; and it is a virtuosity which thereby speaks to a complex interweaving of intertextual and ideological engagement across cultures.[1] This study discusses how such an engagement is enacted in the Gouda translation of Pierre Michault's text, briefly commenting in the first instance on the relationship of the translation to the source text, before focusing on questions of form and versification in the two works. In *Van den drie blinde danssen*, the meaningful contrasts of line- and stanza-length in *La Dance aux aveugles* are recognized and remodelled, and local features of versification in the French text are responded to and extended, in ways that clearly mark the Dutch text as an especially rich example of transcultural translation.

Before discussing these issues, however, an outline of the context in which the two works were produced, and of their content, is in order. Often confused with another author, Michault Taillevent, who worked for the Burgundian court a generation before him,[2] Pierre Michault fulfilled an apparently unremunerated clerical role in the service of Philip the Good, third Valois Duke of Burgundy, and his son Charles, Count of Charolais (the future Charles the Bold), in the period up to 1468.[3] He is responsible for a number of allegorical poetical and *prosimetrum* works, including the *Procès de l'honneur féminin* (after 1461/before 1464),[4] the *Doctrinal du temps present* (1466), as well as the text which concerns us here, the *Dance aux aveugles* (1464).[5] Pierre Michault attests his authorship of the *prosimetrum* in a punning *explicit*, playing on the modesty topos familiar in the literature of the period:

> PIERRE ne peut humeur de basme rendre,
> ne dure teste actaindre a bien hault stile:
> pour ce submés le sens qu'on peut cy prendre
> a tous lisans a qui plaira l'entendre
> par eslever entendement habile,
> les priant tous que par voie docile
> il leur plaise corriger bas et hault
> leur escolier et disciple MICHAULT.[6]

[[This stone/]Pierre can yield no balm, nor make an impression on recalcitrant minds with a lofty style. I therefore submit whatever sense can be gleaned from this to all those who may read it, and will be prepared to heed it by bringing to bear the appropriate understanding. I humbly request of all that, in a spirit of instruction, they kindly correct the errors — wherever they may find them — of their student and disciple Michault.]

The *Dance* obviously enjoyed considerable popularity in court circles and beyond: the work appears in some fourteen extant manuscripts, whole or in part, either as the sole item or in compilations,[7] and in twelve editions printed across a wide geographical area between 1479 (Bruges, Colard Mansion, and Geneva, Louis Cruse) and 1543 (Lyon, Olivier Arnoullet).[8] Further testament to the *Dance*'s popularity and range, of course, is the production and publication of the Dutch translation on which this study is focused. W. J. Schuijt suggests that '[b]lijkens het grote aantal handschriften en wiegedrukken, binnen enkele tientallen jaren vervaardigd, is deze "blinde dans" waarschijnlijk wel een sort "boekhandelsucces" geweest' [as shown by the large number of manuscripts and incunabula [sic], produced within a few decades, this 'blind dance' was indeed probably a 'bestseller' of some kind] (p. xlviii). Here, Schuijt seems to be melding the two separate manuscript and print traditions of the French and Dutch versions of the work in a way that uncomfortably appropriates the French text and denies the diversity of its receptions in different places and times. This is not quite the point, and not quite what I am highlighting here. What I am underlining, rather, is that the popularity of the text was such that a distinct version was produced, which — like the Dutch versions of Olivier de La Marche's *Chevalier Délibéré* and Colijn Caillieu's adaptation of Amé de Montgesoie's *Pas de la mort* — forms part of the cross-cultural traffic that is central to the present volume.[9]

As noted at the outset, a single edition of the translation was printed in Gouda in 1482 by Gheraert Leeu.[10] Leeu began his printing career in Gouda in 1479, and published 69 works there before moving the centre of his operations in 1484 to Antwerp, where he printed some 159 books before meeting his untimely death in 1492 in a fight with his punch-cutter. His output in both centres is primarily devotional and for the most part in Latin, though as is shown in the case of his publication in 1479 of a Dutch-language *Reynaert die vos* and in his translations of French texts like the *Dance aux aveugles*, Leeu also worked in the vernacular, presumably when he saw a market for a particular work.[11] His edition of Pierre Michault's work, *Van den drie blinde danssen*, is the sole translation from French into Dutch that he published in his Gouda period — the Antwerp spell saw two editions of what was presumably the same translation of *Paris et Vienne* in 1487 and 1491, and a Dutch *Histoire de la belle Mélusine* in 1491; and it is the only one of these translations that bears the name of its translator.[12] In a way which mirrors, in sentiment if not entirely in content, the practice adopted by Pierre Michault himself, the *explicit* of the printed translation includes, again in knowingly modest terms, a reference to one 'Martijn':

> Ghi die de penne wel hebt ghedreghen,
> Begrijpt die tot tleeren is gheneghen:
> Dijn scamel scoelkint ende clercxken Martijn.[13]

[You who have wielded your pens effectively, correct the errors of him who is eager to learn: your lowly schoolboy and novitiate Martijn.]

Nothing more is known about the identity of this 'schoolboy and novitiate'; and speculation on whether he is real, or rather a playful device on the part of whoever might have been the author of this translation, is less interesting that what the reference says about attitudes to the work in the context in which it was produced. Unlike the translation of the *Doctrinal du temps present*, which appeared in Dutch as the *Doctrinael des tijts* in 1486 from the Haarlem press of Jacob Bellaert, 'Martijn''s *Van den drie blinde danssen* does not set itself up *as* a translation. Where the faithful rendering in the *Doctrinael* of 'Pieter Michiel''s prefatory dedication to Philip the Good highlights while it reiterates the work's courtly Burgundian provenance,[14] the reframing of authorship here in the *Danssen* divorces the reader and the text from that provenance, and recontextualizes the work for a different public in the urban ambit of West Flanders, and of the *rederijkerskamers*.[15] It would be dangerous, because overly simplistic, to make too much of the urban/courtly distinction in cross-cultural textual traffic in this period, just as it would be to separate too starkly the practice of the francophone poet and the *rederijker*, for the process is precisely one of exchange rather than dichotomies. Nevertheless, questions of authorship and public are central to the changes wrought on the French text by 'Martijn' on a formal as well as a semantic level, as I outline below.

Of course, it is impossible in the modern scholarly context to 'un-know' that what is at issue here is a translation; and on the level of content and of semantics the work printed by Leeu is a very faithful rendering indeed of Pierre Michault's original. Whether in French or in Dutch, the text takes the form of the recounting of a dream-vision in which a figure, known in both versions as the 'Acteur',[16] is 'Actaint au ceur par ung corroux terrestre' (p. 83)/'In therte geraect uut een ardsch verdriet' (p. 6) [Wounded in the heart by a worldly sorrow]. He enters a room divided into three parks in the company of Entendement/Verstant [Understanding]: in these three parks reside blind personified abstractions, respectively Cupido

[Love], Fortune/Fortune ofte Aventeure [Fortune], and Atropos/Dood [Death], who are responsible for governing and even choreographing the world's allegorical dances.[17] In both versions, the visits on which Understanding leads the Acteur are described in prose sections, some of which take the form of lengthy dialogues in which Understanding outlines the moral import of the parks and the dances that take place in them. Each blind figure speaks of her/his powers in a lengthy passage of verse; and verse is also used both in short prefaces to the visits, which we can presume to be the Acteur's *post-hoc* glosses on his experiences, and in a final dialogue between the Acteur and Understanding which supplies the knowledge necessary to thwart the three blind rulers and to remedy the threat inherent in the dances witnessed in the dream. At this most basic of formal levels, then, the Dutch translator of the *Dance aux aveugles* is highly respectful of his source:[18] verse and prose are used for identical purposes as the content of the original is rendered in the reworking; and the only difference in this regard is that 'Martijn' prefaces the translation proper with a *referein* of three sixteen-line stanzas and an eight-line envoi entitled 'Princessen', all with the refrain '[s]cencke den vrouwen den blinden dans' [present the blind dance to the ladies] (p. 3).[19] These verses form a sort of prologue to the work that will ensue, describing its general tenor; they are followed by a prose outline of its content, structure, and form, '[w]elcke materie half dicht, half prose gheordineert is' [which is composed half in verse and half in prose] (p. 5). Beyond this point, however, there is little to distinguish the two texts in terms of their structure; and the same can be said when the French and Dutch versions are compared more closely on a semantic level. There are, however, various elements to note before moving on to an examination of formal concerns in the two texts.[20]

At this semantic level, most of the translational changes wrought upon Pierre Michault's text exemplify the process of 'acculturation', as Jane Taylor has termed the broadly contemporaneous literary phenomenon — and consequent translational practice — of *mise en prose* at the Burgundian court. Taylor describes acculturation as 'a process whereby the socio-culturally unfamiliar is recast in familiar terms, so that the reader can understand systems and phenomena in a source text corresponding to his own ideologies, preconceptions and behaviour-patterns'.[21] Broadly analogous with Lawrence Venuti's concept of the 'domestication' through translation of 'foreign' elements in the source text, this process of acculturation permits both the expansion and the reduction — even the complete excision — of details in the original, in ways designed variously to facilitate the reading experience for the new public.[22] We see a number of these processes at work in 'Martijn''s translation of the *Dance aux aveugles*.

A first example, involving suppression of information on the part of the translator, occurs when the Acteur enters the first park which is inhabited by Love. Looking about, he describes what he sees: a naked prince wearing a crown and sporting wings, a beautiful yet fully clothed maiden, and a mixed pair of minstrels, as well as a phalanx of people:

> Tout ce parc, au demeurant, estoit plain de gens de tous estas et de tous pays, regions et contrees, et voire de nations moult estranges; et y estoient hommes et femmes de plusieurs eaiges, tant Payens, Yndois, Caldees, Juifz, Turcs, Sarrasins

que autres. Et tous dançoient aux sons des instrumens en la presence du jeune prince. (Michault, *Œuvres poétiques,* p. 86)

[This whole park, moreover, was full of people of all stations and from every land, region, and country, and indeed from very remote nations. There were men and women of different eras: there were pagans, Indians, Chaldeans, Jews, Turks, Saracens, and many more. And all were dancing to the strains of the instruments in the presence of the young prince.]

In the French original, as we see here, both the provenance and the religions of the assembled company are noted; in the Dutch translation, by contrast, the crowd is differently depicted. 'Martijn' sets the scene in the same way as Michault, the only difference in the two accounts being that the translator specifies the instruments — 'sacpipe' [bagpipes] and 'luyte' [lute] respectively — played by the male and female minstrels. However, he then introduces the dancers thus:

Al dit parck was andersijns vol volcs van alrehande staten, condicien, lande, conincriken ende vreemde contreyen, also wel van mannen als vrouwen persoenen uut Indien, Caldeen, Macedonien, Syrien, ende Turkien, als duytsche, walsche, overlantsche als nederlantsche tale ende sprake, elc houdende voet naden twee voirscreven pipers ende hoer spel, in die teghenwoirdicheit vanden voerscreven prinche. (*Van den drie blinde danssen,* pp. 11–12)

[Besides, this whole park was full of people of all kinds of stations, conditions, lands, kingdoms, and foreign countries, both men and women; people from India, Chaldea, Macedonia, Syria, and Turkey, and people who spoke Low German, French, Rhenish, and Dutch; each was dancing to the music played by the performers mentioned above, in the presence of the aforementioned prince.]

Like its source, the Dutch version comments on the geographical provenance of the individuals, but offers no counterpart to the 'pagans' mentioned in the French — hence intensifying the concentration on geography, doubtless effected in order to appeal to the new urban audience of the reworking. This hypothesis is supported by the fact that the translator picks up on the French author's allusive 'autres', and adds further, highly specific and familiarizing information about the inhabitants or near-neighbours of his presumed west Flanders base.[23] Recasting the unfamiliar in familiar terms, as Taylor's notion of acculturation would have it, shows the translator engaging cross-culturally with his source, and facilitates his text's appeal in a new context.

The same can be said of those further, more concerted, moments where 'Martijn' expands on the French original to make its 'systems and phenomena' more comprehensible and more palatable to a new public familiar, perhaps, with a different literary tradition. Once Understanding has explained to the Acteur where they are, he notes that Love is wont to declare his power to the people; and '[s]ur ce point, Cupido fit signe que chascun se teust. Lors cesserent les instrumens; et chascun fut assiz pour ouyr la deifique proposition' (p. 88) [thereupon Love gestured for all to be silent. Then the instruments ceased to play; and all were seated to listen to what the deity had to say]. The translator supplies the same basic information, but supplements it:

> Na deser tale ende wedersprake tusschen Tverstant ende den Acteur, Cupido aldus sittende in sinen throon dede een teyken dat elc sweghe. Alsdan hem obedierende, cessieerden die instrumenten; elc koos ruste ende stede om an te hooren Cupido proposicie, voortstel ende redene seer wonderlic verclaert. (*Van den drie blinde danssen*, p. 14)
>
> [After these words exchanged between the Author and his understanding, Love, sitting on his throne, gestured for all to be silent. In obedience to him, the instruments then fell silent; everyone found a place to rest to listen to Love's words, speech, and argument — which was dazzling in its eloquence.]

As befits his godly status, Love sits enthroned, and has both such power that the instruments cease at his bidding and such rhetorical force that all fall silent to hear his top-quality oration. For an urban public better versed in the more community-focused, performative, and competitive *rederijker* culture than in the top-down courtly communication seen via Pierre Michault's introduction of Love, this apparently simple expansion clearly mattered, not least as it provides with its reference to eloquence a neat bit of self-publicity on 'Martijn''s part for the well-wrought words which will follow.

Finally, at this semantic level, it is important to note that changes are made on the part of the translator to the verse sections of this *prosimetrum* allegory as well as to the prose passages, with a similarly acculturating or domesticating function. The following example, in which telling changes are made in the choice of words used, is a case in point. In his oration, Love indicates the ways in which his influence over his subjects can make them behave. Enumerating sardonically the things credulous humans do for love, and especially interestingly for our purposes here, Love indicates not only that lovers write verse for the object of their affections, but states the particular form that these poetic tokens should take: 'je faiz rondeaulx et balades parfaire' [I make people compose *rondeaulx* and *ballades*] (p. 90), *rondeaux* and *ballades* being popular types of fixed-form verse in the later medieval francophone courtly context. The Dutch translator responds creatively, and appropriately, making a small but highly significant change to Pierre Michault's text. In the translation, instead of writing *rondeaux* and *ballades* to their ladies, '[d]een maect refreynen ter eren van haer' [some write *refereinen* in her honour] (p. 20) — using, in other words, the poetic form par excellence of Dutch verse rhetoric in the later fifteenth century, and the form most commonly exploited in rhetoric competitions in the *rederijkerskamers*.[24] With this semantic change the Dutch translator appeals to the formal knowledge of the new public for whom he writes, and ensures that his work corresponds to their 'ideologies, preconceptions and behaviour-patterns', as Taylor has it. This is also true of the way in which 'Martijn' responds, precisely, to the formal challenges of the French text for a Dutch-speaking public; and it is to this that I now turn.

Important recent work by Adrian Armstrong and others has illuminated the previously under-considered role played by technical virtuosity in francophone poetry of the later Middle Ages.[25] Poets at the time were engaged in the production of works that were not only formally innovative in their own right, but also stunningly ambitious when placed (as was common practice) in competitive comparison and exchange with the work of their peers. Pierre Michault is no exception: his work, and perhaps most significantly the *Dance aux aveugles*, shows evidence of a creative approach to form and to versification which mirrors that of his fellow-poets; and it is this creativity to which the Dutch translator responds in his reworking. In the following pages I first outline the way in which Michault himself exploits the possibilities of poetry in the *Dance aux aveugles*, before showing how 'Martijn' exceeds his illustrious francophone predecessor to make of his translation a particularly meaningful example of the cross-cultural literary traffic in the Burgundian Netherlands in the later fifteenth century.

As was noted above, verse is used in three contexts, and under three types, in the *Dance*: for the Acteur's glosses on his meetings with Love and Fortune (there is no standalone gloss given for Death), in the disquisitions of the three blind figures, and in the final explicatory dialogue between the Acteur and Understanding. Distinctions in form and metre, then, are governed by and dependent on character; and these formal and metrical distinctions remain the same in each appearance of the three blind rulers, lending an educational as well as a moral weight to the lines. The Acteur's authoritative pronouncements and warnings, for example, are always presented in long stanzas, either heterometric or with lines containing an odd number of syllables: at their shortest these are at least *douzains*, but can be as long as *vingtains*.[26] His warnings thus acquire an affective force by using forms that, in *seconde rhétorique*, were associated with emotional disorder or excess (heterometric stanzas) or with disruption and lack (heptasyllables).[27] The reader is encouraged via the form to see in his words the outpourings of one who has seen much and, crucially, learned from the experience (a point underscored by the form of Understanding's explanations later, as we shall see), and to learn from them in similar fashion himself.

The blind rulers' speeches, by contrast, all use decasyllables, whether in *huitains*, as in the case of Fortune, or *dizains*, as we see in the pronouncements of Love and Death. In their disquisitions the blind rulers' language is apparently forceful, weighty, and authoritative — elements which would normally be associated with the decasyllable. However, through formal virtuosity and contrast with both the Acteur's lines and the closing dialogue, Pierre Michault undermines these ostensible characterological traits. Just as the heterometric discourse of the Acteur lends credence to his words, so too does the choice of form and metre at the end of the poem when Understanding explains what they have seen to the Acteur using octosyllabic *septains*:

> L'ACTEUR
> J'ay maintenant, loué soit Dieu!
> aucunement la congnoissance
> des trois pars qui sont en ce lieu,
> par ton moyen et pourveance,
> et apperçoy comme on y dance ;
> maiz je te requier que procedes
> a m'enseigner sur les remedes,

> ENTENDEMENT
> Je suis dés pieça disposé
> a mon pouoir de te respondre
> sur ce qui sera proposé
> par toy, pour tes erreurs confondre;
> et, pour mieulx actaindre et apondre
> a tous tes bons propoz et veulx,
> demande tout ce que tu veulx.
> (Michault, *Œuvres poétiques*, pp. 122–23)
>
> [ACTEUR
> Now, praise be to God, I have acquired some knowledge of the three parks in this place through your help and intervention, and I see how people dance here; but I beseech you now to teach me about the remedies for this.
> UNDERSTANDING
> As of now I am willing to answer, as best I can, any questions you may have, to correct your errors. So, ask whatever you want in order that I can respond to all your good intentions and wishes.]

When set against both the shorter lines and the decasyllable, the octosyllable permits two things to happen: firstly, its intermediacy short-circuits the bombast of the rulers' decasyllables, and reveals their words to be intemperate bluster; and secondly, its prestige and authority suggests, precisely, that it is through these measured warnings that the Acteur can gain his own voice of reason.

Two things are at stake here. On the one hand, in Pierre Michault's text narratological, even ontological, issues govern the choice of verse forms and their conventional applications.[28] It is at least partly in relation to one another that the line-lengths acquire their values: by virtue of both their positioning at a point of narrative closure and of their position in the middle of the metrical spectrum as Michault uses it, octosyllables come to strike a happy medium between the 'lacking' heptasyllable and the 'inflated' decasyllable. On the other hand, his formal decisions are rooted in competition with his fellow-poets: in this period, the rules of engagement are laid down to be broken and exploited for poetic gain. We see how this happens intertextually in the francophone context with the *Dance aux aveugles*, via the sense in which it both corresponds to and stands apart from issues in contemporary French verse. Firstly, there are specific precedents for the use of the heptasyllable and of heterometric verse in similar ways to those deployed by Michault in the work of authors such as Christine de Pizan.[29] Secondly, the use of the decasyllable assumes an importance when set against the tendency of authors of the previous generation — such as Alain Chartier and Michault Taillevent — to use the octosyllable in didactic verse: by this contrast decasyllables both appear impressive and take on the pretentiousness seen in the rulers' pronouncements.[30] Further, similar issues of meaningful engagement with convention and of competition, this time both intertextual and intratextual, are at play in *Van den drie blinde danssen*.

In 'Martijn''s translation, the formal contrasts established by Pierre Michault in the French text have clearly been recognized; and they have been compensated for in creative ways in the Dutch reworking. Because it is dependent on stress-patterns rather than on syllable-count, Dutch verse does not lend itself to line-length contrasts in the same way as does French; consequently, the translator conveys the contrasts he has noted, and their value, through creativity with stanza form. While this practice is on the one hand an example of what translation theorists have termed 'compensation' ('a technique for making up the loss of a source text effect by recreating a similar effect in the target text'), it is also crucial evidence of the competitiveness of the Dutch author with both the French author and his own *rederijker* tradition and indeed with himself.[31]

In the French text, as I outlined above, Pierre Michault's basic means of presenting the glosses on Love and Fortune (Death, we recall, is not explicitly explained) are the same in each case: that is, he does so in a formally innovative way via an unequal number of stanzas of varying length, either heterometric or with lines containing an odd number of syllables. Because Dutch is not governed by syllable-count, but because 'Martijn' was a close and subtle enough reader both to identify Pierre Michault's formal dexterity and to wish to respond to it, the translator must find another means to show ingenuity and poetic skill. What happens is that, whereas in the French text the basic principle is the same for each gloss, in the Dutch reworking something different, and very interesting, is done for each ruler.

The Acteur's response to Love, for example, which in the French takes up sixty lines of verse, is accorded in the Dutch seven twelve-line stanzas which rhyme *aabaabbbbcbbc*. Crucially, while the French stanzas are formally unrelated to each other (see n. 26 above), 'Martijn' innovates by developing an enchained sequence, in which the final rhyme of one stanza is identical with the first rhyme of the next. The case of the response to Fortune is similar. Here, where the French verse takes up three *seizains*, its Dutch equivalent constitutes a single *ballade*: a *ballade* in the Dutch rather than French sense, a variant of the *referein* where rhymes were normally the same across the different stanzas, but no refrain was used. In this instance the rhymes of each stanza are different, but the *c*-rhyme of the third stanza is identical with the *a*-rhyme of the envoi.[32] In both cases, in other words, the Dutch sections develop formal relationships between some or all of their successive stanzas that do not exist in the French. Further, Dutch verse does not allow for line-length contrasts based on syllable counts, but the lines used in these instances are much shorter than the standard four-beat lines, having three stresses at most. What this reveals, then, is that 'Martijn' acknowledges and reproduces — albeit only to a limited extent — Michault's line-length contrasts. It is through these features and local formal changes that metrical contrast is both replicated and 'compensated' for: by doing something different with the verse, 'Martijn' responds to Pierre Michault's formal innovation with an extra level of innovation of his own.

A final example illustrates a further, and more interesting, way in which 'Martijn' dextrously and subtly responds to his source, and exceeds its creativity with virtuosity of his own. This can be seen when Death takes the stage. A comparison between this moment in the French and the Dutch texts reveals that the tenor of what appears in the content of both versions is similar, with just some local acculturating changes brought in to appeal to a new public. At the level of form, though, something quite striking is in play. Both versions present their material in a ten-line stanza, but where they differ is in their rhyme schemes: while the French text rhymes *ababccdcd*, the Dutch reworking runs *ababbcbcbc*. In other words, there is one fewer rhyme in the Dutch stanza. Rather than reworking syntax to accommodate both material and the rhyme of the original, as might be seen in some instances of French to Dutch translation in this context at this time, and as the four-beat line would give 'Martijn' enough flexibility to achieve, the translator has set himself the far stiffer technical challenge of using one fewer rhyme for every stanza of a lengthy passage. This is interesting for two reasons. On the one hand, this innovation by 'Martijn' is born out of a recognition of and desire to engage intertextually with another poet's skill and to compensate for it competitively in his own reworking. On the other hand, and more startlingly, this process bespeaks an intratextual understanding of his own practice of translation, for what he is doing here as he responds to the challenge laid down by an unknown predecessor is, moreover, challenging himself and the limits of what he can do with verse.

When viewed alongside the variation in stanza-form discussed above, this innovation signals that we are witnessing in this instance not simply a meaningful relationship between verse forms within the text(s), but — more significantly — that there has been an effort on the part of the translator to devise more complex and more challenging stanzaic structures than in the source as he reworks the text for a new context and a new audience. Furthermore, 'Martijn' brings another degree of formal complexity and poetic innovation to the work by crafting a further (self-referential) narrative level, mediating the first-person account through references to 'den Acteur' [the author] and 'sinen verstande' [his understanding].[33] Thus, ideological concerns are woven into the text through both formal prestidigitation and intertextual engagement across cultures. Far from being a case of 'the blind leading the blind', the example of the *Dance aux aveugles* and *Van den drie blinde danssen* and of their respective authors shows the confluence of the poetic virtuosity attested widely in both regions to be a complex choreography of transcultural translation.

Notes to Chapter 8

1. For an important early study of this phenomenon, see Armstrong, 'Translating Poetic Capital in Fifteenth-Century Brussels', as well as the contributions to this volume by Susie Speakman Sutch and Dirk Coigneau (Chapters 7 and 6 respectively).
2. On Michault Taillevent, who worked in the period c. 1427–48, see Robert Deschaux, *Un poète bourguignon du XVe siècle: Michault Taillevent (édition et étude)* (Geneva: Droz, 1975). On the Michault Taillevent/Pierre Michault confusion, see Arthur Piaget, 'Pierre Michault et Michault Taillevent', *Romania*, 18 (1889), 439–52, and Tania van Hemelryck, 'Le Viel Homme et la mort: observations sur le *Passe Temps* de Michault Taillevent', *Les Lettres Romanes*, 51 (1997), 19–34 (pp. 19–20, n. 2). See also Pierre Michault, *Œuvres poétiques*, ed. by Barbara Folkart (Paris: Union Générale des Éditions, 1980), p. 8.
3. He subsequently moved to work for Artus de Bourbon. See Michault, *Œuvres poétiques*, p. 8, as well as Pierre Michault, *Doctrinael des tijts*, ed. by Schuijt, pp. 56–57, and (the almost identical passage in) Pierre Michault, *Van den drie blinde danssen*, ed. by Schuijt, pp. xv–xviii.
4. Folkart notes that the only means by which we are able to date this work is through an allusion

it contains to the death of the Burgundian poet Martin Le Franc (Michault, *Œuvres poétiques*, p. 10). The reference in the *Procès* does not specify this detail, but Le Franc died in 1461. See Michault, *Œuvres poétiques*, p. 29, as well as Barbara Folkart, 'Le *Procès d'honneur féminin* de Pierre Michault', *Le Moyen Français*, 2 (1978), 3–133.

5. For dating, see Michault, *Œuvres poétiques*, p. 10 and Michault, *Van den drie blinde danssen*, p. xix. The *Complainte sur la mort d'Ysabeau de Bourbon* (1465) has sometimes been ascribed to Michault, but should in fact be attributed to Amé de Montgesoie. For differing positions on the *Complainte*, see Michault, *Œuvres poétiques*, pp. 141–69; Barbara Folkart, 'Perspectives médiévales sur la mort: la complainte de Pierre Michault sur la mort d'Ysabeau de Bourbon', *Le Moyen Français*, 3 (1980), 29–74; Thomas Walton, 'Les Poèmes d'Amé de Montgesoie: *Le Pas de la mort* et *La Complainte sur la mort d'Isabelle de Bourbon*', *Medium Ævum*, 2 (1933), 1–33.

6. Michault, *Œuvres poétiques*, p. 139. Further references are provided in the text. All translations from French and Dutch primary and secondary sources are my own.

7. These are: Geneva, Bibliothèque publique et universitaire, MS français, 182, fols 198^r–230^r; Lille, Bibliothèque municipale, MS 401, fol. 8; London, British Library, MS Harley 4453; Paris, Bibliothèque de l'Arsenal, MS 5113; Paris, Bibliothèque nationale de France (BnF), MS fr. 1119; Paris, BnF, MS fr. 1186, fols 55^r–98^v; Paris, BnF, MS fr. 1654, fols 149^r–187^r; Paris, BnF, MS fr. 1696; Paris, BnF, MS fr. 1989, fol. 1^r; Paris, BnF, MS fr. 5028, fols 237^r–270^r; Paris, BnF, MS fr. 12788; Paris, BnF, MS fr. 22922; Paris, BnF, MS fr. 24442, fol. 67^r; Philadelphia, University of Pennsylvania, Rare Book and Manuscript Library, Codex 947, fols 1^{r-v}.

8. The editions are: Geneva, [Louis Cruse, 1479] (USTC 71368); [Bruges, Colard Mansion, *c.* 1479–1481] (USTC 71369); [Bréhan-Loudéac], Robin Fouquet and Jean Crès, [1485] (USTC 71370); Lyon, [Guillaume Le Roy, 1485] (USTC 71371); Lyon, [Guillaume Le Roy, 1487] (USTC 71372); Paris, Le Petit Laurens, [1495] (USTC 71373); Paris, Le Petit Laurens, [1495] (USTC 71374); Lyon, Pierre Mareschal and Barnabé Chaussard, [1502] (USTC 64728); [Lyon, Pierre Mareschal, 1503] (USTC 64759); Paris, widow of Michel Le Noir, [1521] (USTC 55580); Lyon, Olivier Arnoullet, 1543 (USTC 40236). A further edition, USTC 89964 (Paris, Bibliothèque de l'École Nationale Supérieure des Beaux-Arts, Masson 910), bears no date or publication details.

9. See Susie Speakman Sutch's chapter in the present volume, as well as Armstrong, 'Translating Poetic Capital in Fifteenth-Century Brussels'.

10. The quarto edition (USTC 435522) is now in Copenhagen, Det Kongelige Bibliotek, Inc. Haun., 2753.

11. See Koen Goudriaan, 'Inleiding', in *Een drukker zoekt publiek: Gheraert Leeu te Gouda 1477–1484*, ed. by Koen Goudriaan and others (Delft: Uitgeverij Eburon, 1993), pp. 3–11 (p. 5). See also Lotte Hellinga-Querido, 'De betekenis van Gheraert Leeu', pp. 12–30 in the same volume.

12. The two *Paris et Vienne* translations are, respectively, *Die historie van den vromen ridder Parijs ende van die schone Vienna* (Antwerp: Gheraert Leeu, 1487) (USTC 435854; Paris, BnF, RES-Y2–698), and *Die historie vanden vromen ridder Paris ende van die scone Vienna* ([Antwerp: Gheraert Leeu, 1491–92]) (USTC 436061; Dublin, Trinity College, OLS 178.0.16 no.4 OL Safe). Leeu is also responsible for a Low German *Paris et Vienne* of 1488 (USTC 438824). His *Mélusine* translation is now extant as Brussels, Bibliothèque royale de Belgique, INC B 1.369 (RP): Jean d'Arras, *Historie van Melusine* (Antwerp: Gheraert Leeu, 1491) (USTC 436129).

13. Michault, *Van den drie blinde danssen*, p. 104. Schuijt's 'edition' of the translation is in fact a facsimile (in what Hellinga-Querido, p. 22, notes is the typeface standardly used by Leeu in the period 1480–83 and which resembled 'de Noord-nederlandse boekhand' [the book hand of the northern Low Countries]) of the Gouda edition. Orthography and punctuation have been normalized in accordance with standard editorial practice. All references to the *Danssen* are to the modern pagination of Schuijt's 'edition', and are provided in the text.

14. See Michault, *Doctrinael des tijts*, p. 88.

15. Important recent studies on these contexts and symbioses include: Adrian Armstrong, *The Virtuoso Circle: Competition, Collaboration, and Complexity in Late Medieval French Poetry* (Tempe: Arizona Center for Medieval and Renaissance Studies, 2012); Mareel, *Voor vorst en stad*; Van Bruaene, *Om beters wille*; Oosterman, 'Tussen twee wateren zwem ik: Anthonis de Roovere

tussen rederijkers en *rhétoriqueurs*'; and Small, 'When Indiciaires Meet Rederijkers'.
16. A subtle yet meaningful distinction occurs between the two versions at this point. In the Dutch text a prose preface is supplied to explain what is to follow: a dialogue between 'den Acteur' [the author] and 'sinen verstande' [his understanding] (p. 5). This explanation adds an extra level of third-person narrative mediation to the Dutch text which is absent from the French source.
17. I give the French and Dutch names for the characters here for information; in what follows the English form will be used.
18. In this sense, too, 'Martijn' differs from the Dutch translator of the *Doctrinal du temps présent*, who does not respect the form and structure of his source-text in that passages which were in verse in the original are translated as prose. See Michault, *Doctrinael des tijts*.
19. On the use of refrains (*refreinen/refereinen*) in Middle Dutch, see Dirk Coigneau, 'Les Concours de "referain": une introduction à la rhétorique néerlandaise', in *Première poésie française de la Renaissance: autour des puys poétiques normands*, ed. by Jean-Claude Arnould and Thierry Mantovani (Paris: Champion, 2003), pp. 489–503.
20. There is doubtless scope for much further work to be done on the mechanics of 'Martijn''s translation in comparison with Pierre Michault's original; as such, certain elements, such as mistranslations and the use of loan-words, do not fall into the ambit of this study. For discussions of how such issues are played out in other, contemporary translations, see: Jongenelen, 'Jan Pertcheval's Translation of *Le Chevalier délibéré*'; Jongenelen, 'Pieter Willemsz' vertaling van *Le Chevalier délibéré*'; and Armstrong, 'Translating Poetic Capital in Fifteenth-Century Brussels', as well as Chapter 7 in this volume.
21. Jane H. M. Taylor, 'The Significance of the Insignificant: Reading Reception in the Burgundian *Erec* and *Cligès*', *Fifteenth-Century Studies*, 24 (1998), 183–97 (p. 183). The phenomenon of the *mise en prose* involves the recasting of earlier francophone verse texts in prose for Duke Philip and his bibliophile circle. The texts chosen usually contained themes — for instance, chivalry or genealogy — which were of interest and importance to this court, but by the mid-fifteenth century the language in which they were written was no longer a comprehensible version of French.
22. On domestication and foreignization in translation, see for example Lawrence Venuti, 'The Formation of Cultural Identities', in his *The Scandals of Translation: Towards an Ethics of Difference* (London: Routledge, 1998), pp. 67–87.
23. Schuijt ascribes this provenance to 'Martijn' on the basis of both the morphology and phonology (adduced via rhyme-words) of lexical items found in his reworked text. See Michault, *Van den drie blinde danssen*, p. xlvii.
24. As Dirk Coigneau notes, the *referein* was inspired by the *ballade* of the French tradition. See Coigneau, 'Les Concours de "referain"', p. 490. On the subject of rhetoric in the Dutch context in this period and beyond, see also Moser, *De strijd voor rhetorica*.
25. See especially Armstrong, *The Virtuoso Circle*. See also Armstrong and Kay, *Knowing Poetry*.
26. The form of these pronouncements in his glossing of the encounter with Love, for example, is as follows: a heptasyllabic *douzain* rhyming *aabaabbbabba*; a heptasyllabic *seizain* (*aaabaaabbbbabbba*), a heterometric *vingtain* (*7a7a7a4a7a7a7a4a7b7b7b7b4b7a7b7b7b4b7a*); and a pentasyllabic *douzain* (*aabaabbbabba*). There is no formal connection (e.g. through shared rhymes) between the successive stanzas, a point which becomes relevant in connection with the Dutch translation.
27. See, for example, Pierre Fabri: 'en lay l'en ne traicte que matieres de grande ioye ou de excessiue douleur, et, quasi, comme en furie, les lignes sont ou courtes ou longues, a la volunté du facteur' [in a *lai* [i.e. a heterometric stanza] only matters of great joy or excessive sorrow are treated; and, as if in a frenzy, the lines are either short or long, as the poet wishes]. See Pierre Fabri, *Le Grand et Vrai Art de pleine rhétorique*, ed. by A. Héron, 3 vols (Rouen: Société des Bibliophiles Normands, 1889–1890), II, 51. On heptasyllables, see Adrian Armstrong, 'Printing and Metrical Naturalisation: Jean Molinet's *Neuf Preux de Gourmandise*', in *Essays in Later Medieval French Literature: The Legacy of Jane H. M. Taylor*, ed. by Rebecca Dixon (Manchester: Manchester University Press, 2010), pp. 143–59.
28. On the ontology of verse in this period, see Armstrong and Kay, *Knowing Poetry*.
29. See, for example, the discussion of Christine's use of the heptasyllable in the *Chemin de longue*

estude and the *Livre du duc de vrais amanz* in Armstrong and Kay, *Knowing Poetry*, pp. 180–82 and 183–84.

30. See in particular Armstrong, *The Virtuoso Circle*, pp. 1–69; for a discussion of cross-cultural formal engagement and competition in similar ways to those I outline here, see also Armstrong, 'Translating Poetic Capital in Fifteenth-Century Brussels'.
31. See Harvey, 'A Descriptive Framework for Compensation', p. 66, and Adrian Armstrong's introduction to this volume.
32. Michault's *seizains* all rhyme *aaabaaabbbbabbba*, though different rhymes are employed in each stanza. The first two are heptasyllabic; the third is heterometric, with heptasyllables punctuated by trisyllables in lines 3, 7, 11, and 15. The stanzas of the Dutch *ballade* rhyme *aaabaaabbbbcbbbc*; the envoi, entitled 'Prinche', rhymes *aaabaaab*. On the Dutch *ballade*, see B. H. Erné, 'Rederijkersballaden oude en nieuwe stijl', *De Nieuwe Taalgids*, 65 (1972), 355–63.
33. See n. 16 above.

BIBLIOGRAPHY

Manuscript Sources

Berlin, Staatsbibliothek Preussischer Kulturbesitz
   MS Germ. Qu. 557
Bruges, Stadsarchief
   216
   385
Brussels, Archives de la ville de Bruxelles
   Archives historiques, registre 3413
   Archives historiques, registre 3837
Brussels, Bibliothèque royale de Belgique
   ms. 228
Copenhagen, Kongelige Bibliotek
   MS GKS 79
Douai, Archives municipales
   CC 204
Geneva, Bibliothèque Jean Bonna
   MS Chifflet
Geneva, Bibliothèque publique et universitaire
   MS français, 182
Ghent, Stadsarchief
   Fonds Sint Joris, 155
   Sint Jorisgilde, niet genummerde reeks
Ghent, Universiteitsbibliotheek
   HS 434
   HS 900
   HS G 6112
Glasgow, University Library
   MS Gen. 2
The Hague, Haags Gemeentearchief
   MS 36
The Hague, Koninklijke Bibliotheek
   MS 79 K 10
   MS 130 B 21
Kassel, Universitätsbibliothek
   4° Ms. poet. et roman. 5
Lille, Archives municipales
   15883 (registre aux titres, M.)
   Comptes de la Ville, 16016
   Comptes de la Ville, 16018
   Comptes de la Ville, 16019

Comptes de la Ville, 16020
Comptes de la Ville, 16125
Lille, Bibliothèque municipale
  MS 401
London, British Library
  Add MS 10290
  Add MS 35087
  MS Harley 4453
Mechelen, Stadsarchief
  Titre IX, section 4, tirs et joutes
New York, Pierpont Morgan Library
  MS M 76
Oudenaarde, Stadsarchief
  Oude Archief, gilden 241
  Oude Archief, gilden 507/II
  Oude Archief, gilden 707/II
  Oude Archief, Stadsrekeningen, 1436–1448
Paris, Bibliothèque de l'Arsenal
  MS 5070
  MS 5113
Paris, Bibliothèque nationale de France
  MS fr. 129
  MS fr. 1119
  MS fr. 1186
  MS fr. 1654
  MS fr. 1696
  MS fr, 1989
  MS fr. 5028
  MS fr. 12788
  MS fr. 22922
  MS fr. 24442
Philadelphia, University of Pennsylvania, Rare Book and Manuscript Library
  Codex 947
Rotterdam, Gemeentearchief
  MS 1534
Wolfenbüttel, Herzog August Bibliothek
  Cod. Guelf 84.2.1 Aug 12°

Primary Sources

Acta sanctorum — Januarii tomus secundus, ed. by Jean Bolland and Godfrey Henschen (Paris: Victor Palmé, 1863)

Acta sanctorum — Aprilis tomus tertius, ed. by Godfrey Henschen and Daniel van Papenbroeck (Paris: Victor Palmé, 1866)

Het Antwerps liedboek, ed. by Dieuwke E. Van der Poel, 2 vols (Tielt: Lannoo, 2004)

BARTHOLOMÆUS ANGLICUS, *Van den proprieteyten der dinghen* (Haarlem: Jacob Bellaert, 1485) [USTC 435725]

Dat bedroch der vrouwen (Utrecht: Jan Berntsz, [c. 1532]) [USTC 421111]

Dat bedroch der vrouwen, ed. by W. L. Braekman (Bruges: Marc Van de Wiele, 1983)

BEKA, JOHANNES DE, *La Traduction française de la Chronographia*, ed. by W. Noomen (The Hague: Excelsior, 1954)

BERLAIMONT, NOËL DE, *Vocabulare van nieus ge-ordineert / Vocabulaire de nouveau donné et de rechief recorrigé* (Antwerp: Jacob van Liesveldt, 1527) [USTC 78045]

BOCCACCIO, GIOVANNI, *Des cent nouvelles*, trans. by Laurent de Premierfait (Paris: [for] Anthoine Vérard, [1499–1503]) [USTC 61164]

—— *Vijftich lustige historien ofte nyeuwicheden*, trans. by D. V. Coornhert (Haarlem: Jan van Zuren, for Jean Bellère of Antwerp, 1564) [USTC 411275]

BOUCHET, JEAN, *De loose vossen der werelt* (Brussels: [Thomas van der Noot], 1517) [USTC 436964]

BOUTILLIER, JEAN, *La Somme rural* (Bruges: Colard Mansion, 1479) [USTC 70933]

—— *Somme rurael* (Delft: Jacob Jacobszoon van der Meer, 1483) [USTC 435578]

CAILLIEU, COLIJN, *Dal sonder wederkeeren of pas der doot*, ed. by Paul de Keyser (Antwerp: De Sikkel, 1936)

CALEPINO, AMBROGIO, *Pentaglottos. Hoc est, quinque linguis, nempe latina, graeca, germanica, flandrica et gallica constans* (Antwerp: Gilles Coppenius, 1546) [USTC 66466]

CASTELEIN, MATTHIJS DE, *De const van rhetoriken* (Ghent: Jan Cauweel, 1555) [USTC 400939]

Les Cent Nouvelles nouvelles, ed. by Pierre Champion (Paris: Droz, 1928)

Les Cent Nouvelles nouvelles, ed. by Franklin P. Sweetser (Geneva: Droz, 1966)

CHASTELLAIN, GEORGES, *Œuvres*, ed. by Joseph Marie Bruno Constantin Kervyn de Lettenhove, 8 vols (Brussels: Heussner, 1863–66)

La Complainte de dame Marguerite ([Antwerp: Gheraert Leeu, c. 1491]) [USTC 71327]

Coninck Karel ende Elegast een schone ghenuechlijcke historie ([Antwerp: Jan van Doesborch?, n.d.]), [USTC 424759]

La Couronnation de l'empereur Charles cinquiesme de ce nom faicte a Boloingne la grasse (Antwerp: Willem Vorsterman, 1530 (=1531 n.s.)) [USTC 77906]

Die crooninghe van den keyser, gheschiet te Boloigne la grasse (Antwerp: Willem Vorsterman, 1530) [USTC 400487]

The Deceyte of Women (London: [William Copland for] Abraham Vele, [1587]) [USTC 505398]

The Deceyte of Women (London: William Copland for John Wight, [1558?]) [USTC 505473]

The Deceyte of Women, in Friedrich Brie, 'The Deceyte of Women: älteste englische Novellensammlung (1547)', *Archiv für das Studium der neueren Sprachen und Literaturen*, 84 (1929), 17–52

DESPARS, NICOLAS, *Cronijke van den lande ende graefscepe van Vlanderen van de jaeren 405 tot 1492*, ed. by J. de Jonghe, 4 vols (Bruges: Messchert, 1839–42)

Dits die excellente cronike van Vlaanderen, beghinnende van Liederik Buc tot keyser Carolus (Antwerp: Willem Vorsterman, 1531) [USTC 400512]

Drijderley refereynen ghepronuncieert opte rhetorijck-feest der blauwe acoleyen van Rotterdam (Antwerp: Willem Silvius, 1564) [USTC 407604]

EVERAERT, CORNELIS, *Spelen*, ed. by J. W. Muller and L. Scharpé (Leiden: Brill, 1920)

—— *De spelen*, ed. by W. N. M. Hüsken, 2 vols (Hilversum: Verloren, 2005)

FABRI, PIERRE, *Le Grand et Vrai Art de pleine rhétorique*, ed. by A. Héron, 3 vols (Rouen: Société des Bibliophiles Normands, 1889–90)

FAEMS, AN (ed.), 'Een rederijkersgedicht over de Jonker Fransenoorlog: Achtergronden en editie', *Spiegel der letteren*, 40 (1998), 55–88

Les Fascetieux Devitz des cent nouvelles nouvelles (Paris: Jean Réal [also for Guillaume Le Bret], 1549) [USTC 52757, 11145]

FLORES, JUAN DE, *Histoire d'Aurelio et d'Isabelle, nouvellement traduits en quattre langues italien, espagnol, françois et anglois* (Antwerp: Joannes Steelsius, 1556) [USTC 440651]

Fons vitæ, ex quo scaturiunt suavissimæ consolationes, adflictis mentibus in primis necessariis, ne in adversitate et dolore protinus animum despondeant (Antwerp: Merten de Keyser, 1533) [USTC 437659]

Fons vitæ, ex quo scaturiunt suavissimæ consolationes, adflictis mentibus in primis necessariæ (Paris, [Jean I Savetier]: Richard du Hamel, 1537) [USTC 185860]
FROISSART, JEAN, *Le Joli Buisson de jonece*, ed. by Anthime Fourrier (Geneva: Droz, 1975)
FROST, ROBERT, *Conversations on the Craft of Poetry*, ed. by Cleanth Brooks and Robert Penn Warren, 3rd edn (New York: Holt, Rinehart and Winston, 1961)
Gentsche stads- en baljuwsrekeningen, 1280–1336, ed. by Julius Vuylsteke and Alfons Van Werveke, 3 vols (Ghent: Meyer-van Loo, 1900–08)
GESSLER, JEAN, ed., *Le Livre des mestiers de Bruges et ses dérivés: quatre anciens manuels de conversation* (Bruges: Le Consortium des Maîtres Imprimeurs Brugeois, 1931)
GUICCIARDINI, LODOVICO, *Description de tout le Païs Bas autrement dict la Germanie inferieure, ou Basse-Allemagne* (Antwerp: Willem Silvius, 1567) [USTC 27799]
Die historie van den ouden Tobias ende van sijnen sone den jongen Tobias | L'Historie de l'ancien Tobie et de son filz le jeune Tobie (Antwerp: Jan van der Loe, 1551) [USTC 8864]
Historie van Floris ende Blanceflour ([Antwerp]: Jan van Doesborch, [1517]) [USTC 436979]
Die historie van Peeter van Provencen (Antwerp: Willem Vorsterman, ca. 1517) [USTC 436967]
Historie van Reynaert die vos (Gouda: Gheraert Leeu, 1479) [USTC 435458]
The Historye of Reynart the Foxe ([Westminster]: William Caxton, 1481) [USTC 500045]
HORATIUS FLACCUS, QUINTUS, *Principis & omnium veterum sententiosissimi primae qnatuor [sic] epistolae* ([Deventer]: Jacobus de Breda, 1515) [USTC 420783]
—— *Sermonum libri duo* ('s-Hertogenbosch: Laurens Hayen, 1521) [USTC 410696]
JEAN D'ARRAS, *Historie van Melusine* (Antwerp: Gheraert Leeu, 1491) [USTC 436129]
JEAN DE STAVELOT, *Chronique*, ed. by A. Borgnet (Brussels: M. Hayez, 1861)
Les Joyeuses Adventures et plaisant facetieux deviz (Lyon: [n. pub.], 1555) [USTC 41156]
LA CÉPÈDE, PIERRE DE, *De historie van deme vramen riddere Paris unde vander schone Vienna des dolfijns dochter* (Antwerp: Gheraert Leeu, 1488) [USTC 438824]
—— *Die historie van den vromen ridder Parijs ende van die schone Vienna* (Antwerp: Gheraert Leeu, 1487) [USTC 435854]
—— *Die historie vanden vromen ridder Paris ende van die scone Vienna* ([Antwerp: Gheraert Leeu, 1491–92]) [USTC 436061]
—— *Paris et Vienne* (Antwerp: Gheraert Leeu, 1487) [USTC 70568]
—— *Thy Storye of the Right Noble and Worthy Knyght Parys and of the Fayre Vyenne the Dolphyns Daughter of Vyennoys*, trans. by William Caxton (Antwerp: Gheraert Leeu, 1492) [USTC 438825]
LAET THE ELDER, GASPAR, *Les Pregnostications pour l'an 1493* (Antwerp: Gheraert Leeu, [1492]) [USTC 71221]
LA MARCHE, OLIVIER DE, *Den camp vander doot*, trans. by Johannes Pertcheval (Schiedam: Otgier Pietersz Nachtegael, 1503) [USTC 425427]
—— *Den camp vander doot*, trans. by Johannes Pertcheval, ed. by Gilbert Degroote (Antwerp: De Sikkel, 1948)
—— *Le Chevalier délibéré* ([Gouda: Collaciebroeders?, 1489]) [USTC 71206]
—— *Le Chevalier délibéré* (Schiedam: [Otgier Pietersz. Nachtegael], c. 1498) [USTC 71208]
—— *Le Chevalier délibéré*, pref. by F. Lippmann (London: for the Bibliographical Society at the Chiswick Press, 1898)
—— 'Le Chevalier délibéré par Olivier de La Marche, Schiedam vers 1498', in *Recueil de pièces historiques imprimées sous le règne de Louis XI reproduites en fac-similé*, ed. by Émile Picot and Henri Stein (Paris: pour la Société des Bibliophiles François [Francisque Lefrançois, Libraire], 1923), pp. 241–306
—— *Le Chevalier délibéré (The Resolute Knight)*, ed. by Carleton W. Carroll, trans. by Lois Hawley Wilson and Carleton W. Carroll (Tempe: Arizona Center for Medieval and Renaissance Studies, 1999)

―――― *Le Chevalier délibéré: édition originale, Paris, par Antoine Vérard, 1488; seconde édition, Gouda, Collaciebroeders (?), 1489; manuscrit, Flandres, env. 1484*, ed. and trans. by Sylviane Messerli (Geneva: Fondation Martin Bodmer, 2010)

―――― *Mémoires*, ed. by Henri Beaune and Jean d'Arbaumont, 4 vols (Paris: Société de l'Histoire de France, 1883–88)

―――― *Vanden ridder welghemoet*, trans. by Pieter Willemsz (Leiden: Jan Seversz, [*c*. 1508]) [USTC 420231]

Lanceloet: De Middelnederlandse vertaling van de 'Lancelot en prose' overgeleverd in de 'Lancelotcompilatie': Pars 2 (vs. 5531–10750) met inleidende studie over de vertaaltechniek, ed. by Bart Besamusca (Hilversum: Verloren, 1991)

LEFÈVRE, RAOUL, *Fais et prouesses du chevalier Jason* ([Ghent or Bruges?: David Aubert for William Caxton?, *c*. 1477]) [USTC 71243]

―――― *Fais et prouesses du chevalier Jason* ([Haarlem: Jacob Bellaert, *c*. 1486–88]) [USTC 71245]

―――― *Historie van den vromen ridder Jason* (Haarlem: Jacob Bellaert, [*c*. 1483–85]) [USTC 435612]

―――― *Recueil des histoires de Troie* ([Ghent or Bruges?: David Aubert for William Caxton?, 1474–75] ([USTC 37521]

―――― *Le Recueil des histoires de Troyes* ([Haarlem: Jacob Bellaert, *c*. 1485–86]) [USTC 71249]

―――― *Recuyell of the Historyes of Troye* ([Ghent or Bruges?: David Aubert for William Caxton?, 1473–74]) [USTC 438831]

―――― *Van Jason en Hercules: Die wonderlike vreemde historien* (Antwerp: Jan van Doesborch, 1521) [USTC 410164]

―――― *Vergaderinge der historien van Troyen* (Haarlem: Jacob Bellaert, 1485) [USTC 435730]

LE MUISIT, GILLES, *Chronique et annales*, ed. by H. Lemaitre (Paris: Renouard, H. Laurens, 1906)

MAERLANT, JACOB VAN, *Harau Martin* ([Bruges: Johannes Brito, 1477]) [USTC 71288]

MICHAULT, PIERRE, *La Dance aux aveugles* (Geneva: [Louis Cruse, 1479]) [USTC 71368]

―――― *La Dance aux aveugles* ([Bruges: Colard Mansion, *c*. 1479–81]) [USTC 71369]

―――― *La Dance aux aveugles* ([Bréhan-Loudéac]: Robin Fouquet and Jean Crès, [1485]) [USTC 71370]

―――― *La Dance aux aveugles* (Lyon: [Guillaume Le Roy, 1485]) [USTC 71371]

―――― *La Dance aux aveugles* (Lyon: [Guillaume Le Roy, 1487]) [USTC 71372]

―――― *La Dance aux aveugles* (Paris: Le Petit Laurens, [1495]) [USTC 71373]

―――― *La Dance aux aveugles* (Paris: Le Petit Laurens, [1495]) [USTC 71374]

―――― *La Dance aux aveugles* (Lyon: Pierre Mareschal and Barnabé Chaussard, [1502]) [USTC 64728]

―――― *La Dance aux aveugles* ([Lyon: Pierre Mareschal, 1503]) [USTC 64759]

―――― *La Dance aux aveugles* (Paris: widow of Michel Le Noir, [1521]) [USTC 55580]

―――― *La Dance aux aveugles* (Lyon: Olivier Arnoullet, 1543) [USTC 40236]

―――― *La Dance aux aveugles* ([s.l.: s.n., s.d.]) [USTC 89964]

―――― *Doctrinael des tijts* (Haarlem: [Jacob Bellaert], 1486) [USTC 435827]

―――― *Doctrinael des tijts*, ed. by W. J. Schuijt (Wageningen: Veenman, 1946)

―――― *Le Doctrinal du temps present* (Bruges: Colard Mansion, [*c*. 1479–81]) [USTC 71375]

―――― *Œuvres poétiques*, ed. by Barbara Folkart (Paris: Union Générale des Éditions, 1980)

―――― *Van den drie blinde danssen*, trans. by Martijn (Gouda: Gheraert Leeu, 1482) [USTC 435522]

―――― *Van den drie blinde danssen*, ed. by W. J. Schuijt (Amsterdam: Wereldbibliotheek, 1955)

MOLINET, JEAN, *L'Art de rhétorique*, in *Recueil d'arts de seconde rhétorique*, ed. by Ernest Langlois (Paris: Imprimerie Nationale, 1902), pp. 214–52

―――*Chroniques*, ed. by Georges Doutrepont and Omer Jodogne, 3 vols (Brussels: Palais des Académies, 1935–37)
―――*Faictz et dictz*, ed. by Noël Dupire, 3 vols (Paris: Société des Anciens Textes Français, 1936–39)
MONTGESOIE, AMÉ DE, *Tdal sonder wederkeeren oft tpas der doot*, trans. by Colijn Caillieu (Antwerp: Jan van Doesborch, 1528) [USTC 437415]
Les Mystères de la procession de Lille, ed. by Alan E. Knight, 5 vols (Geneva: Droz, 2001–11)
Nyueuwe sekere ende warachtighe tijdinghen, hoe dat dye hooch gheboren Vorst Ferdinandus tot eenen Roomschen keyser gecoren [sic] is, uutghegeven tot Franckfoort (Antwerp: Jan II van Ghelen, 1558) [USTC 409072]
De onghevaluweirde gauden ende zelven munten van veyl dyverschen conijncryken landen en steden | Les Monnoyes d'or et d'argent non valuées de plusieurs royaulmes pais et villes (Ghent: Josse Lambert, for Symon Vanden Muelien in Bruges, Jaspar Vanden Steene in Ypres, Henric Goysle and Cornelis Vanden Kerckhove in Antwerp, Pieter Hasselt in Brussels, Bartholomeus Jacobszoon in Amsterdam, Pierre Haschart in Lille, and Alexandre Huaul in Tournai, 1544) [USTC 76302]
[*Die ontrouwe der mannen*] (Antwerp: Marten Nuyts, 1543)
Ordonnances de Jean sans Peur, 1405–1419, Recueils des ordonnances des Pays–Bas, 1381–1506, Ordonnances de Philippe le Hardi, de Marguerite de Male et de Jean sans Peur, 1319–1419, ed. by Jean-Marie Cauchies, 3 (Brussels: Commission royale pour la publication des anciennes lois et ordonnances de la Belgique, 2001)
PERGAMENUS, NICOLAUS, *Le Dialogue des creatures moraligié* (Gouda: Gheraert Leeu, 1482) [USTC 57878]
PETRARCA, FRANCESCO (Pseudo-), *Teghen die strael der minnen* (Gouda: Printer of *Teghen die strael der minnen*, [not before 1484]) [USTC 435703]
Recueil des plaisantes et facétieuses nouvelles (Antwerp: Gerard Spelman, 1555) [USTC 56019]
RIJSSELE, COLIJN VAN, *De spiegel der minnen*, ed. by Margaretha W. Immink (Utrecht: Oosthoek, 1913)
Ritmes et refrains tournésiens, poésies couronnées par le puy d'escole de rhétorique de Tournay (1477–1491), ed. by Frédéric Hennebert (Mons: Hoyois-Derely, 1837)
ROOVERE, ANTHONIS DE, *Rethoricale wercken van Anthonis de Roovere, Brugghelinck, Vlaemsch doctoor ende gheestich poete*, ed. by Eduard de Dene (Antwerp: Jan van Ghelen, 1562)
―――*De gedichten*, ed. by J. J. Mak (Zwolle: Tjeenk Willink, 1955)
Le Siege de la ville de Vienne en Ostrice tenu par l'empereur de Turquie (Antwerp: Michel de Hoochstraten, 1529) [USTC 13012]
SOILLOT, CHARLES, *Le Debat de felicité* (Antwerp: Gheraert Leeu, [1489]) [USTC 71473]
Spelen van sinne vol schoone allegatien (Antwerp: Willem Silvius, 1564) [USTC 402938]
Spelen van sinne vol schoone allegatien: Drijderley refereynen (De Rotterdamse spelen van 1561), ed. by Henk J. Hollaar (Delft: Eburon, 2006)
Splendeurs de la cour de Bourgogne: récits et chroniques, ed. by Danielle Régnier-Bohler (Paris: Robert Laffont, 1995)
TERAMO, JACOBUS DE, *Der sonderen troest ofte proces tusschen Belial ende Moyses* (Haarlem: Jacob Bellaert, 1484) [USTC 435684]
THIBAULT, JEAN, *Le Thresor du remede preservatif et guerison bien experimentée de la peste et fievre pestilentialle* (Antwerp: Merten de Keyser, 1531) [USTC 57910]
―――*Le Tresor du remede preservatif et guerison bien experimentée de la peste et fievre pestilentialle* (Paris: Jean Bignon, 1532) [USTC 53820]
Trou moet blijcken. Deel 7: Boek G, bronnenuitgave van de boeken der Haarlemse rederijkerskamer 'de Pellicanisten', ed. by W. N. M. Hüsken, B. A. M. Ramakers, and F. A. M. Schaars (Assen: Quarto, 1997)

Twee uit het Latijn vertaalde Middelnederlandse novellen, ed. by R. Pennink (Zwolle: Tjeenk Willink, 1965)

VANDEKERCKHOVE, SIMON, ed., 'De *Chronike van den lande van Vlaendre*: Studie van het handschrift en uitgave van f° 148v. tot f° 415v', 2 vols (unpublished thesis, University of Ghent, 2007)

Vocabulario para aprender Franches, Espannol y Flamincq | Vocabulaire pour apprendre Franchoys, Espagnol et Flaming | Vocabulaire om te leerene Wallich, Spaensch, ende Vlaemich (Antwerp: Willem Vorsterman, 1520) [USTC 78033]

Vraye et nouvelle election imperialle du tresillustre tresredoubte et tresmagnanime don Fernande roy des Romains de Boheme (Antwerp: Jan van Ghelen, 1558) [USTC 56045]

WILLEMSZ, PIETER, *Vanden ridder welghemoet* (Leiden: Jan Seversz, 1507)

Secondary Sources

ADAM, RENAUD, 'Imprimeurs et société dans les Pays-Bas méridionaux et en principauté de Liège (1473–ca 1520)' (unpublished doctoral thesis, University of Liège, 2011)

ADAM, RENAUD, and ALEXANDRE VANAUTGAERDEN, *Thierry Martens et la figure de l'imprimeur humaniste* (Turnhout: Brepols, 2009)

ALLMAND, CHRISTOPHER, *The Hundred Years War: France and England at War, c. 1300–1450* (Cambridge: Cambridge University Press, 1988)

Archives de littérature du Moyen Âge (ARLIMA), <http://www.arlima.net/il/laurent_de_premierfait.html> [accessed 12 April 2017]

ARMSTRONG, ADRIAN, 'Printing and Metrical Naturalisation: Jean Molinet's *Neuf Preux de Gourmandise*', in *Essays in Later Medieval French Literature: The Legacy of Jane H. M. Taylor*, ed. by Rebecca Dixon (Manchester: Manchester University Press, 2010), pp. 143–59

—— *The Virtuoso Circle: Competition, Collaboration, and Complexity in Late Medieval French Poetry* (Tempe: Arizona Center for Medieval and Renaissance Studies, 2012)

—— 'Boire chez (et avec) Molinet', in *Jean Molinet et son temps: Actes des rencontres internationales de Dunkerque, Lille et Gand (8–10 novembre 2007)*, ed. by Jean Devaux, Estelle Doudet, and Élodie Lecuppre-Desjardin (Turnhout: Brepols, 2013), pp. 237–48

—— '"Half dicht, half prose gheordineert": vers et prose de moyen français en moyen néerlandais', *Le Moyen Français*, 76–77 (2015), 7–38

—— 'Translating Poetic Capital in Fifteenth-Century Brussels: From Amé de Montgesoie's *Pas de la Mort* to Colijn Cailllieu's *Dal sonder Wederkeeren*', *Literature and Multilingualism in the Low Countries (1100–1600)*, ed. by Samuel Mareel and Dirk Schoenaers, special issue of *Queeste*, 22.1 (2015), 47–61

—— '"Imprimé en la ville marchande et renommée d'Anvers": Antwerp Editions of Jean Molinet's Poetry', in *Between Stability and Transformation: Textual Traditions in the Medieval Netherlands*, ed. by Johan Oosterman, special issue of *Queeste*, 23.2 (2016), 123–37

ARMSTRONG, ADRIAN, and SARAH KAY, *Knowing Poetry: Verse in Medieval France from the 'Rose' to the 'Rhétoriqueurs'* (Ithaca, NY: Cornell University Press, 2011)

ARMSTRONG, C. A. J., 'The Language Question in the Low Countries: The Use of French and Dutch by the Dukes of Burgundy and their Administration' [1965], in *England, France and Burgundy in the Fifteenth Century* (London: Hambledon, 1983), pp. 189–212

ARMSTRONG, ELIZABETH, *Before Copyright: The French Book-Privilege System 1498–1526* (Cambridge: Cambridge University Press, 1990)

ARNADE, PETER, *Realms of Ritual: Burgundian Ceremony and Civic Life in Late Medieval Ghent* (Ithaca, NY: Cornell University Press, 1996)

ATILF CNRS/UNIVERSITÉ DE LORRAINE, *Dictionnaire du moyen français*, 2012 version, <http://www.atilf.fr/dmf> [accessed 9 July 2014]

AUER, PETER, 'The Pragmatics of Code-Switching: A Sequential Approach', in *One Speaker, Two Languages*, ed. by Lesley Milroy and Pieter Muysken (Cambridge: Cambridge University Press, 1995), pp. 115–35

BALTHASAR, HERMAN, and OTHERS, *Ghent: In Defence of a Rebellious City: History, Art, Culture* (Antwerp: Mercatorfonds, 1989)

BARBIER, FRÉDÉRIC, *L'Europe de Gutenberg: le livre et l'invention de la modernité occidentale* (Paris: Belin, 2006)

BESAMUSCA, BART, 'The Medieval Dutch Arthurian Material', in *The Arthur of the Germans: The Arthurian Legend in Medieval German and Dutch Literature*, ed. by W. H. Jackson and S. A. Ranawake (Cardiff: University of Wales Press, 2000), pp. 187–228

BILLEN, CLAIRE, 'Brussel-hoofdstad', in *De grote mythen uit de geschiedenis van België, Vlaanderen en Wallonië*, ed. by Anne Morelli (Berchem: EPO, 1996), pp. 203–14

BLOCKMANS, WIM, and WALTER PREVENIER, *De Bourgondiërs: De Nederlanden op weg naar eenheid, 1384–1530* (Amsterdam; Meulenhoff; Leuven: Kritak, 1997)

BOGAART, SASKIA, *Geleerde kennis in de volkstaal: 'Van den proprieteyten der dinghen' (Haarlem 1458) in cultuurhistorisch perspectief* (Hilversum: Verloren, 2004)

BOHEEMEN, F. C. VAN, and TH. C. J. VAN DER HEIJDEN, *Retoricaal memoriaal: Bronnen voor de geschiedenis van de Hollandse rederijkerskamers van de middeleeuwen tot het begin van de achttiende eeuw* (Delft: Eburon, 1999)

BOLTON, J., and F. BRUSCOLI, 'When Did Antwerp Replace Bruges as the Commercial and Financial Centre of North-Western Europe? The Evidence of the Borromei Ledger for 1438', *Economic History Review*, 61 (2008), 360–79

BOONE, MARC, 'Les Gantois et la grande procession de Tournai: aspects d'une sociabilité urbaine au bas moyen âge', in *La Grande Procession de Tournai (1090–1992)* (Tournai: Fabrique de l'Eglise Cathédrale de Tournai, 1992), pp. 51–58

—— 'Réseaux urbaines', in *Le Prince et le peuple: images de la société du temps des ducs de Bourgogne, 1384–1530*, ed. by Walter Prevenier (Antwerp: Fonds Mercator, 1998), pp. 233–47

—— 'Langue, pouvoirs et dialogue: aspects linguistiques de la communication entre les ducs de Bourgogne et leurs sujets flamands (1385–1505)', *Revue du Nord*, 91 (2009), 9–33

——, Thérèse de Hemptinne, and Walter Prevenier, 'Fictie en historische realiteit: Colijn van Rijsseles *De spiegel der minnen*, ook een spiegel van sociale spanningen in de Nederlanden der late Middeleeuwen?', *Jaarboek De Fonteine*, 34 (1984), 9–33

BORCHERT, TILL-HOLGER, 'The Mobility of Artists: Aspects of Cultural Transfer in Renaissance Europe', in *The Age of Van Eyck: The Mediterranean World and Early Netherlandish Painting 1430–1530*, ed. by Till-Holger Borchert, trans. by Ted Alkins and others (Bruges: Ludion, 2002), pp. 32–51

BOS-ROPS, J. A. M. Y., J. G. SMIT, and E. T. VAN DER VLIST, eds, *Holland bestuurd: Teksten over het bestuur van het graafschap Holland in het tijdvak 1299–1567* (The Hague: Instituut voor Nederlandse Geschiedenis, 2007)

BOSSUYT, IGNACE, 'Charles as a Young Man at the Court of Marguerite of Austria', in *The Empire Resounds: Music in the Days of Charles V*, ed. by Francis Maes (Leuven: Leuven University Press, 1999), pp. 85–93

BOUCKAERT, BRUNO, 'The *Capilla Flamenca*: The Composition and Duties of the Music Ensemble at the Court of Charles V, 1515–1558', in *The Empire Resounds: Music in the Days of Charles V*, ed. by Francis Maes (Leuven: Leuven University Press, 1999), pp. 36–45

BOUHAÏK-GIRONÈS, MARIE, and KATELL LAVÉANT, 'Le *Mandement de froidure de Jean Molinet*: la culture joyeuse, un pont entre la cour de Bourgogne et les milieux urbains', in *Jean Molinet et son temps: Actes des rencontres internationales de Dunkerque, Lille et Gand (8–10 novembre 2007)*, ed. by Jean Devaux, Estelle Doudet and Élodie Lecuppre-Desjardin (Turnhout: Brepols, 2013), pp. 67–82

BOZZOLO, CARLA, 'Introduction à la vie et à l'oeuvre d'un humaniste', in *Un traducteur et un humaniste de l'époque de Charles V, Laurent de Premierfait*, ed. by Carla Bozzolo (Paris: Publications de la Sorbonne, 2004), pp. 17–30

—— 'La Conception du pouvoir chez Laurent de Premierfait', in *Un traducteur et un humaniste de l'époque de Charles V, Laurent de Premierfait*, ed. by Carla Bozzolo (Paris: Publications de la Sorbonne, 2004), pp. 53–68

BRAAKE, SERGE TER, and ARJAN VAN DIXHOORN, 'Engagement en ambitie: De Haagse rederijkerskamer "Met Ghenuchten" en de ontwikkeling van een burgerlijke samenleving in Holland rond 1500', *Jaarboek voor de middeleeuwse geschiedenis*, 9 (2006), 150–90

BREUIL, A., 'La Confrérie de Notre-Dame du Puy, d'Amiens', *Mémoires de la société des antiquaires de Picardie*, 13 (1854), 485–662

BRINKMAN, HERMAN, 'De weerklank van de Bourgondische hofliteratuur in het Middelnederlands', *Millennium: tijdschrift voor middeleeuwse geschiedenis*, 8 (1994), 125–33

—— *Dichten uit liefde: Literatuur in Leiden aan het einde van de middeleeuwen* (Hilversum: Verloren, 1997)

—— 'De Brugse pelgrims in het Gruuthuse-handschrift', in *Stad van koopmanschap en vrede: Literatuur in Brugge tussen middeleeuwen en rederijkerstijd*, ed. by Johan Oosterman (Leuven: Peeters, 2005), pp. 9–39

——, ed., *Het handschrift-Jan Phillipsz.: Hs. Berlijn, Staatsbibliothek Preussischer Kulturbesitz, Germ. Qu. 557* (Hilversum: Verloren, 1995)

BROWN, ANDREW, 'Civic Ritual: Bruges and the Counts of Flanders in the Later Middle Ages', *English Historical Review*, 122 (1997), 277–99

—— *Civic Ceremony and Religion in Medieval Bruges, c.1300–1520* (Cambridge: Cambridge University Press, 2011)

BROWN, ANDREW, and GRAEME SMALL, *Court and Civic Society in the Burgundian Low Countries c.1420–c.1520* (Manchester: Manchester University Press, 2007)

BROWN, CYNTHIA J., *Poets, Patrons, and Printers: Crisis of Authority in Late Medieval France* (Ithaca, NY: Cornell University Press, 1995)

BROWN, CYNTHIA J., SUSIE SPEAKMAN SUTCH, and SAMUEL MAREEL, 'Polemics in Print in the Low Countries: *Venegien*: Transcription with Introduction and English Translation', *Queeste*, 19 (2012), 140–72

BRUCH, H., and R. E. V. STUIP, 'Een Franse kroniek van de heren van Brederode', *Holland, regionaal-historisch tijdschrift*, 16 (1984), 35–42

BRULEZ, WILFRED, 'Bruges and Antwerp in the 15th and 16th Centuries, an Antithesis', *Acta Historica Nederlandicae*, 6 (1973), 1–26

BURGERS, J. W. J., ed., *Rijmkroniek van Holland (366–1305) door een anonieme auteur en Melis Stoke* (The Hague: Instituut voor Nederlandse Geschiedenis, 2004)

CAUCHIES, JEAN-MARIE, *Philippe le Beau, le dernier duc de Bourgogne* (Turnhout: Brepols, 2003)

—— '"Service" du prince, "sûreté" des villes: à propos de privilèges délivrés aux confréries ou serments d'archers et d'arbalétriers dans les Pays-Bas au XVe siècle', *Revue du Nord*, 94 (2012), 419–34

CAUWENBERGHE, E. VAN, 'Notice historique sur les confréries de Saint Georges', *Messager des sciences historiques, des arts et de la bibliographie de Belgique* (1853), 269–99

CHOTIN, A. G., *Histoire de Tournai et du Tournésis, depuis les temps les plus reculés jusqu'à nos jours*, 2 vols (Tournai: Massart et Janssens, 1840)

CHRISTIE'S, *Valuable Manuscripts and Printed Books: Auction, London, King Street, Tuesday 24 November 2009*

CLAES, FRANS, *Lijst van Nederlandse woordenlijsten en woordenboeken gedrukt tot 1600* (Nieuwkoop: De Graaf, 1974)

CLARK, WILLENE B., *A Medieval Book of Beasts* (Woodbridge: Boydell and Brewer, 2006)
CLUBB, LOUISE GEORGE, *Italian Drama in Shakespeare's Time* (New Haven, CT: Yale University Press, 1989)
COIGNEAU, DIRK, 'Drie Rijnsburgse refreinen te Rotterdam (1561) en hun Franse bron', *Verslagen en Mededelingen van de Koninklijke Academie voor Nederlandse Taal- en Letterkunde*, 1977, 239–90
—— *Refreinen in het zotte bij de rederijkers*, 3 vols (Gent: Koninklijke Academie voor Nederlandse Taal- en Letterkunde, 1980–83)
—— 'Liefde en lichaamsbeleving op het rederijkerstoneel', *Jaarboek De Fonteine*, 34 (1984), 115–32
—— '9 december 1448: Het Gentse stadsbestuur keurt de statuten van de rederijkerskamer De Fonteine goed. Literaire bedrijvigheid in stads- en gildeverband', in *Nederlandse literatuur, een geschiedenis*, ed. by M.A. Schenkeveld-van der Dussen (Groningen: Contact, 1993), pp. 103–08
—— 'Strofische vormen in het rederijkerstoneel', in *Spel in de verte: Tekst, structuur en opvoeringspraktijk van het rederijkerstoneel*, ed. by B. A. M. Ramakers (Ghent: De Fonteine, 1994), pp. 17–44
—— '*De const van rhetoriken*: Drama and Delivery', in *Rhetoric — Rhétoriqueurs — Rederijkers*, ed. by Jelle Koopmans and others (Amsterdam: North-Holland, 1995), pp. 123–40
—— '1 Februari 1404: De Mechelse voetboogschutters schrijven een wedstrijd uit. Stedelijke toneelwedstrijden in de vijftiende en zestiende eeuw', in *Een theatergeschiedenis der Nederlanden: Tien eeuwen drama en theater in Nederland en Vlaanderen*, ed. by R. L. Erenstein (Amsterdam: Amsterdam University Press, 1996), pp. 30–35
—— '9 december 1448: De statuten van de rederijkerskamer De Fonteine worden officieel erkend door de stad Gent. Rechten en plichten van spelende gezellen', in *Een theatergeschiedenis der Nederlanden: Tien eeuwen drama en theater in Nederland en Vlaanderen*, ed. by R. L. Erenstein (Amsterdam: Amsterdam University Press, 1996), pp. 50–55
—— 'Per haute-couture ten dodendans', *Queeste*, 4 (1997), 84–93
—— '"Den Boeck" van Brussel: Een geval apart?', *Jaarboek De Fonteine*, 49–50 (1999–2000), 31–404
—— 'Bedongen creativiteit: Over retoricale productieregeling', in *Medioneerlandistiek: Een inleiding tot de Middelnederlandse letterkunde*, ed. by Ria Jansen-Sieben, Jozef Janssens, and Frank Willaert (Hilversum: Verloren, 2000), pp. 129–37
—— 'Drama in druk, tot circa 1540', in *Spel en spektakel: Middeleeuws toneel in de Lage Landen*, ed. by Hans van Dijk and others (Amsterdam: Prometheus, 2001), pp. 201–14
—— 'Les Concours de "referain": une introduction à la rhétorique néerlandaise', in *Première poésie française de la Renaissance: autour des puys poétiques normands*, ed. by Jean-Claude Arnould and Thierry Mantovani (Paris: Champion, 2003), pp. 489–503
—— 'Van de *Bliscappen* tot Cammaert: Vier eeuwen toneelliteratuur in Brussel', in *De macht van het schone woord: Literatuur in Brussel van de 14de tot de 18de eeuw*, ed. by Jozef Janssens and Remco Sleiderink (Louvain: Davidsfonds/Literair, 2003), pp. 213–33
COLDIRON, ANNE E. B., *English Printing, Verse Translation, and the Battle of the Sexes, 1476–1557* (Farnham: Ashgate, 2009)
COOMANS, THOMAS, 'Belfries, Cloth Halls, Hospitals, and Mendicant Churches: A New Urban Architecture in the Low Countries around 1300', in *The Year 1300 and the Creation of a New European Architecture*, ed. by A. Gajewski and Z. Opačić (Turnhout: Brepols, 2007), pp. 185–202
CRÉCY, MARIE-CLAUDE DE, *Vocabulaire de la littérature du Moyen Âge* (Paris: Minerve, 1997)
CROENEN, GODFRIED, 'Latijn en de volkstalen in de dertiende-eeuwse Brabantse oorkonden', *Taal & Tongval*, 12 (1999), 9–34

CROMBIE, LAURA, 'Defense, Honor and Community: The Military and Social Bonds of the Dukes of Burgundy and the Flemish Shooting Guilds', *Journal of Medieval Military History*, 9 (2011), 76–96

—— 'The First Ordnances of the Crossbow Confraternity of Douai, 1383–1393', *Journal of Archer Antiquarians*, 54 (2011), 21–28

—— 'Honour, Community and Hierarchy in the Feasts of the Archery and Crossbow Guilds of Bruges, 1445–81', *Journal of Medieval History*, 37 (2011), 102–13

—— 'French and Flemish Urban Festive Networks: Archery and Crossbow Competitions Attended and Hosted by Tournai in the Fourteenth and Fifteenth Centuries', *French History*, 27 (2013), 157–75

CURRY, ANNE, *The Hundred Years War* (Basingstoke: Macmillan, 1993)

DAMEN, MARIO, *De staat van dienst: De gewestelijke ambtenaren van Holland en Zeeland in de Bourgondische periode (1425–1482)* (Hilversum: Verloren, 2000)

—— 'Giving by Pouring: The Functions of Gifts of Wine in the City of Leiden, 14th–16th Centuries', in *Symbolic Communication in Late Medieval Towns*, ed. by Jacoba Van Leeuwen (Leuven: Leuven University Press, 2006), pp. 83–100

DEBAENE, LUC, *De Nederlandse volksboeken: Ontstaan en geschiedenis van de Nederlandse prozaromans gedrukt tussen 1475 en 1540* (Antwerp: De Vlijt, 1951)

DEGROOTE, GILBERT, 'Diets-Bourgondische letteren te Brussel', *Dietsche Warande en Belfort*, 97 (1952), 402–21

—— 'Taaltoestanden in de Bourgondische Nederlanden', *De Nieuwe Taalgids*, 49 (1956), 303–09

DEKESEL, CHRISTIAN, *Bibliotheca nummaria. Bibliography of 16th-Century Numismatic Books: Illustrated and Annotated Catalogue* (Crestline: Kolbe; London: Spink, 1997)

DELANGRE, AGATHON, *Le Théâtre et l'art dramatique à Tournai* (Tournai: Vasseur-Delmée, 1905)

DELLE LUCHE, JEAN-DOMINIQUE, 'Le Plaisir des bourgeois et la gloire de la ville: sociétés et concours de tir dans les villes de l'Empire (XVe–XVIe siècles)' (unpublished doctoral thesis, École des Hautes Études en Sciences Sociales, 2015)

DELISLE, LÉOPOLD, *Catalogue des livres imprimés ou publiés à Caen avant le milieu du XVIe siècle, suivi de recherches sur les imprimeurs et les libraires de la même ville* (Caen: H. Delesques, 1903–04)

DERYCKE, LAURENCE, and ANNE-LAURE VAN BRUAENE, 'Sociale en literaire dynamiek in het vroeg vijftiende-eeuwse Brugge: De oprichting van de rederijkerskamer De Heilige Geest ca. 1428', in *Stad van koopmanschap en vrede: Literatuur in Brugge tussen middeleeuwen en rederijkerstijd*, ed. by Johan Oosterman (Leuven: Peeters, 2005), pp. 59–87

DESCHAUX, ROBERT, *Un poète bourguignon du XVe siècle: Michault Taillevent (édition et étude)* (Geneva: Droz, 1975)

DEVAUX, JEAN, ed., *Littérature et culture historiques à la cour de Bourgogne*, special issue of *Le Moyen Âge*, 112.3–4 (2006)

DHANENS, E., 'Literatuur en stadscultuur tussen middeleeuwen en nieuwe tijd', *BMGN, The Low Countries Historical Review*, 106 (1991), 421–25

Dictionnaire étymologique de l'ancien français, <http://www.deaf-page.de> [accessed 9 July 2014]

DILLON, EMMA, *The Sense of Sound: Musical Meaning in France, 1260–1330* (Oxford: Oxford University Press, 2012)

DIXHOORN, ARJAN VAN, 'Writing Poetry as Intellectual Training: Chambers of Rhetoric and the Development of Vernacular Intellectual Life in the Low Countries between 1480 and 1600', in *Education and Learning in the Netherlands, 1400–1600: Essays in Honour of Hilde de Ridder-Symoens*, ed. by Koen Goudriaan, Jaap van Moolenbroek, and Ad Tervoort (Leiden: Brill, 2004), pp. 201–22

―――― *Lustige geesten: Rederijkers in de noordelijke Nederlanden (1480–1650)* (Amsterdam: Amsterdam University Press, 2009)

―――― 'The Multilingualism of Dutch Rhetoricians: Jan van den Dale's 'Uure van den doot' (Brussels, *c.* 1516) and the Use of Language', in *Bilingual Europe: Latin and Vernacular Cultures. Examples of Bilingualism and Multilingualism c. 1300–1800*, ed. by Jan Bloemendal (Leiden/Boston: Brill, 2015), pp. 50–72

DIXHOORN, ARJAN VAN, and SUSIE SPEAKMAN SUTCH, eds, *The Reach of the Republic of Letters: Literary and Learned Societies in Late Medieval and Early Modern Europe*, 2 vols (Leiden: Brill, 2008)

DOUDET, ESTELLE, *Poétique de George Chastelain (1415–1475): 'Un cristal mucié en un coffre'* (Paris: Champion, 2005)

―――― 'Un chant déraciné? La poésie bourguignonne d'expression française face à Charles Quint', *e-Spania*, 13 (2012) <DOI: 10.4000/e-spania.21220>

DOUTREPONT, GEORGES, *La Littérature française à la cour des ducs de Bourgogne* (Paris: Champion, 1909)

―――― *Les Mises en prose des épopées et des romans chevaleresques du XIVe au XVIe siècle* (Brussels: Palais des Académies, 1939)

DRIVER, MARTHA W., *The Image in Print: Book Illustration in Late Medieval England and its Sources* (London: The British Library, 2004)

DUMOLYN, JAN, 'Une idéologie urbaine "bricolée" en Flandre médiévale: les *Sept portes de Bruges* dans le manuscrit Gruuthuse (début du XVe siècle)', *Revue Belge de Philologie et d'Histoire*, 88 (2010), 1039–84

DUMOLYN, JAN, and ÉLODIE LECUPPRE-DESJARDIN, 'Propagande et sensibilité: la fibre émotionnelle au cœur des luttes politiques et sociales dans les villes des anciens Pays-Bas bourguignons. L'Exemple de la révolte brugeoise de 1436–1438', in *Emotions in the Heart of the City (14th–16th century): Studies in European Urban History (1100–1800)*, ed. by Élodie Lecuppre-Desjardin and Anne-Laure Van Bruaene (Turnhout: Brepols, 2005), pp. 41–62

DUMOULIN, JEAN, and JACQUES PYCKE, eds, *La Grande Procession de Tournai (1090–1992)* (Tournai: Fabrique de l'Eglise Cathédrale de Tournai, 1992)

DÜNNEBEIL, SONJA, *Die Protokollbücher des Ordens vom Goldenen Vlies I, Herzog Phillip der Gute, 1430–1467* (Stuttgart: Thorbecke, 2002)

DUPIRE, NOËL, *Jean Molinet: la vie — les œuvres* (Paris: Droz, 1932)

DUVANEL, MAURICE, PIERRE LEROY, and MATTHIEU PINETTE, *La Confrérie Notre Dame du Puy d'Amiens* (Amiens: Mabire, 1997)

DUVERGER, JOZEF, *Brussel als kunstcentrum in de XIVe en de XVe eeuw* (Antwerp: De Sikkel; Ghent: Vyncke, 1935)

EBELS-HOVELING, B., C. SANTING, and C. P. H. M. TILMANS, eds, *Genoechlike ende lustige historiën: Laatmiddeleeuwse geschiedschrijving in Nederland* (Hilversum: Verloren, 1987)

ERNÉ, B. H., 'Rederijkersballaden oude en nieuwe stijl', *De Nieuwe Taalgids*, 65 (1972), 355–63

ESPINAS, GEORGES, *Les Origines du droit d'association dans les villes de l'Artois et de la Flandre française jusqu'au début du XVIe siècle*, 2 vols (Lille: Raoust, 1941)

FAIDER, PAUL, and PIERRE VAN SINT JAN, *Catalogue des manuscrits conservés à Tournai* (Gembloux: Duculot, 1950)

FOLKART, BARBARA, 'Le *Procès d'honneur féminin* de Pierre Michault', *Le Moyen Français*, 2 (1978), 3–133

―――― 'Perspectives médiévales sur la mort: la complainte de Pierre Michault sur la mort d'Ysabeau de Bourbon', *Le Moyen Français*, 3 (1980), 29–74

FRANSSEN, PETER J. A., '*Dat bedroch der vrouwen*, een onderzoek naar de functie van een 16e eeuwse verhalenbundel I', *Spektator*, 12 (1982–83), 270–89

—— 'Dat bedroch der vrouwen, een onderzoek naar de functie van een 16e eeuwse verhalenbundel II', *Spektator*, 13 (1983–84), 167–81

—— *Tussen tekst en publiek: Jan van Doesborch, drukker-uitgever en literator te Antwerpen en Utrecht in de eerste helft van de zestiende eeuw* (Amsterdam: Rodopi, 1990)

FREEMAN, MARGARET B., *The Unicorn Tapestries, the Metropolitan Museum of Art* (New York: Dutton, 1976)

FRIJHOFF, WILLEM, 'Verfransing? Franse taal en Nederlandse cultuur tot in de revolutietijd', *Bijdragen en mededelingen betreffende de geschiedenis in Nederland*, 104 (1989), 592–609

GABRIËL, RENÉE, 'Boekenlijsten en *Material Philology*: Methodologische overwegingen bij de boekenlijst van Michael van der Stoct (ca. 1394)', *Queeste*, 16 (2009), 83–111

GAULLIER-BOUGASSAS, CATHERINE, *L'Histoire ancienne jusqu'à César ou histoires pour Roger, châtelain de Lille, de Wauchier de Denain: l'histoire de la Macédoine et d'Alexandre le Grand* (Turnhout: Brepols, 2012)

GIJSEN, ANNELIES VAN, 'Katherina Sheermertens, Margarieta van Lymborch, and Margaret of Austria: Literary and Historical Backgrounds in Colijn van Rijssele's *Spiegel der Minnen*', *Publications du Centre européen d'études bourguignonnes (XIVe–XVIe s.)*, 31 (1991), 165–74

—— 'De tussenspelen uit de twee *Handels der Amo(u)reusheyt*', in *Spel in de verte: Tekst, structuur en opvoeringspraktijk van het rederijkerstoneel*, ed. by B. A. M. Ramakers (Ghent: De Fonteine, 1994), pp. 59–86

—— 'Love and Marriage: Fictional Perspectives', in *Showing Status: Representation of Social Positions in the Late Middle Ages*, ed. by Wim Blockmans and Antheun Janse (Turnhout: Brepols, 1999), pp. 227–63

—— 'De amoureuze spelen: De herschepping van klassieke stof op het rederijkerstoneel', in *Spel en spektakel: Middeleeuws toneel in de Lage Landen*, ed. by Hans van Dijk and others (Amsterdam: Prometheus, 2001), pp. 215–27

GIJSEN, J. E. VAN, *Liefde, kosmos en verbeelding: Mens- en wereldbeeld in Colijn van Rijsseles 'Spiegel der minnen'* (Groningen: Wolters-Noordhoff/Forsten, 1989)

GILLIODTS-VAN SEVEREN, LOUIS, *Inventaire des archives de la ville de Bruges*, 9 vols (Bruges: Gailliard, 1871–85)

GODEFROY, FRÉDÉRIC, *Dictionnaire de l'ancienne langue française et de tous ses dialectes du IXe au XVe siècle*, 10 vols (Paris: Vieweg, 1880–1902)

GÖLLNER, CARL, *Turcica: Die europäischen Türkendrucke des XVI. Jahrhunderts. I. Band MDI–MDL* (Berlin: Akademie-Verlag, 1961)

GOUDRIAAN, KOEN, 'Inleiding', in *Een drukker zoekt publiek: Gheraert Leeu te Gouda 1477–1484*, ed. by Koen Goudriaan and others (Delft: Uitgeverij Eburon, 1993), pp. 3–11

GROS, GÉRARD, *Le Poète, la vierge et le prince du Puy: étude sur les Puys marials de la France du Nord du XIVe siècle à la Renaissance* (Paris: Klincksieck, 1992)

—— *Le Poète marial et l'art graphique: étude sur les jeux de lettres dans les poèmes pieux du Moyen Âge* (Caen: Paradigme, 1993)

—— *Le Poème du Puy marial: étude sur le serventois et le chant royal du XIVe siècle à la Renaissance* (Paris: Klincksieck, 1996)

GROSE, FRANCIS, *Lexicon Balatronicum or, A Dictionary of Buckish Slang, University Wit, and Pickpocket Eloquence* (London: C. Chappel, 1811)

HAEMERS, JELLE, 'Philippe de Clèves et la Flandre: la position d'un aristocrate au coeur d'une révolte urbaine (1477–1492)', in *Entre la ville, la noblesse et l'état: Philippe de Clèves (1456–1528) homme politique et bibliophile*, ed. by Jelle Haemers, Céline Van Hoorebeeck, and Hanno Wijsman (Turnhout: Brepols, 2007), pp. 21–99

HANHAM, ALISON, 'Who Made William Caxton's Phrase-Book?', *The Review of English Studies*, new ser., 56 (2005), 712–29

HARVEY, KEITH, 'A Descriptive Framework for Compensation', *The Translator: Studies in Intercultural Communication*, 1 (1995), 65–86

HASSELT, M. VAN, 'A Burgundian Death: The Tournament in *Le Chevalier Délibéré*' (unpublished master's thesis, University of Utrecht, 2010), <http://www.knightorder.org.uk/history/A%20Burgundian%20Death.pdf> [accessed 20 June 2014]

HASSIG, DEBRA, *Medieval Bestiaries: Text, Image, Ideology* (Cambridge: Cambridge University Press, 1995)

HAVE, BEN VAN DER, 'Taalonderwijs: Vier triviumteksten', in *Een wereld van kennis: Bloemlezing uit de Middelnederlandse artesliteratuur*, ed. by E. Huizinga, O. S. H. Lie, and L. M. Veltman (Hilversum: Verloren, 2002), pp. 37–62

HEDEMAN, ANNE D., 'Visual Translation: Illustrating Laurent de Premierfait's French Versions of Boccaccio's *De casibus*', in *Un traducteur et un humaniste de l'époque de Charles V, Laurent de Premierfait*, ed. by Carla Bozzolo (Paris: Publications de la Sorbonne, 2004), pp. 83–113

HELLINGA, LOTTE, 'William Caxton, Colard Mansion, and the Printer in Type 1', *Bulletin du bibliophile* (2011), 86–114

—— *Texts in Transit: Manuscript to Proof and Print in the Fifteenth Century* (Leiden: Brill, 2014)

HELLINGA-QUERIDO, LOTTE, 'De betekenis van Gheraert Leeu', in *Een drukker zoekt publiek: Gheraert Leeu te Gouda 1477–1484*, ed. by Koen Goudriaan and others (Delft: Uitgeverij Eburon, 1993), pp. 12–30

HEMELRYCK, TANIA VAN, 'Le Viel Homme et la mort: observations sur le *Passe Temps* de Michault Taillevent', *Les Lettres Romanes*, 51 (1997), 19–34

HEMPTINNE, THÉRÈSE DE, and WALTER PREVENIER, 'La Flandre au Moyen Âge: un pays de trilinguisme administratif', in *La Langue des actes: Actes du XIe Congrès international de diplomatique (Troyes, jeudi 11-samedi 13 septembre 2003)*, ed. by Olivier Guyotjeannin (Paris: Éditions en ligne de l'École des chartes, 2005), pp. 1–16, <http://elec.enc.sorbonne.fr/CID2003/de-hemptinne_prevenier> [accessed 15 March 2015]

HERK, ANKE VAN, *Fabels van liefde: Het mythologisch-amoureuze toneel van de rederijkers (1475–1621)* (Amsterdam: Amsterdam University Press, 2012)

HINDLEY, ALAN, and GRAEME SMALL, 'Le Ju du Grand Dominé et du Petit: une moralité tournaisienne inédite du Moyen Âge tardif (fin XVe–début XVIe siècle). Étude et édition', *Revue Belge de Philologie et d'Histoire*, 80 (2002), 413–56

Historici.nl: Werken aan de geschiedenis van Nederland, <https://www.historici.nl/resources> [accessed 15 February 2015]

HOMMEL, LUC, *Marie de Bourgogne ou le grand héritage* (Brussels: Goemaere; Paris: Presses universitaires de France, 1951)

HOOCK, JOCHEN, 'Les Berlaimonts: manuels plurilingues à l'usage des marchands (XVIe–XVIIIe siècle)', *Revue de synthèse*, 133 (2012), 273–88

HOOGVLIET, MARGRIET, 'Middle Dutch Religious Reading Cultures in Late Medieval France', in *Literature and Multilingualism in the Low Countries (1100–1600)*, ed. by Samuel Mareel and Dirk Schoenaers, special issue of *Queeste*, 22.1 (2015), 29–46

HÜE, DENIS, *La Poésie palinodique à Rouen (1486–1550)* (Paris: Champion, 2002)

HUMMELEN, W. M. H., 'The Dramatic Structure of the Dutch Morality', *Dutch Crossing*, 22 (1984), 17–26

—— 'The Boundaries of the Rhetoricians' Stage', *Comparative Drama*, 28 (1994), 235–51

—— '*Pausa* and *Selete* in the *Bliscapen*', in *Urban Theatre in the Low Countries, 1400–1625*, ed. by Elsa Strietman and Peter Happé (Turnhout: Brepols, 2006), pp. 53–75

INSTITUUT VOOR NEDERLANDSE LEXICOLOGIE, *De geïntegreerde taal-bank*, <http://gtb.inl.nl/> [accessed 15 February 2015]

JACOBS, JOHANNA, *Sebastiaan, martelaar of mythe* (Zwolle: Waanders, 1993)
JANSE, ANTHEUN, *Een pion voor een dame: Jacoba van Beieren (1401–1436)* (Amsterdam: Balans, 2009)
—— 'Yolande van Lalaing (1422–1497)', in *Yolande van Lalaing (1422–1497): kasteelvrouwe van Brederode*, ed. by Elizabeth den Hartog and Hanno Wijsman, special issue of *Jaarboek van de Kastelenstichting Holland en Zeeland* (2009), pp. 7–36
JANSMA, T. S., *Raad en rekenkamer in Holland en Zeeland tijdens hertog Philips van Bourgondië* (Utrecht: Instituut voor Middeleeuwse geschiedenis; Leipzig: Verlang von Duncker und Humblot, 1932)
JANSON, HORST WOLDERMAR, *Apes and Ape-lore in the Middle Ages* (London: Warburg Institute, University of London, 1952)
JANVIER, A., 'Notice sur les anciennes corporations d'archers, d'arbalétriers, de couleuvriniers et d'arquebusiers des villes de Picardie', *Mémoires de la société des antiquaires de la Picardie*, 14 (1855), 5–380
JESERICH, PHILIPP, *Musica naturalis: Speculative Music Theory and Poetics, from Saint Augustine to the Late Middle Ages in France*, trans. by Michael J. Curley and Steven Rendall (Baltimore, MD: Johns Hopkins University Press, 2013)
JOHNSTON, ANDREW G., 'L'Imprimerie et la Réforme aux Pays-Bas, 1520–*c*. 1555', in *La Réforme et le livre: l'Europe de l'imprimé (1517–v. 1570)*, ed. by Jean-François Gilmont (Paris: Cerf, 1990), pp. 155–86
JOHNSTON, ANDREW G., and JEAN-FRANÇOIS GILMONT, 'L'Imprimerie et la Réforme à Anvers', in *La Réforme et le livre: l'Europe de l'imprimé (1517–v. 1570)*, ed. by Jean-François Gilmont (Paris: Cerf, 1990), pp. 191–216
JONAS: Répertoire des textes et des manuscrits médiévaux d'oc et d'oïl, <http://jonas.irht.cnrs.fr/> [accessed 16 October 2015]
JONCKBLOET, W. J. A., *Geschiedenis der Middelnederlandsche dichtkunst*, 3 vols (Amsterdam: Van Kampen, 1851–55)
JONGENELEN, BAS, 'Jan Pertcheval's Translation of *Le Chevalier délibéré*: *Den camp vander doot* — Source, Translation and Public', *Publications du Centre européen d'études bourguignonnes (XIVe–XVIe s.)*, 43 (2003), 199–212
—— 'Pieter Willemsz' vertaling van *Le Chevalier délibéré*: *Vanden ridder welghemoet* — Dichter tussen bron en lezers', in *Met eigen ogen: De rederijker als dichtend individu (1450–1600)*, ed. by Dirk Coigneau and Samuel Mareel, special issue of *Jaarboek De Fonteine*, 58 (2008), 233–51
JONGKEES, G., 'Het groot privilege van Holland en Zeeland (14 maart 1477)', in *Burgundica et varia*, ed. by E. O. van der Werff, C. A. A. Linssen, and B. Ebels-Hoveling (Hilversum: Verloren, 1990), pp. 48–51
KEESMAN, WILMA, 'Troje in de middeleeuwse literatuur: Antiek verleden in dienst van eigen tijd', *Literatuur*, 4 (1987), 257–65
—— 'Jacob Bellaert en Haarlem', in *Haarlems Helicon: Literatuur en toneel te Haarlem vóór 1800*, ed. by E. K. Grootes (Hilversum: Verloren, 1993), pp. 27–48
KNIGHT, ALAN E., 'Processional Theater in Lille in the Fifteenth Century', in *Le Théâtre et la cité dans l'Europe médiévale: Actes du Vème colloque international de la Société internationale pour l'étude du théâtre médiévale*, ed. by Jean-Claude Aubailly and Edelgard E. Dubruck (Stuttgart: Heinz, 1988), pp. 347–58
KNUVELDER, G. P. M., *Handboek tot de geschiedenis der Nederlandse letterkunde*, 4 vols (Den Bosch: Malmberg, 1971–78)
KOJ, PETER, *Die frühe Rezeption der Fazetien Poggios in Frankreich* (Hamburg: Universität, Romanisches Seminar, 1969)
KOOPMANS, JELLE, 'Rhétorique de cour et rhétorique de ville', in *Rhetoric — Rhétoriqueurs*

—— *Rederijkers*, ed. by Jelle Koopmans and others (Amsterdam: North-Holland, 1995), pp. 67–81

KOOPMANS, JELLE, and OTHERS, eds, *Rhetoric — Rhétoriqueurs — Rederijkers* (Amsterdam: North-Holland, 1995)

KORDECKI, LESLEY, 'Losing the Monster and Recovering the Non-Human in Fable(d) Subjectivity', in *Animals and the Symbolic in Medieval Art and Literature*, ed. by L. A. J. R. Houwen (Groningen: Egbert Forsten, 1997), pp. 25–37

KRAMER, FEMKE, *Mooi vies, knap lelijk: Grotesk realisme in rederijkerskluchten* (Hilversum: Verloren, 2009)

KRONENBERG, M. E., 'Een onbekende Nederlandsche vertaling van *Le Chevalier délibéré*, door Pieter Willemsz. gemaakt', *Tijdschrift voor Nederlandsche Taal- en Letterkunde*, 51 (1932), 178–96

—— 'Fragmenten der Nederlandse vertaling van *Le Chevalier délibéré* door Pieter Willemsz.', *Tijdschrift voor Nederlandse Taal- en Letterkunde*, 69 (1951), 169–79

KRUYSKAMP, C., 'De klucht van koster Johannes', *Jaarboek De Fonteine*, 8 (1950), 25–41

—— 'Een onbekende verhalenbundel van 1543', *Tijdschrift voor Nederlandse Taal- en Letterkunde*, 78 (1961), 161–67

LABARRE, ALBERT, *Bibliographie du dictionarium d'Ambrogio Calepino: 1502–1779* (Baden-Baden: Valentin Koerner, 1975)

LAVÉANT, KATELL, 'The Joyful Companies of the French-speaking Cities and Towns of the Southern Netherlands and their Dramatic Culture (Fifteenth-Sixteenth Centuries)', in *The Reach of the Republic of Letters: Literary and Learned Societies in Late Medieval and Early Modern Europe*, ed. by Arjan van Dixhoorn and Susie Speakman Sutch, 2 vols (Leiden: Brill, 2008), I, 79–118

—— *Un théâtre des frontières: la culture dramatique dans les provinces du Nord aux XVe et XVIe siècles* (Orleans: Paradigme, 2011)

LECUPPRE-DESJARDIN, ÉLODIE, *La Ville des cérémonies: essai sur la communication politique dans les anciens Pays-Bas bourguignons* (Turnhout: Brepols, 2004)

LEERSSEN, JOEP, 'Philology and the European Construction of National Literatures', in *Editing the Nation's Memory: Textual Scholarship and Nation-Building in 19th-Century Europe*, ed. by Dirk van Hulle and Joep Leerssen (Amsterdam: Rodopi, 2008), pp. 13–27

LEFEBVRE, LÉON, *Le Puy Notre-Dame de Lille du XIVe au XVIe siècle* (Lille: Lefebvre-Ducrocq, 1902)

LEFEVERE, ANDRÉ, *Translation, Rewriting, and the Manipulation of Literary Fame* (London: Routledge, 1992)

LINDEMANN, MARGARETE, *Die französischen Wörterbücher von den Anfängen bis 1600: Entstehung und typologische Beschreibung* (Tübingen: Niemeyer, 1994)

LUSIGNAN, SERGE, *Essai d'histoire sociolinguistique: le français picard au Moyen Âge* (Paris: Garnier, 2012)

Luxury Bound: A Corpus of Manuscripts Illustrated in the Netherlands (1400–1550), <http://www.cn-telma.fr/luxury-bound/index/> [accessed 16 October 2015]

MÄND, ANU, 'Saints' Cults in Medieval Livonia', in *The Clash of Cultures on the Medieval Baltic Frontier*, ed. by Alan V. Murray (Farnham: Ashgate, 2009), pp. 191–223

MANTINGH, ERWIN, '"... twelke al gheviel int Spel van Strasengijs": Naar aanleiding van een ongekend drama in Oudenaarde anno 1373', *Queeste*, 7 (2000), 38–50

MAREEL, SAMUEL, *Voor vorst en stad: Rederijkersliteratuur en vorstenfeest in Vlaanderen en Brabant (1432–1561)* (Amsterdam: Amsterdam University Press, 2010)

—— 'Politics, Mnemonics, and the Verse Form: On the Function of the Poems in the *Excellente Cronike van Vlaenderen*', in *Staging the Court of Burgundy: Proceedings of the Conference 'The Splendour of Burgundy'*, ed. by Wim Blockmans and others (Turnhout: Brepols, 2013), pp. 249–54

Mareel, Samuel, and Dirk Schoenaers, eds, *Literature and Multilingualism in the Low Countries (1100–1600)*, special issue of *Queeste*, 22.1 (2015)

Marion, Olga van, 'The Reception of Plutarch in the Netherlands: Octavia and Cleopatra in the Heroic Epistles of J.B. Wellekens (1710)', in *Recreating Ancient History: Episodes from the Greek and Roman Past in the Arts and Literature of the Early Modern Period*, ed. by Karl A. E. Enenkel, Jan L. de Jong and Jeanine De Landtsheer (Leiden: Brill, 2001), pp. 213–34

Maslen, Robert W., 'The Early English Novel in Antwerp: The Impact of Jan van Doesborch', in *Narrative Developments from Chaucer to Defoe*, ed. by Gerd Bayer and Ebbe Klitgard (New York: Routledge, 2011), pp. 137–57

Meconi, Honey, 'Foundation for an Empire: The Musical Inheritance of Charles V', in *The Empire Resounds: Music in the Days of Charles V*, ed. by Francis Maes (Leuven: Leuven University Press, 1999), pp. 19–34

'Medieval Francophone Literary Culture Outside France', <http://www.medievalfrancophone.ac.uk/> [accessed 23 June 2014]

Meeus, Hubert, 'Printing in the Shadow of a Metropolis', in *Print Culture and Peripheries in Early Modern Europe: A Contribution to the History of Printing and the Book Trade in Small European and Spanish Cities*, ed. by Benito Rial Costas (Leiden: Brill, 2013), pp. 147–70

Micha, Hugues, 'Une rédaction en vers de la vie de Saint Sébastien', *Romania*, 92 (1971), 405–19

Miedema, Hessel, *De archiefbescheiden van het St. Lukasgilde te Haarlem: 1497–1798*, 2 vols (Alphen aan den Rijn: Canaletto, 1980)

Morgan, David A. L., 'The Cult of St George c. 1500: National and International Connotations', *Publications du Centre européen d'études bourguignonnes (XIVe–XVIe)*, 35 (1995), 151–62

Moser, Nelleke, *De strijd voor rhetorica: Poëtica en positie van rederijkers in Vlaanderen, Brabant, Zeeland en Holland tussen 1450 en 1620* (Amsterdam: Amsterdam University Press, 2001)

Moulin-Coppens, Josee, *De Geschiedenis van het oude Sint-Jorisgilde te Gent* (Ghent: Hoste Staelens, 1982)

Muller, J. W., 'Gerijt Potter van der Loo en zijne vertaling van Froissart', *Tijdschrift voor Nederlandse Taal- en Letterkunde*, 8 (1888), 264–95

Mullins, Sophie, 'Latin Books Published in Paris, 1501–1540' (unpublished doctoral thesis, University of St Andrews, 2013)

Nicholas, David, *Medieval Flanders* (London: Longman, 1992)

Nieuwstraten, R., 'Overlevering en verandering: De pentekeningen van de Jasonmeester en de houtsneden van de Meester van Bellaert in de *Historie van Jason*', in *Boeken in de late middeleeuwen: Verslag van de Groningse Codicologendagen, 1992*, ed. by J. M. M. Hermans and K. van der Hoek (Groningen: Forsten, 1994), pp. 111–24

—— 'Vervaardigers en bezitters van Raoul Lefèvre's *Histoire de Jason*: Kanalen voor de verbreiding van een idee', *Millennium: Tijdschrift voor middeleeuwse geschiedenis*, 8 (1994), 134–47

Nijhoff, W., and M. E. Kronenberg, *Nederlandsche bibliographie van 1500 tot 1540*, 3 vols (The Hague: Nijhoff, 1923–61)

Oosterman, Johan, 'De fascinerende symbiose van handschrift en druk. Naar aanleiding van: J. M. M. Hermans & K. van der Hoek (red.), *Boeken in de late middeleeuwen: Verslag van de Groningse Codicologendagen 1992*', special issue of *Queeste*, 3 (1996), 76–80

—— 'Oh Flanders, Weep! Anthonis de Roovere and Charles the Bold', in *The Growth of Authority in the Medieval West*, ed. by Martin Gosman, Arjo Vanderjagt and Jan Veenstra (Groningen: Forsten, 1999), pp. 257–67

—— 'Tussen twee wateren zwem ik: Anthonis de Roovere tussen rederijkers en rhétoriqueurs', *Jaarboek De Fonteine*, 49–50 (1999–2000), 11–29

—— 'De *Excellente cronike van Vlaenderen* en Anthonis de Roovere', *Tijdschrift voor Nederlandse Taal- en Letterkunde*, 11 (2002), 22–37

OOSTROM, FRITS VAN, *Court and Culture: Dutch Literature, 1350–1450*, trans. by Arnold J. Pomerans (Berkeley: University of California Press, 1992)

—— *Stemmen op schrift: Geschiedenis van de Nederlandse literatuur vanaf het begin tot 1300* (Amsterdam: Bert Bakker, 2006)

PEETERS, JEAN-PAUL, 'De financieel-economische situatie van de stad Mechelen in het midden van de 14de eeuw (1338–1359)', *Handelingen van de Koninklijke Kring voor Oudheidkunde, Letteren en Kunst van Mechelen*, 108 (2005), 29–60

PETERS, URSULA, *Literatur in der Stadt: Studien zu den sozialen Voraussetzungen und kulturellen Organisationsformen städtischer Literatur im 13. und 14. Jahrhundert* (Tübingen: Niemeyer, 1983)

PETTEGREE, ANDREW, 'Printing in the Low Countries in the Early Sixteenth Century', in *The Book Triumphant: Print in Transition in the Sixteenth and Seventeenth Centuries*, ed. by Malcolm Walsby and Graeme Kemp (Leiden: Brill, 2011), pp. 3–25

—— *The Invention of News: How the World Came to Know About Itself* (New Haven, CT: Yale University Press, 2014)

PETTEGREE, ANDREW, and MATT HALL, 'The Reformation and the Book: A Reconsideration', *Historical Journal*, 47 (2004), 785–808

PETTEGREE, ANDREW, and MALCOLM WALSBY, *NB: Netherlandish Books. Books Published in the Low Countries and in the Dutch Language Abroad before 1601*, 2 vols (Leiden: Brill, 2011)

PETTEGREE, ANDREW, MALCOLM WALSBY, and ALEXANDER WILKINSON, *FB: French Vernacular Books. A Bibliography of Books Published in the French Language before 1601*, 2 vols (Leiden: Brill, 2007)

PIAGET, ARTHUR, 'Pierre Michault et Michault Taillevent', *Romania*, 18 (1889), 439–52

PINCHART, ALEXANDRE, 'Jean de Malines, poète français du quatorzième siècle', *Bulletin du bibliophile belge*, 12 (1856), 28–37

PLEIJ, HERMAN, 'Een fragment van de oudste Nederlandse novellenbundel te Cambridge', in *Opstellen door vrienden en vakgenoten aangeboden aan C. H. A. Kruyskamp*, ed. by Hans Heestermans (The Hague: Martinus Nijhoff, 1977), pp. 142–55

—— 'Ridder Welghemoet in Wenen', *Literatuur*, 4 (1987), 97–98

—— *Nederlandse literatuur van de late middeleeuwen* (Utrecht: H & S, 1990)

—— *Het gevleugelde woord: Geschiedenis van de Nederlandse literatuur 1400–1560* (Amsterdam: Bert Bakker, 2007)

—— *Komt een vrouwtje bij de drukker... Over gezichtsveranderingen van de literatuur uit de late middeleeuwen* (Amsterdam: Bert Bakker, 2008)

—— 'Over Anna Bijns als persoon', in *Met eigen ogen: De rederijker als dichtend individu (1450–1600)*, ed. by Dirk Coigneau and Samuel Mareel, special issue of *Jaarboek De Fonteine*, 58 (2008), pp. 21–44

—— *Anna Bijns, van Antwerpen* (Amsterdam: Bert Bakker, 2011)

POEL, DIEWKE E. VAN DER, 'De voorstelling is voorbij: Vermeldingen van wereldlijk toneel en de casus van *Strasengijs*', in *Spel en spektakel: Middeleeuws toneel in de Lage Landen*, ed. by Hans van Dijk and others (Amsterdam: Prometheus, 2001), pp. 111–32

POP, J., *De spiegel der minnen* (Leiden: Spruyt, Van Mantgem & De Does, 1987)

POPLACK, SHANA, 'Sometimes I'll start a Sentence in Spanish *y termino en español*: Toward a Typology of Code-switching' [1980], in *The Bilingualism Reader*, ed. by Li Wei (London: Routledge, 2000), pp. 221–56

POTTER, FRANS DE, *Jaarboeken der Sint-Jorisgilde van Gent* (Ghent: Hage, 1868)

—— *Geschiedenis der stad Kortrijk*, 4 vols (Ghent: Annoot-Braeckman, 1873–76)

PREVENIER, WALTER, and WIM BLOCKMANS, *The Burgundian Netherlands*, trans. by Peter King and Yvette Mead (Cambridge: Cambridge University Press, 1986)

RAJEWSKY, IRINA O., 'Intermediality, Intertextuality, and Remediation: A Literary Perspective on Intermediality', *Intermédialités*, 6 (Autumn 2005), 43–64

RAMAKERS, BART, *Spelen en figuren: Toneelkunst en processiecultuur in Oudenaarde tussen middeleeuwen en moderne tijd* (Amsterdam: Amsterdam University Press, 1996)

RAPP, FRANCIS, 'Universités et principautés: les états bourguignons', in *À la cour de Bourgogne: le duc, son entourage, son train*, ed. by Jean-Marie Cauchies (Turnhout: Brepols, 1998), pp. 51–65

RAUE, SASKIA, 'Een nauwsluitend keurs: Aard en betekenis van *Den triumphe ende 't palleersel van den vrouwen* (1514)' (unpublished doctoral thesis, University of Amsterdam, 1996)

REID, DYLAN, 'Moderate Devotion, Mediocre Poetry and Magnificent Food: The Confraternity of the Immaculate Conception of Rouen', *Confraternitas*, 7 (1996), 3–10

—— 'Carnival in Rouen: A History of the Abbaye des Conards', *The Sixteenth Century Journal*, 32 (2001), 1027–55

—— 'Patrons of Poetry: Rouen's Confraternity of the Immaculate Conception of Our Lady', in *The Reach of the Republic of Letters: Literary and Learned Societies in Late Medieval and Early Modern Europe*, ed. by Arjan van Dixhoorn and Susie Speakman Sutch, 2 vols (Leiden: Brill, 2008), I, 33–78

REIFFENBERG, FRÉDÉRIC, BARON DE, 'La Fête de l'arbalète et du prince d'amour à Tournai en 1455', *Bulletin de la Commission Royale d'Histoire*, 10 (1845), 255–66

REINTGES, THEO, *Ursprung und Wesen der spätmittelalterlichen Schützengilden* (Bonn: Ludwig Röhrscheid Verlag, 1963)

RENOUARD, PHILIPPE, *Bibliographie des impressions et des œuvres de Josse Badius Ascensius, imprimeur et humaniste, 1462–1535*, 3 vols (Paris: E. Paul et fils et Guillemin, 1908)

RESNICK, IRVEN M., 'Lingua dei, lingua hominis: Sacred Language and Medieval Texts', *Viator*, 21 (1990), 51–74

REY-FLAUD, BERNADETTE, *La Farce ou la machine à rire, théorie d'un genre dramatique 1450–1550* (Geneva: Droz, 1984)

REYNAERT, JORIS, 'Literatuur in de stad? Op zoek naar een voorgeschiedenis van het Gruuthuse-liedboek', in *De studie van de Middelnederlandse letterkunde: Stand en toekomst: Symposium Antwerpen 22–24 september 1988*, ed. by Frits van Oostrom and Frank Willaert (Hilversum: Verloren, 1989), pp. 93–108

RIEMSDIJK, TH. VAN, *De tresorie en kanselarij van de graven van Holland en Zeeland uit het Henegouwsche en Beyersche huis* (The Hague: Martinus Nijhoff, 1908)

ROMAINE, SUZANNE, *Bilingualism*, 2nd edn (Malden: Blackwell, 1989)

RUTTEN, GIJSBERT, ' "Ghelyck wy zien dat de Fransóyzen doen": Dialoog en dialogisme in de *Twe-spraack vande Nederduitsche letterkunst*', *Yang*, 40 (2004), 477–85

SAINT-GENOIS, BARON JULES DE, *Catalogue méthodique et raisonné des manuscrits de la bibliothèque de la ville et de l'université de Gand*, 3 vols (Ghent: Annoot-Braeckman, 1849–52)

SALVERDA DE GRAVE, J. J., *De Franse woorden in het Nederlands* (Amsterdam: Johannes Muller, 1906)

SCHENDL, HERBERT, 'Syntactic Constraints on Code-Switching in Medieval Texts', in *Placing Middle English in Context*, ed. by Irma Taavitsainen and others (Berlin: Mouton de Gruyter, 2000), pp. 67–86

SCHLUSEMANN, RITA, 'De uitwisseling van houtsneden tussen Willem Vorsterman en Jan van Doesborch', *Queeste*, 1 (1994), 156–73

—— 'Buchmarkt in Antwerpen am Anfang des 16. Jahrhunderts', in *Laienlektüre und Buchmarkt im späten Mittelalter*, ed. by Thomas Kock and Rita Schlusemann (Frankfurt am Main: Peter Lang, 1997), pp. 33–39

SCHNERB, BERTRAND, *L'État bourguignon 1361–1477* (Paris: Perrin, 1999)

SCHOENAERS, DIRK, ' "Getranslateerd uuten Franssoyse": Gerard Potter's Dutch Translation of Froissart's *Chroniques*' (unpublished doctoral thesis, University of Liverpool, 2010)
—— 'The Middle Dutch Translation of Froissart's Chronicle (*c.* 1450): Historiography in the Vernacular and the Ruling Elite of Holland', *Dutch Crossing*, 36 (2012), 98–113
SCHOENAERS, DIRK, and HANNO WIJSMAN, 'De *librie* van Batestein: De boeken van Brederode in de vijftiende en zestiende eeuw', in *Yolande van Lalaing (1422–1497), kasteelvrouwe van Brederode*, ed. by Elizabeth den Hartog and Hanno Wijsman, special issue of *Jaarboek van de Kastelenstichting Holland en Zeeland* (2009), pp. 69–98
SCHRIJVER, MARC DE, and CHRISTIAN DOTHEE, *Les Concours de tir à l'arbalète des gildes médiévales: un aperçu* (Antwerp: Antwerps Museum en Archief Den Crans, 1979)
SEGRE, CESARE, *Teatro e romanzo: due tipi di comunicazione letteraria* (Turin: Einaudi, 1984)
SIJS, NICOLINE VAN DER, ed., *Etymologiebank* (2010), <http://etymologiebank.nl/> [accessed 15 February 2015]
SIJS, NICOLINE VAN DER, and ROLAND WILLEMYNS, *Het verhaal van het Nederlands: Een geschiedenis van twaalf eeuwen* (Amsterdam: Bakker, 2009)
SLEIDERINK, REMCO, 'From Francophile to Francophobe: The Changing Attitude of Medieval Dutch Authors towards French Literature', in *Medieval Multilingualism: The Francophone World and Its Neighbours*, ed. by Christopher Kleinhenz and Keith Busby (Turnhout: Brepols, 2010), pp. 127–43
—— 'Johannes Steemaer alias Pertcheval: De naam en faam van een Brusselse rederijker', in *'Want hi verkende dien name wale': Opstellen voor Willem Kuiper*, ed. by Marjolein Hogenbirk and Roel Zemel (Amsterdam: Stichting Neerlandistiek VU; Münster: Nodus Publikationen, 2014), pp. 149–54
SMALL, GRAEME, *George Chastelain and the Shaping of Valois Burgundy: Political and Historical Culture at Court in the Fifteenth Century* (Woodbridge: Boydell Press, 1997)
—— 'Centre and Periphery in Late Medieval France: Tournai', in *War, Government and Power in Later Medieval France*, ed. by Christopher Allmand (Liverpool: Liverpool University Press, 2000), pp. 145–74
—— 'When Indiciaires Meet Rederijkers: A Contribution to the History of the Burgundian "Theatre State"', in *Stad van koopmanschap en vrede: Literatuur in Brugge tussen middeleeuwen en rederijkerstijd*, ed. by Johan Oosterman (Leuven: Peeters, 2005), pp. 133–61
—— *Late Medieval France* (Basingstoke: Palgrave Macmillan, 2009)
SMIT, H. J., ed., *Bronnen tot de geschiedenis van den handel met Engeland, Schotland en Ierland 1150–1585* (The Hague: Instituut voor Nederlandse geschiedenis, 1928–1950)
SMIT, J. G., ed., *Bronnen voor de geschiedenis der dagvaarten van de staten en steden van Holland voor 1544: Deel 2 (1433–1467) Tweede stuk: Teksten* (The Hague: Instituut voor Nederlandse geschiedenis, 2005)
SMIT, W. A. P., *Dichters der reformatie in de zestiende eeuw: Een overzicht met bloemlezing* (Groningen: Wolters, 1939)
SNELLER, Z. W., *Walcheren in de vijftiende eeuw* (Utrecht: Oosthoek, 1917)
SNELLER, Z. W., and W. S. UNGER, eds, *Bronnen tot de geschiedenis van den handel met Frankrijk. Eerste deel* (The Hague: Martinus Nijhoff, 1930)
SNOW, EMILY, 'The Lady of Sorrows: Music, Devotion, and Politics in the Burgundian-Habsburg Netherlands' (unpublished doctoral dissertation, Princeton University, 2010)
SOMME, MONIQUE, 'Étude comparative des mesures à vin dans les états bourguignons au XVe siècle,' *Revue du Nord*, 58 (1976), 171–83
STABEL, PETER, 'Markets in the Cities of the Late Medieval Low Countries: Retail, Commercial Exchange and Socio-cultural Display', in *Fiere e mercati nella integrazione delle economie europee, secc. XIII–XVII: Atti della 'Trentaduesima settimana di studi', 8–12 maggio 2000*, ed. by Simonetta Cavaciocchi (Florence: Le Monnier, 2001), pp. 797–817

——— 'Guilds in Late Medieval Flanders: Myths and Realities of Guild Life in an Export-Oriented Environment', *Journal of Medieval History*, 30 (2004), 187–212

STANGER, MARY D., 'Literary Patronage at the Medieval Court of Flanders', *French Studies*, 9 (1957), 214–29

STEENSEL, ARIE VAN, *Edelen in Zeeland: Macht, rijkdom en status in een laatmiddeleeuwse samenleving* (Hilversum: Verloren, 2010)

STEIN, HENRI, *Étude biographique, littéraire et bibliographique sur Olivier de La Marche* (Brussels: Hayez, 1888)

STEIN, ROBERT, *De hertog en zijn staten: De eenwording van de Bourgondische Nederlanden ca. 1380–ca. 1480* (Hilversum: Verloren, 2014)

STEIN, ROBERT, and JUDITH POLLMANN, eds, *Networks, Regions and Nations: Shaping Identities in the Low Countries, 1300–1650* (Leiden: Brill, 2010)

STROHM, REINHARD, *Music in Late Medieval Bruges*, rev. edn (Oxford: Clarendon Press, 1990)

STRØM-OLSEN, ROLF, 'Dynastic Ritual and Politics in Early Modern Burgundy: The Baptism of Charles V', *Past and Present*, 175 (2002), 34–64

STUIP, RENÉ, 'Histoire des Seigneurs de Gavre dans la bibliothèque d'Antoine de Lalaing en 1548', in *Rencontres de Middelbourg/Bergen-op-Zoom (27 au 30 septembre 1990): les sources littéraires et leurs publics dans l'espace bourguignon (XIVe–XVIe s.)*, ed. by Jean-Marie Cauchies (Neuchâtel: Centre européen d'études bourguignonnes, 1991), pp. 189–98

SUTCH, SUSIE SPEAKMAN, 'Dichters van de stad: De Brusselse rederijkers en hun verhouding tot de Franstalige hofliteratuur en het geleerde humanisme (1475–1522)', in *De macht van het schone woord: Literatuur in Brussel van de 14de tot de 18de eeuw*, ed. by Jozef Janssens and Remco Sleiderink (Louvain: Davidsfonds/Literair, 2003), pp. 141–59

——— 'De Gouda-editie van *Le Chevalier délibéré*: Een boek uitgegeven in eigen beheer', in *Geschreven en gedrukt: Boekproductie van handschrift naar druk in de overgang van middeleeuwen naar moderne tijd*, ed. by Herman Pleij and Joris Reynaert (Ghent: Academia Press, 2004), pp. 137–55

TAYLOR, JANE H. M., 'The Significance of the Insignificant: Reading Reception in the Burgundian *Erec* and *Cligès*', *Fifteenth-Century Studies*, 24 (1998), 183–97

THIENEN, GERARD VAN, and JOHN GOLDFINCH, eds, *Incunabula Printed in the Low Countries: A Census* (Nieuwkoop: De Graaf, 1999)

THIRY, CLAUDE, 'L'Honneur et l'empire: à propos des poèmes de langue française sur la bataille de Pavie', in *Mélanges à la mémoire de Franco Simone* (Geneva: Slatkine, 1980), pp. 297–324

THØFNER, MARGIT, *A Common Art: Urban Ceremonial in Antwerp and Brussels During and After the Dutch Revolt* (Zwolle: Waanders, 2007)

THOMASON, SARAH G., *Language Contact: An Introduction* (Washington, DC: Georgetown University Press, 2001)

——— 'Contact Explanations in Linguistics', in *The Handbook of Language Contact*, ed. by Raymond Hickey (Oxford: Blackwell, 2010), pp. 31–47

TREFFERS-DALLER, JEANINE, 'Borrowing and Shift-induced Interference: Contrasting Patterns in French-Germanic Contact in Brussels and Strasbourg', *Bilingualism: Language and Cognition*, 2.1 (1999), 1–22

Trésor de la langue française, <http://atilf.atilf.fr/> [accessed 9 July 2014]

TRIO, PAUL, 'The Emergence of New Devotions in Late Medieval Urban Flanders (Thirteenth-Fifteenth Centuries): Struggle and Cooperation between Church/Clergy and Urban Government/Bourgeoisie', in *Städtische Kulte im Mittelalter*, ed. by S. Ehrich and J. Obserste (Regensburg: Schnell und Steiner, 2010), pp. 327–38

UNGER, WILLEM SYBRAND, ed., *Bronnen tot de geschiedenis van Middelburg in den landsheerlijken tijd* (The Hague: Martinus Nijhoff, 1926)

Universal Short Title Catalogue, <http://www.ustc.ac.uk>

URWIN, KENNETH, *Georges Chastellain: la vie, les œuvres* (Paris: André, 1937)

VAN AUTENBOER, EUGEEN, *De kaarten van de schuttersgilden van het hertogdom Brabant (1300–1800)*, 2 vols (Tilburg: Stichting Zuidelijk historisch contact, 1993)

VAN BRUAENE, ANNE-LAURE, ' "Abel in eenighe const": Claeys vander Meersch, meesterschilder, en de jonge Fonteine (1448–1476)', *Jaarboek De Fonteine*, 49–50 (1999–2000), 77–94

—— ' "A wonderfull tryumfe, for the wynning of a pryse": Guilds, Ritual, Theater, and the Urban Network in the Southern Low Countries, ca. 1450–1650', *Renaissance Quarterly*, 59 (2006), 374–405

—— *Om beters wille: Rederijkerskamers en de stedelijke cultuur in de zuidelijke Nederlanden (1400–1650)* (Amsterdam: Amsterdam University Press, 2008)

—— 'Princes, Emperors, Kings and Investiture in the Festive Culture of Flanders (Fifteenth-Sixteenth Century)', in *Les 'Autres' Rois: études sur la royauté comme notion hiérarchique dans la société au bas Moyen Âge et au début de l'époque moderne*, ed. by Torsten Hiltmann (Munich: Oldenbourg, 2010), pp. 131–44

VAN DRIEL, JOOST, *Meesters van het woord: Middelnederlandse schrijvers en hun kunst* (Hilversum: Verloren, 2012)

VAN DUYSE, PRUDENS, *Verhandeling over den drievoudigen invloed der rederijkkameren, voorafgegaan door een overzicht harer geschiedenis, tot antwoord op de volgende prijsvraag: quelle a été l'influence littéraire, morale et politique des sociétés et des chambres de rhétorique dans les dix-sept provinces des Pays-Bas et le pays de Liége* (Brussels: Hayez, 1861)

VAN ELSLANDER, ANTONIN, 'De instelbrief van de rederijkerskamer "De Fonteine" te Gent (9 december 1448)', *Jaarboek de Fonteine*, 6–7 (1948–49), 15–22

VAN GENT, M. J., *'Pertijelike saken': Hoeken en kabeljauwen in het Bourgondisch-Oostenrijkse tijdperk* (The Hague: Stichting Hollandse Historische Reeks, 1994)

VAN HOECKE, WILLY, 'La Littérature française d'inspiration arthurienne dans les anciens Pays-Bas', in *Arturus Rex: Volumen 1, Catalogus, Koning Artur en de Nederlanden, la matière de Brétagne et les anciens Pays-Bas,* ed. by W. Verbeke, J. Janssens, and M. Smeyers (Leuven: Universitaire Pers Leuven, 1987), pp. 189–260

VAUCHEZ, ANDRE, 'Saint Homebon (†1197), patron des marchands et artisans drapiers à la fin du Moyen Age et à l'époque moderne', *Académie royale de Belgique. Bulletin de la classe des lettres et des sciences morales et politiques*, 6th ser., 15 (2004), 47–56

VAUGHAN, RICHARD, *Philip the Good: The Apogee of Burgundy*, rev. edn, foreword by Graeme Small (Woodbridge: Boydell Press, 2002)

VELISSARIOU, ALEXANDRA, *Aspects dramatiques et écriture de l'oralité dans les 'Cent Nouvelles nouvelles'* (Paris: Honoré Champion, 2012)

VENUTI, LAWRENCE, *The Scandals of Translation: Towards an Ethics of Difference* (London: Routledge, 1998)

VERBIJ-SCHILLINGS, JEANNE, 'Hofcultuur en hofvermaak: Het Haagse hof in de middeleeuwen (1248–1462)', in *In den Haag geschied*, ed. by Han Foppe (The Hague: Sdu Uitgevers, 1998), pp. 33–53

VERMEULEN, YVES G., *Tot profijt en genoegen: Motiveringen voor de productie van Nederlandstalige gedrukte teksten 1477–1540* (Groningen: Wolters-Noordhoff/Forsten, 1986)

VERWIJS, EELCO and OTHERS, *Het Middelnederlandsch woordenboek*, 10 vols (The Hague: Martinus Nijhoff, 1882–1952)

VESSEM, H. A. VAN, 'De dood van Claes van Ruven', *Haerlem: Jaarboek 1977*, 9–16

De vijfhonderdste verjaring van de boekdrukkunst in de Nederlanden: Catalogus (Brussels: Koninklijke Bibliotheek Albert I, 1973)

VINCKIER, ROMAIN, ed., *Ieper tuindag. Zesde eeuwfeest. Een bundel historische opstellen* (Ypres: Stedelijke culturele raad, 1983)

VOET, LÉON, *The Golden Compasses: A History and Evaluation of the Printing and Publishing Activities of the Officina Plantiniana at Antwerp*, 2 vols (Amsterdam: Vangendt; London: Routledge and Kegan Paul; New York: Schram, 1969–72)

VOOYS, C. G. N. DE, *Geschiedenis van de Nederlandse taal* (Groningen: Wolters-Noordhoff, 1970)

VRIES, JAN DE, and AD VAN DER WOUDE, *The First Modern Economy: Success, Failure, and Perseverance of the Dutch Economy, 1500–1815* (Cambridge: Cambridge University Press, 1997)

WALSBY, MALCOLM, *The Printed Book in Brittany, 1484–1600* (Leiden: Brill, 2011)

—— 'Plantin and the French Book World', in *International Exchange in the European Book World*, ed. by Sara Barker and Matt McLean (Leiden: Brill, forthcoming)

WALTON, THOMAS, 'Les Poèmes d'Amé de Montgesoie: *Le Pas de la mort* et *La Complainte sur la mort d'Isabelle de Bourbon*', *Medium Ævum*, 2 (1933), 1–33

WATERSCHOOT, WERNER., 'Arend de Keysere: Een voorzichtig experimentator', in *Geschreven en gedrukt: Boekproductie van handschrift naar druk in de overgang van middeleeuwen naar moderne tijd*, ed. by Herman Pleij and Joris Reynaert (Ghent: Academia Press, 2004), pp. 119–35

—— '*Dat bedroch der vrouwen* [review]', *Spiegel der Letteren*, 26 (1984), 93–100

WIJSMAN, HANNO, 'Les Manuscrits de Pierre de Luxembourg (ca 1440–1482) et les bibliothèques nobiliaires dans les Pays-Bas bourguignons de la deuxième moitié du XVe siècle', *Le Moyen Age*, 113 (2007), 613–37

—— 'Frank van Borssele en boeken', in *Het kasteel te Sint-Maartensdijk en zijn bewoners*, ed. by Elizabeth den Hartog and others (Haarlem: Kastelenstichting Holland en Zeeland, 2010), pp. 105–68

—— *Luxury Bound: Illustrated Manuscript Production and Noble and Princely Book Ownership in the Burgundian Netherlands (1440–1550)* (Turnhout: Brepols, 2010)

WILLEMYNS, ROLAND, 'Taalpolitiek in de Bourgondische tijd', *Verslagen en mededelingen van de Koninklijke Vlaamse Academie voor Taal- en Letterkunde*, 104 (1994), 162–77

—— 'Laatmiddelnederlands (circa 1350–1550)', in *Geschiedenis van de Nederlandse taal*, ed. by M. C. van den Toorn and others (Amsterdam: Amsterdam University Press, 1997), pp. 147–219

—— *Dutch: Biography of a Language* (Oxford: Oxford University Press, 2013)

WILLIGEN, ADRIAAN VAN DER, *Les Artistes de Harlem: notices historiques avec un précis sur la gilde de St. Luc* (Haarlem: Les Héritiers F. Bohn; The Hague: Martinus Nijhoff, 1870)

WINFORD, DONALD, *An Introduction to Contact Linguistics* (Malden: Blackwell, 2003)

ZINGEL, MICHAEL, *Frankreich, das Reich und Burgund im Urteil der burgundischen Historiographie des 15. Jahrhunderts* (Sigmaringen: Thorbecke, 1995)

INDEX

Abbeville 63
Adelaide of Holland, Countess of Hainaut 15
Albert III, Duke of Saxony 135–36
Albert of Wittelsbach, regent of Holland, Hainaut, and Zeeland 16
Amiens 74–75, 89
Amsterdam 54, 64
Amyot, Jacques 63
Antwerp 3, 25, 54, 56–67, 78, 88, 97–98, 118, 122, 124, 133
Armstrong, Adrian 154
Armstrong, Charles 44, 45
Arras 18, 74
Artois 74, 75
Ath 89

Bade, Josse 57–58
Baertmaker, Jan de 135
Bailleul 88
Bapaume 87
Batestein, castle of 24
Dat bedroch der vrouwen 4, 116, 118–21, 122
Beka, Johannes de:
 French translation of *Chronographia* 24
Bellaert, Jacob 25–27, 33, 38 n. 85, 144, 151
 Der sonderen troest 39 n. 95
 see also Lefèvre, Raoul, *Fais et prouesses du chevalier Jason*
Berlaimont, Noël de:
 Vocabulare van nyeus gheordineert 61–62
Berntsz, Jan 118, 121
Biuyen, Pierre 87
Boccaccio, Giovanni:
 Decameron 106–07, 110–14, 116–19, 120–24, 126
 French translations of *Decameron*, see Premierfait, Laurent de, *Livre des Cent Nouvelles*; Macon, Antoine le
Bonna, Jean 133
Book of Pieter Polet, see Manuscripts, Ghent, Universiteitsbibliotheek, HS G 6112
Boone, Cornelis 77
Bossaert, Jacob 18
Bouchet, Jean:
 Les Regnars traversant les perilleuses voyes des folles fiances de ce monde 62–63
Boutillier, Jean:
 La Somme rurale 32–33, 63

Brabant 13, 15, 17, 25, 29, 30, 31, 71, 78, 80, 107–08, 111, 112, 135
Brain-le-Comte 89
Bread and Cheese Revolt 28, 132
Breda, Jacobus de 58
Brito, Jan 56, 63
Bruges 2, 5, 25, 56, 59–60, 63, 64, 71, 73–76, 78–80, 85, 90–91, 94, 95, 97–100, 108, 116, 150
 Aragonese and Catalan merchant community in 5
Brussels 5, 63, 64, 71, 85, 90, 97, 98, 132, 133, 135, 139, 141, 142–43, 144

Caillieu, Colijn 113, 150
 possible identification with Colijn van Rijssele 110
 Van Narcissus ende Echo 113, 115
Calais 21
Calepino, Ambrogio 62
Cambrai 74
Castelein, Matthijs de:
 De Const van Rhetoriken 113
Cats, Jacob van 27
Cats, Jan van 25, 27, 33, 146 n. 19
Caxton, William:
 edition of *Recuyell of the historyes of Troye* 25–26
Cent Nouvelles nouvelles 4, 106–26
chambers of rhetoric 1, 2, 3–4, 13, 23, 28–30, 33, 71–80, 92, 97, 116, 119, 124, 149, 151, 154
 De Drie Santinnen 116
 De Fonteine 76–80
 De Heilige Geest *or* Heleghe Gheest 4, 76, 78–80, 116
 De Lelie 132, 135–36
 see also *compagnies joyeuses*; *puys*; *rederijkers*; *titels*
chambres de comptes 18–19
Charles V, Holy Roman Emperor 5, 6, 65, 96
Charles VI, King of France 84, 96
Charles VIII, King of France 108
Charles the Bold, Duke of Burgundy 18, 24, 26, 27, 38 n. 87 & 90, 44, 46, 150
Charles, Count of Charolais, see Charles the Bold
Charlotte de Bourbon-Montpensier 24
Chartier, Alain 156
Chastelain, George 1, 3, 42
 Dit de verité 47–48
 Le Miroer des nobles hommes de France 47
 multilingualism of 44, 45–49, 51
Chaucer, Geoffrey:
 The Merchant's Tale 121

Le Chevalier qui fist sa femme confession 116
Coigneau, Dirk 4, 6, 75
Collaciebroeders 132, 133, 134
compagnies joyeuses 74, 77, 78, 80
Coornhert, Dirck 109
Copland, William 118
Coppenius, Gilles 62
Coster Johannes 115
Courolles, Jehan de 71
Crombie, Laura 3–4, 71
Cruce, Andries van der (De la Croix) 20
Cudelier, French entertainer 16

Damme 76
David of Burgundy, Bishop of Utrecht 24
Delft 63
Delft, Dirc van 16
Delft, Treaty of 17
Dendermonde 76
Dene, Eduard de 44
Despars, Nicolas 90
Deventer 56, 58
dictionaries 61–62
Diksmuide 85, 88, 90
Diocletian 86
Dixon, Rebecca 4–5
Doctrinael des tijts 22–23, 31, 33, 39 n. 95, 108, 151, 160 n. 18
Doesborch, Jan van 118–19, 121, 122, 125–26
see also *Dat bedroch der vrouwen*
Dordrecht 89
Douai 90, 99
Doudet, Estelle 45, 46
Dubois, Simon 57
Dupire, Noël 46
Dutch 2, 5, 17, 19–20, 44, 45–46, 50–51, 54, 58, 72–73, 75–77, 79–80, 132–33, 134, 136, 140
see also multilingualism

Een Boer en Meester Marten 115–16
Egmond, Willem van 18
Eleanor of Austria, Queen of Portugal 98
Emerson, Catherine 3
English 3, 5, 7, 118, 120
Erasmus, Desiderius 57–58
Everaert, Cornelis:
 Esbatement van den Visscher 4, 109, 115–17, 126
 Tspel dat ghespeilt was voor de Aragoenoysen 5–6
Excellente cronike van Vlaanderen 91, 94, 96

Ferdinand, King of Bohemia and Hungary, Holy Roman Emperor 67
Flanders 13, 15, 16–17, 19, 23–24, 26, 28, 29, 30, 31, 33, 71, 74, 75, 76–77, 78, 80, 85–89, 95–98, 108, 151, 153
see also Walloon Flanders

Floire et Blancheflor 62
Florent V, Count of Holland and Zeeland 15
Flores, Jean de:
 L'histoire d'Aurelio et Isabelle 64
Fons vitæ 57
Fossetier, Julien 5
Francis I, King of France 5
Frank of Borsselen 29
Franssen, P. J. A. 119, 122
French 3, 6, 16–17, 20, 22–25, 54, 58–61, 71, 73–74, 79–80, 106, 108–09, 132
see also multilingualism
Frisia, 32
Frisian 22
Froissart, Jean 75
 Chroniques 21–22
 Joli buisson de jonece 16
Fruytiers, Jan 4, 123–26
 Ecclesiasticus 124

Geneva 133, 150
George, Saint 84, 86, 89, 90, 97, 98, 99–100
German 5, 9 n. 20
Ghelen, Jan II van 67, 129 n. 47
Ghent 1, 4, 57, 64, 75, 76–77, 78–79, 85–99, 101
 Ghent rebellion 85
Gijsen, Johanna van 109–10
Gouda 25, 27, 28, 108, 132, 133, 134, 135, 149, 150–51
Greek 45, 49, 51, 63
Guelders 13
Guicciardini, Lodovico 61
guilds 71, 72, 74, 75, 77, 84–92, 93, 95, 96–101
Gutenberg, Johannes 56

Haarlem 20, 22, 25–28, 31, 108, 109, 132, 133, 135, 142, 144, 151
The Hague 16, 19, 24, 31, 54
Hainaut 15–16, 25, 74, 75, 80, 107, 108, 135
Halyncbrood, Lodewijk 76
Hebrew 45
's-Hertogenbosch 58, 97
Heynenzoon, Claes 16
Hildegaersberch, Willem van 16
Die historie van den ouden Tobias 64
Historie vanden vromen ridder Jason 26–27, 33, 144
Holland 3, 12–41, 108, 110, 124, 135
 bilingualism in 15–16
 trade relations of 30–31
Holy Ghost 4, 72, 75–76, 78–80
Holy Trinity 4, 76, 78–80
Hoochstraten, Michel de 60
Horace:
 editions of 58
Hulst 88, 101

Immink, Margaretha 109

Index

Isabella of Portugal, Duchess of Burgundy 24
Italian 5

Jacqueline of Bavaria, Countess of Hainaut 17, 21, 24
Jason Master, the 26
Jean, Duc de Berry 106
Jesus Sirach 124
John of Avesnes, Count of Hainaut 15
John the Fearless, Duke of Burgundy 85, 89–90, 100
John I of Holland 16
John, Count of Nevers 16
John, Duke of Touraine 16
Jongenelen, Bas 133, 142
Jonker Fransenoorlog, see Revolt of Squire Frans van Brederode

Kervyn de Lettenhove, Joseph 48
Keyser, Merten de, see Lempereur, Martin
Knuvelder, Gerard 13–14
Kronenberg, Maria 140–41, 142

Ladam, Nicaise 5–6
Lalaing, Guillaume de 24
Lalaing, Yolande de 24
La Marche, Olivier de 45
  Le Chevalier délibéré 4–5, 25, 27–28, 108, 132–44, 150
  Triumphe des dames 108
  see also Pertcheval, Johannes, *Den Camp vander doot*; Willemsz, Pieter, *Vanden ridder welghemoet*
Lambert, Josse 64
Lannoy, Hugues de 24
Lannoy, Jean de 24
Laon 89
Latin 3, 5, 6, 13, 15, 18, 19, 20, 21, 25, 42, 43, 45–46, 48–52, 56, 57–58, 65, 67, 106, 151
  see also multilingualism
Lavéant, Katell 72
Leeu, Gheraert 25–26, 33, 149, 150–51
  edition of *Le dialogue des creatures moraligié* 25
  edition of *Van den drie blinde danssen* 149, 150–51
Lefèvre, Raoul 25, 108, 127 n. 9, 144
  Recueil des histoires de Troie 26, 108, 144
  Fais et prouesses du chevalier Jason 26, 108, 144
  see also *Historie vanden vromen ridder Jason*
Leiden 20, 29, 31, 54, 108, 124
Le Maçon, Antoine 124
Lempereur, Martin 57
Le Muisis, Gilles 91
Leuven 56, 78
Lichtekooi 116
Lille 19, 31, 64, 71, 73, 74, 75, 76, 80, 85–87, 89, 99
Livre des mestiers 30
Loan, Philippe de 107
Louis of Bruges, lord of Gruuthuse 24, 25
Louvain, see Leuven
Lübeck 76

Lyon 57–58, 63, 150

Maerlant, Jacob van:
  Wapene Martijn 63
Mansion, Colard:
  edition of *Doctrinal du temps present* 37 n. 71
manuscripts 24–25, 59, 106, 132, 150
  Berlin, Staatsbibliothek Preussischer Kulturbesitz, MS Germ. Qu. 557: 29
  Brussels, Bibliothèque royale de Belgique, ms. 228: 6
  Copenhagen, Kongelige Bibliotek, MS GKS 79: 9 n. 20
  Geneva, Bibliothèque publique et universitaire, MS français, 182: 159 n. 7
  Ghent, Universiteitsbibliotheek, HS 434: 92–93, 94, 101–02 n. 3
  Ghent, Universiteitsbibliotheek, HS G 6112: 92, 96
  Glasgow, University Library, MS Gen. 2: 9 n. 20
  Gruuthuse manuscript, see The Hague, Koninklijke Bibliotheek, MS 79 K 10
  The Hague, Haags Gemeentearchief, ms. 36: 40–41 n. 117
  The Hague, Koninklijke Bibliotheek, ms. 79 K 10: 74
  The Hague, Koninklijke Bibliotheek, ms. 130 B 21: 24
  Kassel, Universitätsbibliothek, 4° Ms. poet. et roman. 5: 9 n. 20
  Lille, Bibliothèque municipale, MS 401: 159 n. 7
  London, British Library, Add MS 10290: 26–27
  London, British Library, Add MS 35087: 6
  London, British Library, MS Harley 4453: 159 n. 7
  New York, Pierpont Morgan Library, MS M 76: 9 n. 20
  Paris, Bibliothèque de l'Arsenal, MS 5070: 127 n. 17 & 18
  Paris, Bibliothèque de l'Arsenal, MS 5113: 159 n. 7
  Paris, Bibliothèque nationale de France, MS fr. 1119: 159 n. 7
  Paris, Bibliothèque nationale de France, MS fr. 1186: 159 n. 7
  Paris, Bibliothèque nationale de France, MS fr. 1654: 159 n. 7
  Paris, Bibliothèque nationale de France, MS fr. 1696: 159 n. 7
  Paris, Bibliothèque nationale de France, MS fr. 1989: 159 n. 7
  Paris, Bibliothèque nationale de France, MS fr. 5028: 159 n. 7
  Paris, Bibliothèque nationale de France, MS fr. 12788: 159 n. 7
  Paris, Bibliothèque nationale de France, MS fr. 22922: 159 n. 7
  Paris, Bibliothèque nationale de France, MS fr. 24442: 159 n. 7

Philadelphia, University of Pennsylvania, Rare Book and Manuscript Library, Codex 947: 159 n. 7
Rotterdam, Gemeentearchief, MS 1534: 38
Wolfenbüttel, Herzog August Bibliothek, Cod. Guelf 84.2.1 Aug 12°: 9 n. 20
Mareel, Samuel 95
Margaret of Austria 25
Margaret of Burgundy, Duchess of Bavaria 16
Margaret of Holland, also known as Margaret of Bavaria 16
Margaret of York 26
Marguerite de Navarre 124
    L' Heptaméron 124
Martens, Thierry 58
'Martijn', translator 25, 31, 151
    Van den drie blinde danssen 5, 25, 31, 108, 149, 150–55, 156–58
Mary, Duchess of Burgundy 132, 135, 137, 143
masterplots 7
Maximillian I, Holy Roman Emperor 135–36
Mechelen 29, 30, 85, 88–89, 91, 93
Meersch, Claeys vander 77
Melusine 62
Meynderts, Egbert 115
Michael, Saint 98
Michault, Pierre 22, 25, 149–50, 151
    Dance aux Aveugles 25–26, 108, 149–58
    Doctrinal du temps present 22, 25–26, 108, 150, 151
    Procès de l'honneur féminin 150
    see also *Doctrinael des tijts*; 'Martijn', translator, *Van den drie blinde danssen*
Middelburg 31, 33, 110, 112, 114
Molinet, Jean 1–2, 3, 5, 7, 28, 42, 44–51
    Art de Rhétorique 5
    multilingualism of 42, 44–51
    Pater Noster 48–50
    'Response a Anthoine Busnois' 46–47
Mons 80
Montgesoie, Amé de:
    Pas de la Mort 108, 142
multilingualism 1, 5–7, 12–33, 54, 57, 71–73, 76, 79–80, 85–86, 88–90, 92, 101
    borrowings and loans 2–3, 5, 13–14, 19, 21, 22, 27, 28, 29, 136–41, 142
    code-switching 2–3, 14, 17, 19, 21, 42–43, 48–49
    Dutch-French 1–7, 12–33, 42, 45–48, 49, 51–52, 61–67, 71–73, 79–80, 88–90, 101, 133–35, 136–44, 149, 150, 151–58
    Dutch-Latin 13, 18, 49–52
    French-Latin 45–46, 48–49, 51–52
    in poetry 45–52
music 6
    'Flemish Chapel' of Charles V 6

Naaldwijk, Willem van 18
Nachtegael, Otgier Pietersz 6, 132, 133–35, 140

news books 60–61, 65, 67
Nieuwpoort 73
Ninove 89
Nivelles 80
Normandy 74, 75
Nuyts, Marten 122
    see also *Die ontrouwe der mannen*

Die ontrouwe der mannen 4, 121–23
Oosterman, Johan 44
Opstand van het Kaas- en Broodvolk, see Bread and Cheese Revolt
Oudenaarde 71, 73, 76, 79–80, 85, 87, 88, 89, 91, 92, 94, 96–97, 99–100
Oudenburg 76
d'Outremeuse, Jean 91

pamphlets 54
Paris 57–58, 63, 85, 89, 90, 101
Paris et Vienne 62
Pavia 5, 7
Pertcheval, Johannes 132
    Den Camp vander doot 4, 5, 132–40, 142–44
Philip the Bold, Duke of Burgundy 16
Philip of Cleves 25
Philip the Good, Duke of Burgundy 17, 18, 20, 21, 24, 25, 31, 72, 96, 106, 107, 108, 114, 149, 151
    as narrator in *Cent Nouvelles nouvelles* 107, 108
Philip the Handsome, Duke of Burgundy, King of Castile 6, 92, 95, 96, 97, 98, 135, 136
Phillipsz, Jan 29
Picard 15, 17, 19, 108
Picardy 74
Pierre de Provence 62
Pijn, Gijsbrecht 19, 21
Pizan, Christine de 156
Plantin, Christophe 54, 67
Pleij, Herman 14, 133
Pot, Philippe 107
Potter, Gerrit 27
    translation of Froissart's *Chroniques* 21–22, 24, 33
Premierfait, Laurent de:
    Livre des Cent Nouvelles 106, 110, 124
puys 3–4, 74–75, 78–80

rederijkers 13–14, 22, 109, 112, 115, 119, 120, 124, 125–26, 149, 151, 154, 157
Reformation, the 54, 125
Reinoud II van Brederode 24–25, 28
Revolt of Squire Frans van Brederode 27, 28, 29
Reynaert die vos 38 n. 87, 151
Rijmkroniek van Holland 15
Rijnsburg 124
Rijssele, Colijn van:
    Spiegel der Minnen, 4, 13–14, 109–15, 126
    see also Colijn Caillieu

Roovere, Anthonis de 2, 3, 7, 42, 43, 44, 49–51
   Droom van Rovere op die doot van hertoge Kaerle van
      Borgognnyen saleger gedachten 42, 51
   multilingualism of 44, 49–51
   Pater Noster 49–50
   Refereyn van rethorica 78
   Sacramentslof 29
Rotterdam 124–25
Rouen 30, 63, 75, 89
de la Rue, Pierre 6
Ruyven, Elisabeth van 27
Ruyven, Klaas van 27–28, 33, 132, 145 n. 6
Ruyven, Maria van 27–28

Saint-Genois, Baron Jules de 92
Saint-Omer 18, 76
Scheldt 77, 79, 99
Schelle, Pieter van der 91
Schendl, Herbert 43, 45
Schiedam 6, 108, 132, 133, 134
Schoenaers, Dirk 3
Schuijt, W. J. 22, 23, 150
Sebastian, Saint 86
Seversz, Jan:
   edition of *Vanden ridder welghemoet* 132, 139–40
Sidrach 62
Silvius, Willem 124
Sluis 88, 100
Smeken, Jan, *see* Baertmaker, Jan de
Spagnoli, Battista 58
Spain 5–6, 18, 76, 96, 97
Spanish 5, 7, 15
Spelman, Gerard 124
Stavelot, Jean 91
Steemaer, Johannes, *see* Pertcheval, Johannes
Sutch, Susie Speakman 4, 25

Taillevent, Michault 149, 156
Taylor, Jane 152, 153, 154
theatre 2, 4, 5, 7, 71–73, 76–80, 113, 121, 126
   civic procession 71, 73, 74, 80, 85
   farce 115, 116, 117
   landjuwelen 78
   morality plays 119
   Passion plays 73
   tableaux vivants 73, 119
theatregram 6, 7
Thibault, Jean:
   Le Thresor du remede 57
titels 74, 77, 78, 80
Tournai 4, 18, 30, 64, 71–72, 73, 75, 76, 77, 78, 79–80, 84–85, 87, 88, 89, 90, 91, 92–94, 95–96, 98, 100
trade 1, 30–31, 54–61, 65, 67, 92, 98
Tuscan 106
type 65, 67, 132, 134, 159 n. 13

Utrecht 24, 29, 97, 118

Valenciennes 73, 75
Van Bruaene, Anne-Laure 3, 29
Van Eyck, Jan 76
Vele, Abraham 118
Velissariou, Alexandra 124
Vérard, Anthoine 63, 108–09, 110
   edition of *Cent Nouvelles nouvelles* 108–09, 110, 126 n. 1, 128 n. 23
versification 5, 28, 51, 72–73, 94–95, 113, 125, 149, 152, 155–58
   acrostic 48–50
   ballade (Dutch) 29, 73, 95, 157
   ballade (French) 29, 124, 154
   chanson 6
   chants amoureuses 71
   chant royal 71, 75
   decasyllables 155–56
   heptasyllables 155–56
   heterometry 155–56, 157
   hypometry 48
   metre 47, 155–57
   octosyllables 93, 132, 155–56
   prosimetrum 5, 149–50, 154
   referein, refrain, or *refrein* 73, 74, 77, 79, 120, 123–26, 152, 154, 157; see also *ballade* (Dutch)
   rhyme 3, 14, 47–48, 51, 91, 94, 95, 97, 113, 146 n. 13, 157–58
   rondeau 29, 154
   rondel (Dutch) 29
   stanzas 95, 124, 125, 133, 134, 137, 141, 143, 149, 152, 155, 157–58
      douzain 155
      huitain 155
      seizain 157, 160 n. 26
      septain 155
      vingtain 155
   stress-based verse 5, 156–57
   virelai 29
Vienna 133
   siege of 60–61
Vorsterman, Willem 65, 95, 98

Walloon Flanders 17, 74, 75
Walsby, Malcolm 3
Wassenaar, Willem van 40
Watervliet, Hieronymus Lauweryn van 6
Wervik 71
Wight, John 118
Willemsz, Pieter 135
   Vanden ridder welghemoet 4–5, 28, 132, 133, 135–36, 139–44
William VI, Count of Holland 16
Wolfert VI of Borsselen 24

woodcuts 61, 64, 65–67, 94–95, 108, 118, 132–33, 134, 137, 140

Ypres 32, 64, 71, 72, 73, 74, 75, 76, 78–80, 85, 87, 88, 90

Zeeland 3, 13, 15, 24, 26, 28, 30, 31, 32, 33, 110, 114, 135
Zomere, Willem de 71
Zwolle 56, 58

www.ingramcontent.com/pod-product-compliance
Lightning Source LLC
LaVergne TN
LVHW061251060426
835507LV00017B/2015